Drop Shipping and eCom

What you need and where to get it.

Myths, Pros and Cons, Mistakes to Avoid.

Drop shipping suppliers and products, payment processing, ecommerce software and set up an online store all covered.

by

Christine Clayfield

- Author of "From Newbie To Millionaire". Search for it on Amazon or buy it as an eBook on www.FromNewbieToMillionaire.com

- Author of "Finding Niches Made Easy. 177 Free Ways to Find New Hot Profitable Niches". Search for it on Amazon or buy it as an eBook on www.FindingNichesMadeEasy.com

- Creator of www.WorldwideSelfPublishing.com Video Tutorials

Published by IMB Publishing 2013

Copyright and Trademarks

Disclaimer and Legal Notice

Quick Overview of Chapters

Table of Contents

Acknowledgements

I've said my big thank yous in my first book "From Newbie To Millionaire," so I will keep these short and sweet.

Thank you so much to my dear darling husband. Without your support, I would not have been able to build my Internet marketing business.

Thank you to my two beautiful, intelligent twin daughters for being such respectful young adults.

Thank you to my four stepchildren for continuing to look after your twin stepsisters.

Thank you to you, the reader, for putting your trust in me and buying this book. I hope this book will guide you and inspire you in your eCommerce or drop shipping venture.

I don't have any other people to thank as everything I know about internet marketing, I've learned on my own, by practicing, making mistakes and by working hard.

Foreword

Hello fellow Internet marketer,

Well, I guess you ARE an Internet marketer or you are planning to sell online, as you've picked up this book!

Throughout this book I will refer to you as an Internet marketer; when you run online shops, everything is done online, therefore you are an Internet marketer.

I have been an Internet marketer for over 7 years now and I absolutely l o v e it.

Let me tell you first what I am not:

- I am not a computer geek.

- I am not a computer programmer.

- I am not an IT consultant.

- I am not a computer science diploma holder.

- I am not a super duper clever person (I never did well at school).

I started with NO experience, NO support, NO training, NO special skills but figured it all out on my own and ultimately started to make money online.

But this is what I am:

- I am a hard worker.

- I can read, analyse and learn quickly.

- I am eager to earn money.

- I have determination.

- I believe in what I want to achieve.

- I have a business mind and I can spot money-making possibilities.

- I will not give up until I have reached my goal.

If you are a person with the same thinking, you are on your way to earning money online.

> **The quality of most people's lives are a direct reflection of their expectations.**

> **TOP TIP:** Learn from the people who have proven that they know what they are talking about. Never take tips and tricks from somebody who is not experienced.

I strongly believe in this tip, whatever business you are in: always learn from people who have proven that they know what they are talking about. Ask yourself: "Did they prove that they know their stuff?" or "How much money has he/she earned?"

I am not here to boast about my income, but it is important to mention so you know that I do practice successfully what I preach. I bank £83,000/$150,000 per month, that is £1,000,000/ $1,800,000 per year from multiple streams of income. Part of that income is drop shipping and eCommerce.

I started with absolutely zero experience or knowledge and I am living proof that with enough determination and the right information, anyone can make money online. It has been hard work but hey, in what other business would you not have to work hard to get these kind of results?

Want proof of my income? Simply visit www.FromNewbieToMillionaire.com and opt-in to see my bank account. I promise I will not flood your inbox with crappy affiliate links—that's just not my style! My income does not come from sending affiliate links to my subscribers but from multiple sources of income of my own products.

It is my aim with this book to give you enough information to make you ready and confident to start your first website and…start selling. I have tried to give you a good idea of what drop shipping is all about and how everything works. It is too complicated to tell you every single thing you need to know, as some things you can only learn by practicing them, no matter how well someone explains it to you.

eCommerce is time consuming and there is a heck of a lot to take in, but if you break it into manageable chunks, you can do it too. To start with, you will not make any money sitting on your backside; you will have to put in some time and effort. After a while, though, you WILL be sitting on your backside and earning money. I will never say that making money on the Internet is easy because it isn't. Well, it isn't at the beginning, but once you start to make money, you will enjoy the Internet and realise its power.

Do you need a lot of money to start with? No, you don't. You might not need a lot of money, but you do need time. If you are not going to put in any effort, you will not make any money. Do bees get honey without work? No, they don't.

No Bees No Honey - No Work No Money

I am planning to make videos about drop shipping and eCommerce, showing you step by step how to set it all up, upload products, connect everything to shopping cart, merchant account, etc…I will set up a shop and record it all on video so you can SEE how it is all done.

If you are interested in this, please visit www.DropshippingAndEcommerce.com/yesvideos.html.

If I have a lot of people asking for the videos, I will do them and you will be notified when they are ready.

I hope you will enjoy reading this book, and I hope your drop shipping/eCommerce venture will be profitable.

Good luck! I wish you all the success you need to succeed!

My warmest regards,

Christine Clayfield

Author, Entrepreneur, Infopreneur, Internet Marketer, Book Publisher, Public Speaker.

My Other Products

Below you find a list of my other products that are Internet marketing/office related.

1) *My bestselling book* "From Newbie To Millionaire"

Buy the **eBook** here: www.FromNewbieToMillionaire.com

Buy the **hard copy book**: search for it on Amazon

---

2) My bestselling book "Finding Niches Made Easy. 177 Free Ways to Find New Hot Profitable Niches".

Buy the **eBook** here: www.FindingNichesMadeEasy.com

Buy the **hard copy book**: search for it on Amazon

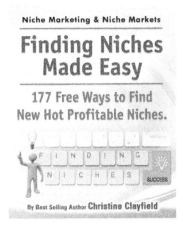

3) My Self Publishing Success System explained step by step in video tutorials

I publish a new book, on average, every 6 weeks. These books are all in different niches and I outsource all aspects of the book, including writing and cover design, except for the publishing, which I do myself. Buy the video tutorials to watch online: www.WorldwideSelfPublishing.com

4) My Break Reminder Software

I have to try and reduce the time I spend on my computer due to a neck injury (you will read about it later). I used to use www.workpace.com, which is software that forces you to take breaks whilst on your computer. I had my own simplified version developed, which you can buy here: www.BreakReminderSoftware.com.

5) My Repetitive Strain Injury Book

The real-life stories in the book will make you think and will, hopefully, make you take regular breaks on your computer/mobile phones, etc.

The book is aimed at anyone who use our much-loved electronic gadgets too often, too long, without taking breaks. Nobody warns people about the permanent damage it can do to your body.

Buy the **hard copy boo**k: search for it on Amazon by author Lucy Rudford (pen name)

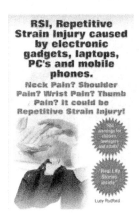

6) *My Print Screen Software*

When I was looking for a very simple screen printing software application, without all the bells and whistles, I couldn't find it, therefore I had my own developed. I use it every single day and don't know how I could ever be without it.

You can buy it here: www.PrintingYourScreen.com

 Printing Your Screen, Screen Capture

The Software that Makes Printing Screen Shots And

Saving Screen shots *instant*.

7) *Print a Kindle eBook*

I don't like reading from a screen and searched A LOT for a reliable solution to print a Kindle book. You can grab your copy here free: www.HowToPrintAKindleBook.com.

How to print a kindle book from your PC. If you are like me and you prefer reading books from paper, this is for you. Before I knew how to print a Kindle book, I never bought any Kindle books, now I do because I print them and read them.

Please note there is a one-time charge of $29.99 / £19.00 to buy the Kindle Converter that I recommend in order to convert your Kindle to a pdf format that you can print. However, you have 5 days to test the product free. This converter is not my product and I don't earn any money from it if you buy it but it is a product that actually works.
Works on PC, windows explorer. I have not tested it an an Apple computer.

More information about me:

www.ChristineClayfield.com

For more information about how you can make money as an affiliate selling my products, please refer to the end of this book.

Important to Mention

There are a few important things you need to know before we start digging into drop shipping and eCommerce.

- My mother tongue is not English and for the first 30 years of my life I spoke only Flemish (I am from the Flemish part of Belgium, not the French part) until I met an English gentleman, who is now my husband. For that reason, if you do find some grammatical errors in this book, I apologise. This book has been proofread, but perfect proofreaders are very rare to find. It is not my goal to write a "perfect English" book, instead it is my goal to write an informative book that will help you to build a successful eCommerce business.

 - Readers who have read my book "From Newbie To Millionaire": you will find that I repeat some of that information in this book, but not much. You can't run a profitable drop shipping business without knowing the keys to success in Internet marketing, therefore I have to explain some Internet marketing issues in this book.

- Internet marketing is really well explained in my book "From Newbie To Millionaire". If you can afford it, get yourself a copy. People call it The Internet Marketing Bible. Check out the reviews on Amazon: it's not me saying it is a really good book!

- You can build a drop shipping / eCommerce business gradually, no need to quit your day job from the start! You can start building your online store by working just 2 to 3 hours per day.

- Whenever I say "Google your keyword" (A keyword is whatever someone types into the search box in a search engine), what I really mean is search for your keyword in whichever search engine you want.

The same applies for whenever I say "Google it"—what I mean is look it up on the web. According to statistics, Google owns the largest share of the search engine market, followed by Yahoo! Search, Bing, Ask and lots of other smaller search engines. See the pie chart below. Source: *www.writeonpointseo.com*

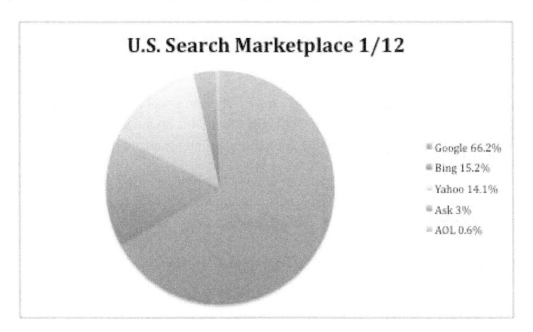

- This book is also based on trying to please Google with our websites, but a lot of the search engines apply the same methods to decide which pages display for a certain keyword, although all search engines have their own algorithms (the formula that each search engine uses to evaluate web pages and to determine if their relevance and value are good enough to be shown in the searches). Consequently, whatever techniques that I use for ranking will work for most search engines.

- At times in the book I mention the same thing twice or more. There are two reasons for doing this: firstly because I firmly believe that repetition makes you remember things better, and secondly because some readers might only read a few chapters in this book and not understand that particular chapter when reading it should I have left certain information out.

- I have put prices in £ and $ to make it easy for UK readers and USA readers. Please note sometimes the £ prices will be correct and converted to $ and sometimes the other way around. As I am in the UK, lots of websites immediately display their prices in £, even if they would be displayed in $ if you visit the same website in the USA. The prices can vary as they are converted at today's rate. You will, of course, have a good idea what the approximate price is that I talk about.

- I live in the UK, so this book is written in English spelling, therefore you will see colour instead of color, optimise instead of optimize, socialise instead of socialize, etc.

- At the time of printing this book, all websites were fully functional and prices mentioned were correct. If you come across a website, a plugin, etc. that is no longer available (the Internet changes all the time), I suggest that you search online for an alternative.

- I don't endorse any of the websites I mention in this book, nor can I tell you which one is "THE" best supplier to work with or "THE" best eCommerce software to use as it all depends on your products, your priorities, your taste, etc.

Why I had to reduce my drop shipping business.

My income from drop shipping was, in 2011 and in 2012, much larger than what it is now, in 2013. I'll explain: soon after I was diagnosed with a neck problem (see further), I had to leverage my time to reduce the time I sit on my computer. Running several drop shipping sites is time consuming. I did an analysis on how many hours I would work on all my multiple streams of income compared to the income it would give me. The loser in my analysis was drop shipping and the winner was self publishing. As a result of that, I decided to sell some of my drop shipping/eCommerce sites and create an alternative income flow that would require less work, resulting in less time on my computer.

For that reason, I have been concentrating on self publishing. It was my aim to within 2 years earn the same from self publishing as I did with drop shipping. I've done that.

Now you could say just outsource the drop shipping work, but that is not so simple, as sometimes you need to speak to your customers directly, take care of returns, make sure the customer gets a credit, etc. I always took care of my drop shipping sites myself and I didn't really want the headaches of outsourcing it. Most affordable outsourcers are in Philippines, etc., and I am in the UK, therefore customer services or phoning customers occasionally is a problem.

I always like to prove what I say, so here is proof. Below you see two screenshots from Streamline - My Merchant Account, or the company I use to charge people's credit cards.

- The first one is sales of £76,695.05/$124,334 in November 2012; that is a good month (November and December are usually good months due to Xmas sales).

- The second is sales of £40,678.63/$65,951 in August 2013. At the time of writing, I do not have September 2013 or later yet, so I am showing the latest month I have received from Streamline.

Don't worry if you don't understand all the details on the screenshots, I will explain them later in the book, just look at the total, which is circled.

streamline

Charge Details

Invoice Number
Charges for November 2012

Your Merchant ID
Store Trading Name

Cards Acquired		Number of Transactions	Charge per Transaction p	Value of Transactions £	Transaction Charge Rate	Transaction Charges	VAT Code
MasterCard Cr Per	Purchases	33		8,245.26	2.225%	183.46	
MasterCard Signia	Purchases	1		9.29	2.719%	0.25	
MasterCard World	Purchases	10		4,467.23	2.719%	121.46	
Visa Credit Personal	Purchases	12		2,086.61	2.494%	52.04	
Visa Debit	Purchases	201	37.880	50,279.60	0.0%	76.14	
	Refunds	1	37.880	(151.26)	0.0%	0.38	
		202		50,128.34		76.52	
Dr MasterCard EEA	Purchases	1	36.880	226.87	0.0%	0.37	
MasterCard Business	Purchases	6		3,714.37	2.4%	89.14	
MasterCard Corporate	Purchases	3		436.78	2.4%	10.48	
MasterCard Fleet	Purchases	3		1,005.17	2.4%	24.12	
Visa Business	Purchases	4		3,807.01	2.4%	91.37	
Visa Corporate	Purchases	7		2,306.11	2.4%	55.35	
Maestro UK (DOM)	Purchases	1	34.000	202.01	0.0%	0.34	
		283		76,695.05		704.90	E

streamline

Charge Details

Invoice Number
Charges For   August 2013
Page

Your Merchant ID
Store Trading Name

Cards Acquired		Number of Transactions	Charge per Transaction p	Value of Transactions £	Transaction Charge Rate	Transaction Charges	VAT Code
MasterCard Cr Per	Purchases	11		4,299.62	2.225%	95.67	
MasterCard World	Purchases	4		367.00	2.719%	9.98	
Visa Credit Personal	Purchases	7		765.38	2.494%	19.09	
Visa Debit	Purchases	132	37.880	31,400.94	0.0%	50.00	
MasterCard Business	Purchases	1		108.86	2.4%	2.61	
MasterCard Corporate	Purchases	2		392.41	2.4%	9.42	
MasterCard Fleet	Purchases	3		1,129.18	2.4%	27.10	
Visa Corporate	Purchases	5		1,829.77	2.4%	43.91	
Maestro UK (DOM)	Purchases	2	34.000	385.47	0.0%	0.68	
		167		40,678.63		258.46	E

As you can see, the difference between November 2012 and August 2013 is £36,016.42/$65,951!! In one month!! That is a LOT of money! But that was my aim and I am earning the difference from self publishing books. So I am not worried and I am happy with that. I can always set up new eCommerce websites should I wish to do so and hire full-time staff to look after them, but I have enough on my plate right now! One of them is finishing this book. :-)

The lesson to be learned, so YOU don't have to sell your websites:

You need to look after your health! Believe me, I know!

Consider this a very important message from one Internet marketer to another. Believe me, I have learned the hard way. For years I sat working on my computer for hours and days in the wrong position, in the wrong chair, without any breaks. On some days, I would switch my computer on at 8 am and work on it until 1 am the next morning. My punishment for this: I have been diagnosed with cervical spondylosis (a non-curable condition) in my neck, with disc space between C5, C6 and C7 most affected. Want proof? Here it is. As I always like to prove what I say, here is an x-ray and MRI scan of my neck. You can see on the first picture that the space between disc C5 and C6 is thinner than all the other spaces. The second picture shows a bulging disc putting pressure on the spinal cord and its nerves fibers. Permanent nerve damage can be caused when a bulging disc in the neck is compressing a nerve for a long period of time.

 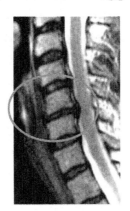

Now I cannot work on the computer as much as I would like to because when I do, my neck starts to hurt, my arm goes "dead" and I lose part of my grip and feelings in my arm. I have two choices: work a long time and give myself pain or work less and have no pain. As health is more important than money, I obviously choose to work fewer hours. I can still work long hours on the computer but certainly not as long as I would like to, in order not to make my condition worse. I am not telling you this out of self-pity as I am very happy with what I have achieved. ***I am telling you this so you don't make the same mistake.***

I am a professional, full-time Internet marketer and always will be, as I **love** it. The fact that I cannot work as much as I would like to is not a major disaster for me, because a lot of my sites/products will provide me with income on autopilot for many years to come, and I do have staff members. ***Please, please pay attention to the following. What I am about to say truly is very important for your health***.

I feel that it is my duty to tell everybody in an office environment about the dangers of working constantly on a computer. I would not want you to make the same mistakes as me. If somebody had told me seven years ago what I am going to tell you, I would not have a problem with my neck now. As an Internet marketer, you will be sitting in front of the computer for hours and hours and maybe even days. **Most people think that an office environment is a place with very low risk of injury. I thought the same until I had excruciating shoulder pain (cause by pinched nerves in my neck) when I woke up one day. The truth is a lot of musculoskeletal disorders are caused in office environments. These disorders develop because of repetitive strain to the body's muscles, tendons, ligaments, joints and nerves. Back, shoulders, neck, arms and hands are the most commonly affected from computer injuries (work-related musculoskeletal disorders).**

The two most important things that you need to know:

1. Make sure that you are sitting in the correct position on your computer. Search for "correct posture at a computer" and you will find a lot of information. Search for "ergonomic office chair" and change your office chair if you have to.

2. Make sure you take regular breaks. Staring at a computer screen with your head and neck always in the same position is very straining for your neck.

I use my own developed software, www.breakremindersoftware.com, and in my opinion this should be installed on each computer that is sold anywhere in the world. It is not available for Apple computers. www.workpace.com is similar, more sophisticated software and I believe available for Apple computer. The software monitors the time you work on the computer and it alerts you when you need to take a break. It shows you general exercises that you can do while sitting on your chair. You can set it to block your keyboard during breaks so you cannot work. My settings are as follows:

- I have a break for 20 seconds every 10 minutes and I've set the software so that my keyboard is blocked. Therefore every 10 minutes I do some gentle neck exercises.

- I have a 10-minute break every hour and my software is set so my keyboard is blocked, which forces me to get up and do something else for 10 minutes.

If you can afford it, invest in www.breakremindersoftware.com. It is the best piece of software available for an office environment. You have been warned: install it as a matter of urgency. If you cannot afford it, force yourself to take regular breaks. There are similar programs on the market. Simply search for "office timers" or "office break timers". www.workpace.com is another good one that I've used.

Sorry to have to be the one to tell you, but i-Pads, laptops and mobile phones are a lot worse for your neck than a normal computer screen. This is because your face is always pointing downwards, so your neck has a lot more strain on it.

Also, finger arthritis is predicted to be a major worldwide problem in years to come, as people use their phones for too long. The finger movement involved in texting and moving a mouse causes Repetitive Strain Injury, resulting in arthritis for a lot of people.

You can read real-life shocking stories about Repetitive Strain Injury in my book "RSI Repetitive Strain Injury" search for it on Amazon. The author is Lucy Rudford, my daughter's pen name.

Correct posture at the computer: **Bad posture at the computer:**

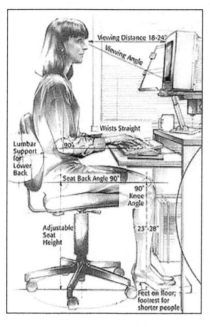   

(Source: www.ergonomics-info.com)

Please do not ignore this message, it really is very important,

I cannot stress it enough!

Important to mention: drop shipping and eCommerce can work for you, but make sure to take regular computer breaks. I have learned my lesson the hard way! If I would have taken regular breaks, I would not have a neck injury, and I would have continued with all my drop shipping/eCommerce businesses.

If you only have 1, 2, 3 or 4 sites, it will be easy to manage, but there was a point where I had 15 eCommerce/drop shipping sites and that was just too many, therefore I sold a lot of them.

Chapter 1 - It Won't Be Easy and It's Time Consuming!

- It Won't Be Easy!

- You are probably thinking about getting into drop shipping because you've heard it is easy. You've heard you can just sit back and relax while the money rolls in. Most drop shipping pitches focus on just that: ease and no effort. You'll have the money in no time to pay off your mortgage, student loans or your car. These pitches claim you can start selling a variety of products tomorrow. Unfortunately, this is not true. Get the wrong shopping cart software and you will never earn a penny. We are all brainwashed with hype and false information. Lots of shopping carts look impressive on paper but lack crucial tools. Lots of companies try to lure you in with $200 Google Adwords coupons or free gifts, etc.

Over 40,000 online business fail every year and the owners simply give up. That is a fact.

95% of Internet markers fail and never earn a penny. That's another fact.

While it is true that drop shipping is a great way to make money and is legitimate, it is not true that you are going to get rich overnight. Instead, you will learn how to sell products to make a profit and have your own online business. It will take hard work, knowledge, planning, time and effort. If you can deal with that, then let's begin.

Whatever you've heard, whether it is all easy are not, I bet you are very excited to start your own online niche shop!

I am doing exactly the same in this book as I did in my book "From Newbie To Millionaire"—telling you that you CAN make a lot of money with Internet marketing/drop shipping/eCommerce, but it won't be easy and it will take a LOT of time before you start earning a decent income, e.g. £1,200/$2,000 per month net.

I am also telling you, right at the beginning of this book: you *will* need some money; if you have no money at all available, don't even think about starting an eCommerce business as you simply can't do it without some money. You will have monthly expenses for your hosting, your payment processor provider, etc…all will be explained later. If you want to build a *professional* online store, you *will* have monthly expenses.

You have to look at your online venture as a ***real*** business, with overheads, profits to calculate, taxes to pay (hopefully anyway), and work to be done. The difference with a brick and mortar business is that you won't need ***that*** much money ***and*** you can be successful much quicker because of the power of the Internet.

I am proud to be different from most Internet marketers with their overhyped stuff! I am telling you exactly as it is: I am not promising you that success will be easy, but I am promising you, if you are prepared to put in the work, and if you choose a profitable niche, that you can earn a lot of money.

When you build a house and you don't structure it properly and use the right bricks to support it, the house will collapse. Exactly the same applies for your eCommerce business: if you build it the wrong way, with the wrong ingredients, it will also collapse.

eCommerce software is not simple push-button software, it is more like an airplane: if you want to fly, you need to learn everything there is to know about flying. If you want to build a successful online business, you will need to learn everything about the software that you decide to use.

Now don't get me wrong, it is NOT my aim to convince you not to start an online store! I just want to make sure that you understand the things that can go wrong and the issues that you will have to deal with. eCommerce and drop shipping are not the path to overnight success, but they can lead to earning LOTS of money. Once you've read this book, you will know all the things that are involved with building an online store. If you feel you can cope with all that, you can be successful!

- It Is Time Consuming!

Drop shipping can be extremely profitable, if done correctly, but also very time consuming. Please be aware of that before you start. Here are only a few tasks that are time consuming that you are probably not considering when thinking of setting up a drop shipping site:

- Monitor your sales.

- Watch back orders and make sure to ship them on time before you have an annoyed customer.

- Analyse your sales with analytic reports, e.g. see which product is not selling and change the price to see if it makes any difference.

- Tweak your product mix.

- Run promotions on a regular basis to wake up "sleeping" customers and create extra sales that way.

- Watch the stock—especially if you sell products with an expiry date. You might have to throw a lot of stock away if you don't monitor your stock levels.

- Your supplier will change his prices; you will have to change your prices too.

- Your supplier changes their return policy; you will have to change yours too.

- Damaged stock to sort out.

- Your transport company changes their prices; you will have to change yours too.

- Products are being discontinued, thus you will have to discontinue your products and do everything you can to sell your existing stock.

- There might be a fault with a product, so you have to recall all the products you've sold.

- Your supplier has shipped the wrong product to your customer and you will have to keep the customer happy.

- Paperwork! Paperwork! Yes, there is a lot of that to be done! It could be that you will be invoiced per shipment. You need to keep a record of which invoice goes with which order. You need to reconcile your drop shipper charges to make sure they are all correct. Your bank statement will show an income of "X" amount, usually put in your account daily. You need to keep record of your daily sales to make sure you can reconcile that "X" amount against all the sales, and the totals need to match or your accountant won't be happy!

- Your drop ship supplier does not respond to your questions and you have to email or phone them several times.

- Your drop shipper cannot give you tracking of a shipment, so you can't give an answer to your customers.

- If your drop shipper does not have an automated process for orders, you will have to put in each order manually and send to them. Errors are easy to make this way, creating even more work to solve the errors.

- A customer orders a product and your supplier failed to tell you that the product is no longer available. Now you've got an order but you cannot fulfill it and you will have an unhappy customer.

- Your drop shipper has shipped the goods and has included HIS company name on the paperwork instead of yours. You need to contact the supplier and tell them it is unacceptable.

- Your drop shipper has shipped goods and has included YOUR trade invoice with the goods instead of the invoice with the prices that your customer has to pay. Again, you need to take necessary steps to make sure it doesn't happen again.

- You will have to deal with failed deliveries e.g. the shipping company tried to deliver a product and no one was home. You need to contact the customer to arrange a mutually suitable new delivery date. You need to contact your supplier to give them the new date.

You will always have a To Do List!

- Support in general can take up a lot of your time.

You can outsource all or part of your support, against a fee. Visit these for more information:

www.kayako.com

www.getsatisfaction.com

Let me give you three scenarios, each of which happened to me. I could give you 20 scenarios, but I think you will get the picture after reading just three.

Scenario 1 - Card declined

In this scenario, you have a physical credit card terminal to charge your customer's card and get authorisation from the customer's bank.

- You've received an order.

- You have to charge the customer's credit card.

- The card declines.

- You try again three times, thinking you have done something wrong when entering the card information, but the card declines each attempt you make.

- You contact the customer on a Monday.

- You have not heard from the customer on a Wednesday, so you contact him/her again.

- The customer contacts you on Thursday saying sorry, there were no funds but funds have now been put in the bank.

- You try to charge the card again.

- Card is declined.

- You try again three times, thinking you have done something wrong when entering the card information, but the card declines each attempt you make.

- You contact the customer again, saying the card has been declined again.

- The customer contacts you 4 days later to say sorry and gives you another card to charge.

- You try to charge the card again.

- Card is declined.

- You try again three times, thinking you have done something wrong when entering the card information.

- You contact the customer.

-The customer says sorry again and gives you another card as she really likes the handbag and wants it.

- The card goes through—you've got a sale!

- You order the handbag from your supplier.

- The supplier tells you that the product has been discontinued!

Lots of work, lots of hassle, no sale and believe me, the customer will tell you that you are unprofessional and will never order from you again!

Scenario 2 - Drop shipper does not reply

- You send an email to your drop shipper with questions a customer has asked as she wants to buy a product.

- Drop shipper doesn't respond after two days.

- You get an angry email from your customer saying you haven't replied yet.

- You email drop shipper again asking why they haven't answered yet.

- Another three days and no answer.

- Customer emails again—even angrier, saying what an unprofessional company you are.

- Customers orders item somewhere else.

- Bad review about you to follow, etc…

- Nothing you can do about it!

A customer was lost forever and a drop shipper also lost my business after this incident.

Scenario 3 - Goods sent to the wrong delivery address

- Day 1: You've shipped a toaster to a female customer.

- The transport company has delivered the goods to the wrong address. Delivery went to Bull Road number 214 instead of Bull Road 241! Clear error made by the person who delivered the goods. Not your fault, not your customer's fault.

- Day 4: Three days after delivery date, your customer emails you asking where the hell her order is. Email arrives at 6 pm.

- You tell her by email it was shipped and delivered because your software tells you it was delivered.

- Day 5: She calls you a liar!

- You phone the courier company and check. They confirm it was delivered to the correct address and signed by "John Samuels".

- You tell this to your customer and she says there is no John Samuels at her address.

Day 6: You receive a call from Mr. Samuels (who lives at number 214) at 6 pm saying he has received a toaster and he never ordered one!

TOP TIP: Do what I do: I always send out all my orders with a fluorescent sticker on each box, saying: "If package is undelivered or delivered to the wrong address, please contact 0111 123 456"

- Day 7: You contact your transport company explaining what happened.

- You contact your customer explaining what happened and she says: "I don't believe it! I have already ordered another toaster from a professional company."

- Day 8: Your transport company has investigated, and the driver went to do a fake delivery to the same address and admitted it was his fault and he delivered the goods to number 214 instead of 241. You are not charged for the delivery of that product.

- Day 9: I ask my transport company to put in writing what happened so I can use it to show my customer.

- Day 10: I ship a box of chocolates to my customer with the apology letter from the transport company and with a handwritten letter to apologise.

- Customer emails me saying how much she appreciated that gesture.

Five days later I received an order from the same customer for £200/$324, and she still orders from me, three years later.

It won't be easy, it is time consuming, but the good news is: ***it is possible.***

Start working on it and you'll get there through making errors and learning from them. If you are not happy with where you are now, change things and start something new. Maybe you will love drop shipping and eCommerce!

Your life does not get better by chance,   **it gets better by change!**

You will make mistakes. The worst mistake you can make is not to make any!

It is important you learn from your mistakes and not give up, but:

When you lose,   **don't lose the lesson!**

Chapter 2 - Good Customer Service Is Crucial!

Good customer service is crucially important to succeed. That's why I am mentioning this in the beginning of this book.

The customer is King and the customer is always right are two things you will have to believe in. Of course, the customer is not always right and their comments, complaints and demands can be unpleasant to deal with, but they are your customers!

You will have customers returning goods saying:

- "My coffee pot does not match my wall paper."

- "My shoes don't match my watch."

- "I've read the book and I didn't like it."

So if you don't like dealing with these kinds of support issues, don't start an eCommerce business, because you WILL have to deal with customers.

To build a sustainable, profitable business, you need your customers to come back to you again and again. To achieve this, impress them with an extraordinary customer experience. You WILL impress them with this, as usually customers experience awful customer service by most companies. Be different!

Offer your products at a good price, get them out quickly, and bend over backwards to offer very friendly customer service throughout the fulfillment process.

I once saw this sign:

Complaints department is on the 45th Floor.
Elevator is out of order!

Love it!

I believe in this: if your customer is not happy, most of the time it is YOUR fault. You have done something wrong that gives a customer a reason to complain. Most complaints are things like this:

- someone did not respond to an email

- the information on the product on the web did not correspond to the product received

- the wrong price was charged

- the wrong quantity was shipped

- duplicated order received

- wrong shipping address input by customer

- the transport company delivered to the wrong address

- goods did not arrive

- the goods were damaged

- the goods got lost in transport

You see, in a lot of these cases, you could have avoided the complaint.

I am starting from the point of view that 98% of your customers buy goods because they want them, and they all want just that: order, pay and receive the goods. Done. Everybody happy.

However, there are customers (the other 2%) who buy goods, just to send them back and ask for a refund. They buy again and send it back again for a refund.

Some customers buy clothes, wear them for an occasion, and return them for a refund. These things are simply reality, like it or not. I know customers who have a tagging gun, so they can take the labels off the clothing and simply put the tags back on with their tagging gun. When you receive it back, it looks like the item is brand new, but sometimes…you can simply smell it has been worn! BUT the customer has the benefit of the doubt, and the dress does indeed look brand new, with tags on, so you don't have a choice but to refund the item.

> **TOP TIP**: If you have your own eCommerce shop (not a drop shipping website) and you have staff, always have a picker and a packer! The picker picks the goods from the warehouse (which could be your spare bedroom, of course), and the packer does two things: 1) checks that the picker picked the correct goods and the correct quantity and 2) packs the goods to ship. Never let one person fulfill an order as everyone makes mistakes, but in this case, a lot of mistakes can be avoided.

Here are a few rules that I apply when it comes to customer services.

- Design your site with your customers in mind.

- ALWAYS, ALWAYS put yourself in your customer's shoes, whatever you do.

Yes, you do see a picture of shoes in a drop shipping book! Just so you remember to practice this principle, whatever you do in business: put yourself in your customer's shoes!

- Treat your customers the same way you want to be treated yourself.

- **Be** your customer, e.g. place an order on your site and see what your customer sees.

- Think like your customer.

- Surprise your customer with a free gift or an unsolicited coupon.

- Empathy is extremely important in whatever business you are in. Empathy means to recognise your customer's emotions. Try to understand what your customer is feeling, why they complain, etc.

-ALWAYS, ALWAYS apologise to your customer for what has happened. Even if you think the customer is wrong, they think they have a reason to complain, so you need to apologise.

- Listen to your customer; let them ramble on (they do sometimes), and when they have finished their story, tell them calmly that you are sorry for what has happened. Tell them you are not perfect, but you will put it right for them.

- Keep a list of your customer's complaints so you can learn from them and avoid the same thing happening to another customer.

- Respond IMMEDIATELY to a complaint.

- Don't EVER promise anything you can't do. Customers like it when they can say, "You promised me..." It puts them in a strong position to ask for extras from you.

- Respond IMMEDIATELY to a customer's email. Not in an hour, not later in the day—immediately! The customer will be VERY impressed by this, and you will have a better chance of keeping the customer happy and therefore ordering more from you.

- If a customer complains, that does not mean they will never order from you again. Providing you deal with the complaint promptly and solve the problem, the customer will be happy. Most customers experience awful customers service, so be different: be GOOD at customer service.

- All customers are humans who make mistakes, so you can make mistakes too. If you admit immediately that you made a mistake and that you will resolve it immediately, your customer will appreciate that.

- VERY IMPORTANT: make a tray with customer's complaints. Don't think, "I'll remember to deal with that", because you won't. Go over the tray at least twice a day to see if you can do anything else in the process of the complaint solution. Your complaints tray should be empty most of the time!

- Keep your customer updated at all times. If you promised them an answer by 5 pm and you rely on other people, send the customer an email at 4 pm saying: "Sorry, I haven't got your answer yet, I will update you morning. Customers appreciate that.

- Don't keep a customer on hold for too long and if you do, play some on hold music, otherwise customers don't know if they are still connected.

- Don't say, "Our terms and conditions say that...." Who reads them anyway? Customers don't like hearing this at all. They will immediately dislike you.

- Don't EVER shout and DON'T ever lose your temper.

- If you promised to call your customer, you MUST call them, even if you haven't got the solution yet. Tell them you are working on trying to get it resolved.

- Don't ever take it personal!

- Send a handwritten "sorry note" with the replacement item if the wrong item was sent.

- ALWAYS give your customer something as your way of saying sorry.

Give your customer something to "make up" for what happened. That will make them feel good; they will love it and they will appreciate it! Some examples are:

- a discount voucher for their next purchase.

- a gift card. You can get these at www.incomm.com. Make sure your software can cope with gift cards.

- a flower (got to be careful with this one not to start an argument in a marriage. :-))

- a discount voucher for a friend.

- a free set of batteries.

- a free charger.

- an extra bag of sweets free—if you sell sweets.

- or even a box of Belgian Chocolates! Go the extra mile, buy a box of chocolates and ship it to your customer with a sticky note saying "Sorry". People love it!

> **TOP TIP:** Identify your best customers. These are your most profitable ones, who come back to buy from you again and again. Work very hard to keep them happy. People are naturally proud to be special. Tell them they are a VIP customer and invite them to VIP-only sales.

Exceptions to the rule: very awkward customers, customers that you hope will never order from you again. That's indeed how awkward some customers can be, but you are still not ever allowed to lose your temper! Don't be afraid to fire the very annoying ones who waste your time and cost you money all the time.

If you have staff: make sure they believe in all the above principles and apply them accordingly.

People will not remember what you sell, what price you are selling it for, but they will remember your attitude.

> **99% of what people remember about you is your attitude.**
>
> **Attitude is a little thing,**
>
> **that makes a huge difference in your sales.**

Chapter 3 - What Skills Do You Need to Succeed?

Are you dreaming of your own mansion, like many other people do? Are you hoping to retire early? Perhaps you just want to earn a nice income to be able to pay for all your expenses AND have some disposable income as well. Everyone these days wants to sell on the Internet! But the question is, can you do it? Can anybody build an eCommerce site? Can anybody be an Internet marketer? You *will* be an Internet marketer, as you are selling online.

As an online shop manager, you will have countless jobs to do: managing payment processes, managing pictures, sourcing new products, writing new content, coordinating logistic providers, putting new products on your website, calculating your product prices and profit margins, etc…

1. Comparison to running a "normal" business?

All you need is a computer and an Internet connection to make money online, right? Well, I am afraid it's not that simple. In my opinion, anybody with a tiny little bit of business acumen and common sense can make money on the Internet. A person with a lot of business attitude and business knowledge has a better chance of making it. The buying attitudes, reasons and motives of customers buying on the web are very similar to the ones buying on the High Street. Many business principles can be applied to both marketing online and offline, so people who are aware of these business principles are just one step ahead of others. Having said that, you certainly do not need business knowledge to make it. It is just an advantage and not a necessity.

The traditional elements of marketing are the "four Ps". These also apply to Internet Marketing (IM) businesses. The point I want to get across here is that IM is comparable to doing business outside the Internet. An Internet business is like running a normal business; it will need your full-time attention to succeed.

Here are some business terms that are very well known in the marketing/business world outside the Internet and can also be applied to the Internet Marketing environment.

a) The 4 Ps are:

- **Product**. Your product is whatever you are selling, online or offline.

- **Price**. Your price needs to be realistic compared to comparable products on the market, in our case on the web.

- **Placement** is about your distribution channels. Where and when are your products going to be available? There is one big difference here with normal marketing because products are available online 24/7.

- **Promotion** is your channels of communication with your customers and prospects.

If there is a problem somewhere with your sales, on the web or outside the web, you need to investigate each P to see which is causing the problem.

b) AIDA

A = Attention. Get your visitor's attention, in our case by building an attractive online store.

I = Interest. Get your visitors interested in what is on your site.

D = Desire. Give your visitors the desire to click on the order button.

A = Action. Your visitor takes action and clicks on your order button.

c) 80/20 rule

80% of your sales come from 20% of your customers applies very often in any business environment. This also applies in keyword research, as 80% of your sales will come from 20% of your keywords that you've used. It is therefore important to look after that 20% of your customers and to focus on the important 20% of your keywords.

d) Rule of 10

A sales representative can get 100 prospects gathered at an exhibition. Out of these 100 prospects, he might get ten more interesting leads, and out of those ten leads one person will buy his product. If he is lucky, the sales rep could get between 2% and 5% of sales out of his 100 prospects. That is a principle that I have always applied in all my businesses.

How does this work in Internet Marketing? If 100 people view your product online and one person buys your product, you have a conversion rate of 1%, which is acceptable in Internet Marketing (IM). A realistic IM conversion rate is between 1% and 5%. 10% conversion rate is very good and not very common.

e) Know your competitors

Knowing your competition is vital whatever business you are in. Later in the book, I will give you some tools to "spy" on your competition.

f) Supply and demand—pricing policy

If a manufacturer makes a product and there is strong demand and no competition, they will probably sell the product with a high profit margin. If other manufacturers start to produce similar products and bring them to market, the first manufacturer will probably have to reduce his price, as it is likely that the other manufacturers will have a lower selling price.

The same applies for your products: if you find a niche and there is no competition, you can sell your product for a high price. If twenty other people sell exactly the same product at a lower price, you might have to lower your price to stay competitive in the market.

g) Benefits, benefits, benefits

When selling any products, you HAVE to concentrate on what the benefits are for the customer when purchasing the product. If you are selling a product online, exactly the same applies: benefits, benefits, benefits. Don't say: "This is a good quality chair". Instead, say: "Your back pain could disappear forever with this chair". Focus on what it does for your customer!

h) Only two sales

There are only two reasons for sales in any sales environment, on the web or outside the web:

- A solution to a problem

- A fulfillment of a need or dream

i) Put on other people's shoes

If you want to be in business you need to put yourself in your customer's shoes. What would you like to see if you were a potential customer? Look at the world, your product, your product description, etc. as a potential customer. If you visit a website, what would you like to see? Develop the website in that way.

j) KPI indicators

KPI stands for Key Performance Indicators—also called Key Success Indicators. These are used a lot in businesses outside the web environment. As an Internet marketer, you also need to analyse as many aspects of your website as possible and try to improve it all the time. Just like the giant supermarkets know more about your spending habits than you do, you need to try to find out what the searching habits of your customers are. The purpose of a KPI is to measure a certain activity, analyse the data and learn or improve.

k) Last but not least: **Your USP = Unique Selling Point.** What is unique about your product? How do you stand out from your competition?

2. What skills does an Internet marketer need?

My success in the IM world did not come overnight. I have read, I have analysed, I have tried, I have learned, and what I've learned, I've put into action. I have made lots of (expensive) mistakes.

You can forget about working only one hour a day to earn millions. That is living in a dream world. If you are prepared to spend a lot of time on the computer and if you are prepared to work hard and learn from your mistakes, you have a good chance of making it. However, you will have to learn a lot of skills in a short time in a very competitive business.

To succeed on the Internet you need to have some knowledge in a variety of fields. There is no need to be an expert from the start in all the different fields, as you will learn as you go along. Any business owner will tell you that it is hard work running a company. The same applies for an IM business. If you are planning to do all the work yourself, without outsourcing any of it, you will need some skills from all the professions listed below. To succeed, you will need a mixture of these 25 skills:

- **Website builder.** You will need these skills as that is the aim of the game: build a website that will sell your products. In order to build good websites, you will also need lots of the skills listed below.

- **Graphic artist.** You will have to be creative in how you arrange the layout of your website. You must think about where to put images and text. You have to know what colours match and what colours clash when seen together. You have to know what typeface to use and what size the typeface should be.

- **Computer expert.** You don't really need to be an expert but you certainly need to have some computer knowledge. You will have to be able to work with different software programs (such as graphic layout programs and graphic design programs), as you will need to resize pictures or reduce their resolution. Knowledge of some basic HTML, a web coding language, is an advantage but not a necessity.

- **Marketing expert.** You need to have some marketing knowledge. It will be a huge advantage if you know what the 4 Ps, AIDA, Maslow's triangle and market segmentation are. When your website is designed, you need to know what your target market is, who your target customers are, and who your competition is. Not only do you need to know about it, but you also have to be able to analyse the information to your advantage.

- **Salesperson.** You need to know how to sell, what price to sell for, and who to sell to. One big advantage: you do not need to wear a smart suit, shiny shoes, red socks or a polka-dot tie ☺.

- **Accountant**. You need to work out your profits and you need to know how to calculate 65% profit on a product. You need to know how much profit is left after you've deducted your purchasing prices, your shipping costs, etc.

- **Mathematician**. You need to work out conversion rates and use spreadsheets to work out a total of your profits.

- **Writer.** You need to write content for your site and write product descriptions.

- **Photographer.** You need to work with photographs, so you will need some basic photo editing skills to know what resolution means, what pixels are, how to save a photograph as a JPEG, and so on.

- **Logo designer.** You will need to design a header for your site. You can also outsource this.

- **Psychologist.** You need to know about your customers' behaviour. Analyse in what style to write and to sell for your target customers. You need to realise that selling to teenagers and silver surfers is different, and you must adjust your style of writing accordingly.

- **Behaviour analyst.** You need to know where on your screen to put a "buy it now" button. You need to know which part of your screen your visitors look at first, according to studies.

- **Video expert.** You are likely to work with videos, so you need to know the best format to save a video for the quickest download. You need to know what MPEG and WAV mean.

- **Typist.** You need to be able to type more than five words per minute. If you are a very slow typist, you are losing valuable time.

- **Logical thinker**. You need to think about the logic of the page order on your site. Also, think about whether your text flows logically.

- **Businessperson.** You need the business instinct to spot money-making opportunities and exploit markets. You will need to make business decisions and foresee any changes needed, and be able to adapt to those changes.

- **Analyst.** You need to analyse information from several sources, put it all together and make decisions based on your analysis. Ask yourself: what market are you selling to? Who are you are selling to? What are they buying? Are they spending money?

- **Organiser.** You will, without a doubt, need some organisational skills. You need to organise the files on your computer in folders. You will need a system to instantly find a password when it's required. You will need to organise your orders: shipped, not shipped, problems, etc....

- **Risk taker.** You need to be able to make calculated risk decisions in case you are going to spend money on paid traffic methods.

- **Copywriter.** You need to be able to write in a style that makes people order from you. The ability to write interesting sales copy is very important.

- **Researcher.** You will need to research your niche and be able to conclude what is important information for your potential customers.

- **Planner.** You need to be able to plan when you will design your site, when you will drive traffic to it, and when you will try paid traffic.

- **SEO expert**. The most important thing for your website is to rank highly in Google search results pages, therefore SEO (Search Engine Optimisation) knowledge is essential. I'll talk about SEO later.

- **Webmaster.** You will need to be able to publish your site to the search engines. You need to know what an IP address is and what hosting means.

- **Judge.** You need sound judgment and the ability to recognise a lie. There are lots of scam artists on the web who are often very convincing.

So there you have it! That is 25 skills that you will need to become a successful Internet marketer. And I am not joking. To become successful, you need a blend of these skills, abilities and talents. Most of all you need entrepreneurial flair and business instinct. Maybe now you understand why most online businesses fail and why a lot of people give up. Even if you will be using ready-to-use templates and software or an online shop, you will still need the majority of the skills above. Even if you decide to outsource everything, you still need to know all the basics about IM, as you will have to check and correct the work delivered to you by outsourcers.

But there is hope: you do not need all these skills from the start, but you will need most of them to become a successful Internet marketer. Fortunately, you can learn a lot of these skills by reading about them. No one was born wise; it comes from making more good choices than bad ones and learning from the bad ones. In the beginning, you will probably, just like me, feel like you're not getting anywhere, but be positive and stay focused and keep your spirits high.

I want to say a few more words about **Judgment** (the 25th skill), as it is especially important. You need to STOP living in a dream world and STOP believing the overhyped sales letters. I am not saying you DO believe them, but if you do, you must STOP it. Right Now. Here are some rules to believe in, starting today.

- If it is too good to be true, it IS!

- Get rich quick schemes DO NOT EXIST and DO NOT WORK. EVER! I don't care who promises you what. If you do believe in these, sweet dreams!

- No one can guarantee you success, and if anyone does, run fast in the opposite direction!

- Pushing 1, 2, 3 buttons does not work either, EVER.

- Don't believe anyone will hold your hand all the way! YOU will have to do the work and figure out things for yourself OR wait four weeks to get a response to your support ticket.

- If you desperately need a lot of money immediately, don't start an online business—or any business, because building a business takes time.

Doing business online involves work and determination.

Successful people are successful because they have put in the work!

If you only remember one thing after reading this book, it should be this: take action. Start now, set a goal for yourself.

Do not wait; the time will never be "just right". Start where you stand, and work with whatever tools you may have at your command, and better tools will be found as you go along. *Napoleon Hill*

Skills + action = success

TOP TIP: write down what you are going to do and tell your friends what your plan is. Did you know that you are 49 times more likely to get something done if you write it down? On top of that, you are 49 times more likely to do it if you tell all your friends that you are planning to do it. That is 2,401 (49 x 49) times more likely to get things done if you write it down AND tell your friends. You know what to do.

On top of the blend of skills, you will also: Be prepared to work hard; Be determined and persistent; Have a strong money-earning desire; Have the willpower to keep going when things go wrong; Be willing to outsource; Invest your profits in your next project; Focus on one thing at a time.

Be like a stamp: stick to one thing until you get there.

Now, let's talk about eCommerce and Drop Shipping!

eCommerce Drop Shipping

All covered in this book:

Shopping Cart

SEO

Security

eMail Marketing

Keep a Record of Everything

What Niche?

Skills Needed

Profit Margins

Domain name

eCommerce Software

Traffic

VAT/TAX

Web Design

Keywords

Hosting

Picking Shipping

Templates

Legal

Merchant Account

Requirements

Selecting Products

Payment Gateway Watch

Competition

and a lot more....

Chapter 4 - Facts, Myths And Mistakes To Avoid.

1) What is eCommerce?

You may have heard of eCommerce before, but it's important to define it. eCommerce (or electronic commerce) is a broad term used to describe the selling of products or services on the Internet. It involves digitally enabled commercial transactions between companies and individuals. Established businesses that have "brick and mortar" stores or online-only stores—operated by large businesses or a single individual—can all participate in eCommerce. Basically, anyone with a computer, a website, and a product can participate and benefit from eCommerce. Yes, this means you! This ability to create a website and sell products online can generate you lots of profit, right from the comfort of your own home! The number of people who buy online is increasing every day.

eCommerce occurs when someone makes a sale or an online purchase. It is certainly going to expand and grow as more and more people get access to Internet, have their own computer and are generally more accustomed to buying products or services online. Global eCommerce is expected to reach $1.4 trillion in 2015! Today, people don't necessarily have to own a computer to participate in eCommerce! They can make purchases over the phone!

eCommerce is a constantly growing business, but there is no easy-to-follow roadmap for success. Everything that I know, I've had to figure out on my own.

The possibilities of eCommerce are endless. Generating value for other people can help you generate a lot of money online. However, there are a couple of things that you should know to effectively participate in eCommerce.

A big advantage of eCommerce is its ubiquity: this means products can be available and ordered everywhere, at all times—no need to walk into a physical store to order. You can order from your laptop or mobile phone, whether you are on the train or sitting in your kitchen.

Another great thing about eCommerce is its global reach: you can literally reach billions of customers, all over the world.

The first thing you need to have is an actual website, so that people will be able to log on to the Internet, go to your Internet address, and review what you have to offer—and buy! The next thing you need to create is a way for people to pay you, collect funds, and to notify you when they purchase an item—otherwise known as a payment platform. Of course, you will need a product to sell. And lastly, you need to generate a way to ship or deliver your product to each of your customers when they order from you. You can ship the product yourself or someone else will ship the product for you. This is where "drop shipping" comes in, as will be explained further.

To give you one of my own examples: www.liquorice-licorice.co.uk is one of my (small) eCommerce sites. So if you like liquorice, you know where to get it! It's not a drop shipping website but an eCommerce website, and I buy the goods wholesale (more about this website later in the book).

Amazon is one of the most successful eCommerce websites. Amazon has over 144 million customers and employs over 43,000 people!

Another successful eCommerce site is www.hayneedle.com.

Different types of eCommerce

There are different types of eCommerce, distinguished by the market relation or who the website is selling to.

- B2C - Business-to-Consumer: A website that sells consumer goods directly to the consumer, e.g. Amazon.

- B2B - Business-to-Business: A company producing boxes sells those boxes to companies that needs boxes to ship their goods.

- C2C - Consumer-to-Consumer: Where consumers (people) sell items to other people, e.g. Ebay, Craigslist, any auction site.

- M-commerce - Mobile eCommerce: When someone uses a mobile phone or a tablet to order a product.

- Social eCommerce: Facebook is an example of this; it has online shopping tools.

2) What is drop shipping?

Wikipedia: "*Drop shipping is a supply chain management technique in which the retailer does not keep goods in stock, but instead transfers customer orders and shipment details to either the manufacturer or a wholesaler, who then ships the goods directly to the customer. As in all retail businesses, the retailers make their profit on the difference between the wholesale and retail price.*"

Here's another definition: It's a method of selling an item whereby an individual retailer will advertise, sell, and collect the money, then contact a larger merchant or warehouse where the item is actually stored and have them ship the item to the consumer for a percentage of the profit. The consumer usually does not know that the larger merchant or warehouse is involved in the process at all. This is a great way to start a home-based Internet business!

The parties involved:

1. **The manufacturer**. This is the company that manufactures the product. He or she does not sell direct to the public or to retailers/websites. However, some do.
2. **The distributor or drop shipper.** This is the company that buys the product from the manufacturer in bulk and supplies it to the resellers and retailers.
3. **The retailer.** YOU. This is the company that sells the product on their website. The retailer orders the product from the distributor as they are sold, and the distributor ships the product to your customer.

Sometimes the manufacturer and the distributor are the same company.

The people involved:

1. **The Seller -** You!

2. **The Buyer -** Someone who's looking for what you're selling.

3. **The Supplier -** The person who stocks and sells the item you're selling.

The thing about drop shipping is that you never even have to see the products. There is no pre-purchasing products to stock until they sell. Instead, the products stay with the supplier and you create a website, blog or auction to sell the products. Once the products sells, you place the order with your drop shipper and they will ship the product directly to your customer—there is no middleman!

So, you never have to have inventory crowding your home. All you do is partner with a wholesale drop shipping supplier and list their items for sale on your site. Once someone orders a product, you forward information to the supplier for fulfillment. You pay for the product and the supplier ships the item directly to your customer from their warehouse.

Drop shipping can be a VERY profitable business. It may take some time to fully grasp it all, but once you have your website set up with products from reliable suppliers, and you've decided on your card processing company, all you need is traffic to your sites. Drop shipping is a category in the eCommerce or "shopping cart software" side of Internet marketing.

Drop shippers do the time consuming research for you and provide you with products and their lists and catalogues with products available to you at trade prices.

The big advantage is you pay your suppliers the buying price for a certain product but YOU can decide the selling price. With this in mind, you are in total control of your profit margins. Remember that you need to carefully study the competition and not overprice the products or potential customers will look elsewhere.

Here's how drop shipping works step-by-step:

1. You find a supplier who can drop ship your product.

2. You set up an account with the supplier.

3. You receive images and descriptions of the product you want to sell from the drop shipper. Usually you can simply download these from their website.

4. You create an offer for that product, displaying it on your own website or an online marketplace, such as eBay.

5. Customers visit your site or marketplace, thanks to a number of techniques that you implement to bring traffic to your site.

6. Customers look at what you have to offer them and make a purchase if they like what they see. The item is paid for in full by the customer.

7. You receive the order from the customer and charge your customer for the goods.

8. You send the order to your drop shipping company, along with the customer's shipping information.

9. You will be charged the price of the product in the drop shipping company's catalog, and in most cases you will also be charged a drop shipping fee per order. You pay for that item in full, usually by credit card, unless you have a credit account with the supplier. Your profit is the difference between this price and the price your customer has paid for the product on your website.

10. The drop shipping company (which is also the supplier) fulfills the order and ships it to the customer.

11. Your name and address is (should be) on all the paperwork that is sent with the order, so your drop shipper is unknown to your customer and you are the only point of contact for your customer.

12. The customer then receives the product.

13. Order done.

It starts all over again for your next order.

The customer who ordered the product will think that you have done all the work: stock the product, ship the product, etc. Most customers don't know that drop shipping even exists.

Sounds easy, huh? While it may sound easy, not every aspect of the drop shipping process is easy. You need to choose a product with a healthy profit margin so that you will actually make money off the product that you sell. A profit margin is the money that you have left after expenses have been fully paid. In other words, it is your sale price of the product minus what you pay for the product and minus the expenses to fulfill the order (more about this later).

You may have heard that it is difficult to truly find a good profit margin; however, when research is done correctly, you can easily find items with a solid profit margin that will guarantee the success of your business. This is just one of the many things about drop shipping that you will learn in this book as we move forward.

I wrote earlier about how important customer service is: you must always keep in mind that your customer does not know that the product they have bought from you is being shipped by a drop shipper. You are your customer's point of contact, so your customer will reach out to you in case of a problem. For this reason, it is important to work with a drop shipper that solves problems quickly and has a good customer service system, because often you will have to contact your drop shipper first before you can solve the problem with your customer.

Tell your customer you will take care of the problem and then contact your drop shipper to work out the resolution with them.

A drop shipping site looks like any other "shop" on the internet and the visitor will not know that it is a drop shipping site. As with all websites, the problem will be to get traffic to your drop shipping site (SEO is also very important, e.g. naming your product with a keyword), but once your customers find the site and start ordering, you can make a lot of money with drop shipping. If you don't know what SEO is, it is very clearly explained in my book "From Newbie To Millionaire".

Is Amazon a drop shipper?

Some people ask me if Amazon is a drop shipper and in a way, they are, as you can send Amazon products and they will ship them for you if any products are sold, but I will not talk about Amazon as a drop shipper in this book. This book is focused on having your own website and working with a drop shipper.

This is how Amazon works, if you become an approved Vendor.

1. You send your products to Amazon. 2. Amazon stores your products. 3. Customers order your products. 4. Amazon picks and packs your products. 5. Amazon ships your products.

You can also become an Amazon reseller, where you list the products, Amazon takes the money and you ship the product yourself.

You can find more information here:

http://services.amazon.co.uk

http://services.amazon.com

The responsibilities of the drop shipper are:

- Supply goods at decent prices

- Inform the retailer of any price changes ahead of time

- Provide product information, prices and pictures

- Delivery good quality products

- Make sure the products are available to the retailer

- Ship ordered products quickly

- Ship the product with the retailer's paperwork

- Provide good customer service

- Notify retailers of any changes, stock availability, pricing, etc.

The responsibilities of you, the online shop:

- Make sure you follow all the terms in the contract with your supplier

- Use the correct picture and description on your website

- Provide great customer service

- Sell at a decent price

- Charge the customer for the goods

- Double check that you send the correct details of the order to your drop shipper

3) The difference between drop shipping & eCommerce

eCommerce is a great way to generate money through your own website, with your hand in each part of the sales process:

- source, investigate and select the product

- take a picture of the product

- make the title description for your product

- decide your selling price

- put the product on your website

- purchase the products wholesale

- stock the products

- collect the money when you get an order

- deliver the product to the customer.

eCommerce: you do everything yourself from A to Z.

Drop shipping: you will receive all pictures, information, etc. from your drop shipper. The only thing you need to do is charge your customer's card and all the rest is done by the drop shipper.

Why drop shipping and eCommerce?

Today, it is fairly difficult to find anyone who regularly uses a personal computer that hasn't already purchased a product or service online. The fact is that every day, more and more people use the Internet to buy the things they need and want, easily, safely and conveniently from their own home. Since the Internet is accessible to anyone in any part of the world, an online business has unlimited potential to reach customers in any region of the globe.

This new computer usage is great news for budding entrepreneurs because it can give them the potential to offer their very own product—or variety of products—to their customers from the comfort of their own home! Imagine, making great money by providing any number of great products, right from your kitchen table! Yes, it's possible!

4) What do you need to start up?

To sum up, here are the basic items you need to participate in eCommerce:

- A website

- Products that you buy yourself (if you are setting up an online store and buy products wholesale) or you become a drop shipper

- A payment processing platform or merchant account

- A payment gateway

- Customers!

- An auto responder (explained further)

And that's it! That's all you need to create your own eCommerce business! It may look simple, but as you will find by reading this book, it isn't always that simple. I will discuss each of these in greater detail so you will not only have a good understanding of what you need, but you will be ready to move forward with your plan for your own eCommerce business and start making yourself some money.

What is an auto responder?

The words auto responder are linked to an opt-in box and email marketing. Here's the explanation of what they mean

- What is an opt-in box?

An opt-in box is another way of saying "somewhere for your visitors to enter their email address to receive updates and emails from you". Once a visitor has given you their email address, they have "opted-in". An opt-in box normally resembles the layout of the examples below:

Wikipedia definitions:

Opt in email is a term used when someone is given the option to receive "bulk" email, that is, email that is sent to many people at the same time. Typically, this is some sort of mailing list, newsletter, or advertising. Obtaining permission before sending e-mail is critical because without it, the email is Unsolicited Bulk Email, better known as spam.

There are several common forms of opt-in email:

Unconfirmed opt-in

A new subscriber first gives his or her email address to the list software (for instance, on a web page), but no steps are taken to make sure that this address actually belongs to the person. This can cause email from the mailing list to be considered spam because simple typos of the email address can cause the email to be sent to someone else. Malicious subscriptions are also possible, as are subscriptions that are due to spammers forging email addresses that are sent to the email address used to subscribe to the mailing list.

Confirmed opt-in (COI) or double opt-in

A new subscriber asks to be subscribed to the mailing list, but unlike unconfirmed opt-in, a confirmation email is sent to verify it was really them. Many believe the person must not be added to the mailing list unless an explicit step is taken, such as clicking a special web link or sending back a reply email. This ensures that no person can subscribe someone else out of malice or error. Mail system administrators and non-spam mailing list operators refer to this as confirmed subscription or closed-loop opt-in.

Some marketers call closed loop opt-in "double opt-in".

The term double opt-in was coined by marketers in the late '90s to differentiate it from single opt-in, where a new subscriber to an email list gets a confirmation email telling them they will begin to receive emails if they take no action. This is compared to double opt-in, where the new subscriber must respond to the confirmation email to be added to the list.

Some marketers contend that double opt-in is like asking for permission twice and that it constitutes unnecessary interference with someone who has already said they want to hear from the marketer.

The term double opt-in has also been co-opted by spammers, diluting its value.

Opt-out

Instead of giving people the option to be put on the list, they are automatically added and have the option to be taken out.

End of Wikipedia definitions

Here is an example what a confirmation request email may look like after somebody opted-in to receive a newsletter:

> **IMPORTANT: Just one more step before you can get my newsletter.**
>
> ## Click on the Link in the Confirmation Email!
>
> - Check your inbox for your confirmation email. Click on the link in the email to verify your subscription.
> - If your confirmation email isn't in your inbox in 15 minutes, check your spam or junk mail folder (sometimes they get put there by mistake).

As an Internet marketer, you should always try to get double opt-ins by sending your opt-ins a confirmation email—see the above screenshot. Your opt-ins are then telling you twice that they want the information: first when they opted-in and a second time when they received the confirmation email and clicked the confirmation link.

Double opt-ins are better, as the chances of the emails ending up in your visitor's spam box are smaller. However, in my experience, a heck of a lot of emails (that I signed up for with double opt-in) end up in my spam box anyway.

This is called building a list that you can use for email marketing. You have a list of 1000 people if 1000 people have opted-in.

- What is email marketing?

Email marketing is one of the best ways—if done correctly—to keep existing visitors coming back and to market your offers directly to their inboxes. All you need to do is send the people who opt-in an email on a regular basis with affiliate links that will earn you money. The people that will receive your emails have given their permission, so it is permission-based email marketing and for this reason is not categorized as spam. Predictions are that in 2013 some 400 billion emails will enter inboxes every day. As much as 75% to 80% are spam or unwanted emails.

In the offline world: to sell a product, you sell yourself first. People have to like the salesperson that is sitting on the other side of the desk, otherwise the customer will not order. This is the same in IM: with email marketing you have a chance to build a relationship with your customers. Give them good content or interesting freebies and they will start to like you, giving you a better chance of selling to them. Lead generation is huge on the Internet.

> **TOP TIP:** you can buy email addresses these days. My advice: don't! They are always untargeted addresses and I have never earned any money with them.

- *What is an auto responder?*

An auto responder is a software program that automatically sends out emails on a pre-scheduled basis to all opted-in people on your list.

Once you have built a list, the idea is that you send them some freebies or send them a newsletter or an affiliate link etc. You can't possibly do all this manually each time you receive a new opt-in. An auto responder does this automatically for you. Let's say you want to create a five-part email course. You set the intervals for the emails, say once a day. All you need to do is type in the emails once in your auto responder software and your list will get an email once a day. Anyone joining your list will automatically be sent those emails for the next 5 days.

So the owner of the list uses auto responder software to set up a sequence of emails that go out at regular intervals.

You must have an auto responder when you have an opt-in box on your website.

You will have seen these messages at the bottom of your emails:

To unsubscribe or change subscriber options visit:
http://www.aweber.com/z/r/?jAx.....

When you click on that click, you will be unsubscribed. By law you need to put an unsubscribe button at the bottom of each email you send. If people no longer want to receive your emails and click unsubscribe, your auto responder will remove that person automatically from your list and your next pre-scheduled email will no longer be received by the person who has unsubscribed.

- *Which auto responder is best?*

The best email auto-responder on the market, in my opinion, is www.aweber.com, but a good, free alternative is www.mailchimp.com (if using a limited list).

Here's a list of some well-known automated email auto responders:

www.aweber.com RECOMMENDED

www.getresponse.com

www.1shoppingcart.com (expensive)

www.infusionsoft.com (expensive)

You have to make sure that you use a professional auto responder service because that way you are protected from spam complaints. If you can provide proof of subscriber opt-in, you are in a strong position.

I am not going to go into more detail about email marketing, as I could write a whole book about that. Google the subject to find more information.

Important to mention: some eCommerce software platforms have their own auto responder build in and if you wish to do so, you can use theirs. The downside of doing that is in the event you want to stop working with that eCommerce software, your database of customers (or your list) will be lost, and you have to start all over again with building a list. However, some auto responders have the capability to import lists.

Can You Start a Drop Shipping Business?

You now know what drop shipping is and maybe you are thinking that you can't possibly do it. Maybe you think you are too young or too old, don't have enough experience, or aren't tech savvy enough.

Lucky for you, no experience is necessary and there are no pre-requisites—no age requirement and no degree needed. Whether you want to sell a few things to make some extra money for an emergency fund or for the holidays, or if you want to open a full-fledged eCommerce drop shipping store so that you can quit your day job and work from home, anything is possible.

So, no matter what your current situation is, you are a candidate to start your very own drop shipping business; and with this book, you will learn everything you need to know about getting started.

Types of Drop Shipping

Ultimately, there are two types of drop shipping. The first is where you can do niche research to find a top-selling niche/product that you can make money with and then create your own website to sell that product or products. By doing it this way, you'll need to learn about payment processors (merchant accounts) and shopping cart services.

This option means YOU are in control of the payments and you will immediately receive the money from your customers. This is the way I set everything up.

The second is finding a drop shipping company that, for a small fee, will give you everything that you need to get started—the website, access to products, etc. All you need to do is get traffic to your site to sell those products, which are pre-loaded onto a pre-made website just for you.

Not sure which one you want to do? Not to worry, we'll discuss them both and provide options for both types of drop shipping so that you can make an informed decision.

5) You must make a mini business plan

I am not going to show you how to do a "proper" business plan, as I assume you are trying to earn money whilst working at home. In that case, you are not going to have massive overheads like most businesses have that are not home based.

The absolute minimum you must do is make a simple spreadsheet and see how much profit you can realistically make and when you will start to make a profit. A mini business plan will show you how long you will have to invest money before you will start to make a profit.

Even if you don't need money from the bank, and even if you will be the only person who ever reads it, you must make a mini business plan. Don't start doing business online without it.

You need to have an idea of how many products you are planning to sell. Even if you work with drop shippers, a lot of them will ask for a forecast of how many items you are planning to sell. You need to have an idea of how much profit you can make before you start your new venture. You might find that when you have done your forecasts, you are not going to make any money!

This is what your mini business plan should include:

- What do you plan to sell?

- Why are you doing it?

- Who will you sell to?

- Who is your competition and how can you beat them?

- What marketing will you implement to sell your products?

- Who will do all the work and why are they qualified to do the work?

Information about figures, sales, etc.:

- How many products do you think you will sell over the next year? What is your target?

- What are you going to do to make the target?

Missing a target is NEVER the target's fault!

- How much profit are you planning to make?

- What is the average selling price of your product?

- What is the average shipping cost of your product?

- Are there any other taxes, e.g. duty, import taxes, etc.?

- What is the average packaging cost of your product?

- What are your monthly overheads? These are costs that you will have regardless of whether you are selling anything or nothing, e.g. merchant account and payment gateway charges, etc.

- Make a list of all the one-off set-up fees that will influence your profit.

- Your business plan will show all your expenses and estimates of your sales for one year, organised per month.

- Don't kid yourself, put down realistic figures!

- Make a spreadsheet and add up all your expenses for the next year.

Add up the total sales you are projecting. Take your total sales figure and take off your total costs and see what profit you will make.

What is Your Gross Profit?

You will need to know your gross profit and net profit to run a business and to make a business plan, as these are important financial concepts.

Calculate Your Gross Profit

Description	Amount
Total Sales, Excluding VAT	200,000
Cost of Goods Sold	120,000
Credit Card Fees	4,000
Gross Profit	76,000

Simply substract the cost of the goods from the total sales to determine your gross profit. Your gross profit in the above example is 76,000.

Calculate Your Gross Profit Margin

Description	Amount
Gross Profit	76,000
Total Sales	200,000
Gross Profit Margin	0.38
Gross Profit Margin Percentage	38%

Divide the gross profit by the total sales will give you your gross profit margin.
To calculate your gross profit margin percentage, simply multiply your gross profit x 100.

In order to get a better gross profit margin, you can either raise the price of your products or you can try and buy the products cheaper from your suppliers.

Your net profit is your gross profit minus all expenses deducted. That is your net profit before tax. You pay the tax on that amount and you are left with your net profit after tax.

Calculate Your Net Profit

Total Sales, Excluding VAT	200,000
Cost of Goods Sold	124,000
Gross Profit	**76,000**

Operating Expenses:

Salaries - Always Pay Yourself!!	40,000
Rent and Rates = None as you work from home	0
Office Expenses e.g. toners, printers, letterheads, etc..	1,000
Utilities: heat, light and power	1,200
Internet fees eg. merchant account, gateway, hosting	1,000
Motor expenses	1,000
Loans	3,000
Packaging expenses	2,000
Accountant	1,000
Bank Charges and Interest	200
Transport costs	3,000
Insurance	800
Bad Debts - customers that didn't pay you	200
Depreciation	2,000
Total Operating Expenses	**56,400**

Net Profit Before Tax	**19,600**
Tax at 20%	3,920
Net Profit After Tax	**15,680**

To calculate your Net Profit before tax, substract the Total Operating Expenses from your Gross Profit.

Some people use the term Operating Profit = Gross Profit - Operating Expenses

Note: I am not an accountant, but I believe the above spreadsheets are correct.

Cash Flow Is a Killer!

There are a lot of businesses going under, and very often it is because of one or more of these reasons:

- growing too quickly

- bad management

- not enough customers

- not controlling expenses

- too much competition

- cash flow problems

Cash flow is the flow of money in your company: money going out, money coming in. Bad cash flow means a shortage of funds, liquidity problems, e.g. no money in the bank to pay your rent or your suppliers. If a business is out of cash, it will become insolvent. A cash flow forecast shows you the likely movement of cash in and out of the business.

Here are a few things you can do to keep a positive cash flow or to improve your cash flow:

- Sell all your slow-selling stock FAST. Even if you have to sell it at a loss; at least you will get the money in your bank, thus improving your cash flow situation.

- As you will be collecting money online with your eCommerce business, you will receive the money immediately when you have a sale. Try to get a credit account with your suppliers where you pay your supplier 30 days after their invoice date. This will create positive cash flow.

- If you do give credit facilities to your customers, you MUST have a strict payment policy and follow up to make sure the customer pays you ON TIME. Never give a customer more than 30 days to pay, and try to get credit from your suppliers for 60 days.

- Reduce your costs.

- Delay payment of suppliers. However, this is not a good idea if you want to work with that supplier in the future, as next time he might demand payment in advance.

- Don't expand—solve your cash flow problems BEFORE you expand.

- Minimise the wages you draw from your company for a while.

- Improve your profit margins.

Here is an example of a cash flow forecast for 12 months, downloaded from www.microsoft.com. You might not be able to read the next page, but you can download this for free at www.microsoft.com. Search for "cash flow forecast".

Cash Flow Forecast – 12 Months

Month:	Pre-Start	1	2	3	4	5	6	7	8	9	10	11	12	Totals
Receipts														
Cash sales	0	0	10,020	10,855	12,525	14,195	15,865	18,370	21,710	24,215	26,406	28,808	33,066	216,035
Collections from credit sales	0	0	0	251	418	501	501	585	752	752	1,002	1,002	1,166	6,930
New equity inflow	0	0	0	0	0	0	0	0	0	0	0	0	0	0
Loans received	0	16,700	0	0	8,350	0	0	8,350	0	0	8,350	0	0	41,750
Total Receipts	0	16,700	10,020	11,106	21,293	14,696	16,366	27,305	22,462	24,967	35,758	29,810	34,232	264,715
Payments														
Cash purchases	0	401	326	166	131	237	166	149	149	166	113	113	167	2,284
Payments to creditors	0	1,203	978	499	392	713	499	446	446	499	339	339	503	6,856
Salaries and wages	0	6,304	5,120	2,620	2,058	3,728	2,620	2,336	2,336	2,620	1,780	1,780	2,631	35,933
Employee benefits	0	3,152	2,560	1,310	1,029	1,864	1,310	1,168	1,168	1,310	890	890	1,315	17,966
Payroll taxes	0	1,051	853	437	343	621	437	389	389	437	297	297	438	5,989
Rent	0	5,253	4,267	2,183	1,715	3,107	2,183	1,947	1,947	2,183	1,483	1,483	2,192	29,943
Utilities	0	1,021	830	425	333	604	425	379	379	425	288	288	426	5,823
Repairs and maintenance	0	584	474	243	191	345	243	216	216	243	165	165	244	3,329
Insurance	0	1,021	830	425	333	604	425	379	379	425	288	288	426	5,823
Travel	0	1,240	1,007	515	405	734	515	460	460	515	350	350	518	7,069
Telephone	0	1,043	847	434	341	617	434	387	387	434	295	295	435	5,949
Postage	0	438	358	182	143	259	182	162	162	182	124	124	183	2,499
Office supplies	0	949	770	394	310	561	394	352	352	394	268	268	396	5,408
Advertising	0	6,938	5,635	2,883	2,285	4,103	2,883	2,571	2,571	2,883	1,959	1,959	2,895	39,545
Marketing/promotion	0	5,439	4,418	2,261	1,776	3,217	2,261	2,016	2,016	2,261	1,536	1,536	2,270	31,007
Professional fees	0	1,751	1,422	728	572	1,036	728	649	649	728	494	494	731	9,982
Training and development	0	26	21	11	9	16	11	10	10	11	7	7	11	150
Loan repayments	0	0	0	0	0	0	0	0	0	0	0	0	0	0
Tax payments	0	25,050	0	4,175	10,000	0	0	10,000	0	0	21,325	0	0	29,225
Capital purchases	0	0	0	0	0	0	0	0	0	0	0	0	0	41,325
Total Payments	0	62,864	30,716	19,891	22,346	22,366	15,716	24,016	14,016	15,716	32,001	10,676	15,781	286,105
Cashflow Surplus/Deficit (-)	0	-46,164	-20,696	-8,785	-1,053	-7,670	650	3,289	8,446	9,251	3,757	19,134	18,451	-21,390
Opening Cash Balance	0	0	-46,464	-66,860	-75,645	-76,698	-84,368	-83,748	-80,429	-74,983	-62,732	-58,975	-39,844	-747,413
Closing Cash Balance	0	-46,164	-66,860	-75,645	-76,698	-84,368	-83,748	-80,429	-74,983	-62,732	-58,975	-39,844	-21,390	-768,803

6) Drop shipping vs. wholesaling

The battle between drop shipping and wholesaling has been going on for some time now. The winner of this battle depends on your individual preference, amount of capital that you have to work with, and the type of product that you are hoping to sell.

First of all, you need to understand the difference between manufacturers, wholesalers and drop shippers.

A manufacturer is the company that actually produces the product.

A wholesaler is a company that buys directly from the manufacturer, adds on a profit and sells the product to the retailer, you. The retailer can be a website, i.e. an online store.

A drop shipper is a company that will ship a product for you directly to your customer. The drop shipper will have that product in their warehouse.

The drop shipper can be a manufacturer or a wholesaler.

Any of these—wholesaler, manufacturer, drop shipper or retailer—can act as a drop shipper. Collectively, all these are called "suppliers" throughout this book.

Just because someone claims to be a drop shipper doesn't mean that you are getting the goods at wholesale prices. It is up to you to investigate the pricing.

Is it better to buy from a drop shipper than a wholesaler? Well, that depends on the capital you have to buy stock, on the space you have to store products, and on the time you want to spend shipping sold products.

If you have an eCommerce site and you are planning to use drop shipping, you MUST work directly with the REAL wholesaler in order to build a successful eCommerce business.

Most of the time, you CANNOT buy from a real wholesaler if you are not a legal business! Most wholesale companies that let you buy products from them without

proving to them that you are a business are NOT real wholesalers. That's my experience.

It is possible to obtain a list of wholesalers from The National Wholesalers Association.

In a few bullet points, if you buy from a wholesaler:

- You will get lower prices, as drop shippers usually buy the goods from a wholesaler or a manufacturer.

- Most of the time, a wholesaler will require proof of you owning a business and tax ID.

- A wholesaler does not drop ship (most of them don't) so you have to ship the product to the customer yourself.

- Wholesalers have a minimum order quantity, e.g. £500/$800 or one pallet or minimum 10 cases, etc.

- You need storage space for the stock you buy.

> As a general rule: you will earn more if you buy products wholesale as you will be able to buy the products cheaper. When you use a drop shipper, you will usually earn less. With wholesale you will need the money to buy the goods and you will need the space to store the goods.

Let's look at some details.

a) The thing with wholesale

To put it in one sentence: wholesale is where you buy products at a wholesale price, stock them and sell them from your own stock. No need to say that you will need the money to buy stock, and usually the more stock you buy, the cheaper the price will be, therefore the more profit you can make. So you need a lot more money when you practice wholesaling compared to drop shipping.

People who buy wholesale often don't do drop shipping but do eCommerce: buy stock, sell it from their own website, charge the customer and ship the goods directly to the customer. In this case, it is impossible to set up a business making money on autopilot with hardly any work, as you need to do all the work yourself.

By purchasing products wholesale, you will have more control over your products and what you can offer to your customers, but you also have a larger initial investment. It isn't very often that you can just purchase a single item wholesale. In most cases, you'll need to order five or more of the same item or purchase products in a pack or a crate. For example, you'll typically have to order six pairs of jeans or six shirts rather than a single piece.

Your commitment is larger as well, as you'll need more time when it comes to order fulfillment. The saying "time is money" is relevant here. The time you spend packaging and shipping customer orders is time that you could have spent working on various other parts of your business.

As previously mentioned, you will have more control over the items you have in stock when you purchase wholesale. You also don't have to worry about an item being out of stock, as you'll know exactly how many products you have on hand.

Furthermore, wholesale offers more flexibility in the way you sell your product. It creates an easy way to provide customers with promotional offers. For example, since you have control over your customer's order and how and when it is shipped, you can offer promotions for free shipping for customers who spend £31/$50 or more. It also provides you with the ability to offer promotional materials inside your packages. You can even add an extra "thank you" note in the package to your customer thanking them for their purchase with you.

Unlike drop shippers, wholesalers may offer you the chance to apply for a line of credit. Some wholesalers will eliminate the minimum order requirements once you make your first purchase. Some will also allow you to mix and match on your order when it comes to color and style.

b) The good with drop shipping, compared to wholesale

With drop shipping, you won't have to have an inventory on hand. Therefore, there is no large investment upfront nor does a warehouse have to be purchased or rented in order to store the products that you are selling. In addition, no packaging or shipping materials need to be purchased, nor do you have to spend time packaging and shipping the items sold.

Since you don't have an inventory on hand, the product lines that you sell are flexible. In other words, let's say that you are selling a particular product, such as umbrellas, but they aren't selling well. You can simply remove the item from your website or remove the listing from eBay (or another auction site) and you are done with it. There's no need to worry about what you are going to do with that unsold inventory of umbrellas because you don't have any inventory! This of course applies when you buy from a drop shipper, not when you've bought your products wholesale and stock them yourself.

If you choose wholesale, this means you are buying the products yourself and stock them. If the product does not sell, you will have to sell them with a loss or never sell them at all. Of course, the money you invest in stock that you can't sell will eat your profits away.

If you have a very reliable drop shipper, drop shipping is great fun: you can focus on marketing your site whilst your drop shipper will take care of shipping and warehousing.

c) *The downside to drop shipping, compared to wholesale*

- The downside with drop shipping is that the price isn't nearly as good as it would be if you were to obtain products via wholesale. While drop shipping prices can be good for some products, other products are cheaper when you purchase wholesale. For example, when purchased wholesale, an item may be 50 percent lower than the retail price of the item, but when purchased via drop shipping, that same item may only be 25 percent cheaper than the retail price.

- Most drop shippers will charge a fee on orders, which can take a huge chunk out of your profits; however, not all drop shippers do this. In fact, many drop shippers only charge a one-time upfront membership fee. Ultimately, it's all in the drop shipper that you choose, but we'll get to that later.

- Another downfall with drop shipping is the supply of products. You don't have a lot of control over product availability when drop ship. You may not receive any notice at all— and if you do, it may be very little—when a particular product runs out. You have absolutely no influence as to how many products the drop shipper keeps on hand or even when a product line is changed. It is possible for items to be completely cut off and discontinued. The bad part of this is that this could happen to any product, even the product that you sell really well and you have absolutely no say in it at all. If you buy your products wholesale, you DO control your own stock levels.

- You also do not have any control over the shipping process. Drop shipping could ultimately cause problems for returns and there is absolutely no control over how or when a particular item is shipped to a customer. Some drop shippers will allow for you to use your company name on packaging. Other drop shipping companies may ship orders with their company name, causing confusion when your customer receives the product since the company name is different e.g. the customers ordered from your website www.niceshoes.com and the paperwork comes from www.dropshippingshoes.com . This will be confusing.

- It is important that you check with the drop shipper to make sure that your company name will appear on a receipt inside the package or on the outside of the package.

- When returns come into the picture, drop shippers may allow customers to return the item directly back to them, while others may require that the item be shipped to you first. This can result in some expensive shipping costs, especially if the item is relatively large or heavy. Drop shippers often have limitations as to which locations they are willing to ship their items to. In other words, if you plan on selling products internationally, outside of the U.S., you may find it more difficult to find a willing drop shipper.

- There is also a lot of competition with drop shipping, as hundreds of websites might be selling exactly the same product; these days, the criteria to be accepted by a drop shipper are easy to meet.

- Your drop shipper might cease to trade and your business will suddenly not create any more sales. You will need to find new suppliers, set up new products, etc.

d) So, what is best: wholesaling or drop shipping?

There are a number of factors that you should consider before making the decision to purchase your products from a drop shipper or a wholesaler.

- Are You 100 Percent Sure?

First things first, are you 100 percent positive about the product or products that you want to sell in your online store or on your website? If you've dreamed about selling a particular type of product for years and you've done adequate market research to determine that there is enough demand and not too much competition for you to sell this product and make a profit, then choosing to purchase the item wholesale may be in your best interest. However, if you think you might want to sell other products, or there is even the slightest chance that you may want to offer your customers different items, then you may want to use a drop shipper so that you don't have to purchase several different items initially and take the chance of not being able to sell the products, causing you to be stuck with them on hand.

- Is Your Product Available?

Next, you want to consider whether or not your product is available via a drop shipper and/or a wholesaler. As a general rule, virtually any product can be purchased through a wholesaler, but it's a different story with a drop shipper. Brand name products are more often sold via a wholesaler, although there are restrictions on resale since there are exclusive distribution rights. To get around this, you can purchase and resell refurbished or overstock items. Clothing textiles are also more often sold via a wholesaler. Clothes are generally sold in packs of six, 12 and 20 at very low prices, sometimes with shirts being as low as £1.80/$3 a piece, with jeans running typically around £6/$10 per piece.

- Can You Afford a Wholesaler?

We've discussed that purchasing wholesale can generally get you lower prices per item. However, you have to have the capital upfront to make the initial investment. Because of this, you may need to opt for a drop shipper to start your online business. If you don't like using a drop shipping method, then you can always switch over to purchasing products wholesale after a few months of drop shipping when you've had the chance to build up enough profit to actually invest in the purchase of wholesale products.

When I first started, I would make money and re-invest that money in order to expand my business. This is a business principle that applies in every business, online or not: make profit and rather than pocket the profit, re-invest it with the aim of making more profit.

- How About Using Both?

More often than not, many online eCommerce stores choose to purchase via wholesale and also use a drop shipper. In a number of cases, you may find that you want to use a drop shipper for most of your products, but for your best selling items, you may want to purchase wholesale so that you can get them at a better price and ultimately make a larger profit.

> **TOP TIP:** Start with drop shipping and if you start to make money, consider buying wholesale.

Typically, when you first start out, drop shipping is the preferred method. As you learn more about the business and your products, you can switch over to wholesale for all of your products or just for certain ones.

Confused? That's okay. Here's an example to explain things a little better for you. You'll see that in the example below, it is more profitable for you to purchase bedding sets wholesale. However, due to the cost of shipping and packaging materials, you would lose money if you were to purchase coffee makers wholesale; therefore, it would be in your best interest to use a drop shipper for these.

Note: This is all assuming that you are not storing items in a rented or purchased building and that your products are being stored in your basement, garage or somewhere free of charge. If this is not the case, you would have much larger expenses therefore you would need to sell a lot more to cover your expenses before you make a profit.

Example 1, bed set:

Assume a bedding set sells at 230.00 retail price ($ or £ doesn't matter in this example).

Purchasing Wholesale

115.00 Purchase Price

+ 0.00 Storage Cost

+ 4.00 Packaging Materials

+ 12.00 Shipping Cost P&P

+ 15.00 Time Spent - 15.00 per hour

146.00 Total Cost

84.00 Your Profit (230.00 - 146.00)

****

Purchasing Via Drop Shipper

230.00 Bedding Set - retail price

150.00 Purchase Price

+ 5.00 Drop shipping fee

+ 12.00 Shipping Cost P&P. Your drop shipper will charge you shipping cost.

167.00 Total Cost

63.00 Your Profit (230.00 - 167.00)

As you can see, it is more profitable for you to purchase the bedding set via wholesale rather than via a drop shipper.

Example 2, coffee maker:

Assume a coffee maker sells at 79.99 retail price ($ or £ doesn't matter in this example).

Purchasing Wholesale

50.00 Purchase Price

+ 0.00 Storage Cost

+ 6.00 Packaging Materials

+ 12.00 Shipping Cost P&P

+ 15.00 Time Spent - 15.00 per hour

83.00 Total Cost

-3.01 Your LOSS (79.99 - 83.00)

****

Purchasing Via Drop Shipper

56.73 Purchase Price

+ 2.00 Drop shipping fee

+ 12.00 Shipping Cost P&P Your drop shipper will charge you shipping cost.

70.73 Total Cost

9.26 Your Profit (79.99 - 70.73)

As you can see, you don't make any profit if you purchase the product via wholesale as your expenses are too high as you HAVE to add your time, your wages.

Conclusion: selling "cheaper" items is often not profitable when you buy wholesale as you have to do the work and therefore pay yourself to do the work.

Where to find wholesalers?

Lots of wholesalers are not very good in their SEO (Search Engine Optimisation), so they are not easy to find in Google. Search for:

- "bath foam" wholesaler

- "bath foam" reseller

- "bath foam" bulk

- "bath foam" distributor

Some ways to find products to sell if you are NOT doing drop shipping:

- direct enquiries: contact manufacturers directly—search for them

- go to trade shows and exhibitions

- buy some trade magazines

- physically knock on company doors

We will talk about directories to find wholesalers later.

7) Exposing the facts related to drop shipping

Let's look at some facts regarding drop shipping before we talk about some myths that are often related to the process of drop shipping and the business that surrounds it.

Purchasing and re-selling products and services online has become popular in recent years. More and more people turn to the Internet to make their purchases, even on the most common household items. Therefore, it is really no surprise that drop shipping businesses are popular with individuals looking to secure their financial future. By having a drop shipping business online, you are gaining exposure that a brick-and-mortar retail store could not have. However, to be successful, there are some facts you should be aware of and some steps that you should take, as you will have competition.

a) No overnight success

A snap of your fingers won't make you a millionaire—even though we all wish it could. The same can be said with the drop shipping business. As with any business, you can't get rich overnight. It will take time and effort on your part, especially with a drop shipping business. Now, in the long run, a drop shipping business can be very profitable, but it can only be profitable if you take the necessary steps for your business to actually make money.

b) Quick and easy to get started

For the most part, this is one myth that can be debunked. Getting your drop shipping business will take a little bit of time, especially if you tackle it all on your own rather than selecting a pre-made website with pre-loaded products to sell; however, ultimately, once you are used to it all, it will become easy. The best thing about a drop shipping business is that it is not very expensive to get up and running and begin seeing profit.

c) Decent income? Yes!

Unlike many at-home business opportunities, drop shipping is a legitimate way to actually make a decent amount of income from home with little initial investment. Some drop shipping and eCommerce sites are known to make six or seven-figure incomes; however, this isn't something you should expect as you first start out, as you'll need to effectively market your site/store in order to gain traffic and potential customers. Every person is different, and therefore the actual success (or failure) will vary from person to person.

d) Drop shipping with eBay and Amazon

While it is possible to make a sufficient income from drop shipping with a variety of products on Amazon and eBay, it is still recommended that you sell products from your own personal website—either one that you create from scratch or one that you purchase ready-made and pre-filled with products from a drop shipping company. Some will find they can sell their products with ease via eBay and Amazon, while others will find that their products simply do not do well on those sites. Generally, it has nothing to do with you and just has to do with the product and the current market (or lack thereof) for that particular product.

e) *Small percentage of unhappy customers*

As a general rule, you won't find yourself caught in a mess between yourself, your drop shipping company/product supplier and a customer. There are no more unhappy customers in the drop shipping industry than there is in any other industry. This is, of course, assuming that you offer quality customer service, provide accurate details to your customers about your products, and purchase your products from a reliable drop shipping source that updates stock frequently and ships quickly.

All in all, a drop shipping business can be very lucrative if done appropriately and can provide you with the personal freedom and the ability to lead a good life financially and otherwise.

8) Myths associated with drop shipping

As with most things, there are a numbers of myths associated with drop shipping, from not being able to make money with this strategy to it not being easy to find wholesale suppliers. Here are four of the top myths associated with drop shipping:

- It's impossible to make money with drop shipping.
While some products will have lower profit margins than other products, it is 100% possible to make money in the drop shipping business. Believe it or not, many businesses, retailers and corporations—both small and large—utilise drop shipping. This is one of the reasons why retailers can offer such a diverse selection of products to their customers, because they are using a drop shipping service.

It is true that most individuals cannot make drop shipping work because they are unable to meet the product purchasing requirements of wholesale distributors. If you are part of a larger picture, then drop shipping can be used. By joining as a member of a drop shipping service, you are in the group with hundreds and thousands of other members that use the same service—and likely, same products. This ensures that minimum purchasing requirements are met, allowing for you to sell your product on your own site for a low price and make a decent profit.

- For minimal work, you will make a very large amount of money.
While it is true that you will do less work and make money, it isn't accurate to say that you will work very little and make huge amounts of cash. You see, you save time by not having to package and ship out orders to customers, but that saved time is used in other areas of your business, such as generating traffic to your site to get those sales. You spend time researching products, listing products, building websites and advertising. So, it's safe to say that you will be working hard. Any successful business requires hard work and dedication—a drop shipping business is no different.

- Drop shipping and wholesale providers will work with anyone and everyone.
This couldn't be further from the truth. Some wholesale providers require a hefty up-front fee, large orders and minimum order quantities. Because of this, these providers must be selective in who they work with, as they must only work with people that will ultimately meet their requirements and needs.

Luckily, this isn't something you have to deal with in your drop shipping business. You can sign up with a variety of drop shipping services that have taken care of all the previously mentioned stuff for you. You can sign up and have access to products and be able to order without having to meet a minimum order amount or having to purchase large quantities of an item. You can simply order one item when it sells on your site without needing to purchase multiple items. Drop shipping services charge a one-time fee or a monthly fee to cover the costs that they pay to ensure you have the best quality products at your disposal from a selection of top-notch wholesalers.

Selecting a first-rate drop shipping service for your business is one of the many things that will ensure your business's success.

- Drop shipping is everyone's one-stop solution to product sourcing.
Unfortunately, there is no magic solution to product sourcing, although many believe drop shipping fits the bill. Drop shipping is practical for a number of online businesses, but that doesn't mean it is the right answer for anyone and everyone. It all depends on what you

are actually looking for. If you are looking for in-demand brand name products with images and descriptions given to you and the ability to sell products at any given time, then drop shipping may be ideal for you. Drop shipping is also for those who want to sell products, but don't want to have to deal with inventory and up-front costs associated with having in-stock products. If you don't want to have to deal with inventory and the shipping of products, then drop shipping is an excellent choice for you.

Lack of money is one of the most common reason why individuals can't start a business. Fortunately, drop shipping makes it so that money is not an issue. While you may be out of some money when finding a drop shipping service and setting up your website, you are only spending a fraction of the cost that you would be if you had to purchase inventory to have in stock. As long as you have motivation and determination, drop shipping can help you succeed with your very own online business.

9) Pros and cons of drop shipping

The Pros

The benefits of a simple process like drop shipping are outstanding. For a nominal membership fee to the site, you can gain access to a wide variety of benefits:

- Minimal financial risk overall; you don't need a lot of money to start.

- Easy to get started.

- Minimal out-of-pocket expenses.

- No overheads, work from home.

- Large selection of product to choose from.

- No buying products in advance.

- No storing inventory.

- No managing or even handling inventory.

- No trips to shipping companies (USPS, UPS, FedEx).

- No getting orders ready for shipment.

- You can copy the pictures from their websites so there is no need to know about photography.

- YOU can decide how much you sell the product for. The drop shipper might give you a RRP (Recommended Retail Price), but you don't need to stick to that price.

- You can copy the product's name and description from the drop shipper BUT I don't recommend you that. Give it your own name and descriptions, with keywords, which I will explain later.

- Save time and money—not to mention space, inconvenience and more!

- Get started immediately with 24/7 access to high quality, profitable products.

- Be YOUR boss, set YOUR hours, and work from YOUR home.

- Easy to scale. If you run your own company and fulfill orders yourself, you will have twice the work if you have twice the orders. That does not apply in drop shipping as most of the work is done by your drop shipper.

- It's a trusted model. There are big stores online that use drop shipping because then they don't have the hassle of inventory.

Ultimately, you won't need thousands of dollars to stock up on products to start your store. Instead, you will simply order an item when a customer orders it from you. And because you don't have to pre-purchase inventory, you can offer your customers a wider selection of items. With that being said, the risk of starting an online business is greatly reduced since you won't be pre-purchasing merchandise. If you don't sell something, you don't have to worry about the money you spent buying the product because you never bought it! But, as with anything, there are a few pitfalls to drop shipping as well.

The Cons

- Lack of control on packaging, shipping and more.

- Issues with out-of-stock products; syncing inventory is not always real time.

- You have no control over inventory management.

- You rely on someone else to fulfill your orders.

- Higher prices than when purchasing wholesale and in bulk.

- Lower, sometimes awful, profit margins.

- Possibly have to deal with returns.

- There will be loads of competition from stores selling exactly the same products.

- Shipping can be complex. If you will work with multiple suppliers, which you are likely to do, the products on your website will be sourced from different suppliers, making it more complicated to keep a record of your shipping costs. If a customer places an order on your website for three products and you buy those products from three different suppliers, you will have 3 shipping costs to pay for and you can't pass these charges on to your customers.

- Everyone makes mistakes, so your drop shipper will make mistakes in processing orders. You will have to apologise to your customer, even if you didn't make the mistake.

All in all, you can see that the advantages quickly outweigh the disadvantages. Drop shipping is certainly not a stress-free way to earn a lot of money. The drop shipping model has some great advantages but also comes with some complexities and problems you need to be aware of.

However, with some great planning and knowledge of the problems involved, you can build a profitable drop shipping business.

10) Important things to know and do

These four things are very important to know or do if you want to reach success in your drop shipping business.

- Choosing a Drop Shipper That Meets Your Needs.
Every individual person is different and will have different goals as they start and operate their drop shipping business. It is important to become familiar with your goals and needs so that you can choose a reliable drop shipper that can ideally meet them. Be aware that there are lots of Internet cowboys out there trying to make money from you but not giving you anything of value. Find a drop shipping company (which will likely result in a one-time nominal fee for access) that will provide the products to you at a reasonable price, offer a variety of marketing, security and website tools and features, and provide you with a large list of wholesalers and drop shippers that have been pre-screened and reviewed to ensure their reliability and credibility in the drop shipping industry.

- You MUST Make a Test Order When Working With Wholesalers.
In the event that you decide to work with wholesalers instead of drop shippers (or even if you work with drop shippers), you must make a small sample order to test their service. This will help you in your identification of the reliable and honest drop shipping companies and wholesalers. It also gives you an idea of estimated shipping times, which is important when you are counting on someone else to ship the order to your customer. During this test order, make sure to look closely at the packaging label to see if they utilise blind labeling, or if they are using their own distribution center labels.

Ask a friend to order something from your site—you pay him, of course, for the purchase he made. See how quickly he gets the product from the drop shipper. Put yourself in your customer's shoes; remember the picture of the shoes? By making a test order, you can see what your customer will experience when placing an order.

- Market Your Drop Shipping Site.
While this isn't necessary until you have your business and site up and running, it is a necessary step to ensure that you actually receive customers, make sales and generate revenue. You can't simply expect to create your site and have visitors flowing in one after another immediately. You must market your website (there are free ways to do this, by the way, such as forums, guest blogs, article marketing and more) in order for your business to

receive visitors and convert those visitors into customers. There are over 100 traffic methods in my book "From Newbie To Millionaire".

- Keep Lines of Communication Open at All Times.
Like any business, there can be delays or potential problems with items. It is important that you provide your customers with your contact information and let them know that you will take care of their needs. By being available for contact, you are ensuring that your customers will have a more enjoyable experience with you and your drop shipping business, which will lead to positive word-of-mouth marketing (free, by the way) attracting more customers. All in all, it's important to keep your customers happy. Keep your customers informed, even if the problem is not solved yet. Send them a message: "I did not forget you, I am working on the problem…" or something along those lines. Keep your customers updated with what is going on. NEVER should customers ask you why they have not heard from you yet.

11) 20 drop shipping mistakes to avoid

Drop shipping is a powerful endeavor, if the proper amount of planning and research is done. While it's always helpful to know what to do when starting your first-ever drop shipping business, it's just as valuable to understand a few things that you shouldn't do. Although some of these may seem like common sense, the sad, unfortunate truth is that a number of optimistic entrepreneurs will still make silly mistakes. Here are a few mistakes that you should avoid when entering the drop shipping business.

Mistake #1 – Don't sell products that have no potential buyers.
Unfortunately, it happens. Plenty of people have failed with their drop shipping business because their initial product or product niche was something that didn't interest many people. It may seem great to you, but you aren't selling it to yourself—you are selling this product to the world over the Internet. Others must agree that the product is great or it won't sell, and your drop shipping business will sink. The best way to avoid this is by choosing a product or product niche that you believe would sell really well and ask your family, friends and co-workers to see what they think about the product. While everyone isn't going to like it, you will get a good idea of whether or not it's a solid product idea or if you need to do research to find a new product/niche to drop ship.

Don't ever forget:

- It is not important what YOU like, it is important what your customer likes.

- It is not important what YOU would buy, it is important what your customer would buy.

Mistake #2 – Don't go overboard with your website at first.

While it's great to be optimistic, that great attitude should be put on hold just a bit to ensure you don't rush into anything. You see, your drop shipping business may take off in a second, but there's also the possibility that the product or niche you have chosen to drop ship and sell won't work. If the latter is the case, then you'll have to re-design everything, so it's better not to put a lot of time, effort and money into your initial website until you can see that the products will sell. I'm not saying you should have a Plain Jane website, as this could turn customers away, but just don't spend thousands of dollars getting your site up and running. Build a website that is professional from content to design and proceed with the necessary steps to generate targeted traffic. If your site gets traffic and sufficient sales, then that's great and you can move forward with improving your website. Be careful and hedge your bets wisely.

Flash ain't cash: a brilliant looking website with all the bells and whistles doesn't mean it is going to make you money.

Mistake #3 – Don't ever start your business without researching first.

From understanding what drop shipping is to knowing how to get your website up and running, it is important to research, research and research. This book will tell you everything you need to know about starting a drop shipping business, but there may be a few things that you want to research on your own. This is especially true when it comes to marketing, as this book only speaks of this sparingly.

Remember: failing to plan is planning to fail.

Mistake #4 – Avoid purchasing products that are at or close to retail price.

Some drop shipping companies will try to scam you by making you think you are getting a good deal, but in reality, it simply sucks. If the discount you are getting is about 10 percent, you can rest assured that you won't really make any profit. In drop shipping, there are expenses: overheads, shipping, VAT, etc. All of this must be factored in. Will these costs be covered with that 10 percent discount and still make you a profit or are you going to be in the red in the end?

Find products that sell well and have a significantly high profit margin. Competition on certain products can be tough and having some leeway in the price that you can sell your product for can really help. You simply can't afford (literally) to purchase products that you have to sell at an inflated price, keeping you well below your competition in sales.

Mistake #5 – Not checking ahead of time if there is sufficient inventory.

The best drop shipping companies have systems in place to notify their customers when a product is reaching a dangerously low stock. However, some do not offer this luxury. In fact, you could find a supplier that doesn't offer real-time updates, which would result in a sale that you must refund. Check in regularly with your drop shipping supplier to ensure that they have plenty of stock. While this isn't necessary every day, it doesn't hurt to do it a couple of times a week and definitely check it right before days when you expect to receive lots of orders e.g. when you are doing a special promotion.

Mistake #6 – Working with the wrong suppliers.

Sadly, there are many suppliers that are not experienced in the industry, unreliable or dishonest.

You have to be really careful when choosing suppliers, as some may appear to be pretty reliable and honest, but they have no intention of helping you if you have problems with the product or anything else. There are also suppliers that won't ship in plain packaging or aren't willing to put your name on the shipping label. Instead, they put their contact details on the outside of the package, resulting in your customer buying directly from them for future orders. These suppliers also often sell to both retailers as well as end users, which is just another reason to stay away from them.

You are doing the work trying to get buyers and when you have a sale, they won't become repeat customers from you, but their next order will be directly with your supplier. That's why it is very important to do a test sale. As a general rule, this mistake applies to those looking for suppliers on their own rather than working through a drop shipping company. It's always in your best interest to work with a drop shipping company that takes care of virtually everything for you or to work with a well-known, reliable wholesale or drop shipping directory.

Mistake #7 – Purchasing or promoting uncompetitive products.

No matter how much you may like a product, if it is too expensive, unpopular and/or of inadequate quality, you need to stay far, far away. Whether you are selling on Amazon, eBay or your own personal website, you are going to be in competition with other sellers and websites to obtain customers and sales. Therefore, you need to obtain and sell products that are high quality, competitively priced and popular so that you can beat your competition; otherwise, you won't make a profit with your drop shipping/wholesale business.

Mistake #8 – Choosing the wrong hosting

Once you have decided on your domain name, which is the name of your site, such as www.yourdomainnamehere.com, you need to make sure that somebody will host your website. This means somebody has got to store your website somewhere so people can access it. When you have built a website on your computer and it has been published to the web, people need to be able to see it. If 1,000 people want to look at your site, they won't come to your home or office to do it, so you need to have a place where your site is "hosted" so that all 1,000 people can look at it at the same time. This is what a hosting company does; they will give your site a space on their massive computer servers so people can view it. You pay the hosting company a fee to host, or store, your site.

When choosing a hosting company, you need to look at two factors: web disk space and bandwidth.

Another reason why you need a hosting company is because of the bandwidth (see explanation below) on your computer. If you host your website yourself and have an internet connection speed of 1MB on your home computer, it will take a long time for a customer to download a video (assuming you sell videos). A hosting company might have a 250MB internet connection speed, meaning your customers can download the video much quicker.

Choose your hosting company carefully. You can spend a heck of a lot of time designing your site, but if it is slow to load due to a poor hosting plan, visitors will move on to another site. I recommend strongly not using the free or very cheap web hosting companies. The speed of loading of your website is crucially important to your success. Have you ever opened a site and closed it because it took too long to load? I know I have. You certainly don't want this to happen with your site. Consider hosting as one of the very important foundations of your success so NEVER go for the unknown, cheap hosting deals.

You can buy a domain name from one company and have the hosting done by another company. Personally I prefer to use the company I bought my domain from to do the hosting as well.

If you have an Australian website and you are targeting a market in Australia, it is always best to choose a hosting company with an Australian server. If you are based in USA, choose a hosting company with a USA based server and so on. This can be important for search engine ranking purposes and for the loading speed of your site.

- What is bandwidth and what is the difference between it and web disk space?

This often confuses IM newbies.

What is 'disk space'?

Disk space is also called data storage or hosting space. It is the amount of data that the hosting provider allows you to store. Images, audio files, visual files, multimedia files and graphics all take up a lot more space than simple text. If your site has 20 pages of mostly text, your total disk space needs will probably be under 1MB. If you have a site with lots of graphics and multimedia, you need a lot more disk space.

TOP TIP: To find out how much disk space you need for your website, simply put all your website files into one folder on your PC. Right click the folder and choose 'properties', which will show you the total space needed to store your website.

What is 'bandwidth'?

Bandwidth is the amount of traffic that your hosting company allows between your website on their server and the visitors to your website. It is a measure of total data transferred in one month to and from your site. Each time a visitor looks at your site, it is downloaded from your hosting company to be viewed on the internet. If you go over the amount of bandwidth with your hosting company they could charge you an extra fee; visitors might not be able to see your site or it will be downloaded very slowly.

Think about bandwidth as cars on motorways (highways in the US). If you are the only car on the motorway, you can drive quickly, but the more cars, the slower you're forced to go. You are also not able to overtake another car when you are stuck in a queue. With low bandwidth, your visitors cannot download things quickly and will be stuck in a queue when wanting to download a file if two people want to download it at the same time.

How much bandwidth do you need?

For most small businesses or personal sites 2GB of bandwidth per month is usually enough. Most hosting companies will include this in their cheapest package. Traffic to your site is the number of 'bits' that are transferred on the Internet. One gigabyte (GB) is 1,024 megabytes. To store one character, one byte of storage is needed.

- Imagine that you have 100 filing cabinets in your office.

- Each of these filing cabinets has 1000 folders in it.

- In each folder there are 100 papers.

- On each paper are 100 characters.

- The total of all these is 1 GB (100x1000x100x100).

How much bandwidth you need depends on what type of website you are building. If people can download MP3 songs or videos from your website, and you are expecting a lot of visitors, you will need a very high bandwidth because each MP3 song is, on average, about 4MB. A long video in High Definition can be up to 1000MB or 1GB. In this case, if you only have a bandwidth of 1GB, when two customers want to download a 1GB video, they cannot do it at the same time. Remember, in my comparison with motorways and cars, you cannot overtake a car when in a traffic jam. The second one in the queue will probably receive an error message. This will result in your customer having a negative impression of your site, which of course you must avoid. If you are expecting ten thousand visitors to your site per day, you need to choose the correct bandwidth plan with your hosting company. Most hosting companies offer the facility to start with low bandwidth and upgrade it at an extra cost.

Companies offer a variety of bandwidth options in terms of your monthly gigabyte allocation.

Working out how much bandwidth you need is not as simple as calculating how much disk space you need. But the following formula will give you some idea: Size (or disk space) of all your web pages including all graphics X numbers of visitors you expect each day X number of pages your visitors will view X 30 days per month = total monthly data transfer, or bandwidth.

The number of emails that you send also counts in the bandwidth. If you often send hundreds of emails with very large files attached, it will count towards your bandwidth usage.

If your website gets lots of visits per month, through Google or from affiliates sending traffic to it, you need more bandwidth, not necessarily more space.

Having said all the above about hosting, quite a few hosting companies now offer unlimited bandwidth and unlimited disc space.

Mistake #9 – Underestimating costs associated with drop shipping
While it can be relatively cheap to start a drop shipping business, you will still incur start-up expenses. Never underestimate these costs. Starting a drop shipping business, just like any other business, means you need some money to start. You don't have to pre-purchase your inventory with drop shipping, but there are still other expenses to consider, e.g. hosting, website design, merchant account fees, etc. I will discuss all expenses later.

Mistake #10 – Do not rush into drop shipping

While you may be in a bad financial situation and you need money **now**, it is important not to rush into things when it comes to setting up your drop shipping business for success. Most people are unsuccessful with drop shipping because they rush into everything. They think if they quickly put a product on Ebay or Amazon, the sales will start rolling in. Sure, you may get lucky and the product sells the first day you have it listed, but it is unlikely and it isn't going to happen every single time.

By rushing into things, you lack the proper knowledge to truly create a successful drop shipping business. More than likely, you have no idea what products to choose or what niche to select, as the niche ideally needs to be low competition yet high demand. Choosing random products and just going for it hoping for the best is not the way to tackle your new business. You may need to sell your products quickly to get money, but if you don't learn the things you need to know, such as choosing the right drop shipping niche and how to generate traffic to your website, you won't sell many products and you most definitely won't see long-term success.

Mistake #11 – Going live before testing is done

One of my students asked for help. He said he did everything according to the book and his website was shown on the first page for his keywords, but he simply did not get any sales.

The very first thing I do when I hear that sort of problem is check his order buttons. Each time I tried to order any product I received an error: "There is an error processing your order, please contact the webmaster." The problem was that he simply did not link his order buttons to his merchant account.

I don't mind helping people, but that's what I call wasting my time!

Lesson to be learned: you must do some test orders for a few products, just to make sure everything works. Place an order pretending you are the customer. Read all the confirmation emails your customer will receive and see if there's room for improvement. Pay for the goods, do the WHOLE procedure from ordering a product until you receive it.

Most eCommerce software will have a "test" button on the site, but even after I have tested with that button, I still do a "real" test order for some products, as I believe what I SEE, not what I hear or have been told.

Mistake #12 – Choosing the wrong niche

Don't pick a niche that is too broad or has too much competition. As a beginner, it will be impossible to beat the big boys. Investigate your niche really well and analyse how you can beat your competition, which we will discuss later.

Mistake #13 – Work with poor quality eCommerce software

You will find out as you read through this book that there are many choices for software, but you must be aware that there are a lot of cowboys trading on the web, selling you poor quality software that will load very slowly, etc…don't fall for the very cheap or free options.

Mistake #14 – Trying to please everyone

I don't know the exact secret to success, but I DO know the reason for failure: trying to please everyone.

Whatever anyone tells you, investigate thoroughly what you are planning to do, and if you believe in it all, go for it and ignore what other people say. Only learn from people who have proven that they know what they are talking about. Don't take lessons from a 99p Kindle book, as that will probably not contain anything really valuable for you.

Mistake #15 – Poor keyword research and SEO

You will learn later how important SEO is. I can tell you now that it is crucially important if you want to rank in Google on the first pages. You need to spend A LOT of time doing your SEO.

Mistake #16 – Not focusing on profit

Don't focus so much on sales and product availability that you forget about profit! You must investigate your pricing properly. How much profit can you make? Will your profits cover your overheads? I strongly believe in a small turnover and big profit margins as compared to a large turnover and small profit margins.

Mistake #17 – Poor customer service

A lot of your customers should become repeat customers—depending on what you sell, of course. If you don't treat your customers with the respect they deserve, they will not come back AND they will certainly not provide word of mouth advertising for you.

Mistake #18 – Underestimating the competition

Always, always watch what your competition is doing. They will try and beat you, but you must try and beat them! I will talk more about this later in the book.

Mistake #19 – Choosing the wrong eCommerce platform

As you will read later, there are lots of choices to build your eCommerce shop. Sign up with a few for a free trial and see if you like the platform.

Mistake #20 – Set it all up and just sit back and wait

I have left the most important mistake for last. Most people quickly set up a website and hope the customers will automatically arrive and the orders will start flooding in. No way—won't work! You need planning, a strategy for success BEFORE you start building your store. If you can't effectively market your business and attract customers to your store, you won't make it, unless you will find an incredibly good niche without any competition at all.

You need traffic or visitors to your site! Don't expect them to just knock on your door to buy your stuff.

Conclusion:

Homework was dreaded in school, but it's necessary to do your homework to ensure your success in drop shipping. Be sure to read online reviews from previous sellers and customers of wholesalers and drop shippers, investigate their history and contact them directly with any questions and concerns that you have. Initial due diligence will ensure fewer headaches in the future.

Ultimately, these mistakes could determine the success or failure of your business, so it's important to stay clear of the above-mentioned problems.

12) How to avoid drop shipping and suppliers scams

Regardless of what you are doing online, whether it's purchasing a weight loss product or choosing a drop shipping service, there are going to be fraudulent sites that are simply there to take your money. They'll be online one day, and the next, they'll be gone. Luckily, though, when choosing a drop shipping service, there are several things you can do to ensure you are not a victim of a scam artist.

Ongoing Fees. Real wholesalers don't charge a monthly fee. If you come across a supplier that charges you a monthly fee, it is likely not to be a legitimate company. There are exceptions.

Important to mention here is that there is a difference between suppliers and suppliers directories. These directories will charge you a monthly fee or a one-time fee. It does not mean that the directories are not legitimate.

Scour the Site—Inside and Out! Look at the site. I mean, really look at the site. Don't just glance at one page or two pages and assume it's good to go. This is a very common mistake amongst individuals looking to start a drop shipping business. This results in paying a couple hundred bucks of your hard-earned money for services that you never receive. And guess what? There's not a thing that can be done about it.

So, before committing to any paid subscription, look at the site in-depth. Don't just read the benefits and features page. You need to look at everything from the benefits and features to the FAQs. On the FAQ page, you will be able to find all the basic information regarding the service. In most cases, you can get a true feel of how the company runs its business.

Usually, when you come across a site that is full of advertising, that website is not going to be any good to you. These sites concentrate on earning money from advertising.

Require Proof. The majority of legitimate wholesalers will require proof that you are a legal business. Most of the time, they will ask you this before you can set up an account with them and before you can see the price they charge you for their products.

Call Them. A good way of finding out if you are dealing with a legitimate supplier is to call them. If no one ever answers the phone number that is displayed on their website, they might not be legitimate.

Check Out the Blog. If the company that you are considering using has a link to a blog, make sure to look at it. This will also give you more information about the company. In most cases, the blog will provide you some inside secrets as to how they work and how you can make a profit. Don't expect every single secret to be shelled out that easy, though! They expect you to work hard for your money!

Testimonials. Never, ever trust the testimonials of a drop shipping service or any other service or product on the Internet. In most cases, testimonials are written by employees of the company themselves or they paid someone to write up fake reviews to create a better reputation for their service/product. While this may not be true for every single product or service out there, it is majority of the time. What company is going to publish negative reviews on their site?

Even if the website has an area to leave comments and reviews, the webmaster will usually approve the comments first before publishing them. He or she will just delete the negative comments.

Terms and Conditions. This is by far the most important. Read the terms and conditions thoroughly. This is the small print that they don't expect you to read. Probably 98 percent of the time, the "I Agree" checkbox is checked without even reading the terms and conditions. They expect you to do this, but it is one of the worst things you could do.

In the terms and conditions, especially with drop shipping services, there is vital information regarding refund and warranties. In many cases, there will be a disclaimer in the terms and conditions stating that the company is not responsible for lost or damaged packages while in transit and when delivered. They also often state that they will not help you in the replacement or refunding of the product.

The Verdict. Finding reliable suppliers can be a bit tricky. However, if you take the necessary time to read the fine print and investigate potential suppliers, you should be able to pick the good ones from the bad ones.

Chapter 5 - What Niche?

In my book, "Finding Niches Made Easy", I explain finding a niche in a lot more detail.

Your niche is the type of product you will sell, e.g. you can be in the animal niche and sell dog food. You can be in the car niche and sell car accessories, etc…

A niche is a small part of a topic or subject. A car market is a niche: that is a niche where all people are interested in cars. Mercedes is a sub niche from the main niche (a niche within a niche), as it is a manufacturer of cars. You can keep digging deeper into a niche: a yellow Mercedes would be another sub niche of the Mercedes niche. A yellow Mercedes with yellow leather chairs (digging deeper again) would be a micro niche in that sub niche. In this book I will sometimes talk about sub niches and micro niches that have the potential to make money. I will simply use the term "niche" throughout this book.

Recap:

Market or niche: Car

Sub niche: Mercedes

Micro niche: Yellow Mercedes

Here's another example:

Market or niche: Tennis

Sub niche: Serving

Micro niche: Serving left-handed

The Internet is ideal for finding niche markets. A few things you can do to find a niche:

- Join forums

- Join groups

- Join communities

- Join chat sites

- Join social websites

- Join hobbyist forums

- Buy some magazines

- Browse manufacturer's sites

- Talk to people

- Look around you

- Analyse everything, wherever you are

- Ask everyone you know if they have been looking for something and can't find it easily

- Go to article websites and randomly read some articles

- Go to exhibitions

- Go to trade shows

In "the olden days" you would have to go to exhibitions, join clubs, phone people or write thousands of letters in order to find people who love yellow Mercedes'. All you need to do these days is Google Yellow Mercedes and it's likely that you will find potential customers. And the extra bonus? You can sell to people all over the world.

Why are micro niches of significant importance? Research has proven that when people do not *immediately* find what they want on a site, they will leave it. Take our example of Mercedes: a searcher types in "yellow Mercedes" and comes across a site that has not focused on the keywords yellow Mercedes. He sees all red, black and blue cars and leaves the site. The next site he comes across shows four pictures, all with a yellow Mercedes. He will no doubt have a look on the site because he knows that it contains relevant information.

Here are some more examples of niches, just so you get the picture: piano players, twin mums, translators, model train builders, yoga trainers.

Sub-niches would be: standing-up piano players, twin mums over 40, Spanish translators, and so on.

1) Choose a niche market over a generalized product store

You might have an idea to sell a product; lots of people have ideas all the time, but having an idea is simply not good enough! You need to investigate to see if your idea will make you money! Your light bulb needs to be filled with money!

Every single big thing and every single BIG company started with an idea! You might be "The next big thing". Believe in your product, believe in yourself and make it happen!

You need to have the drive! You need to believe you can do it!

One of the first mistakes that newbies to the eCommerce industry make is deciding to create a store that sells a little bit of everything—kind of like Walmart or Tesco in the UK. While it may sound like a good idea because you have a large selection of products and virtually anything that someone might need, you'll have the problem that you can't offer rock-bottom prices for products like other general stores, such as Walmart.

Price isn't everything, though. You can offer perks that Walmart might not be able to, such as free shipping, superior customer service, a more diverse product selection, free t-shirts, coupons, informative articles, etc. All of this will be discussed later. Right now, you need to select a product.

You need to sit down, brainstorm and choose a niche market. You see, Walmart may have a wide selection of items, but they don't carry everything. For every product, there are a number of styles and Walmart doesn't carry. This is where you can triumph—with specialization.

a) *Difference between elastic and inelastic demand*

There are two types of market demand: elastic and inelastic. The former is when a product is widely available with a wealth of substitutes, and because of this, demand drops when prices are raised. In other words, when a product is available everywhere, you aren't going to make much profit, if any at all, because mega retailers, such as Walmart or Tesco, can sell this product for much cheaper than you can.

An inelastic demand is when a product is not available everywhere you turn and has fewer substitutes as well as suppliers. Therefore, this product is in higher demand and higher prices won't matter because customers will still pay it since the item is hard to come by. My own website www.liquorice-licorice.co.uk is a good example of this.

b) *Expert specialization is your key to success*

By specializing in a particular niche, you can become an expert, which will lead to more sales in the long run, as you'll become an authority seller for that particular niche. You must perform research in order to determine the best products that will satisfy your demographic, and you'll need to learn what brings in visitors. This is the key to your success, because if you can't please your demographic while capitalizing on your niche, it's a failure.

Ideally, you need to develop a passion for your product, but this is not always needed to make money with your niche. If you are able to work with a niche that you are already passionate about, then that is fantastic, but you may find that your favourite hobby is a very saturated market. However, you can always develop a new passion..

This is probably the most challenging hurdle for someone looking to start an online business, but it is also the most important. The reason for this is because the success of the niche that you choose will determine whether you succeed or fail in your drop shipping business. Your niche is what makes you your money, so it is important that you choose the right niche—one that has realised profitable success online.

While it is helpful in some cases to choose a niche that you are passionate about, when you first start out, it is probably better to choose a niche that you know will be profitable. Of course, if you can find products to sell that YOU are personally interested in, that would be better. Personally, I don't like liquorice, but I know thousands of people do as I sell liquorice on a daily basis.

The niche that you love may not even be available for drop shipping, or there may not be much demand for your passion. After all, you aren't doing this to develop a new hobby or to expand on your current hobby: you are looking into the drop shipping eCommerce business because you want and/or need to make money. But, if you can find a niche that is profitable and you are passionate about, then it's a win-win situation for you!

A recommended book on this subject is "The Zulu Principle: Making Extraordinary Profits from Ordinary Shares", by Jim Slater (available on Amazon).

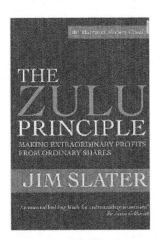

Although this book is about trading shares, the message in this book is very clear: you can become a leading expert in any niche or micro niche in a very short time just by studying and analysing that niche. Slater applies his method by specialising in a certain type of share and situation surrounding that share. The book is all about finding a niche and then attempting to dominate it. Slater suggests that you need to become an expert in your niche, and your expertise will enable you to outperform the markets in niches neglected by others. The same principle applies on the web; if you, as an Internet marketer, can find a lucrative niche and specialise in it, you can make money. The ability to find a niche and dig deeper into that niche is an extremely good skill to have as an Internet marketer.

I have been in business for over 30 years, and I have always believed in this: if you want to buy something and you cannot find it easily, you can assume that other people are looking for it as well, therefore there is a market for it! I have set up businesses in the past based on that principle. You will read about it later in this book.

That is also the reason why I wrote my book "From Newbie To Millionaire", because I bought lots of books and some things where still not clear to me. Therefore, I wrote the book I couldn't find myself.

c) *Why it's important to have knowledge of your niche*

By being knowledgeable of your niche market, you can:

- Effectively choose the right suppliers

- Adequately choose the perfect product line

- Create a visually appealing website

- Confidently interact with customers

- Successfully add valuable website content

2) How to choose your niche

Things to think about when choosing your niche

You should always keep in mind the reasons why people spend money. Purchases are made for one of the following reasons (in all walks of life, not just online):

- To solve a problem they are having
- To fill a basic need

- For convenience
- To give them peace of mind
- Increasing their image or ego/peer pressure/showing off
- For their entertainment
- To make them wealthier (this could mean either saving money or making money)
- For knowledge
- To replace something they've lost or broken
- For value—people can't resist bargains

Check points for your niche

- Always check if your niche is in a market where people are spending money.

- Make sure whatever you sell is a long-term product in the market, unless you are happy selling products that are only popular in the short term, or are seasonal.

- Do the customers that you are targeting have money to spend? There is not a lot of point selling luxury yachts to homeless people.

- Is there already too much competition? This will be covered later in the book.

- Is your niche a growing market?

- Is your product easily available in people's local shops? In that case, they will just buy it in the shop.

- Sell product that will make you a good profit, with a good markup.

- Can you sell the product for a high enough price, e.g. £1.25/$1.99 profit is not going to make you a millionaire.

- Are your products manageable in transport? According to UK law, one box can be a maximum of 25 kg if you use couriers, e.g. FedEx. This is to protect the delivery people who have to carry the products on their own. If your products are heavier, it will cost you a lot more to ship them.

- Does your product solve a pain or solve a problem? Or is it just a fashion item?

- Do your products have a short expiration date? (Never a good thing as you might get lumbered with lots of throw-away stock.)

- Make sure there are no legal limitations to sell your product, e.g. certain chemical products and food. Some products have restrictions and regulations.

- If you sell food, you might get a visit from the Food Standard Inspection to make sure you play by the rules.

- Can you build a big business with your product as you grow?

If you prefer to sell products that you are interested in yourself, analyse these questions:

- What are your hobbies?

- Do you have any special skills?

- Do you have any special knowledge?

- What do you like to read about?

a) Niches NOT to pick

Before we look into what niches to pick, let's have a look at what niches to avoid if you are a newbie in the field. There are many gurus who tell you to pick a popular niche: health, wealth, books, electronics, insurance and so on. I disagree. I never pick these niches because it is an enormous task to rank highly for them.

The subjects listed below are subjects that I do not recommend for a newbie. Reason? With these subjects/niches, it is almost impossible to beat "the big boys". Let the "big boys" play the "big game". If you want to open a grocery store in the USA, you do not want to compete with Walmart and the like. It is impossible and a losing battle. It is better to accept that you cannot compete with them and start a very specialised food store instead. The same applies for websites: the enormous companies spend enormous amounts of money to rank in Google on the first page, or they spend an even bigger amount of money on advertising. Insurance companies employ extremely clever webmasters. I wouldn't like to compete with them, and I recommend you don't waste your time either.

15 years ago it was relatively easy to build a website on insurance and rank on the first pages, but in 2013 that is an almost impossible task, unless you are very experienced.

Here are my top 10 niches to avoid. It is the list of the niches that I do not recommend for newbies:

- Insurance

- Debt consolidation

- Mortgages

- Loans

- Real estate

- Computers

- Automobile

- Forex (Foreign Exchange online trading)

- Booking holidays online

- Making money online

Here are the top four that most gurus say to try:

- Dating and relationships

- Health and fitness

- Lifestyle

- Self-help

If you can find a *micro* niche with potential in one of those four niches, that might be do-able.

Niches NOT to pick because of homonyms or "double keywords".

Suppose that you think "How to get rid of a mole in your garden" could be good keywords, and you are planning to sell products for getting rid of moles. When you type "mole" into Google, you will see that some websites are about moles as skin growths, and some websites are about moles in the garden. This is what I call a "double" keyword: a word with a double meaning, also called a homonym.

Homonyms generally include two categories of word types: homophones and homographs.

Homographs are words that are spelled the same but have different meanings. Here are a few examples:

Mole: an animal/a skin growth

Parrot: a bird/a wireless device

Suit: a piece of clothing/to fit in with

Canary: a bird/Canary Islands

Homophones are words that sound the same when you pronounce them, but have different meanings, e.g. allowed and aloud, buy and bye. You see it gets complicated, that's why I call them "double keywords".

I never build websites with double keywords because there will be "double" competition on Google and other search engines. Websites not even related to yours will rank. Why make it more difficult than it already is to rank in Google?

b) *Thinking outside the box*

Personally, I always think like there is no box!

When choosing your niche, you want to choose one that is going to make you money. Therefore, you don't want to choose the most popular niche out there. A "hot" niche is going to do you no good because the competition is going to be so incredibly fierce that you'll do good to get one or two visitors to your site a month. You could probably make it work if you offered your product cheaper than your competition, but that would make the profit margin so low that it's likely that you won't be making any money once all is said and done.

Therefore, you want to think outside of the box, but not so outside of the box that no one will ever visit your page because they won't need your products.

c) Adding value

When choosing a niche, you want to be able to add value—not in terms of money, but in terms of helpfulness. When customers go to the web to search for a product, they are generally trying to solve a problem. So, if you can provide them with a product while solving their problem at the same time with informative content on your site, you'll be able to charge a premium while also offering expertise and clarity to the customer, which will help them make a well-informed decision.

d) Maximizing value

To truly add value, you need to choose a product that will be easy to add value to. In order to do this, you can search for a niche that is a bit confusing. If a product is confusing, it gives you room to provide a clear, concise explanation to your customers. When you educate your customers, they are able to understand the product better, which makes them more likely to pay a higher price for the product.

The same can be said for a product that requires multiple components or requires a difficult installation. In most cases, customers have no idea which components are compatible with their product. By educating your customers and making it clear to them what it is that they need, you will add value. Furthermore, by outlining clear instructions for installation, your customer will feel as though you truly helped them, which will add overall value.

e) Little competition

I am afraid a good niche idea is not good enough! You need to investigate your potential sales and you need to investigate your competition. You most definitely want to choose a niche that is not over-saturated with competition. You can use the Google Keyword Planner to help assess the competition by inputting your product into the search field.

Google Keyword Planner is a free tool that lets you find out how many people are typing in a certain keyword per month.

You need to sign up for a Google Adwords account (a Google advertising platform, explained in more detail later) to be able to use Keyword Planner. However, the Keyword Planner tool is free and you don't need to spend any money with Adwords to be able to use the tool. Search Youtube for videos how to use Keyword Planner. Sign up here:

www.adwords.google.com

www.adwords.google.co.uk

Importance of long tail keywords.

First of all you need to understand a bit more about keywords.

A *keyword* is whatever you type into the search box in a search engine. *Keyword research* is using a set of tools to discover what keywords people are searching for. If we know this, then we can build a site that targets people's searches.

Long tail keywords are keywords with multiple words in them, sometimes called golden keywords. These types of keywords are less searched for, less popular and less competitive, but when you target these keywords collectively, they can drive a lot of traffic to your site. These keywords are very specific to what you are selling. Long tail keywords are also cheaper per click if you use paid traffic.

If you were looking for information on how to cook a fish pie, what would you search for? Would you search for "fish pie"? No, you'd more likely search for exactly what you want: "how to cook a fish pie".

This is an example of a long tail keyword. These kinds of keywords will have fewer searches than short, single-word keywords, but the person searching will be looking for something more specific, which is good for us: it means we can build a site that perfectly suits what they're looking for! Google shows the keywords that the searcher typed in

bold. Subconsciously, people will first click on the websites that show their keyword in bold. **Long tail keywords have a much better conversion rate than short keywords because you will get quality targeted traffic. People type in exactly what they are going to buy and land on your site.**

TOP TIP: Always try and rank for long tail keywords.

If you could buy the domain name www.howtocookafishpie.com, that would be your first step towards success. But you must follow all the other rules for success; a good domain name by itself is not enough to make it in the Internet world.

It is much better to rank for lots of low competition, long tail keywords than not to rank for highly competitive short keywords. You will find these long tail keywords with the keywords research tools, discussed later.

For instruction purposes, let's say that you want to sell weight loss supplements. You would input the keywords "weight loss supplements" into the appropriate field in Keyword Planner, as shown below, and click "Get ideas".

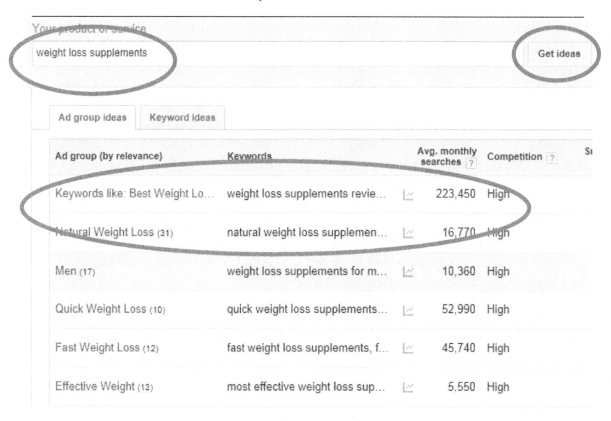

Next, you'll want to look at the average monthly searches that the keyword has, in our case 223,450.

If it is more than 10,000, go to Google and type in the keyword. While Keyword Planner says the competition is high, you can see how many sites approximately you would be competing with by a quick Google search. The competition for the keyword "weight loss supplements" can be seen at the very top of the search results, as shown in the screenshot below.

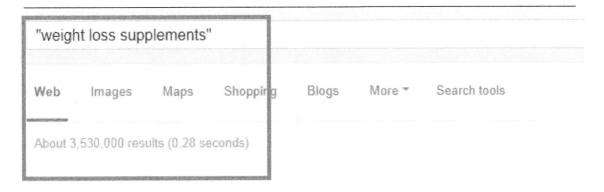

Back to Keyword Planner: When you click on "best weight loss....", as shown below, you will get different keywords.

When you click on "best weight loss....", this screen will follow:

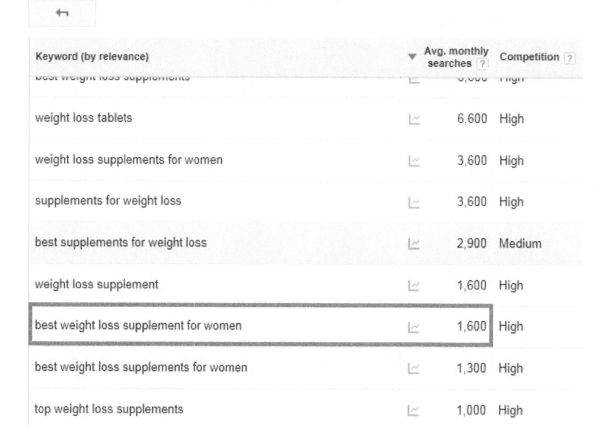

Ad group: **Keywords like: Best Weight Loss Supplement**

Keyword (by relevance)		Avg. monthly searches ?	Competition ?
best weight loss supplements		8,000	High
weight loss tablets		6,600	High
weight loss supplements for women		3,600	High
supplements for weight loss		3,600	High
best supplements for weight loss		2,900	Medium
weight loss supplement		1,600	High
best weight loss supplement for women		1,600	High
best weight loss supplements for women		1,300	High
top weight loss supplements		1,000	High

Note that you can see the search results for long tail keywords. Have a look at the keyword "best weight loss supplements for women" and paste that into the search in Google.

You can see that the numbers of results is immediately a lot lower, so it will be an easier job to rank for that keyword.

While the competition is still higher than you would like, it is better than the first keyword you tried.

f) Consider your own previous purchases

Another way to brainstorm possible niches is by considering your previous online purchases. Look back to the purchases you've made in the last year or so. Because you bought them online, there's a good chance other people buy these same products online, too. These products are generally a niche market, which we've previously discussed is what you need to be targeting. This is because when you purchase online it's because you want to get the best possible price for a product, you simply don't have time to get to the store locally (yes, even though it's local), or you are purchasing an unusual, specialised product that simply can't be found at your local mall.

Some common products that may be purchased online could include:

- Video games

- Books (new and used)

- T-shirts

- Movie tickets

125

- Shoes

- Gift baskets

- Jewelry making supplies

- Baking supplies

- Confectionery

Actually, EVERYTHING is now for sale online.

As you can see, some of these aren't so specialised and are actually generalized, common products, but some are indeed more specific. If you go deeper into your purchases, you may find that some purchases were even more specific. For example, what type of t-shirt did you buy? Maybe it was a "funny t-shirt" or a "religious t-shirt," both of which are specialised niche markets. What about the shoes? Who were they for? Were they a special kind, a special colour maybe?

You'll have to do the research to learn whether or not it is a specialised niche market which is worth your time or not. But the thing is, when you do this type of brainstorming, you come up with a wide variety of products that may or may not represent an expanded, specialised or contracted niche market. For example, if you were to take the gift baskets, you could contract that to baby shower gift baskets or wedding anniversary gift baskets. Alternatively, you could expand the idea of the religious t-shirt into a religious website.

The point here is for you to think as busily and creatively as you can. Once you've got a variety of ideas from this brainstorming exercise, you can start researching the market demand of each one of the ideas to see if it is even a possibility. I mentioned at the beginning of this book that, if you have an entrepreneurial spirit, you have more chance of becoming a successful Internet marketer. This is certainly a good example of that.

g) *Expanding on your inspirations*

Now that you've brainstormed a few ideas, you want to keep in mind that not every product or niche is appropriate or available for resale. Take the movie tickets, for example. If there is no supplier, you simply can't sell the product. With movie tickets, it's unlikely that you'll find a supplier, and if you can find a supplier, there may be certain restrictions and limitations.

With some items, you may find that the manufacturers of a product maintain small operations. In other words, there are relatively few workers making the product, which decreases your ability to get an item quickly and dramatically decreases the likelihood of drop shipping. Then, there's wholesale. Because the item is produced by few people, it may not be an item that they can offer at wholesale prices. Some industries lack the aspects you need to make a product work for drop shipping or for wholesale.

You are also going to have do market research on a niche. This is going to be discussed shortly, and we will go into detail about how you can determine whether a certain niche is going to be profitable for you with little competition, or if the niche is over-saturated and offers low profitability, if any at all.

Once you've completed your research, you may find that you have several niche markets left to choose from. How do you choose? It may come down to the best supplier that you can find, which will be discussed later.

h) What is your USP?

Your USP is your Unique Selling Point(s) or Proposition.

There might be hundreds of websites selling the same product that you are selling. Why would customers buy from you? What is so special about your product or your service? You need to be different from your competitors; you need to be Unique.

Your Unique Selling Point point can be:

- your price

- your customer service

- your niche

- your transport cost

- extra detailed product description

- return policy

- exclusive products

- your website

Whatever you think your USP is, make sure you make this very clear to your customers when they visit your site.

Your USP will make you STAND OUT, which is always a good thing. "Never follow the crowd" is what I strongly believe, whatever the business.

i) Do your SWOT Analysis

SWOT stands for Strengths, Weaknesses, Opportunities and Threats.

- Analyse what your strengths are—closely related to your USP.

- Analyse what your weaknesses are.

- Analyse your market opportunities.

- Analyse your threats - usually your competition.

j) Niches for repeat sales

If possible, try and find a niche that will create repeat sales, e.g. books, clothing, health products, vitamins, magazines, knitting material, craft material, etc. That way, once you have a customer, they will re-order all the time and you don't have to do anything to get those customers back, providing you treat your customers as if they were King, because they are King!

k) Look at the selling price!

I am leaving the most important thing to look at for last!

It's no good selling £1.25/$2 items, as you will simply have to sell too many to make a decent profit.

Let's have a look at my own website, www.liquorice-licorice.co.uk. There are many online shops selling liquorice in 100gr bags. I have decided to sell most of my liquorice products per kilo (2.20 pounds) instead, differentiating me from my competitors. Not many other companies sell liquorice by the kilo, in fact, I haven't come across any other company.

Have a look at this comparison:

Selling price

Price of my competitor's 100gr bags: £1.50/$2.40 (that would be £11.50/$20.40 per kg)

Price of my 1 kilo bag: £12.94/$20.95

Total selling price when 100 products sold

Total price for my competitor: £150/$240 (£1.50/$2.40 x 100)

Total price for my product: £1,294/$2,095 (£12.94/$20.95 x 100)

Profit per 100 sold:

Assume 50% profit for ease of calculation, but you can easily add more profit for sweets (80% and more), providing you buy from the right suppliers.

Total profit for 100 sales for my competitor: £75/$120

Total profit for 100 sales for me: £647/$1,047

BIG difference! That is £572 / $972 more profit for me.

> **The most important thing to remember here is that I have EXACTLY the same amount of work to do as my competitor! Interesting, hey!**

3) Test if your products will sell.

- When I first started in Internet marketing, I used to build mini websites, after having done my keyword research. I used to put affiliate links on those websites, selling eBooks for which I would receive 50% commission.

The eBooks started to sell from some websites.

From a commercial point of view, I soon realised that if it would be MY book I was selling instead of someone else's book, I would earn 100% instead of 50%. That's how I first started in publishing books. I would outsource the writing of the book for the eBooks that started to sell from my websites and put MY book on my website instead.

A few examples:

www.HowToRacePigeons.co.uk

www.PeafowlsPeacocksandPeahens.com

www.HowToKeepMicropigs.com

www.MicroPigshed.com (which sells all the version of the books)

These books are available as eBooks, as hard copy books on Amazon, as Kindle books, AND I have affiliates selling it for me. Scroll down to the bottom of the sales page on the above mentioned sites to find the affiliate page.

Why am I telling you this? Well, you can apply the same principles to your eCommerce or drop shipping site: test if the products will sell and if they do, create your own store. When you have found what you *think* is a good niche, find an online store with an affiliate network that already sells these products. Another thing you can do is start selling a product as a drop shipper and if the products sell well, buy them wholesale and earn more profit.

You could build a mini website and sell those products from your website. You might be selling your competition's products, but that's OK, you will still earn some money. IF the products start selling, you can build your own online store.

Now I personally have not done this for my online stores, but you could consider doing this just to find out if your products will sell. The downside of this is that you will have to learn about affiliate marketing.

- Another good way to test your niche is to sell your products face to face to start with to see if they sell. Many years ago, before I had my liquorice website, I used to go to markets and sell liquorice at markets! Yes, with a market stall! Me! I used to buy the liquorice in Belgium and sell it in England. I am talking many, many years ago, before I had an Internet marketing business! When I moved to England, people told me liquorice does not sell in England, but I wanted to prove them wrong by testing the market. I was surprised and astonished at how much liquorice I sold every Tuesday and Thursday at the market. I use to sell over £1000/$1600 PER DAY! That's when I decided that English people DO love liquorice. I decided a few years later to sell liquorice online - when I became an internet marketer - and this is my site: www.liquorice-licorice.co.uk that sells liquorice by the kilo. I will tell you later (under the SEO section) which keywords this site ranks for in Google.

- Last example to test if your product will sell: Richard Reed, the founder of "Innocent Smoothies", went from market stall to half a billion dollars! He started in 1999 with a market stall selling what is now the number one smoothie brand. He sold his business to Coca Cola at over half a billion dollars, and he remains on the board as a minority shareholder! He started to test his sales at a local market!

Here are a few ways to get ideas for your new site or to find out if your idea has potential.

In my book "Finding Niches Made Easy", there are 177 places listed where you can find niche ideas.

- Google search: if you search for your niche keyword and all the sites on the first three to five pages are sites with hardly any content or no keyword in the domain name, that is a very good start. This might mean that it will be easy for you to rank, but you'll need more investigation before you can decide.

- Google Alerts. Sign up to www.Google.com/alerts and get emailed at regular intervals whenever anyone blogs or talks about your niche. If there's a lot of movement, then it may be a good niche. Even if you have decided on your new niche, I suggest that you keep Google Alerts on because it flags blogs, forums and more that are relevant to your niche each time you receive an alert. Each time you see a new blog in your niche, write the blog domain name on your to do list as you can get links from the blog once your own website is developed.

- Google Trends. Have a look on Google Trends (www.Google.com/trends) for hot searches and hot niches. Google Trends is very interesting. You do not want to start a new niche that has gone down in search consistently for the last two years. Google Trends has clear graphs, so in a matter of seconds you can see if your niche is potentially a good one. For instance, you might see on the graph that your keyword is seasonal or that it gets peak searches only in two months of the year. The graph below shows "stand up comedy" as a consistent niche for over six years.

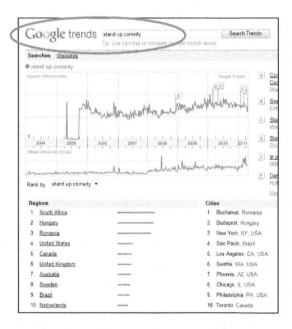

- Google Zeitgeist. Fastest rising and fastest growing niches: www.Google.com/zeitgeist. Find out what people have searched for.

- Yahoo Buzz. Find out what people are talking about: www.news.yahoo.com.

- Lycos. Find out what the latest trends and hot topics are: www.lycos.com.

- eBay. Visit www.listings.ebay.com to see which categories are best sellers.

- Toluna. http://uk.toluna.com/test is a website where brand new products are tested. You can get great ideas here. Some products might never be released, but other products will have huge potential for a website. A website with a product name as a keyword in the domain name is always good but make sure to check the legalities and trademarks.

- Alexa hot urls: www.alexa.com/hoturls.

- Pricegrabber. Visit www.pricegrabber.com to search for keywords and sort by Popularity. Find a product and do your research in Keyword Planner to see how many people are searching for it.

- Amazon Top 100. Go to www.amazon.com. This is an excellent way to identify hot new markets. This is updated hourly. Choose a category from the drop down menu, e.g. electronics. Type in your keyword and click "Bestsellers". This will show you the Top 100 bestselling products in that category.

Each time you dig deeper into a specific category, it will show you the best sellers.

- Magazines. www.magazines.com will give you a list of almost every magazine there is. People who publish magazines have done a lot of research and concluded that there is a market out there for that subject. Find a niche and do your research with Keyword Planner to see if people are searching for that niche.

- Will your eBook be in a popular niche? Find out:
http://www.barnesandnoble.com/bestsellers or www.ebooks.com

Do a search in your niche. If no eBook is listed and there are a lot of searches per month, you might have found a winner.

4) What sells best online?

This is a list of the products that sell best online as of September 2013:

1. Books (that's why I am publishing niche books)

2. Computer Hardware (that's why I am selling end of line PC's and printers)

3. Computer Software

4. Apparel

5. Toys/Video Games

6. DVDs

7. Health and Beauty

8. Consumer Electronics

9. Music

10. Jewelry

11. Office Supplies

12. Home Decor/Linen

13. Flowers

14. Sporting Goods

15. Footwear

16. Small Appliances

17. Tools and Garden

18. Gifts

If your niche is not listed above, it doesn't meat it won't sell! Lots of products and niches are not listed here, but you can still make LOTS of money. There was no demand for a tablet when they first came onto the market! There was no demand for mobile phones when they first came out!

5) What are the Top 20 brands in the world?

According to branding consultancy company Interbrand, these are the Top 20 brands in the world:

1. Apple ©

2. Google ©

3. Coca-Cola ©

4. IBM ©

5. Microsoft ©

6. GE ©

7. McDonalds ©

8. Samsung ©

9. Intel ©

10. Toyota ©

11. Mercedes Benz ©

12. BMW ©

13. Cisco ©

14. Disney ©

15. HP (Hewlett Packard) ©

16. Gillette ©

17. Louis Vuitton ©

18. Oracle ©

19. Amazon ©

20. Honda ©

- You can see the Top 100 here:

http://www.interbrand.com/en/best-global-brands/2013/Best-Global-Brands-2013.aspx

- Perhaps you can find related products to sell, e.g. spare parts, end-of-line products, etc.

- Start working YOUR brand and maybe you will be included in this list one day!

How do you know if your niche will make you money? Well, you don't know and you can't find out until you test it. The tips you've read will increase your chances of succeeding and help you to make an informed decision.

Chapter 6 - Selecting Products to Sell.
1) What to know before selecting products to sell

Once you have determined your niche, you will be selecting a drop shipping company and deciding on products to sell. But, before we jump into all that, let's discuss a few tips on selecting the best products to drop ship. Your product line will probably change throughout the year, especially to offer holiday items or a brand-new item, and you'll be taking products off your site that aren't selling. This is just a natural process for an online business, so don't let it worry you.

TOP TIPs:

- You need to try and cut out any middlemen when sourcing products. You need to be as close to the manufacturer as you can to maximize your profit. The web is full of middlemen.

- You MUST try and work directly with genuine wholesalers. Anyone that gets between you and the wholesaler will make a profit, therefore your buying price will be more.

Regardless, though, you've got to start somewhere, right? So, just how do you choose the best drop shipping product or products to go with? If you've selected your niche market (or have a couple to choose from), then you can just brainstorm products that would be part of that niche market.

Consider looking at several wholesale providers of products and discover the hundreds of thousands of products you would be able to buy and sell. Often, a wholesaler will sell you a bundle of products at a steep discount. The price you sell on your site would be the retail price. Often, people charge anywhere from 20% to 300% of the price they buy the product for. So for example, if you buy a product that costs £6.25/$10 per item from a wholesale distributor, you might consider turning it around and selling it for £12.50/$19.99 at a 100% profit margin.

Remember, you still need to pay for the website and all the transaction fees, including shipping (you may also charge a shipping fee through your shopping cart), and of course, you want to make a profit!

You need to know all these to be able to decide your selling price:

- Wholesale price or your buying prices from a drop shipper

- Fixed costs: your transaction fees and expenses

- Variable costs, e.g. advertising

- Your desired profit

a) Watch out for drop shipping agents!

The Internet is full of companies pretending to be real drop shippers. They do give you access to one or a few real drop shippers, but they are middlemen. They will charge you a monthly fee to get access to the real drop shippers. These agents work all over the web and lots of people fall for them, therefore your competition will be enormous, as thousands of online stores will be selling the same product from the same drop shipper that they recommend to you.

These agents will make you think they have a warehouse full of products, but they don't.

Drop ship agents operate this way:

- They contact a few REAL wholesale drop shippers and ask them for pictures and information about their products and tell them they can help selling the products. Professional wholesalers will not work with these agents, but there are wholesalers that do.

- They put those products on their website, pretending that they are a real drop shipper with a big warehouse.

- When you place an order with these agents, they will simply give it to the real drop shipper and they will ship the order to your customer.

- Some of these agents even tell you they are an agent but that it makes sense to work with them, as they "centralise" your orders and shipping.

These agents are not illegal and from a commercial point of view, I guess good for them, but these are not the people you want to work with.

b) Watch out for broker networks!

Broker networks can be compared to MLM—Multi-Level Marketing. The big problem with these networks is that you must buy thousands of dollars of product before you can become a broker yourself, and you will try to sell products to other brokers. These brokers tell you they are the wholesale supplier, and when you look at their sites, that's indeed what it looks like: a wholesale supplier. Often these networks won't even let you apply unless they know you have thousands of dollars to waste. These networks are legal, but this is NOT direct wholesale supply, which is what you are looking for.

These networks also sell their customer's details to Internet marketers, so you will be flooded with crap in your inbox (aka SPAM!).

c) Don't ever buy lists

When you type in "list of wholesalers" in Google, you will come across websites that sell you a directory of wholesalers. Don't ever buy these. These are usually well out of date, and those websites have been selling the same list for 5 years! There MIGHT be the odd genuine list, but it's very difficult for you to find these.

d) Watch out for FREE drop shipping sites.

There are several drop shipping websites that are FREE for you, giving you thousands of details for drop shippers and wholesalers. These websites are usually NOT the ones to use. What these companies usually are aiming for is to get a lot of people visiting their site so that they can sell advertising space to other companies. That's the way those free websites earn money.

139

> **TOP TIP:** Don't work with or buy anything from drop shipping/wholesale websites that have a lot of advertising on them.

e) Watch out for middlemen

There are companies that claim to be drop shippers but are not. They are middlemen. A middleman is someone who positions themselves between the real drop shipper or distributor and you, the seller. A middleman gets their products from a drop shipper that you can easily work with directly, so you will have less profit as the middleman will take profit as well. Before you decide on a drop shipper, check that they buy directly from the manufacturer.

f) Watch out for review sites.

Since I have been an Internet marketer, I have never believed in review sites, as I realise that the people who develop the sites are not putting the "real winners" on the top. Instead, the websites for which they earn the most commission from as an affiliate, are listed as the winners.

In drop shipping, there are scams going on with websites recommending THEIR OWN product to be the best. You, as the visitor, do not know that the company on the top of the review is actually owned by the same people that have built the review website.

So if you come across a review site for drop shipping, chances are that the company that wins the review is the owner of the site! So they are giving their own company the best review!

g) Watch out for drop shippers with fees

Here are some general rules for spotting scam drop shippers. Scam drop shippers:

- can charge a monthly fee

- can charge an annual fee

- can charge a set-up fee

- usually have more expensive prices for the products than the real drop shipper

Directories are different, as they usually charge a fee.

h) Drop shipping for affiliates

If you don't know what affiliate marketing is, my book "From Newbie To Millionaire" explains this really well.

I could write another book about affiliate marketing, so it is impossible to explain it all here. Affiliate marketing means basically selling stuff for other people and earning a commission on the sales. Your affiliate is the person who sells for you and who you will pay commission.

An affiliate network is software that controls everything: how much you sold via your affiliates, how much commission you have to pay them, when to pay them, etc.

www.amazon.com is a good example of a successful affiliate merchant business, which launched in 1996. They now have over 400,000 affiliates (Amazon calls them associates).

www.amazon.com and www.comparethemarket.com are probably two companies that you have heard of before, but you never realised that they make money in affiliate marketing.

To find websites that have an affiliate program, search in Google for "your keyword + affiliates", e.g. "blueberry jam + affiliates". Visit the websites and scroll to the very bottom of the home page, where the link to the affiliate page usually is.

Some trustworthy affiliate networks:

- www.affiliatewindow.com

- www.clickbooth.com

- www.linkshare.com

- www.affiliatefirst.com

- www.commissionjunction.com

- www.JVZoo.com

- www.shareasale.com

To find more affiliate networks, visit some well-known stores and scroll to the bottom of their websites to find which affiliate network they have signed up with. Pretend you are signing up as an affiliate to see who they work with. You can count on those affiliate networks being reliable, otherwise the BIG guys wouldn't be using these companies.

2) Things to consider when selecting products

a) *Start Small*

While you may want to start off with something popular, such as diamond jewelry or 3D televisions, you need to start smaller than that. Just because you sell a large, expensive item doesn't mean that there is more money to be made this way. Until you've been able to build a name for yourself and a positive reputation, it is wise to start small. As a general rule, the best drop shipping products when you first start out will generally be between £18.80/$30 and £62/$100…and even up to £125/$200. Now, because you are selling smaller, lower-priced items, you may think there isn't a large profit margin, but you'd be surprised just how much you can make on smaller items. For example, you can probably gain access to purses for £12/$20 and re-sell them for £50/$80. That's a pretty steep profit margin. But if you were getting cameras for £180/$300 and selling them for £250/$400, there's not as much profit there.

Most of my eCommerce sites (before I sold them) had profit margins between 50 and 200%!

My advice is to start with lower priced products, just to see if you like the whole drop shipping principle. That way, if things go wrong, e.g. return of the product, it will not cost you that much money. If you start with selling belt buckles at £5/$8 each, it won't cost you much money to take the product back in stock, but if you start with selling £300/$480 products, it will cost you a lot more!

b) *Profitability of the product*

When choosing your product, you must consider how much money you can earn. If the product is too cheap or too expensive, then you may not be able to make much of a profit. If you are going to have to sell hundreds of one item just to make a profit, then you need to choose a new product. Expensive products cost more to ship and are more difficult to sell. They also need a huge image of security or else you won't sell anything. In other words, while you could sell LCD TV's and diamond jewelry online, it is likely that you will want to give your business some time to grow a name for itself and build an image of security before you tackle that section of drop shipping.

The laws of supply and demand very often will determine the price of a product.

If demand is high and supply is low, you can easily sell at a higher prices. When lots of people want the product and it is difficult to find, charge more.

If demand is high and supply is high, you can't charge that much as your competition will be greater. So, if many people are selling a product and lots of people are buying it, you can't charge that much.

Find products that people are looking for and give it to them.

In business you get what YOU want
by giving other people what THEY want.

You always need to study the competition before selection your product; that is THE most important thing to do before you decide which product to sell. You can learn a lot from other shops that sell the same product. Investigate:

- The prices other shops charge.

- The supply of the product: is it easily available for you to buy?

- How are the other shops marketing themselves?

- Do the other shops rank in Google for their product?

However, it is not always a good idea just to lower your price to be able to beat the competition. It is no good selling products and not making a profit!

Ultimately, you want to get started with products that range anywhere from £18/$30 to £94/$150 or so at retail price. These products will have a good enough profit margin, but they won't be so pricey that your customers are leery of making a purchase with a new online business.

Once you are more experienced, I advise you to sell more expensive products.

Keep in mind, though, that not all products are sold with huge profit margins. Some products sell really well, but the profit margin isn't great. For example, because of the amount of competition in electronics, you won't be able to make a whole lot of money off your sales—regardless of the price of the item. What I'm trying to get at is that just because an item is expensive doesn't mean that it is the most profitable.

Make charts similar to the ones shown below to determine how profitable a product will be.

21pc Barber Buzz Set (Retail Price 30.00)	
Product Purchase Price:	17.41
Drop Ship Fees:	0.00
Total Cost:	17.41
Profit:	12.59

Bagless Canister Vacuum (Retail Price 140)

Product Purchase Price:	101.28
Drop Ship Fees:	0.00
Total Cost:	101.28
Profit:	38.72

Sleeping Bags (Retail Price 55.00)

Product Purchase Price:	12.52
Drop Ship Fees:	4.00
Total Cost:	16.52
Profit:	38.48

You'll notice that the least profitable item is the medium-priced item and the most profitable comes in at a tie at the most expensive item and the least expensive item. So, as you can see, the most expensive item isn't always the best drop shipping product to make money off of, but neither is the least expensive. It takes research to determine the best possible product with a good profit margin. It all depends on the product, its demand and much more.

Keep in mind that lots of drop shippers charge a drop shipping fee per order, between £1/$1.60 and £3/$4.79

On top of that, your merchant account fees need to be added, but more about that later.

c) Product demand

If not enough people want your product, you are not going to sell much. It is as simple as that. You need to do your keyword research to see how many people are searching for it.

If you only sell in the UK, it's no good idea selling snowboards in the summer, nor is it a good idea to sell bikinis in the winter. You simply KNOW in advance you won't sell well, as there won't be any demand for the product.

d) Product availability

There are ultimately two different kinds of availability: the availability to those who want to purchase it and the availability to you for you to re-sell. Both are important, but the latter is especially important, seeing as not all products are actually available to be resold.

For example, when you start brainstorming drop shipping product ideas, you'll quickly think of brand name products; however, many of these products are not available at a wholesale price or to be resold. Plus, if you do find a name brand product that can be resold, you'll likely need to purchase in massive quantities or have a super huge line of credit. In addition, it may be limited to brick-and-mortar locations, which your drop shipping business does not have. Of course, there are some brands that you can find at discounted prices or find overstock or refurbished items that you can re-sell, but most of them are unavailable for this. So, when brainstorming ideas, try to steer clear of brand name products.

e) Check your competition

If you find 100 websites selling the same product you want to sell, forget it and investigate another product. This certainly applies when you are new to eCommerce or drop shipping. More about investigating your competition in other parts of this book.

If all the websites on the first 2 pages are well-known names in the industry, you will also have an almost impossible task to beat them.

f) Create or manufacturer your own product.

Of course, creating or manufacturing your own product is not easy, but it's by far the best option. Having YOUR own product is always the best and easiest way to earn money on the Internet, and YOU will earn more money, which is the most important factor. You can also let affiliates do the selling for you, giving you more income on autopilot. You can work with dealers who will stock and sell your products in their physical shop or on their website.

If you can create or manufacture your own product to sell or have a product manufactured especially for you, it will limit your competition and you will be able to set your own prices, so maximising your profits!

I believe in the principle: if you can't find what you are looking for, produce it yourself as it means other people are looking for it as well. I always like to prove what I say, so here are some examples of my own, and I'll explain why I have created these products.

1) My Newbie book. I wrote my book "From Newbie to Millionaire" because I couldn't find what I was looking for. I wanted to buy a book that would explain exactly how Internet marketing works and how to earn money—written *in very simple, easy to read style*. I bought lots of books, but decided there was a shortage on the market for a book like the one I've written. That's why it has been selling so well for over 2 years and continues to sell well. I knew the book would sell well because I knew other people were looking for it, simply because I was looking for it. You can assume if you are looking for something, other people are as well.

2) My Self Publishing Videos. I published my video tutorials at www.worldwideselfpublishing.com for the same reason: everything out there about self publishing books is all delivered with puzzle pieces missing. I knew many people were pretty annoyed about this and were getting very fed up buying overhyped stuff that simply does not deliver the promises made on the sales letters. I had been looking for a *complete* self publishing course but couldn't find it, therefore I created it myself. It has been selling much better than I ever thought (being a high-end product). I receive orders on a daily basis and I don't even know where the orders are coming from! Nice! I am not boasting, that's not the sort of person I am! I just want to get the message across that you can do stuff too. I am nobody special and don't have any special skills. Everything I know about making money online, self publishing, and eCommerce, I've learned from practicing and making mistakes.

3) My Break Reminder Software. I used to use www.workpace.com, which is software that forces you to take breaks whilst on your computer. I had my own simplified version developed, because I couldn't find it myself; you can buy it here: www.BreakReminderSoftware.com.

4) My Print Screen Software. When I was looking for a very simple screen software application, without all the bells and the whistles, I couldn't find it, therefore I had my own developed. I use it every single day and don't know how I could ever be without it. You can buy it here: www.PrintingYourScreen.com.

The 2 last products were developed by a developer on www.elance.com for £180/$300! These products have a ONE-OFF creation cost and all the ones you sell are 100% profit, once you've covered your initial investment. So if you have an idea to make some software, go for it!

5) This book. The reason why you are reading this book is, again, because I couldn't find what I was looking for. I've bought lots of books about eCommerce and drop shipping, but NONE of them were a satisfying read for me, and they all had lots of puzzle pieces missing. After years of experience with eCommerce, I decided to write a book about it.

6) My Baby Respiration Monitor. When I moved from Belgium to England, my twin daughters were 6 months old. They were born premature, therefore I rented a baby respiration monitor (or breathing monitor) in Belgium when they were born. It is a device that detects a baby's breathing pattern and it is known to help prevent cot death. I couldn't find an affordable baby respiration monitor in the UK (they were all £600/$950 and up and I didn't have any money then so couldn't afford one) and soon discovered there was a BIG gap in the market for such monitors.

It was my goal to change that and so I did! There was me, just moved to another country, and I was going to change the baby monitor market! I knew I had a huge task ahead of me.

I borrowed some money from my mum and I went to over 30 manufacturers to discuss the possibilities to manufacturer a monitor for me. After almost one year of searching, I found one.

I went to a leading London hospital with a baby care unit to find out what was important for them. What did I have to develop for them to consider buying it? I took all their suggestions into account and discussed them with the manufacturer.

It was not easy to get the product approved to sell in the UK market as several certificates were needed by law. The product needed to be tested to European Medical Standards. The product needed to be TUV (a European approval label) approved. Two years later my product was launched: The RM25 Respiration Monitor.

The RM25 is fully certified to European Medical Standards:
EN60601-1: 1992. IEC601-1:1988 (BS5724 PART 1:1989)
Emission Standards:
EN55011 Emission Standards
EN500 82-1 Generic Immunity Standard
IEC 601-1-2 Immunity Collateral Medical Standard
TUV Approved. Certificate No. S 9472093

The deal I made with the manufacturer is that they would manufacture the product and do nothing else. I would do ALL the selling. It was my aim to sell to the public and to the hospitals, and I started by putting small ads in various baby magazines and sales started to come in!

To sell more, as I started to realise the power of selling on the Internet about 7 years ago, I set up a website for it: www.physicalstate.co.uk. It is a very ugly-looking website! It was one of the first websites I built. The checkout page is the ugliest one I've ever seen! Read on to learn why I never made it look better.

Seven years ago, my website ranked for the keywords "baby breathing monitor "or "baby respiration monitor", as it was very easy to rank in those days. I sold some monitors, but not many.

What happened next? Lots of hospitals with a baby care unit started to approach me, as they were very interested in buying the product, because my product was half the price of the ones they were buying. I used to send out free trial monitors to hospitals as I KNEW the monitors were very good quality. Hey, I was using it for my own babies, so I wasn't going to use just ANY monitor! It HAD to be reliable and good. It is TUV approved and has lots of other certificates to prove it was a product suitable to sell for its purpose.

As a result of the fact that I was sending out free trial monitors to hospitals, all the hospitals were very happy with the monitor and they started to order them! Word of mouth kicked in as the hospitals have regular meetings with each other. I needed to become an approved NHS (The UK's National Health Service) supplier, but that was pretty easy, as the hospitals wanted my product.

The product was in high demand because of the very competitive price, and also I had built in some features that other products on the market did not have. Because it became, and still is, a high demand product, I can sell it with a good profit margin.

What happens now? Although the original plan was to sell it directly to the consumer via ads in magazines and later through my website www.physicalstate.co.uk, I now sell it to hospitals and THEY are doing the selling for me: mums and dads whose babies are premature can see that their baby uses the RM25 Respiration Monitor in hospital, and they ask the hospital where to get one. I never have to do a thing to sell a monitor.

The hospital gives the parents details of the Lullaby Trust. www.lullabytrust.org.uk: The lullaby trust used to be CONI (Care Of Next Infant). This is an organisation that provides support for anyone affected by a sudden infant death or for anyone who had a premature baby. The organisation also advises new parents on the best ways to put a baby to sleep to minimise the risk of cot death. They work closely with the NHS and are present in hospitals and health centers, they work all the time with midwifes, pediatricians, doctors, etc... They order LOTS of respiration monitors from me to give to parents. The Lullaby Trust is present wherever babies are born, so all parents hear about my monitor through Lullaby Trust; once they have their baby. The monitor was designed for premature babies but a lot of parents use the monitor on their baby, just for peace of mind, if their baby was not born premature.

 The monitor is now sold by several organisations and by dealers, and I never do a thing to create the sales. I just ship the monitors (well, my secretary does) when I receive orders and charge the customers, of course.

Search for "RM25 Baby Respiration Monitor" and you will see that my monitor is also available on these sites (these sites are buying the monitors from me, they are not my sites):

- www.babymonitorsdirect.co.uk

- www.anawiz.com

- www.babysecurity.co.uk

- www.monitormybaby.co.uk

- www.babymonitoring.co.uk

- www.Amazon.co.uk

- www.twenga.co.uk

- www.play.com

- www.ebay.com

- www.medicare.ie

- www.theshop4gifts.co.uk

- www.cruxbaby.co.uk

etc....

It is also listed on lots of comparison sites. Don't ask me how it got there, as I have no idea. :-)

The best thing: ALL people selling the RM25 Respiration Monitor ANYWHERE in the world, HAVE to order directly from me. 17 years after the monitor was launched, it is STILL selling well!

The above story is why my ugly-looking website www.physicalstate.co.uk is still ugly:

- I developed it "quickly" to test the market and never touched it again, as sales were created from different angles.

- It shows up in searches on page 7 onwards for the keyword "baby respiration monitor", therefore hardly anyone ever visits it. Maybe one day I will improve the look of the site and improve the SEO but it is not a priority as other web sites and the Lullaby Trust are selling the monitor for me.

In case you are an expectant parent, here are some specs about the monitor:

- Supplied with mattress pad (no contact with baby) <u>AND</u> a body sensor.
- Tried, tested, certified and approved product.
- Used in many hospitals and homes worldwide.
- Dedicated professional breathing monitor.
- Has a low breath alarm, extra early warning of problems.

I hope from what you have read about it, you know you can trust that it is a reliable monitor, as The Lullaby Trust gives it to parents. You can also download a hospital user list from my ugly website.

I never planned to write over 3 pages about my monitor, but in order for you to understand the complete picture and the potential business you can create by having your own product, I decided I had to write it.

The conclusion of my monitor story and an important point for you to remember: after my initial investigation, I decided there was a gap in the market and that there would be high demand. The product sold itself! **Others are now doing the selling for me! YOU too can find gaps in the market and create your own product!**

A good idea without business skills is not a good idea.

By the way, just in case you are wondering, the Streamline screenshots in the beginning of this book do NOT include monitor sales as all sales are invoiced and paid into my bank account by bacs or wire transfer. The monitor sales are dealt with in another company (I have several companies), not my internet marketing company. It has nothing to do with my Internet Marketing business as those days, I was not a full time Internet marketer. But I guess you could say that it was a taste of selling products online for me, as in the beginning I did sell monitors from my ugly website.

I did find some other gaps in the market and acted upon them by finding products to sell, but I guess you don't want to hear another story about that! It would fill up another 4 pages in this book, and it's not about me, it's about you in this book, as I want YOU to succeed in eCommerce. Let's turn back to selecting products to sell.

g) Exclusive pricing or distribution

If at all possible, find some good products to sell and negotiate exclusivity, like I did with my respiration monitors. You can sell for a higher price that way. I have done that for a few more products that I sell. Here's my story…only joking! I am not going to write another story about one of my products.

You've read under the skills you need to succeed, in the beginning of this book, that you need entrepreneurial flair and business instinct to succeed. Finding gaps in the market, creating your own product and negotiating exclusive distribution are certainly good examples of that.

h) Take shipping into consideration

Because you will be selling online, you'll need to consider the fact that the price will be inflated by the cost of shipping from you (or the drop shipping company) to the customer. Ultimately, the price for a product, shipping included, should equal the same price as what the product would be at a brick-and-mortar store. If you have a rare product or a product that is sold in limited quantities locally, then the demand will be greater online, meaning that you can sell it for an increased price, as people will be willing to pay a little extra for the product as they have the convenience of ordering it online.

i) Specialization is OK – recommended, actually

While not everyone picks one specific niche and sticks with it, you will find that you can compete better in a specialised niche. General stores that sell virtually everything will have to compete with other stores similar to them, such as bigwigs Walmart, Target and Tesco in the UK, making it virtually impossible to really make a profit. For that reason, a specialised niche is beneficial. You can write articles and blogs that are related to your product(s), thus improving your SEO, generating quality traffic, and building a solid relationship with customers. Try a product that is related to a certain theme or hobby.

j) Multiple suppliers

It is a good idea to source products that multiple suppliers stock. That way, if one suppliers does not have the product in stock, you can use the other supplier.

k) Product life cycle.

Investigate your product life cycle. Perhaps people will stop buying it after a certain time.

l) Investigate your supplier

You are going to need a supplier, so make sure you check them out. Do they have support? How big is their product range? Are they reliable? How long have they been trading for?

m) Check patent

Make sure you are not selling a patent-protected product. That can get you into serious trouble with some heavy fines to pay.

n) No-compete clause

Some suppliers will ask you for a no-compete clause. This means you are not allowed to sell another similar product on your website. Let's assume you want to buy pink candles from your supplier, if he asks for a no-compete clause that means you cannot sell any other pink candles on your store. Not many suppliers will ask for this, but if it does happen to you, now you know what it means.

o) *Private labeling*

If you have the capital and you have big dreams, you can ask the manufacturer if they can produce the product for you with private labeling. You might not realise it, but private labeling is all around you, every day of your life. So what is private labeling? Well, when you go to the supermarket and you see a pot of vitamins on the shelf from a leading manufacturer and next to that pot is another pot, looking pretty much the same size and shape, but the label on it says "Walmart's Vitamin C" or "Tesco Vitamin C"—that is private labeling. The manufacturer of the vitamins has made a deal with the supermarket to produce the vitamin for them, BUT instead of putting their own label on it, they put the supermarket's label on it.

Wikipedia says: "Private label products or services are typically those manufactured or provided by one company for offer under another company's brand. Private label goods and services are available in a wide range of industries from food to cosmetics to web hosting etc. They are often positioned as lower cost alternatives to regional, national or international brands, although recently some private label brands have been positioned as 'premium' brands to compete with existing 'name' brands."

So, if you come across a lipstick you like to sell and you think you can sell a lot of it, contact the manufacturer and ask how much you need to have your label printed on the lipstick.

The problem is that usually you need to order a large quantity, e.g. 10.000 lipsticks.

The big advantage of private labeling is that you won't have competition; the disadvantage is that many people prefer to buy from major brand names, so you need to really promote your lipstick in order to sell.

There is a whole lot more to be said about private labeling, so if you are interested, research the subject.

p) *Find out how others advertise the product*

Type in a keyword that people would type in to find the product you are selling and see if many people are advertising your product on Google in the form of paid advertising.

Type in exactly the same keyword in one, two and three weeks' time. If the same advertisers are still advertising, they are probably making money. If they have disappeared, chances are they decided the advertising is not earning them any money.

The websites as outlined in the screenshot below are all websites that are advertising for the keyword "purple duvet cover".

If too many companies are advertising for your keywords, that won't be good either, as the price per click will increase, making it more difficult for you to make money. Each time someone clicks on your ad, you have to pay Google money.

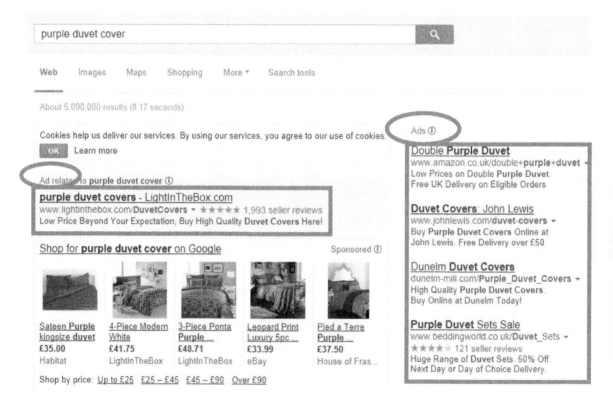

Don't only look at Google, though, to see how others are advertising your product. You need to research everywhere on the web.

q) How does intellectual property affect you?

(All text underneath "How does intellectual property affect you?" is by *Jeff Knight, Vice President of Marketplace, Doba. source: www.doba.com*)

IP, or Intellectual Property, according to the World Intellectual Property Organization, "refers to creations of the mind: inventions, literary and artistic works, and symbols, names, images, and designs used in commerce." There are two categories of IP: Industrial Property and Copyrights. Industrial Property largely refers to inventions, or patents, trademarks, designs, and other works used in commerce. Copyrights are focused on literary and artistic works.

As the Internet has grown and become an important part of how information is disseminated and shared – IP has become an ever-increasing issue. As an eCommerce retailer, IP and the regulation of IP rights effects all aspects of your business. For this reason, I am going to give a brief and general overview of IP issues and how they affect your business.

Before starting, I want to emphasize again that IP is very complicated and a heavily debated area – and this part of the book will only provide a general overview. I will provide URLs at the end to assist with gathering additional information. Second, there is a lot of debate over how to regulate IP, the value of the regulations, and the motivation behind IP laws – we will only skim the outsides of the debate. Largely, for our purposes (i.e. Doba, retailers and suppliers, and IP regulators); we all share a common goal even if at times we are inconvenienced by the regulations.

What are examples of IPs in your day-to-day business?

Most of the images, copy, brand names, MAP (Minimum Advertised Price) policies, channel restrictions (no eBay, brick and mortar only, etc.) – are all examples of IP. Every item that you list on eBay or place on your website, is subject to IP regulations. For most retailers, they are only aware of how IP affects them when they are notified they are in violation. The report is usually followed by the eBay listing being removed, a legal cease and desist letter or in most cases, an email explaining whose IP rights are in question and what you must do to be in compliance.

Truthfully, very few retailers using Doba's platform have had this experience. Before the product is added to Doba's platform – agreements over the supplier's rights and responsibilities are in place to help proactively alleviate questions. Even with the best efforts of Doba and the suppliers, however, there are still situations that arise. Why does this happen? While Doba is authorized to provide you with the product information and images – we couldn't possibly inform every brand/manufacturer of every retailer on Doba's platform. In addition, within a manufacturer's organization are different groups selling to different channels and at times, there can be overlap and even conflicting policies.

Digital Millennium Copyright Act

In 1998, the United States Senate passed the Digital Millennium Copyright Act (DMCA). The DMCA criminalized the act of using technology to circumvent access control protecting IP, as well as the creation of technology or devices that are used to circumvent control. An important aspect was that the DMCA criminalized the act whether the copyright was infringed at all. In addition, DMCA steepened the penalties for copyright infringement on the Internet. DMCA enforcement has ranged from catching pirating (music, software, etc.) to frivolous patent lawsuits of large retailers over common use technology like shopping cart processes. Criticism has focused on the concept of a government, albeit briefly, granting a monopoly over technology thus inhibiting enterprise. Other critics argue that DMCA discourages research and other non-commercial activities. Finally, and most important to Doba users, the DMCA has made it extremely easy for IP rights holders to force websites and retailers to remove content. If a website receives a notice that it is in violation, the website can remove the content or link without being held liable. Essentially, there is no incentive for the website to question the notice, even if the rights are in question, because the website's liability is limited by the removal.

From eBay to Google, the largest technology websites have developed similar polices – if a violation is reported, remove the content and let the publisher of the content work it out with the assumed IP rights holder.

What should you do if you are notified?

Chances are that every retailer will face a situation where IP rights will be in question. What should you do if you are notified? While you may wish to push back or fight the report – Doba would recommend suspending the listing while you gather more information. Next, contact the party and ask for specifics on what content is in violation, how you can verify it is in violation and if it is in violation, how can you correct the violation. In addition, please let Doba know so we can work with the supplier to resolve ongoing issues.

Understand that very few IP rights holders will contact you directly. Larger manufacturers will use a third party enforcement agency or a legal firm to monitor and protect their IP. One of the largest companies in the online space is NetEnforcers. Doba has had many positive interactions with them and we have found them to be a reputable company genuinely interested in protecting their clients and helping retailers in violation get back in compliance. There are many other companies and each will take a different approach. It is important to understand that while the tone of their correspondence may be very accusatory and cold – in the end, the company has most likely not singled you out. I think the positive to take out of a situation is, if a manufacturer cares enough to protect their brand and retailers to hire a third-party; you should look into possibly becoming one of their approved dealers. Overall, getting manufacturer authorization is a good idea for brands you intend on focusing on – many manufacturers have additional marketing and incentives for retailers who comply and meet their program requirements.

eBay and IP

If your eBay auction is suddenly cancelled or you receive a cease and desist letter, don't panic. Look at the global situation; contact the people reporting the violation and move ahead. eBay created its VeRO (The Verified Rights Owner Program) program to help IP rights holders and sellers manage and proactively solve issues. On the VeRO program pages, eBay gives details of how to be in compliance and even lists all manufacturers who do not allow their goods to be sold on the eBay platform.

Here are some places to visit for more information Intellectual Property:

The eBay VeRO program is located at:
http://pages.ebay.com/help/tp/programs-vero-ov.html
Google's DMCA policy:
http://www.google.com/dmca.html
World Intellectual Property Organization:
http://www.wipo.int/about-ip/en/
NetEnforcers:
http://www.netenforcers.com

3) Brainstorming drop shipping product ideas

Now that you know the basic guidelines for choosing a drop shipping product, all you need to figure out is which product you are going to sell. While you don't have to set anything in concrete just yet, you just want to brainstorm a lot of ideas right now. Get a piece of paper or pull up a blank document in Microsoft Word and start thinking.

There are thousands and thousands of items that you can sell online via drop shipping or wholesale methods and gain a significant profit. Sometimes it can help to review a list of items to really get your creative juices flowing. So, in case you need some help getting your brain going, you'll find a list of prospective drop shipping product ideas on the next pages. All of these have seen success in the drop shipping industry; however, I can't guarantee that you'll experience success with them. It takes time and effort on your part to make a product profitable, but with the right tools, such as those outlined throughout this book, you are on the right track to making the product that you choose (as long as it meets guidelines) a success for your drop shipping/eCommerce business.

Your success depends on a number of factors, such as the products that you choose, how cheap you can buy your products, how much profit you can make, how effectively you market your site and products along with a number of other variables.

Here are some ideas to help you get started:

Popular Drop Shipping Products to consider:

- Adult products—sex always sells!

- Art supplies

- Baby products

- Bamboo products

- Beading supplies

- Belt buckles

- Boat parts and accessories

- Body building products, e.g. protein shakes and supplements

- Cake decorating supplies

- Camping gear

- Christian and religious items

- Christmas products

- Clocks (Cuckoo, Grandfather, etc.)

- Collegiate and professional sport themed items

- Computer accessories

- Confectionery

- Crafting supplies

- Dance shoes

- Die cast toys and models

- Doll clothes

- Emergency and survival kits

- Environmentally friendly items

- Fishing gear

- Fitness products

- Fondue sets

- Free from products: free from sugar, milk, gluten, etc...

- Gardening items

- Gift baskets

- Gourmet coffee

- Gourmet cookies

- Hair accessories

- Hats

- Helicopter parts and accessories

- Hunting gear

- Jewelry

- Kitchen items

- Laptop bags

- Left-handed products

- Luxury bedding

- Make up

- Manicure and pedicure supplies

- Martial arts equipment

- Massage products

- Maternity clothing

- Moccasins

- Model trains

- Motorcycle accessories

- Movie themed items

- Nanny cameras

- Night lights

- Organic products

- Plus size clothing

- Poker products

- Robotic toys

- Scarves and gloves

- Science kits

- Security cameras

- Snorkeling gear

- Solar items

- Spa items

- Sports memorabilia

- Supplements and vitamins

- Swords

- Tall people's products

- Tea and tea sets

- Tie-dye kits

- Toys

- T-shirts (themed, funny, etc....)

- Vegan products

- Wallets

- Water bottles

- Wedding favours

- Wine accessories

4) What to look for in drop shipping services

Selling online does not have to be difficult. In fact, that's what a drop shipping service is for: to make things easy for you when selling online. You want to look for a service that offers solutions based on your individual needs. There are some drop shipping services that will take care of everything from returns and inventory updating to tracking packages. However, there are some out there that will only provide you with access to a directory of suppliers and products and not a single thing more. For some, the latter is fine, but for others, they want the whole shebang.

I fell for a few scams myself; being a very suspicious person, I still fell for them, so be careful out there and research, research, research before deciding to select a company to work with.

When looking at drop shipping services, you want to have a close look at the terms and conditions. While the service may sound all hunky dory from the homepage, the terms and conditions may outline a whole other story. The terms and conditions are the real deal, though, no matter what information is on the homepage and sub-pages.

In just a moment, we are going to have a look at the best drop shipping services out there. Some will provide you with only products while others will provide you with everything you need. In fact, some will even offer you a fully set up and automated website so that you can get started immediately.

However, if you decide to do some of your own research, here are a few criteria to look for when evaluating online drop shipping services.

Features. Some drop shipping services will offer a variety of features, while others will only have a limited feature set. The more features that there are, the less that you actually have to deal with on your own, resulting in less stress on your part. Not only will more features ease your stress levels, but it will also help you make more profit.

Tools. This is just like the features. The more tools that a drop shipping service offers you, the less you have to deal with on your own. This means you can relax more, stress less and watch the money start rolling in.

Customer Support. First-rate drop shipping services will provide you with plenty of support. The best ones will provide support for your customers as well. You want to ensure that, when you need help, you will be helped quickly, efficiently and professionally. Some services will only offer telephone support while others will offer phone, e-mail and live chat support. The more options that are available, the more you can tell that the service wants to ensure their clients remain loyal to them.

Never work with a service that offers no way of contacting them, as this is a good sign that they are a scam.

Check Inventory. On most drop shipper's websites, you can view the number of products in stock at any given time. I advise to always work with a drop shipper that has a mechanism in place to check inventory. Don't do business with a company that does not have this.

Note that some drop shippers require a tax ID or a business license and won't do business with you if you don't have these. Many drop shippers just need your name, address and credit card details, but if you want to work with the best companies, it is always better to start up a business.

If you do have a tax ID or a business license, you will be able to buy from more wholesalers and make a bigger profit that way rather than buying from drop shippers.

You have to think and decide for yourself if you want to build a business or if you are just going to do this as a hobby. You probably will not make much money just doing it as a hobby, though. Running a drop shipping site or eCommerce store will need your full time attention in order to earn a lot of money.

Important note: there are two kinds of drop shippers: the private brands ones—these are the ones that are OK to work with. Then there are the ones who charge you a monthly membership fee—these are the ones not to deal with. These last ones usually sell direct to the public themselves, so you will be in competition with them.

The "good ones" usually don't sell to the public and only sell to people like you.

Often, the "good ones" have a MAP policy: Minimum Advertised Price. This means you are not allowed to sell a product with a RRP (Recommended Retail Price) of £300/$500 for £200/$336 just because you don't mind a lower profit margin. They want to protect their goods/brands.

5) What is a light bulk supplier?

You will certainly come across the term light bulk. This can be compared to wholesaler, but you don't need to buy so much in one order. This also means that usually the product will be a little bit more expensive compared to if you would buy the same products wholesale. Many drop shipping websites also have a Light Bulk Section. This is where you will find suppliers for when you want to hold your own stock and ship to your customers yourself. www.worldwidebrands.com has a Certified Light Bulk section. Be aware, as there are a lot of "Large Volume Wholesalers" online where the minimum order is likely to be £625/$1000, and they rarely work with online sellers, so you are on your own if you have a problem. On the other hand, Certified Light Bulk suppliers usually have a minimum order that is lower, e.g. £313/$500 or less, and they are "Online Selling Approved", so they can help you with problems.

6) Sourcing your products – drop shipping services

Several years ago, only a few companies would drop ship, but now there are plenty of wholesale drop shipping companies out there. It is therefore important to choose a renowned company.

Whoever you decide to work with, make sure that you work with certified drop shippers. You don't have to worry about keeping stock. These certified drop shippers will give you a photo that you can use on your shop and when you make a sale, they will ship it direct to your customer. Certified drop shippers will also give you REAL wholesale prices, and they don't have monthly fees or set up fees.

Please note that for some drop shippers, you need to set up your website FIRST before they will approve you. Some of them will ask you questions, such as how are you going to send traffic to your site, how will you make sure you have good customer service, etc. However, most drop shippers will approve you quickly to sell their products.

If they ask to view your websites and you haven't got one yet, here's what you can do. Sign up for a free trial with any of the eCommerce software companies, e.g. Shopify, and set up a "quick store" by choosing a free store theme. Add pages like "Shipping and returns", "Contact us", and upload some products on it. Put some products on your store: don't worry, nobody is going to find your store yet!

Here are some of the best drop shipping companies out there—they are well known, reliable and reputable. I have listed some pros and cons at the beginning of each site, underneath the name.

I do not endorse any of these companies or directories, I am simply giving you some options.

So how do these directories make money?

- They charge a one-off fee to join.

- The suppliers have to pay a fee to be listed.

> **TOP TIP:** Sign up for a 7-day trial and buy your Xmas gifts—or any gifts—
>
> at wholesale prices. :-)

Let's look at some companies. Pricing of the all these websites are correct at the time of printing.

Important to mention: when you will research these companies, or any other companies mentioned in this book, it could be that you find some negative things about them. All the sites that I mention, I have either used myself or I know people who have used them with success. The problem with searching for reviews online is that very often, the competitors of the company that you are investigating, will say they are scam and then put a link of their own company, saying: "This company is much better to deal with, click here"! That's the negative side of these review sites as anyone can leave any comment with any username and you have no idea who that username is or what company he is from or works for. You just never know. To find out if they are any good or not: you've got to use the companies you are thinking of using yourself to judge them.

a) *Worldwide Brands - I highly recommended this one*

www.worldwidebrands.com is a supplier directory.

- Made for online sellers

- Return policy varies for each supplier

- No monthly fees

- Very large selection of products

- Millions of WBI-Certified (Worldwide Brands Inc.) wholesale products to sell online. I believe they are the largest drop ship directory on the web. You won't find a better source of genuine wholesalers ANYWHERE on the web. It's mostly USA certified drop shippers, but they also have international sellers.

- They also have a Light Bulk Wholesalers section if you don't want to do drop shipping.

- They publish only genuine, verified drop shippers and wholesalers.

- They add new suppliers weekly.

- They have lots of training videos.

- They have an exclusive members-only forum.

- Instant Market Research. I love this about Worldwide Brands: They have analysed the potential of the product you are thinking of selling. They give you an analysis percentage (from 0% to 100%) of that product's chances of success on the Internet. They give you, in a matter of minutes, details about demand, competition, advertising, etc…and they generate an Instant Analysis for you. This feature saves you HOURS AND HOURS of research!

With an A+ rating with the Better Business Bureau (BBB), Worldwide Brands is by far the most trusted drop shipping company in the industry. They have a wide variety of educational and market research tools and features to help you get your drop business off the ground; however, other drop shipping services provide a much more extensive variety of tools and features that may prove to be more helpful in getting your business going. They don't actually ship anything, but they provide a huge directory of verified wholesalers and drop shippers. The companies listed on their site pay a fee to be listed.

Supplier and Product Availability. They offer a wide variety of drop shippers and wholesalers that are WBI-certified and products are available in "light bulk" for those that want to have small amounts of inventory on hand.

Every one of their wholesalers meets these criteria:

- They will NOT charge you an account set up fee to do business with them.

- They are ALL genuine factory-authorised wholesalers or the actual manufacturer.

- They ALL carry only brand new, factory warranted products.

-They ALL know they are listed in the WorldWideBrands's directory, so they are expecting calls from people like you, wanting to start up an online store.

There are literally millions of different products that are available to be sold online in your store. Worldwide Brands offers a monthly newsletter as well as updates. They have some of the best wholesalers and products available, with many of the products being perfect to sell on Amazon or eBay, not to mention on your own site. As with any other site, you want to keep an eye on profit margins, as some products and categories will be better than others. Most importantly, it is definitely not a scam.

Returns. One problem with using Worldwide Brands as your drop shipping supplier is that the returns policy varies. The actual return policy isn't with Worldwide Brands as it is with the supplier that you purchase your products from. Therefore, the return policies will vary from one supplier to the next.

Pricing and Payment Plans. Probably best of all, there are no monthly fees. However, there is a price to pay: a one-time fee of £187/$299.00. Ultimately, though, the price is well worth it, as they offer a large number of features for the one-time fee. If the price is a little steep all up-front, they do offer a payment plan where you can pay £62/$99 up front and then make two monthly payments of £70/$110.00 to pay the lifetime membership in full.

This is what they say on their website:

WBI Certified™ **Dropshippers**	VS	Fake "dropshippers" you find online
✓ No Monthly Fees		$10 - $100 Monthly Fees
✓ No Annual Fees		$50 - $200 Annual Fees
✓ No Setup Fees		Additional Setup Fees
✓ 100% Wholesale Pricing.		Wholesale + Markups.

b) Doba

www.doba.com is a suppliers directory.

- Only for USA

- No returns

- Trial period

- No long-term contracts—pay as you go

- eBay Certified Service Provider

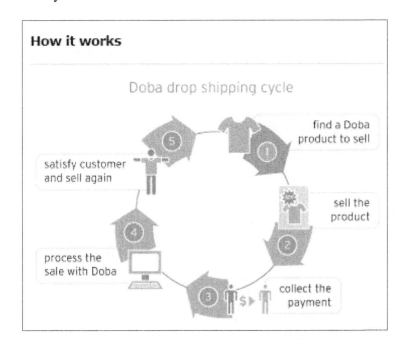

Doba is another great drop shipping company that offers a variety of products—over 1.5 million to be exact. Doba is recommended by Shopify, as well as many other well-known eCommerce companies. Most data is updated in real-time, and the company is a member of the BBB (Better Business Bureau), which is encouraging when dealing in this industry.

With that accreditation, you can rest assured this company is no scam and is truly a trustworthy drop shipping company.

Doba is a drop shipping agent who sits between you and the wholesaler. You work directly with Doba, but they don't hold any inventory. Doba passes your order to the wholesaler, who will deliver the product to your customer. You can always find a product on Doba and try to find the supplier directly, as you will get better prices that way.

Doba has over 2 million products in the product catalogue. Their platform is extremely easy to use.

You can sign up if you are in the UK, Australia or anywhere else in the world, but their drop shipping program only operates in the USA; this means that all suppliers listed on Doba only ship within USA.

This is what Doba says about who and what they are: "*You often hear the terms 'supplier', 'wholesaler', 'distributor', and 'manufacturer'… for the purposes of this article we are going to clump them into one term, supplier, since they are closely related to one another. Simply stated a drop shipper is a supplier who will drop ship items for their clients, the people that actually run retail stores selling products to the public. A drop shipper is the one who actually stores, packages and ships the actual products. By this definition Doba is not a drop shipper. In fact, Doba is not a supplier, wholesaler or distributor either for that matter. Doba is a company that has online software which allows online retailers (people looking for products to sell) to connect with several different suppliers (who provide drop shipping and therefore can also be called drop shippers). To see how our service works in detail try viewing our short tour, it is a really quick and helpful way for both suppliers and retailers to understand how our service actually works. If you just want to read (or skim if you're in a hurry) about it see our how it works page.*

Retailers can search, browse, and even filter through the entire catalogue to find products they want or need to sell. And almost any drop shipper can setup a data feed to get their product catalogues on Doba's site. Another slick advantage with Doba's site is that retailers can also place their product orders through our site. This way retailers don't have to go to separate drop shippers' websites to place their customers' orders.

Sign up for our free trial to test it out first before you decide if you want to use it.

In conclusion, Doba is NOT a drop shipper. We are a service that helps connect retailers and wholesale suppliers together more efficiently than they can on their own. Drop shippers are the ones who actually store, package and ship goods right to the retailers customers. This saves the retailer a lot of expense and a lot of hassle."

Helpful Tools. With Doba, you locate and set up accounts yourself with suppliers and have the ability to negotiate prices with them. Doba also offers a push-to-marketplace tool that allows easy posting of products to eBay, Facebook and other online auction sites. There are no minimum orders and you can place your order online without having to call or fax in your order.

Product Prices. While this is one of the best drop shipping sites for beginners, the prices can be a little bit high when compared to other drop shipping services, resulting in less profit. It's really just a trial and error process to find products that will be truly profitable. Despite some of the products being more expensive, Doba is better than the majority of its competitors in the market. It's an excellent way to get your feet wet.

Returns. One problem with Doba, when compared to other drop shipping services, is that you have to deal with returns yourself, as they don't handle the process for you. This can cause you a headache and more hassle than you would like. If a customer wants to return a product, it is up to you to accept it or not, but keep in mind that Doba will not accept the product back. You will need to re-sell it or be at a loss.

Tracking and Updates. Doba offers tracking information so that you can follow items as they leave the warehouse and travel to their destination. They also have a process that automatically updates prices and inventory. Shipping and tax can be calculated up-front prior to selling the product so that your buyer can be charged accordingly.

Training Tools. Doba has an extensive training library that features articles, tutorials and webinars to help you with your drop shipping business. You'll even gain access to weekly e-mails that emphasize the bestselling products. With this site, you'll also get a special price for Terapeak, which is a really cool, easy to use research tool to investigate your pricing, market, competition, etc...

Customer Support. Doba's customer support team is very responsive. In some instances, they have answered in as quickly as an hour, although the timeframe for which they say they will get back to you is one business day. You can contact Doba via e-mail, and their website offers a physical address in Utah.

Free Trial and Monthly Fees. Doba offers a free trial, so you can try it out for free and see how you like it before you make a full-fledged commitment, as the monthly fee is £38/$59.95 per month. It's a great way to get started in the drop shipping business, but after you start noticing success, you may want to find a site with more affordable products so that you can gain more of a profit. The free trial limits how many products you can have in your inventory and how many products you can push to your marketplace, e.g. eBay or Amazon.

You can upgrade to Doba Advanced for £44/$69.95 per month, which gives you 250 products in your inventory list and 10,000 imports to your website or marketplace.

There is another upgrade available for £56/$89.95 per month, which gives you 1000 products in your inventory list and 25,000 imports to your website or marketplace.

You can also pay an annual fee or a lifetime fee. Here's an overview of the upgrades:

Upgrade to Doba Advanced or Doba Pro

Choose a membership that fits your eCommerce needs.

Your Doba Limited membership ($199 value) gives you access to over 60,000 drop ship products at wholesale pricing from four of Doba's most reliable suppliers. You can sell Doba products online or even buy products at wholesale for yourself family and friends! You also have access to 100s of product sourcing articles, educational webinars, as well as step-by-step tutorials on how to get started. You can also upgrade your membership to Doba Advanced and Doba Pro to get more products, more selling tools, more education. Doba Advanced and Pro members have more opportunities to make money selling on eBay, Facebook, Amazon, Craigslist or their own Webstore.

	doba advanced	doba pro
Monthly Rates	○ $69.95/month	○ $89.95/month
Annual Rates	○ $629.55/year ˄	○ $809.55/year ˄
Lifetime Rates	○ $1,099.95 Lifetime ˄	○ $1,299.95 Lifetime ˄

c) Inventory Source

www.inventorysource.com

- No returns

- Free access with limited use of all features

- a BBB-approved company

With well over half a million products in their database, Inventory Source is another great company in the drop shipping industry.

Returns. With Inventory Source, you won't run into extra fees because you work directly with the sellers. However, because of this, Inventory Source does not offer a warranty or a return policy. Therefore, you will need to work directly with the seller if a product is damaged upon arrival or if the customer wishes to return it. This might be something you want to speak to the seller about before listing the product for sale on your website.

Monthly Fees and Plan. All services at Inventory Source are on a month-to-month basis and start as low as £15.60/$25 per month. You can gain access to Inventory Source for free, but you won't be able to place any orders.

Here's a look at what Inventory Source offers in terms of packages:

- **Free Account**. This plan gives you limited access to Inventory Source at no charge. You will receive access to the member's area, tutorials and training. You'll also be able to view product information and have the ability to contact suppliers at your discretion. You will receive the monthly newsletter, e-mail alerts and free sales and e-mail support.

- **Download File Package**. In addition to all of the above, you will get access to integrated image and product files with new and active filters for Amazon, eBay, Yahoo Stores, Excel and much more. For a one-time £22/$35 programming fee, you can access CSV or XML feeds that are fully customisable for marketplaces, store platforms or other needs. You will have free e-mail and phone technical support. You will gain access to a product filter and custom category tool as well as a tool for custom pricing. You will receive alerts when new products become available and improved HTML formatting to avoid value issues (descriptions, categories, weight, etc.). This plan is available for £15.60/$25.00 a month for the first supplier and for each additional supplier, it costs £9.40/$15.00. Custom files are accessible for £9.40/$15.00.

- Full Automation Package. In addition to all of the above, this plan gets you automated product information and image uploading as well as automatic updates regarding inventory directly applied to your site. This helps you to avoid out-of-stock incidents and negative feedback. You'll even get automated uploading of new products from your suppliers to your site. This plan costs £31/$50 per month for the first supplier and £18.80/$30 for each additional supplier. You must have an existing website for this plan. Custom files can be obtained for £6.25/$10.

- Hosted Website Bundle. In addition to all of the above, this plan will provide you with dedicated hosting, a shopping cart, e-mail, SSL and platform support. This plan is available for £31/$49.95 per month for the first supplier and £18.80/$30.00 for each additional supplier. All items are included in this price and there are no extra fees. Custom files are accessible for £6.25/$10.

All of this can be a bit confusing, so if you need help, just sign up for the free access and let Inventory Source know about your goals, needs and how much experience you have with drop shipping so that they can work with you to design a package that is perfect for you and your business.

Optional Services. In addition to providing drop shipping services, Inventory Source also offers custom service packages that will help your business.

- Logo Design. To have Inventory Source design a logo for your drop shipping business, you will shell out £62/$99. That's not a bad price, but you could get it done for cheaper.

- Custom Graphic Design. If you need a custom graphic designed, Inventory Source can do that for a charge.

- Custom Website Template Design. This costs £438/$699, which is cheaper than some services online, but more expensive than others. Make sure you ask which platforms are available.

- Complete Custom Website Setup Package. This will cost £1,505/$2,400, but you'll get a unique website design and virtually everything you need to build credibility for your business. Again, make sure you ask which platforms are available.

Ultimately, their designs are pretty good, but if you can find top-notch work cheaper, then go for that.

Available Tools. The drop shipping service offers feeds and updates that are fully customisable for different marketplaces and come with push button controls for marketplaces such as eBay, Amazon, Nextag, etc. Fully automated, Inventory Source will update your site automatically with new images, quantity available, current price and more as the information is received. If you have your own products, you can upload them to your site one at a time or in bulk.

Automatic Updates. You will automatically be notified when new products become available, prices change or inventory stock changes. It's common for manufacturers and suppliers to increase a product's price, and with the automated system that Inventory Source has, you'll be notified immediately of this change so that you can alter your product's price on your site accordingly. Alternatively, the service has an option that you can set up to alter your price automatically so that you don't have to manually take care of it or worry about a product selling for the old price before you have a chance to get online and change it.

Other Features. Inventory Source can help you locate the best sellers, with hosting options and integration. They offer a variety of tools that will help you create a great space to sell your drop ship product. Once you have a website created, Inventory Source will provide you with shopping cart software that makes organization of your products easy and provides a simple checkout process for your customers.

Inventory Source has an extensive FAQ section. While they may not offer returns or warranties, because they locate trustworthy suppliers for you, you will be able to speak directly with the suppliers, negotiating prices and possibly getting cheaper prices than what they have listed.

Ultimately, Inventory Source may not be as great as some of the other drop shipping services, but they offer constant updates, help on creating your website and all the necessary tools to create a successful drop shipping business.

d) SaleHoo

www.salehoo.com is a suppliers directory.

- Free trial

- Ready websites

- Find suppliers of brand-named goods

- Also have suppliers that supply in small quantities

- Join SaleHoo Community

SaleHoo has a user-friendly interface, a number of features and tools for success and a large number of suppliers with good-priced products. There are more than 8,000 security-screened suppliers and over 1.5 million products to choose from to sell on your drop shipping website. Their products range from lingerie to electronics. They have a little bit of everything, but if you can't find the product or niche that you are looking for, contact SaleHoo and they'll do their best to try and find a legitimate, reputable supplier for you.

Free Trial and Pricing. SaleHoo lets you test the waters with a free trial of their supplier and product directory. This helps you in many ways, because you can see whether they even have the product or niche available for drop shipping before you pay the price for membership. While you won't be able to view contact information for the suppliers or place an order, you can get a good idea of whether or not they have enough products for your particular niche to make this service worthwhile.

The price of SaleHoo is £42/$67 PER YEAR, which gives you access to the supplier directory, training material and members' forum. If you catch it at the right time, you may even get free access to SaleHoo Research Labs, which gives you insight into how many people are selling particular niches and products that will be the most profitable.

When you first sign up, you can get the web store for free for 1 month, to see how you like it. After the free trial, you are charged £17/$27 per month.

Ready-to-go Web store. If you want to get your site up and going instantly so that you can start selling products without a waiting time, then you may want to consider choosing the web store that SaleHoo offers. There are a number of benefits with the SaleHoo web store that many other drop shipper services offering turnkey websites do not offer, such as built-in search engine optimisation. You can choose your design from a large variety of ready-made templates.

The site is optimised for ease of use, so that buyers can easily find what they are looking for the moment they land on your website. It is also easy to set up and easy to use.

Educational Tools. They offer a variety of educational tools and articles that will help you along the way. SaleHoo will hold your hand until you feel safe enough to let go and continue on your own. There is information available to help you learn about avoiding fraud, selling on eBay, and what items are good to sell for profit and where the best place is to sell them. There's also plenty of free information regarding sourcing products, scam prevention, importing and shipping and setting up your business the right way.

Customer Support. SaleHoo's customer support staff are very experienced and dedicated to ensuring that SaleHoo customers are satisfied every step of the way. There is an FAQ page if you want to try and find the answer yourself. If you want more immediate support, you can contact SaleHoo via telephone. If you'd rather not speak on the phone, you can contact them via e-mail for support. Plus, you have access to a support forum where the experienced staff members of SaleHoo will answer questions that are posted.

e) Drop Ship Access

www.dropshipaccess.com

- Free trial

- Automatic updates

- Automatic ordering

- Does return but with a re-stocking fee and some items are excluded from returns.

- Integration to Ebay and Yahoo small businesses

From books and music to electronics and software to lingerie and jewelry, Drop Ship Access gives you access to over 1.8 million different products at wholesale prices.

Free Trial and Pricing. You can gain access to Drop Ship Access free for seven days, during which you can view all the products that are available. The free trial will not give you access to product prices. Pricing ranges from 30 to 70 percent of MSRP (Manufacturer's Suggested Retail price).

After the free trial, you are charged £31.30/$49.95 per month. You have to give them your card details when you sign up for the free trial, so make sure to delete your membership before the free trial expires.

Push to eBay. Drop Ship Access comes equipped with a push to marketplace service for eBay. You can easily post items for sale on eBay, and when an item is running low on inventory, you'll receive a notification via e-mail.

Automatic Updates. Once you add products to your website, you don't have to worry about them going out of stock and still showing for sale on your site, as Drop Ship Access offers automatic updates. This means that you don't have to manually update your inventory. When a product runs out of stock or a price increases, it will be updated on your site automatically.

Automatic Ordering. What's really neat with Drop Ship Access that I haven't seen available with other drop shipping services is that they offer automatic ordering. What this means is that when your customer places an order, the information is sent directly to Drop Ship Access without you having to place the order manually yourself. All you have to do is review the information to make sure it is correct and approve the order.

Returns and Warranty. If an item arrives to your customer damaged, defective or as the wrong item, Drop Ship Access will take care of it. Now, if your customer simply does not like the item that they received for whatever reason, it may be returned, but depending on the item, there may be a restocking fee of between 15 and 20 percent. Due to the nature of the items, lingerie and jewelry may not be returned. You should always contact Drop Ship Access prior to simply returning a product to ensure that they will accept it.

Educational Material. There's plenty of educational material available through Drop Ship Access, including eBook and articles.

f) Dropship Design

www.dropshipdesign.com

- Ebay certified

- Ready-made websites available

- They handle returns

- They drop ship to USA, Canada and UK and have 2 different plans for this. They also drop ship to other countries, but you need to contact them for this.

- Not very good prices for some products

Probably one of the most advanced drop shipping companies out there right now, Drop Ship Design is considered one of the best companies to work with when you are opening a drop shipping business. They don't accept money orders (BACS payments) or checks as a form of payment, but that is not a big problem as all online shoppers have their credit/debit card or PayPal account ready. Let's delve right in and find out what Dropship Design can offer you and your drop shipping business.

If you are looking for an easy way to get into the drop shipping business, then Dropship Design is a good starting point. Dropship Design is eBay certified, making it incredibly easy to list and sell any products on the well-known auction site. Plus, you have immediate access to the company's database of products, which ultimately means that there is no waiting time for the products to be shipped. These are just two of the valuable features that come with Dropship Design.

Dropship Design Plans. There are four plans that are designed to suit any seller's needs, from the most amateur drop shipping seller to the most experienced seller. Here's a look at the plans:

- **Basic Plan**. Available at a lower price than the other packages, the basic drop ship plan is a very simple plan with few features. You will gain access to more than one million products that are available for drop shipping. There is no push to marketplace or website builder with this package. It is available for a **one-time fee** of £31.35/$49.99. There are absolutely no monthly fees and no hidden fees or drop ship charges.

- **Ebay Plan**. Specifically designed to work in conjunction with eBay, the second drop ship plan creates an eBay wizard that helps you create and manage your eBay auctions quickly and simply. With this plan, you will be able to push products directly to your account with eBay and begin to sell those products within mere minutes. Once an order is placed and sold, the product will be shipped out immediately by the drop ship company. This is available for a **one-time fee** of £62/$99.99. There are no monthly fees to worry about.

- **Data Feed Plan**. This plan allows you to download descriptions and images of all of the available drop shipping products into a CSV file, which can then be viewed in Excel. Daily updates are always applied. You can then take this information and upload the data onto your own website, auction site, Amazon, etc. There is no monthly fee, just **a one-time set-up fee** of £92/$149.99.

- Website Plan. You get a website that is loaded with all their products. The website is customisable, and you can accept card payments and PayPal.

The domain name is free, and your emails are free.

This will cost you a **one-off fee** of £92/$149.99 and after that a monthly fee of £18/$29.99, but you get the first six months free.

Returns. With Dropship Design, you don't have to handle returns, as they handle the entire process for you. If an item arrives damaged or the customer simply isn't satisfied with the product that they ordered, you never have to deal with it. You can continue on with the rest of your business while Dropship Design handles everything for you.

Unlike many other drop shipping companies, your orders can be placed online. There is no need to call or fax in your order.

Automatic Updates and Tracking. Dropship Design sends automatic updates regarding the inventory and prices of the products. This results in you having more credibility as a seller with your customers, as you are less likely to be selling a product that is no longer in stock. You will always be notified when a product of yours is out of stock or is getting low. In addition, when a product is shipped from the drop shipping company, you will receive a tracking number that you can share with your customer. This ensures that you and your customer both know where the product is at all times.

Helpful Tools. Dropship Design has a very informative page with various FAQs. If you are unable to find the answers you are looking for there, they offer a live chat service so that you have access to a representative who can answer your questions within mere seconds. Alternatively, you can e-mail them, but you'll be waiting 24-48 hours to receive a response.

US, UK and More. Dropship Design is available to those looking to start a drop shipping business in the United States or the UK, as well as many other countries, as DropShip Design is available in more than 225 different countries. They are known to provide fast international drop shipping services. Dropship Design has a wide variety of products, ensuring that you find something that is worthwhile and profitable to sell. While there are many great drop shipping companies out there that you can partner with, Dropship Design is definitely one of the best.

g) DropShippers.com

www.dropshippers.com

- Free trial available

- USA and UK

- Own web store

- Automatic updates

- Tracking available

- 24/7 support

- Lifetime membership with a one-off fee

www.dropshippers.com offers a number of more advanced tools and is not necessarily recommended for a beginner. However, if you are a quick learner, then it may be okay. Nonetheless, it's one of the best and most reputable drop shipping services out there today, and is worth your consideration, whether you choose to use it to get your business started or you switch to it after you get some money rolling in.

Available for use in the United States and the United Kingdom, Dropshippers.com offers access to 3.5 million products. They say they have the largest wholesale directory in the world—a claim that they proudly stand by. They are so positive that their database is the largest, that if you can find a competitor with a larger directory of wholesale products, they'll give you £62.70/$100 towards your membership with them!

Plans and Prices. There are three different plans available and then a combo plan that includes all three original plans. Here's a look at each one of them:

- **Directory Plan**. This plan gives you access to the directory of all their products. You can reach out to suppliers and make your own deals with them. You'll have access to drop shippers and wholesalers as well as discounted closeout and surplus items. You can get the directory plan for a £62/$99 **one-time fee** and no monthly expenses.

- **Auction Plan**. With this plan, you can sell your items on eBay, but don't have to worry about doing the heavy lifting. You sell, notify Dropshippers.com and purchase the product. Dropshippers.com ships to your customer. You will gain access to numerous eBay tools as well as research reports designed for the auction seller. This plan costs a **one-time set-up** fee of £94/$150 and does not require a monthly fee.

- **Website Plan**. This plan gives everything you need to get your drop shipping business started. You will have an entire storefront without putting an ounce of effort into creating it. You can customise the site any way you wish in terms of design, products sold and domain name. Products will be pre-loaded as picked by yourself, and the design can be customised through the installed Control Panel. They'll even set-up a merchant account for you through Meritus. Website hosting is free of charge for the first 90 days. This is all for a **one-time fee** of £124/$199, and no monthly fees are associated with this plan except for the cost of hosting.

- **Combo Plan**. This plan gives you all of the above in one convenient package for £187/$299 as **a one-time fee**. You'll gain access to backend customer support that is only available to those who purchase the combo package.

Free Trial. Dropshippers.com offers a seven-day free trial so you can check the service out and see if it's what you are looking for before you commit to an up-front set-up fee.

Automatic Updates. Dropshippers.com offers automatic updating of their product inventory and prices. If a product that you have on your website for sale begins to run low in stock or runs completely out of stock, and even when the product has been re-stocked, you'll receive a notification informing you of such information. When you receive these inventory alerts, you are able to remove the product from your online shop to avoid someone purchasing an out-of-stock product.

Tracking. The service also ensures that you can keep track of each and every order, as you'll be provided with tracking information. You'll know when the product has been packaged and shipped. You'll be able to follow it to each shipping processing stage. You'll know exactly when it has been delivered to your customer.

h) Wholesale2b

www.wholesale2b.com

- Ebay certified

- Easy to use

- Turnkey websites available

- No Tax ID required

- Returns allowed

- Not that many features and tools available

Incredibly easy to use, Wholesale2b offer a variety of features and tools to help you get your drop shipping business and site up and running quickly. While their features and tools do not outrank some of the other drop shipping services, nor do they have as many products as some other services (about 1,500.000 products), the service is easy to use and offers superb customer service. It is considered to be one of the easiest drop shipping services to get your drop shipping business started and growing.

Plans and Pricing. Wholesale2b has three different plans available offering different features. Here's a detailed look at each of them:

- **Drop Ship eBay Plan**. This plan gives you access to all the service's drop ship products and has a push-to-eBay tool allowing you to easily post products for sale on eBay in the US and the UK. Their eBay tool is certified by eBay and allows you to push a single product or items in bulk. You choose the price that you sell the item for. You'll get access to 240 different auction templates so that your auction can be set apart from the rest with a different look. There is no limit on how many products you list for auction/sale on eBay. This plan is available for a yearly fee of £62.70/$99.99 or a monthly fee of £15.60/$24.99.

- Drop Ship Website Plan. This plan gives you access to all products. Domain name, e-mail address, admin dashboard, hosting, daily updates and customizing tools are all included in the price. This gives you a turnkey website so that you don't have to go through the tedious process of setting up a website on your own. This is helpful when you aren't sure what you are doing and you want to ensure that all products on your site are kept up to date in terms of stock and pricing. The site can be customised so that you focus on a niche rather than just a general store. All you have to do is choose the products you want and they will create a website for you. This plan is available for a yearly fee of £187.50/$299.99 or a monthly fee of £25/$39.99.

- Drop Ship Data Feed Plan. This is a data export plan that gives you access to all the available products. You will get product descriptions in a CSV file and product images in a zip file, although you can get them in a number of other formats, if needed. Daily updates are included in this plan, so you'll always know when products are low in stock or completely out of stock to avoid unhappy customers. Some shopping carts require a data feed in order to import products onto your site, so if this is the case for you, you'll need this data feed. Alternatively, they are used to push the products and relevant information to various marketplaces, such as Amazon, Bonanza and other third-party auction sites. This plan is available for a yearly fee of £94/ $149 or a monthly fee of £15.60/$24.99.

US, UK and More. Wholesale2b ships anywhere in the United States and Canada and most international countries, including the United Kingdom. Once a product is shipped by the supplier, you will receive a tracking number, giving you the reassurance that your product is on its way to your customer and knowledge of exactly where the shipment is. Wholesale2b offers a warranty that will cover damaged goods and a return policy that allows returns within 30 days from the date of delivery.

Helpful Tools. Wholesale2b offers a FAQ page that has answers to basic questions. If you need further assistance, you can create a support ticket.

Free Trial. You can sign up for a free account that allows you to view the products and their prices. Should you decide that Wholesale2b is for you, you can activate your full account with re-selling capabilities by purchasing one of the three plans described above.

i) Sunrise Wholesale Merchandise

www.sunrisewholesalemerchandise.com

- USA and Canada only

- Limited products

- Access to "only" 10,000 brand name products

- Monthly subscription

Sunrise Wholesale Merchandise has been in business for 13 years and has an A+ rating from the BBB. Sunrise Wholesale Merchandise has products of good quality, although if you are looking to sell automotive or apparel, this drop shipping service isn't for you, as they are not available. For the most part, this service specialises in home and beauty products, such as bath and body products, jewelry, candles, gifts, décor, furniture and toys. When compared to other drop shipping services, they don't have as many products available for drop shipping nor do they have as many helpful tools and features.

Tracking, Returns and Automatic Updates. Among the features that Sunrise does have are instant access to drop shipping products at discounted prices, online ordering, and a 30-day return policy. You will always receive a tracking number when your orders have been shipped so that you can stay up to date on where the package is in the shipping process. There are also automatic notifications to inform you about a product's inventory status to ensure that you are never selling a product that is no longer available.

Turnkey Website Option. Sunrise will help you build a website to sell your products on so that you don't have to tackle that on your own. But, unlike other services, you cannot customise the design of the site; however, there are plenty of templates that you can choose from. If you choose this route, your site will be up and running within minutes of providing all the necessary sign-up information. Once you get to your site, you can add and remove any products, change categories, etc.

eBay Auction Wizard. Sunrise Wholesale Merchandise also comes with an eBay Auction Wizard, making it easy to sell merchandise on eBay. This is handy if you want to sell on your own website and eBay.

Free Trial and Monthly Fees. While you can get free access for a week, there is a monthly subscription fee of £18.78/$29.95. If you choose to opt for a pre-loaded website from Sunrise, you'll be paying £31.32/$49.95 a month. You can pay once per year and that will cost you £62/$99. There are no per-order drop shipping fees.

Free Inventory Files and Method of Payment. When you sign up, you will gain access to free inventory files that are provided to you in either XML, Excel or CSV format. These files are updated on a daily basis. Sunrise allows payment to be accepted via debit/credit card and PayPal, just like the other services; however, Sunrise differs in the fact that they also accept payments via money order (BACS) and eCheck.

Customer Support. If you need help, you can contact Sunrise via phone or e-mail. If you'd rather find the answer on your own, you can search their FAQ page.

US and Canada Only. One thing with Sunrise Wholesale Merchandise is that they only ship to the United States and Canada, so if you are in the UK or you plan on selling internationally (other than the US and Canada), then this service is not for you.

Free Trial. Before you pay for the service, a seven-day free trial is available for Sunrise. This allows you to test the waters instead of jumping right in—the water may just not be right for you.

j) Product Sourcing

www.productsourcing.com

- Fewer tools available

- No returns and no warranty

- You can only sell in USA

If you are looking to save money and don't mind having less features and tools at your disposal, then Product Sourcing may be a good service. Many refer to Product Sourcing as a downgraded version of Doba.

Free Access. Regardless, though, they have a decent selection of drop ship products and provide a decent service overall. The site allows free access in viewing their product catalog and even allows you to start selling products. However, the free account has limited access. You won't be able to use their push to marketplace tools and a number of features, such as all the educational articles and tutorials, are not available unless you upgrade to a premium account.

Returns and Warranty. Basically, Product Sourcing gives you what you need to simply get by. There is no warranty or return policy. If a product is lost or damaged, they state in their terms and conditions that neither they nor the manufacturer are responsible. So, if a customer receives a damaged item, their package is lost or they are simply not satisfied with their product, you are responsible to take action, as you will not receive any assistance from Product Sourcing. You may try contacting the manufacturer of the product and see if they'll help you out, but there is no guarantee that they'll oblige. Therefore, it will essentially be your decision to take the loss or keep an unhappy customer who might spread the word about your poor service.

Tracking and (Lack of) Automatic Updates. Product Sourcing does offer you tracking information when a product has been shipped so you can keep track of the package as it is on its way to its destination. There are no website building, custom pricing or custom design features, nor is there an automatic update tool that will keep you in the loop in terms of pricing and current inventory of your items. They simply say it's your responsibility to stay on track with this information.

Plan Pricing. The free account gives you limited access, but there is a Pro account that you can gain access to which will give you accessibility to various tools, features and educational tools in addition to a lot more products and suppliers. The Pro account costs £25.00/$39.95 per month, £188/$299.95 a year, or £564 $899.95 for a lifetime membership.

k) Other Drop Shipping Services

While the above-mentioned drop shipping services are the best of the best, there are a few more that are worth mentioning and checking out:

Wholesale Central - www.wholesalecentral.com A directory, free to use as it charges their supplier to be listed.

Aid & Trade - www.aidandtrade.com A directory of legitimate, reliable drop shippers.

True Dropshippers - www.truedropshippers.com A directory of wholesale products.

Urban Load - www.urbanload.com

Electronix HQ - www.electronixhq.com

Plum Island Silver - www.plumislandsilver.com

Hienote - www.hienotedirectory.com

Focal Price Dropshipping - www.focalprice.com

National Dropshippers - www.nationaldropshippers.com

7) UK specific drop shipping services

While some of the previously mentioned drop shipping services cater to the US and the UK—among other countries—there are some drop shipping services that are actually based in the UK and cater more to UK customers than others. Drop shipping businesses are just as popular in the UK as in the US, so here are a couple of the most popular services offered in the UK.

a) ATS Distribution

http://www.atsdistribution.co.uk

- Only UK

- Different accounts available

- Templates available

- Automatic stock updates

Whether you are just starting your drop shipping business or are looking for some more products to have at your fingertips, ATS Distribution is one of the best drop shipping services in the UK. Offering a wide variety of products as well as some valuable features, ATS Distribution has three different plans you can choose from to get your business going and offering plenty to your customers. I have used ATS distribution successfully but there a lot of negative reviews about this company online. I can only say that it worked for me!

Before you actually pay any fees, you can sign up for an account and view prices; however, no ordering can take place until you've paid for one of the memberships.

Products Available. ATS Distribution may focus on electronics, such as chargers, batteries and accessories, but they also offer a wide range of products including toys, kites, umbrellas, pet gifts and baby carriers. If you go searching under the categories, you'll notice most of them are limited to about 10 items, but the product information is very detailed, ensuring that you understand everything there is to know about an item.

Pricing and Plans. There are three levels of plans that you can choose from. There is a Dropshipping Account, Standard Account and Website Account.

- Dropshipping Account. This plan costs a one-time fee of £40/$64. There is no minimum order. You can have the items delivered to yourself, or you can have them drop shipped to your customer. There are also plenty of shipping options to choose from. Orders are only accepted online and must be paid for at the time of ordering.

- **Wholesale Account**. This account requires that you have the items delivered to your doorstep rather than your customer's. This is ideal if you want to take part in drop shipping, but want to ensure that the products are accurate before you send them to your customer, or if you want to have some inventory on hand. This account requires a minimum order of £50/$80. Products can be shipped next day within the UK for less than £8/$12.75. Compared with the drop shipping account, prices are a bit cheaper, likely because of the minimum order required. Orders can be taken by phone or online.

- **Websites Account**. For a set-up fee of £79/$126 and a monthly hosting fee of £9.99/$15.95, you can have your own website that is ready to go. The site is customisable, fully integrated with the 4,500-plus products that ATS Distribution offers, and gives you the opportunity to begin selling products immediately with limited to no hassle. You can even add your own products from other services. The set-up fee covers the costs of the domain name, site testing, website creation, secure payments, initial logo creation, domain configuration, control panel configuration, static IP, e-mail control panel, and unlimited tech support. Stock levels are updated automatically every 20 minutes to ensure accurate numbers are shown to your customers.

Shipping Locations. If you were planning to sell internationally, you'll have to go with another service, as ATS Distribution only permits items being shipped within the United Kingdom. Shipping takes two to five days for Royal Mail first class. Extra charges may be necessary for shipping to Scottish Highlands and Northern Ireland, among other areas. Same-day shipping is generally available if orders are placed before 2 pm.

Returns. While many services require that you deal with returns on your own, ATS Distribution helps you out here by dealing with the returns. This leaves you to concentrate on other aspects of your drop shipping business.

Help and Support. You can find answers to most of your questions on your own by searching the FAQ section, which is pretty detailed. You can learn how to order, add funds, add images and much more, such as tips for pricing, invoicing and billing. You can reach customer support via telephone (tech and member support), e-mail or post.

The Verdict. All in all, ATS Distribution is a great place to get started for your drop shipping business in the UK with its wide feature set, affordable packages and extensive customer help and support. Keep in mind, though, if you wanted to sell your products internationally, you will need to choose a service other than this one.

b) More UK drop shipping services

Here are a few more UK drop shippers that you could consider:

- www.wholesaledeals.co.uk

- www.esources.co.uk

- www.ukdropshipgroup.com

- www.dropshipland.com

- www.dropshipkids.co.uk

- www.puckator-dropship.co.uk

- www.dropshipforum.co.uk = forum

8) Various websites that drop ship

You don't necessarily have to sign up with a drop shipping service to be able to take part in this part of the online business industry. In fact, there are plenty of business websites out there that will drop ship their products. Each will have their own set of rules that you'll need to read up on, but here's a list of several companies that are willing to drop ship their products.

- **Alternative Health Care** – Natural remedies, herbs, organic skin care, sports nutrition, vitamins, supplements and more. www.althealthcare.com

- **Anatex** – Educational children's toys, such as puzzles, games and learning toys. www.anatex.com

- **Aura Fragrance of Paris** – Perfume and cologne for men, women and children. www.aurafragrancesofparis.com

- **Big Discount Fragrances** – Perfume, cologne, hair products, skin care products and more. www.bigdiscountfragrances.com/wholesale/

- **Cutting Edge Products** – Security products. www.cuttingedgeproducts.net

- **Fish Click** – Fishing tackle products. www.fishclick.com

- **Fitness Cash** – Sporting goods. www.fitnesscash.com

- **Guardian Survival Gear** – Emergency survival kits. www.wholesalesurvivalkits.com

- **Hobby Tron** – RC cars, planes, trucks, boats, kites and more. www.hobbytron.com

- **Halloween Select** – Halloween costumes, decorations and goodies. www.halloweenselect.com

- **iiSports** – Products for martial arts, airsoft and paintball. www.iisports.com

- **Pet Stores USA** – Pet supplies and products. www.petstoresusa.com

- **Real Action Paintball** – Paintball products. www.rap4.com

- **RMF Scrubs Wholesale** – Lab coats and scrubs. www.rmfscrubswholesale.com

- **Safety Technology** – Tasers, stun guns, hidden cameras as well as surveillance systems. www.safetytechnology.com

- **Sos Eyewear** – Sunglasses. www.soseyewear.com

- **TeeShirtsRock** – T-shirts. www.teeshirtsrock.com

- **Upright Golf** – Golfing products. www.uprightgolf.com

- **Viking Wholesale** – Swords, knives, cutlery and more. www.vikingwholesale.com

- **Vitabase** – Vitamins. www.vitabase.com

- **WMS Clothing** – Lingerie, jewelry, shoes, handbags and more. www.wmsclothing.com

9) Buying products wholesale

In the event that you actually have the money to spend on inventory, you may want to consider purchasing items wholesale to ensure that you have products in stock for your customers when they order. While it is rare, a glitch could occur in the drop shipping/eCommerce system and inventory numbers may not be updated appropriately, resulting in your customer ordering a product that is really not in stock. If you had purchased this item wholesale, you'd have it in stock ready to ship to your customer.

Buying wholesale is not for everyone, but if you have the funds to do it, it is a good idea as you can buy cheaper, therefore earn more. I've compiled a list of some of the top websites where you can buy products via wholesale prices. Some of these are focused on particular niches, while others have almost every niche you could possibly think of.

If buy wholesale, you would set up an eCommerce site and not drop ship unless you have decided to sign up with a drop shipping site that also allows you to sell your own stock.

Important note: always pay by credit card when buying from these companies, as there are a lot of cowboys trading that will take your money and never send you the goods. If you pay by credit card, at least you are insured, but if you pay by wire transfer or BACS, you cannot get your money back if things go wrong.

You can search for wholesale products by typing in "your keyword" + wholesale, which will likely bring up some companies that sell your products at wholesale prices. Here are a few websites that sell at wholesale prices.

- **DHGate** – Everything from clothing and jewelry to electronics and home and garden products. www.dhgate.com

- **AliExpress** – Everything from clothing and jewelry to electronics and home and garden products. www.aliexpress.com

- **AliBaba** – Everything from clothing and jewelry to electronics and home and garden products. www.alibaba.com. Word of warning: there are A LOT of scammers on Alibaba that take your money and you never see any goods. Make sure to thoroughly research the company you are planning to buy from.

- **OC Surplus** – Everything from clothing and jewelry to electronics and home and garden products. www.ocsurplus.com

- **Wholesale Fashion Square** – Women's clothing and accessories. www.wholesalefashionsquare.com

- **Apparel Showroom** – Women's clothing and accessories. www.apparelshowroom.com

- **Cosmopolitan Cosmetics** – Perfume, hair products and more. www.cosmopolitanusa.com

- **BooJee Handbags** – Handbags and accessories. www.boojeehandbags.com

- **Buy 4 Less Electronics** – Cameras, phones, tablets and more. www.buy4lessinc.com

- **Noah's Ark Distribution** – DVDs, books, and more. www.shopnoahsark.com

- **Wholesale DVDs for Less** – DVDs, cloth diapers, flameless candles and more. www.wholesaledvdsforless.com

- **DMA Incorporated** – Sporting goods, RC toys, tactical gear, gun accessories and more. www.dma-inc.net

- **Self Defense Supply** – Self-defense products. www.selfdefensesupply.com

- **Master Cutlery** – Swords, knives, daggers, air guns, crossbows and more. www.mastercutlery.com

- **Novelty Wholesale Company** – Ideal for gifts, this UK-based company is reliable; I have worked with them. www.noveltywholesale.co.uk

10) What margin and what price do you sell your products for?

Can you sell your products online and beat Tesco's or Walmart's price? Sure you can.

Here's how to do it:

- Find a bank willing to loan you a few billion.

- Find an international architect and start building warehouses all over the world.

- Travel around the world to do deals with the best manufacturers at rock bottom prices.

- Buy 157 trucks to take care of your transport.

- Buy millions worth of products and start stocking your warehouses.

- Spend millions on advertising.

See, it is easy after all! I've presented you with your step-by-step plan to do it. :-)

Now back to the real world: of course you can't beat a super market price!

- You need to source your products, if possible, direct from wholesale suppliers to cut out any middlemen. That's your best chance of selling at very competitive prices.

- When you have found a product and a supplier you are going to work with, they will give you a price list which will show your buying prices and the suggested retail price (SRP). Some suppliers also have a MAP price, this is the Minimum Advertised Price. This means you are not allowed to sell the product anywhere for less than the MAP price. This is very interesting for you, as it means you will be able to compete with the big boys if they sell the same product.

If you DO sell underneath the MAP price, the supplier will no longer work with you. What some companies do is display the MAP price on their website, give their customer a discount and sell the product with a discount. That way, they are selling under the MAP price.

- The most important thing to remember here is: price your product for PROFIT, not with the intention of selling a lot but with the intension to maximise profits. I guess that's why you are reading this book, to make a profit, right?

Price for profit, not for volume.

It is easy to lower your prices, and your customers will love it, but it is not so easy to increase the price once it is on the web: your customers will notice it. That's why it is very important to get your price right from the start.

- In order to price your product, you need to know your costs first, so make sure you know exactly how much your expenses are and what your profit margin has to be to cover those expenses.

You DON'T have to be the lowest price!

No that's right, you DON'T have to be the lowest price! A clean and attractive website with brilliant customer service will impress your customers more than saving a dollar.

- As a general rule, you can price your products higher if there is high demand and low competition AND if you think there is a market for your products.

When I first priced my liquorice products, on www.liquorice-licorice.co.uk, I thought by myself: "How much are people willing to pay for very salty liquorice that you cannot get on many online shops?" I had a figure in mind and thought, "Surely I cannot price it that high!", but I did and the products are selling well.

It is best to set your prices high; this way, you can give people a discount voucher should you not create any sales. Announce something like "20% discount on all orders this week" and see if it makes a difference. If you start with a very low profit margin, you can't offer any discounts. People love buying at discounted prices; we all love a bargain!

- If you are selling to students, who don't have a lot of money, price as low as possible, while still keeping a good profit margin. However, if you are selling helicopter parts to people who own helicopters, it is obvious that these people have more money to spend.

- Look at the prices your competitor is charging! If possible, beat your competitor's prices or sell at the same price. Lots of customers look at price comparison sites these days. You can do the same: go on comparison sites and see how much similar products sell for.

- If you always have the cheapest price on the comparison sites, customers will eventually stop comparing prices and automatically order from you again because they will think you are the cheapest all the time. Of course, being the cheapest goes against what I just said about pricing for profits, but maybe you can be the cheapest for a few products...and still earn a lot on other products.

- You might sometimes think reading this book that I say price high enough for profit and then I say price as cheap as possible. The reason for this is that there simply is no rule for pricing, as it depends on what niche you are selling. Just put your entrepreneurial hat on, and if you can get away with charging a lot, start high and don't question it.

- So, what is a "normal" profit markup or profit margin for an online shop? I am sorry, but there is no such thing as a "normal" markup. It depends on what industry you are in, where you are located, what you are selling, who you are selling to, how much you are selling for, etc. Profit margins can be anything between 10 and 400%! I suggest you NEVER sell anything under 25% profit margin, but I do know people who do.

Most drop ship margins range from 25 to 75%.

An average, generally accepted profit margin is between 20 and 60%. In the clothes sector, it is often 100% or more (e.g., buy clothes from India bulk for 0.50c per piece and sell them here for 4.95 each!).

- If you have a mailing list, you can ask the advice of people on your list by sending them a survey. You can do this with www.surveymonkey.com. Ask other people what price they would be prepared to pay for your prestigious-looking mugs.

A product is too expensive when the value is too low.

- Let's have a look at pricing from a drop shipper's point of view. So in this example, you are going to be the manufacturer and you are planning to supply a drop shipper. Drop shipping often has a 50% above wholesale format. This is how the pricing is calculated, at 50% margin.

A simple formula for wholesale pricing: manufacturing cost x 2 = wholesale price x 2 = retail price, or price you sell the item for on your store. Always take production cost into account when working out your wholesale price. This includes insurance, wages, handling, etc. You need to know how much it really cost to produce the product.

Here's a simple example:

- Your product cost 4.00 to produce

- Add 1.00 to cover your insurance

- Add a 1.00 inflation coverage

- Add 2.00 for your wages

- Total cost per product: 8.00

Double it = your wholesale cost = 16.00

Double it = your retail cost (RRP) = 32.00

- You can calculate your selling price "the easy way": take your purchasing price and double it or add 70%, 80% on it, whatever you can get away with to make it a sellable product. Doing it this way, you assume that by selling a lot of products, all your expenses will be covered. I must be honest and say that I sometimes do practice this method, but there is a better way.

In order to work out what price you are going to sell your product for, ideally you should calculate all expenses related to the price of your product and calculate your price that way. Most people don't do it this way and I must be honest, I don't always do it this way either but if you do, you know you will make a profit, even if you only sell one product.

The following spreadsheet is an example of how to work out the total cost of your product and include the shipping price into the price you will sell the product for. If you are using a drop shipper, you will also have to add the drop ship cost per order, if your drop shipper will charge it to you, which most of them will do.

Calculate Total Cost of Product

Purchasing price of product	5.00
Packaging expenses e.g. cardboard, bubble	0.20
Import Cost per unit	0.30
Duties/Customs	0.40
Credit card processing, 2% on selling price	0.50
Shipping Cost	4.50
Handling Cost: your wages for packing the product	4.00
Total cost per product	**14.90**
Selling price	19.97
Profit per product	**5.07**

You can see 5.07 profit is not a lot of profit per sale if you sell your product at 19.97!

This is assuming you do free shipping, if you charge for shipping, your profit will be 4.50 more, so 9.57.

TOP TIP: never pad shipping fees. Your customers are not stupid. They know it does not cost £15/$25 to ship a small camera! This will cost you more money in lost sales than you would ever make on the extra shipping charge.

See what your drop shipper charges you for shipping and charge exactly the same to your customer; maybe add a little bit to cover your drop shipping charge per order.

Important to know: your drop shipper will charge you a drop ship fee "per address". This means if your customer orders 1 product, your drop ship fee will be e.g. 2.00, but if that same customer orders 5 products and you purchase all 5 products from the same supplier, your drop ship fee will still be 2.00.

If you ship the product yourself, include the packaging material in your charge; that's why it is called P&P—Postage and Packaging.

- Internet customers are used to paying P&P. Some of the biggest online stores use drop shipping and charge the drop ship fees to the customer as a P&P charge.

- What I usually offer is "Free shipping if you order over X amount", and I display that clearly on my website. This works and a lot of people will order more until they reach that "X" amount to avoid P&P.

- And then there is VAT/TAX!

So many people don't think about this. Check the legalities in the country you are in. Some products are VAT-FREE. Find out which ones they are.

If you are not VAT registered, you don't have to worry about this, but hopefully your turnover will be so high that by law, you will have to be registered. If you don't register when you reach the threshold, you will get a heavy penalty charge for forgetting it or ignoring it!

If you **are** VAT registered: when you sell a product for £62/$100 on your website and your purchasing price is £37/$60, that does not mean your profit is £25/$40, as the £62/$100 will include your VAT/TAX, which you will have to pay to the government.

Of course, you can claim the VAT back (when you are reaching the VAT threshold) on your expenses, e.g. packaging materials, office furniture, etc...

Check where you live when you have to register for VAT/TAX.

If you are VAT registered, you will have to charge VAT to your customers and include that in your selling price. The VAT rate in the UK is 20%. This means that your price will increase by 20%. That is a lot, but you HAVE to take this into account.

If you are selling to other businesses that are VAT registered, this is not a problem as they will be able to claim the VAT back on the purchases they make.

Usually, if you export, no VAT is charged, or at least that is the case in the UK. You need to check in your country when you have to charge VAT and when VAT does not apply.

Once your sales volume is so high (hopefully soon), you will have to investigate VAT more, as it is simply not possible to explain it all in this book. After all, this is not a "How does VAT work" book.

- All eCommerce software will have a Tax Settings screen, where you tell the software if the prices displayed on your site are including VAT. You can also set the countries for which you need to charge VAT. Here are screenshots from EkmPowershop:

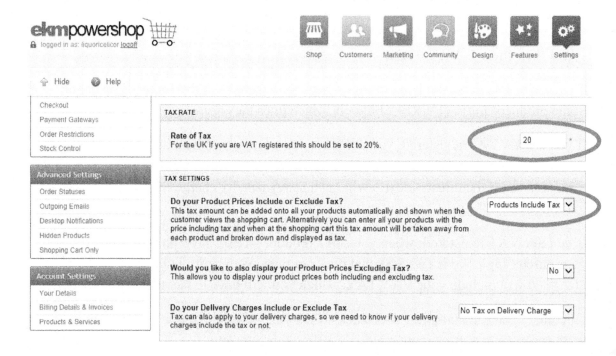

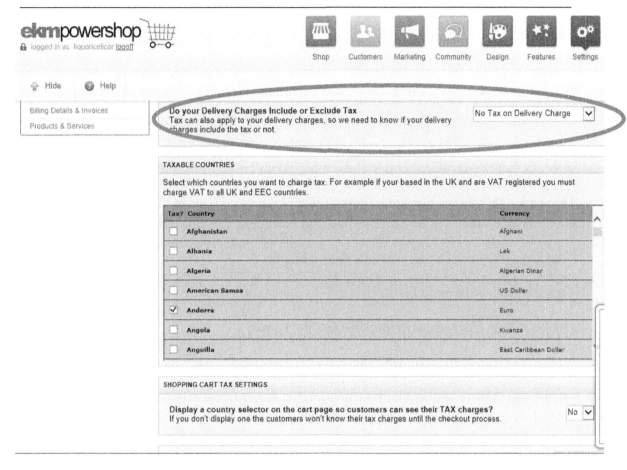

Conclusion: to decide on your price, remember these:

- Price for profit, start high, you can always lower it.

- Investigate your competition.

- Don't forget about the VAT if you are VAT registered.

Always show the selling price incl. VAT on your shop so the customer does not get any surprises at the check-out, when the VAT will be added and the customer did not count on that.

11) Your product description is important

You can copy the title and the product description from your drop shipper's website BUT I recommend you change that. Don't just copy that text, but re-word it and put keywords in it.

Also, never just copy someone else's text (who is selling the same product) word for word, as that is considered copyrighted material and it's against the law to copy it.

There are a few things that are important when you write your product description. This is the description that will be displayed next to or underneath your product.

- use keywords (see further) in your product name.

- put the product name in bold.

- make a short crispy description; also use keywords.

- make a longer description with more details and again,use keywords.

- make sure, where applicable, you mention the dimensions/ sizes of the product. This is very obvious for clothing, but if you sell chairs, tables, etc…you need to list all the dimensions so your customer will know immediately if the item is suitable.

- How much do the maintenance products cost, e.g. printer cartridges?

- Add-ons. Does the product need anything else to work, e.g. batteries? Are they included? How many? Which type?

If the add-ons are not included, mention it clearly and offer them as an upsell.

- Put a "View larger image" on if possible.

- Put the order button, e.g. add to cart, on the right hand side of the image.

- Put like buttons below the image or on the right.

- Tell it like it is. If your product has a negative side, mention it in the description! This will minimise returns.

- Show it as it is. Don't show a picture with a red ribbon around the candle if it will be delivered with a green ribbon! This may sound stupid, but it is important. Your customer orders the product thinking they will get exactly the same as shown on the picture on your site. Sometimes customers are difficult and this will result in a reason for your customer to ask for a discount or a refund.

- Learn from the "big boys" like Amazon, Debenhams, Asos, New Look, Harvey Nichols, etc.

Here is an example of a good product description as seen on Debenhams.com:

Your customers must also be able to view all these quickly and easily; you can create an information page per product for this or display the information somewhere else:

- Contact information

- Delivery costs

- Payment facilities

- FAQ

- Privacy Policy

- Reviews of your company

- Security information

- Is VAT/TAX included in your product prices? Customer hate surprises at the checkout, so if TAX is not included, tell them so where the price is displayed.

Please note that the information pages (Privacy Policy, etc.) are not used for SEO purposes, so it is not important to use keywords on that page.

12) What reference number for your product?

Good eCommerce software should give you the possibility to give your product an internal reference as well as a customer reference number. Even if you use software that doesn't have this feature, there are a few things worth mentioning.

- If possible, put a keyword in the reference number.

- Don't make your reference number too long, e.g. 100/394858/DC/758/H2. That is just annoying for everyone involved.

- Make it clear from the reference numbers from which supplier you have bought the products. This will make things soooo much easier when you print reports and analyse your sales.

Your supplier could be called Johnson Drop Shipping. You can use JD in your reference numbers. That's what I do, e.g. your reference number could be JD786.

TOP TIP: Make the last or first two characters of your reference number the first two letters of your supplier or any two letters, just so you recognise the supplier.

TOP TIP: if you deal with people on the phone or people can order over the phone: DON'T use these letters in your reference numbers, as they can easily be mistaken on the phone, resulting in you shipping the wrong product.

- M and N. A customer might order your reference MD346 and you might send your reference ND346 instead.

- F and S. An F sounds like an S on the phone and the other way around. This saves you having to constantly ask: Is that an "S for Sierra" or an "F for Foxtrot"?

- O. The letter O is very often mistaken for the number 0, depending on which typeface you use and O can indeed look like a 0.

Make it easy for your customers. Remember, always put yourself in your customer's shoes. If you would have to phone or email about your product, which reference number would you rather quote: 100/394858/DC/758/H2

or

JD786?

Chapter 7 - Shipping, Returns and Back Orders.

1) Shipping your product

If you work with a drop shipper, this will not apply to you, but if you have your own stock and run an eCommerce site, you or a staff person will have to ship your orders.

Before you ship, you MUST double check or triple check the order to make sure you've got everything right: colour, quantities, size, etc...

Who do you ship with?

I can only speak about the UK in this chapter as I ship from the UK. I personally ship with FedEx or UPS and in my experience, they are both very reliable. Other good ones are: DHL, Royal Mail, Parcelforce.

Whatever shipping company you use, things WILL go wrong now and again. Things like:

- parcel delivered too late

- parcel delivered to the wrong address

- parcel got lost

- parcel damaged

- parcel refused by customer

As these are things out of your control, the only thing you can do is solve them as soon as possible. The sad thing, though, is that even if it is not your fault, your customer will blame you!

The way Royal Mail has changed its pricing recently, I hardly ever post anything. IF your parcel is under 1 kg and not too big, Royal Mail might be the cheapest way to go, but in any other case, Royal Mail is just too expensive. They look at the weight AND the size to price their parcels.

Here are a few important things regarding shipping:

- Always insure your goods (usually transport companies/couriers do this anyway as a standard rule).

- Make sure what you ship is actually insured! In the small letters of the contract with the shipping company, it will exclude some products from their insurance!

- Negotiate prices. Couriers are always happy to have your business and usually they will drop the price IF you ask.

- Some couriers will give you a printer to print out the labels to put on the packaging. Negotiate when you start working with the courier that they supply the labels and toner for the machine free of charge.

- Negotiate a better price once you reach a certain number of parcels, e.g. when you start working with them, say: "When I reach 10 parcels per day, can we agree that you give me a better price?"

- ALWAYS, ALWAYS ship parcels in a way that they can be tracked, e.g. Royal Mail Recorded Delivery, Courier. Never just post goods if the value of the product is over £10 / $16. Of course, if you have sold a product for £2/$3.30, it doesn't make a lot of sense of sending it recorded as your profit will already be extremely small for that sale. Most customers are honest but there are always customers that will tell you they haven't received the product, even if they have. If you send goods with POD (Proof Of Delivery), you will avoid this from happening to you.

- Use a courier that has software so you can check the tracking online.

- Don't use the cheapest courier; often a reliable one is much more important.

- Make sure you include all paperwork in the parcel.

- Most companies put in a return form—I know as I order a lot online—but I don't personally do this with my liquorice site. I think this depends on what you are selling. If you are selling clothes or shoes, as people cannot try them on before they order, you have to make returns easy and put in a return form in the parcel.

- The cost for one parcel can vary a lot: anything between £4.95/$7.90 and £19.95/$32.00, depending on the weight, the number of boxes per consignment, the speed of the delivery (1 day, 2 days, etc…), and so on.

- If you are selling small items that are not fragile, you can use the courier's own bags, and then sending a parcel will be very cheap, e.g. £4.95/$7.90.

- The location from where you invoice your customer and where you will ship to are important. Some countries have extra charges and taxes. This can vary from the location you ship and the location you ship to. An example is India, which has Octroi charges. You have to understand the law of the country you are shipping to before you ship to those locations.

TOP TIP: Buy all your packaging products, e.g. cardboard boxes, tape, bubble, etc., from a manufacturer, not a middleman. Tell the manufacturer you will sell his products on a website. You can save lots of money that way. It is worth setting up a website, e.g. www.packaginggalore.com, and sticking a few packaging products on it to show the manufacturers that you do have a website that sells packaging products. The hosting of the website will cost you a little bit of money per month but you will save THOUSANDS on packaging products if you can buy them direct from the manufacturer.

Will you ship internationally?

Selling internationally on the web is not as simple as it may sound. Customers prefer to shop in their own language and pay in their own currency. There are legal aspects and taxes to take into account.

Your shipment charges will be high, so you need to sell reasonably high-priced products to make a good profit. Having said that, I have customers in the USA, Denmark, Switzerland, etc... who order for £50/$80 worth of liquorice and they are prepared to pay £80/$128 transport costs. Hard to believe, but true!

And of course, you will need eCommerce software that can display your prices in different currencies, even if the language is in English.

I cannot advise you on whether or not to ship internationally, as it depends on what products you sell, but as all good shopping carts will have that feature, I suggest you try it and see what happens. I use FedEx International or DHL to ship the goods to any destination in the world. Your customer will usually receive the goods the next day if based in Europe.

2) How to handle returns

Returns are a hassle for everyone involved in the process. It's as simple as that. Try to minimise your returns by giving very clear product descriptions.

Returns are the one thing that most people are concerned about when they want to start a drop shipping business. For the most part, the decision as to how you handle returns will be up to you, although some drop shipping services that you choose to work with may handle returns for you. It is very important to know your drop shipper's return policy before you sell their products.

If you don't want to deal with returns, DON'T set up an eCommerce or drop shipping business, because you WILL have returns.

Every online shop has to make returns easy, as your competition is doing it, therefore you will have to do it. It is part of online shopping, like it or not.

Be aware: IF you have lots and lots and lots of returns, your merchant account can close you down, and you can't sell another thing by credit card! Merchant accounts exist for one reason: to make money. If they can't make any money from you because of constant refunds, they don't want you as a customer. You've put in a lot of work to get a merchant account, and now they are closing you down? Business is tough! Everywhere! For this reason, it is important that you do everything you can to minimise returns.

- You could state on your website that all sales are final and that returns are not allowed. However, this would be against the law. By law in the UK and in some countries, your customer must have a period to ask for a refund. You need to investigate what the law says about this in your country.

- If you make it more difficult for your customers to return products, very often they will keep them rather than having to contact you and ask for a return number, etc. If it is a hassle for them and items are inexpensive, many people just won't bother. That's why I don't always include a return form when I ship orders. I do always provide a telephone number and email address so customers need to contact us to arrange a return.

- You could allow returns to be sent back to the supplier, assuming that they are willing to take returns, of course.

- You could have your customer return the product to you, and you either take the loss or send it to the supplier for a refund, or re-sell it from your website and ship it yourself. If you ask your customer to return the product to you, make sure to inform them that YOU will credit the customer for that expense.

- If you have sold a £9/$15 product and your customer wants to return it to you, it will cost you approximately £16/$25 to have a courier collect it and deliver it back to you. This is what FedEx calls a "reverse delivery", and you have to pay the delivery charge twice: once to collect from your customer and the second time to deliver the product back to you. That is a lot of hassle and expense for a product you've sold for £9/$15! Returns are just a pain and very often will cost you money.

TOP TIP: Before you agree to a refund, ask your customer if they are happy with a discount, e.g. a 25 or 30% discount. Many customers will be happy with that, and you still earn a little bit of money and don't have the hassle of a return. A discount is always better than a refund.

---

a) Permitting direct returns with the supplier

Most drop shippers will have the products sent directly back to the supplier. However, this can't always be done. For this to happen, the supplier must allow for returns to be sent to them. Usually, most suppliers will allow returns for damaged products or wrong items. Some will allow returns for certain types of products. In other words, never tell your customer to return a product to so-and-so address when you aren't even positive that they'll accept the product back with no problem. Otherwise, you'll be in a huge pickle.

Ultimately, the best way to go about all this is to have the customer contact you in regards to the return and have you approve it before they send the product back to the address provided. This just gives you more control over the return process, ensuring that every step is taken accurately. However, most big companies include return papers with the shipped goods.

As a general rule, though, when a customer wants to return a product, you'll need to contact the supplier for approval. If approved, you'll receive a return authorization code to make the process quick and easy. This code will need to be sent to your customer, as they'll need to send it with the item when they return it or else the return may not go through.

Make sure you tell your customer returns have to be done in a way that your customer can obtain proof of delivery e.g. by recorded delivery, by a transport company, etc..

b) Controlling the return process yourself

Some prefer to have the items returned to them before the item actually goes to the supplier. This is definitely recommended if the product is relatively expensive. Ultimately, it provides you more control over the entire return process but you'll also be out more on shipping costs.

Regardless of who sends in the return, it needs to be equipped with a tracking code so that no one can say that they sent it when they didn't. If you have it shipped to you before you send it to the supplier, you may want to charge a nominal restocking fee to your customer to cover some of the costs associated with the double-shipping. However, most customers don't like this.

If you are running an eCommerce business and buy from a wholesaler, of course all goods need to be returned to you.

c) The problem with "all sales are final"

While you may think this option is all well and good, the truth of the matter is that this actually poses a huge risk to the success of your business. You see, if you inform your customers that they cannot return a product under any circumstances, the trust that you need to build with them is essentially gone forever.

You will have accept returns if the product arrived damaged or if the wrong product was shipped. Neither of these problems are the customer's fault.

Overall, it's fine to say all sales are final, but you should have a few exceptions, and you have to realise that you will have fewer sales when you have a no-return policy. It is important to remember though that all the big, well known online shops have an easy-no-quibble-return policy.

d) A few final thoughts on the returns process

Let's say that your supplier permits returns within 30 days after purchase or confirmation of delivery. You may want to make your returns allowed within 20 days. This ensures that there is plenty of time to get the return in within the 30 days that the supplier allows.

If the supplier charges a restocking fee, make sure to charge that to your customer to ensure that you aren't out more money than you need to be because your customer wanted to return an item. In fact, saying you charge a restocking fee will generally cut down on the number of returns, because no one wants to pay that extra money on a product that they realised they don't actually want.

Make sure that the same details your supplier gives you are accurately provided to your customer. For example, many suppliers will take returns on certain items, but they must be unopened and clearly unused. This is information that is important to display to your customers; otherwise, you'll be the one at a loss in the event that your supplier will not accept the product as a return.

If you use more than a single supplier, just make sure that you take the restrictions of each supplier and combine them into one clear and concise return policy. This cuts down on any confusion if you were to say that for this product, your return policy is this, and for that product, it is that. If one supplier is stricter on returns, go with that information, as it would be better to be strict about everything than to run into problems down the road. It just keeps things simpler for you and your customers.

Ultimately, when creating your return policy, make sure that it contains the items that are allowed to be returned, why the items can be returned, and the period of time allowed for returns to be processed.

In summary:

- Don't be afraid of permitting the return of items. While it doesn't happen every day, it is possible for customers to be unhappy with the items that they receive. This is especially true if you order the wrong product from the drop shipper or the wrong product is sent in error by your supplier.

- Take the time to thoroughly look over the return policy of your supplier(s). If you are using multiple suppliers, combine their return policies to create one clear policy for your customers.

- Never actually post the address for returns on your site. You want the customer to get in contact with you first so that they can give you the reason for their return. This gives you the chance to validate the reason for return. Once validated, you can then send them the return address, authorization number, and any other necessary information they may need to ensure the return is processed quickly and properly. If the customers has to contact you to organise the return, you also have the chance to offer your customers a discount in return for them to keep the product.

- If the item up for return is expensive, you may have your customer send the item to you instead of directly to the supplier. This gives you a chance to inspect the product first-hand and resolve any issues while the product is in your hands.

- Always make sure the returned item goes back in stock. Most software does this automatically, but you might have to put it back in stock manually.

- Don't forget that even if you think the customer does not deserve a refund and you won't give it, your customer might go directly to the credit card company and demand a refund that way. This is more hassle and paperwork for you, as you will have to send the credit card company copies of all correspondence so they can decide if the customer deserves a refund.

- For most drop shipping companies, the shipping and handling fee is non-refundable. This is one reason why you need to offer your customer a discount rather than immediately do a refund.

- Most drop shippers will need you to contact them to obtain an RMA (Return Merchandise Authorisation) number. You can ask your customer to return the product DIRECTLY to your drop shipper, in which case you need to give the customer the RMA Number and MAKE SURE your customer puts that number on the package when returning it.

> **Top Tip:** If something has gone wrong or the customer wants to return the goods because you have done something wrong, NEVER make the customer pay for returning the goods.

It WILL happen that you don't earn any money from returns, but that's just the way the business works! There are no set rules for returns, so it is up to you to decide.

3) How to handle back orders.

A back order is an item that you cannot supply as you have mistakenly sold it whilst is was not in stock. The drop shipper will get it back in stock when he orders more stock from the manufacturer.

Back orders create unhappy customers, so the best way is to avoid them at all times. If you do have a back order, contact your customer and tell them that they bought a very popular product and you sold out faster than you expected.

You can offer your customer:

- keep the order in back order until the product comes back in stock

- replace it with a similar item

- refund the order

Whatever you do:

- don't talk your way out of a refund if that is what the customer wants. Customer is King, remember.

- Solve the problem quickly and in a professional manner.

Lots of people will talk about you online IF they have a negative experience, so if they are not happy with your service or the way you treated them with the back order situation, they will be doing plenty of negative advertising, which is the last thing you want as it will damage your business.

Chapter 8 - Setting Up Your Drop Shipping Account and Selecting Products to Sell.

For illustration purposes, I'm going to show you how to set up an account with www.doba.com. You can go along with me as I set it up to set up your own, or you can just come back to this section once you are finished with the book and you are certain drop shipping is right for you.

It is *incredibly easy* to sign up, choose products, and get images and descriptions to put on your website.

On Doba, you have nothing to lose, as you can sign up for a 7-day free trial. So, you aren't out any money at first to see how it works. So, once you click on the 7-day free trial button on the homepage of Doba, www.doba.com you are taken to a page to sign up with your e-mail address and are requested to create a password.

After you've clicked "Try if free", you will be taken to this page.

Free trial benefits

- Instant access to 2,055,360 name brand products
- **Largest selection** of products available from any single drop ship source
- Doba is the only dropshipper that's an **eBay® Certified Service Provider**
- 33% - 75% average product margins
- **No risk!** Sell first, buy later

Name and Address

FIRST NAME	
LAST NAME	
COUNTRY	United Kingdom ⌄
ADDRESS	
TOWN/CITY	
POSTAL CODE	
PHONE	

Next

Go ahead and type in your e-mail address and create a password. You'll then be taken to a page where you'll need to input some of your personal information: name, address and phone number. You might get a little frightened because they ask for your credit card information and you thought you were signing up for a free trial. You really are signing up for a free trial, but they will charge your credit card if you forget to cancel within the first seven days.

Just remember to cancel within the first seven days if you decide that you don't like Doba, or if drop shipping just isn't your thing. It is very *easy and very quick to cancel* your account, so don't worry about giving your CC details. All you need to do is click on your account, and there is a button that says "cancel my account".

We stand behind our services
and our guarantee

If for any reason you are not 100% satisfied with your trial membership, simply notify us within the first 7 days, and you won't pay a cent.

Your free 7-day trial membership will begin when you click Start Membership. If you are enjoying Doba, do nothing, and your membership will automatically continue for as long as you choose to remain a member at a rate of $59.95 per month. See Terms of Service for complete membership details. No commitments, no hassles. Cancel any time Monday - Friday, 7:00am - 7:00pm, Mountain Time.

By clicking the Start Membership button, you acknowledge that you have read and agree to the Doba Terms of Service.

Questions?

As a Doba member, you will have access to our on-site support team by phone and live chat from 7am to 7pm MST, M-F.
For more information, click the "Contact Us" link after you've logged in to your account.

Why do you need my credit card?

We need your credit card to set up your account and verify your information. If you decide to cancel during your trial, your card will not be charged.

After you've filled in all the above details, you will get the "Congratulations" screen:

CONGRATULATIONS

Your Startup Account

Account

You are now a Doba Startup member.

Account Contact

Please print this page for your records.

GB

For your records we have emailed your login information to you.

Phone

Billing Profile

Thank you for signing up with Doba.

Help us personalize your Doba experience by
answering the following 8 questions:

1. What category of products are you interested in selling? (you can choose more than one)

☐ Apparel, shoes & jewelry   ☐ Games, movies & music   ☐ Home, Garden & Living   ☐ I'll sell anything that will make money
☐ Electronics & computer   ☐ Books   ☐ Kids, baby & Toy
☐ Automotive, tool & industrial   ☐ Health & Beauty   ☐ Outdoor & sports

2. Do you have a website?

○ Yes - If Yes, what is your website URL?
○ No
○ In Progress

3. If you have a website, what shopping cart technology are you using?

Feel free to go ahead and fill out the questions that are presented to you on this page. Alternatively, you could opt not to fill these out right now and just click on the Get Started button at the bottom of the page.

On the next page, you can request to receive a Free Instant Website Report. Fill in any domain name to receive it; it's free, so why not.

FREE Instant Website Report

Customers are searching online for your products. **Be found first!**

✔ **Your Search Engine Ranking** Is your site optimized for Google, Yahoo and Bing and what ranking do they give you?

✔ **Competitor Analysis** How your website compares with your online competition.

✔ **Keyword Analysis** What keyword phrases potential customers use to find you online and how you rank with these keywords.

✔ **Free Consultation** Ensures that your website is optimized for search engine traffic and customers.

Higher search engine rankings significantly increase website *visibility, taffic, and sales.*

Take the first step to increasing your online sales.
Get your **FREE Website Report** today!

Domain Name:

That's it: sign up is done in a matter of minutes! You will receive an email confirming your account information.

You'll next be taken to a page that shows the different categories of products. If not, just click on "Catalog". You can begin here, or you can enter a search term if you know exactly what you are looking for. For educational purposes, we'll use the "Kids, baby and toy" category.

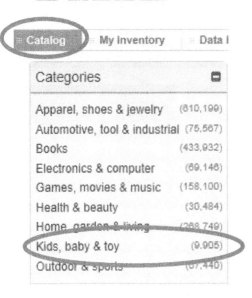

Once you click on that category, you are presented with a list of products. Find one that you fancy. I am going to choose the "Cook Together Kitchen" and click on that product.

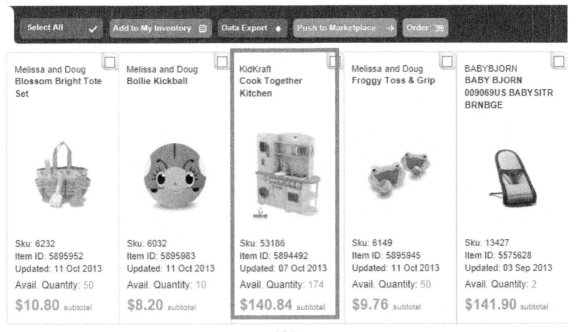

Now you see more details about the product, and you can calculate how much you will earn when you sell one.

Let's have a look how much the cost is of your kitchen and how much you will earn. All these figures are displayed on the above screenshot.

$136.84 is the Wholesale Price—this is your buying price

+ $4.00, the Drop Ship Fee

$140.84 is your total price excluding shipping costs

+ $43.05 is your shipping cost

$183.89 is your total cost including shipping

226

$259.90 is the MSRP = Minuimum Suggested Retail Price. You don't HAVE to sell the product for this price. You can sell it for more or less as there is no MAP price, or Minimum Advertised Price.

Let's say you sell it for the MSRP of $259.90: what is your profit?

$259.90

- $183.89, your total cost including shipping

$76.01 is what you will earn when you sell one. Not bad. That is a 29% margin (76.01/259.90).

Also note that there are 174 items in stock. If this said 3 items in stock, I would NOT choose this product, as it will probably be sold out soon. Around Xmas, when toys sell really well, I would also not choose this product, as 174 items in stock is not enough.

1) Add To Inventory List

If you want to put this product on your website, simply click on "Add to My Inventory", and you will be asked to give your Inventory List a Name. I will call it "Kids toys", so I will put all my kids toys in this Inventory List.

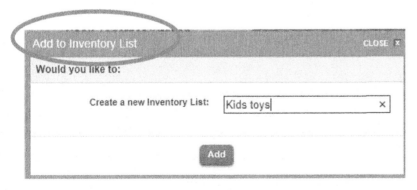

Your Inventory List will be created:

You'll notice that during your free trial period, you can only export 10 items, but that's enough to let you know whether this is something that you want to continue with after the 7-day trial.

The Data Export button is used when you want to transfer information to your own marketplace, such as your website, or save information on your computer. If you look at the drop down list for the format, you will notice that there are a ton of options. More than likely, the hosting provider that you use has a shopping cart feature that is listed here. If that is the case, that is the format you would choose. This would ensure that once you downloaded and saved the data into an Excel spreadsheet that it would be easy to upload to your website.

Now you need the details of the product to be able to put it on your store. Click "Data Export" and you will be asked in what format you want to download. I always choose "Product Comma Delimited" so I can import the data easily in Excell.

Click "Save and Download" or "Download Only". I always click the first one.

You will be asked to save or open the file. I always click on Open and then save the file to my computer.

Do you want to open or save **export_20131012042403.csv** from **doba.com**?   Open   Save ▾   Cancel   ×

The file will open in Excel—in my case—and now I have all the product info handy, e.g. product name, product description, etc. DON'T just copy this info, but re-word it to create unique content for search engine purposes.

supplier_id	drop_ship_fee	supplier_name	product_id	product_sku	title	description
89	4	Hood	5212527	53186	Cook Together Kitchen	Get out your chefs hat and apron, beca

Now click on "Download image" underneath the product, and it will be downloaded to your computer.

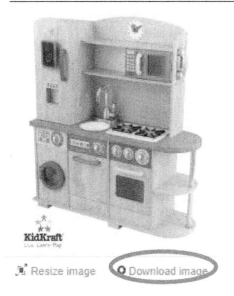

How easy is that? That's all you need to do. Now you can put all the information on your store simply by importing the image and the description, etc. from within your eCommerce software.

2) Push to Marketplace

You can also push your product to Marketplace. This means importing the details to eBay or Amazon.

Click on " Push to Marketplace" and this screen will appear:

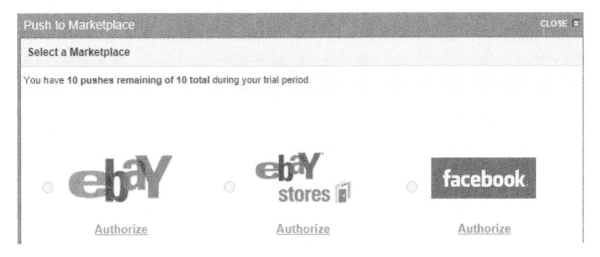

Select the one you want. I have clicked on "Authorize" underneath eBay.

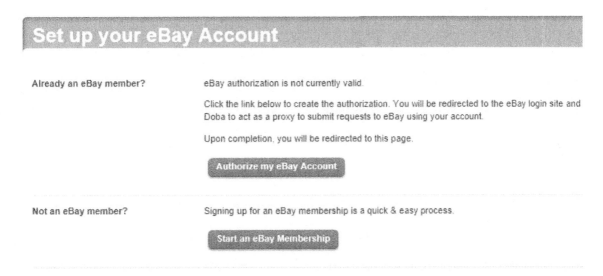

You have 10 pushes available during your trial period. This is what you should see.

Here, you'll need to authorize your eBay account or create an account with eBay. Since I already have an account, and hopefully, you do as well, we are going to click on "Authorize". If you don't have an eBay account, that's okay, because it's really easy to get started.

I'm signed into eBay and this is what appears:

Grant application access: Doba

Ready to use Doba? Great! We need your consent to share your eBay data. Don't worry, we won't share your eBay password. You can change this any time by editing

Please take the time to read Doba's terms of service and privacy policy, because these policies will apply when you use this service. Remember, we don't manage polic

By clicking on the "I agree" button, you're allowing us to link your eBay account with Doba.

I agree   No thanks, take me to the Application's website or eBay homepage

Obviously, you want to grant permission, so click on the I Agree button.

You'll then be taken back to the Doba site, where you'll need to input some personal information, such as your postal code and PayPal address.

eBay Settings

* Postal Code:	
* Country:	US
* PayPal Email:	
Username	jim111922
Authorization Expiration	2014-05-28 09:43:33
Renew Authentication	Renew Authentication

Save Settings

Go ahead and input this information and click save. You can then continue on to list the item on eBay.

3) Order products to be drop shipped.

Let's assume you have received an order on your website for 2 items that are on your website: the Kitchen and ABC Blocks. I have added ABC blocks to my Inventory List.

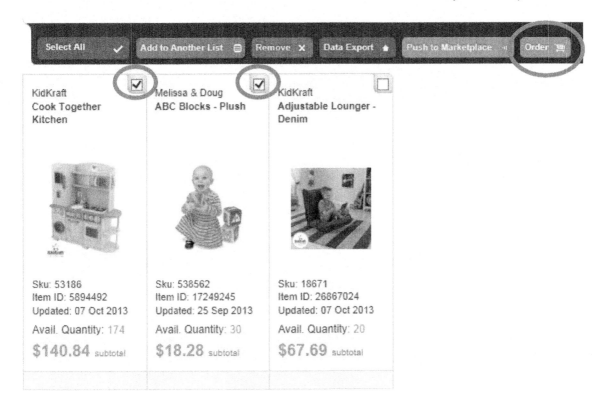

Simply tick both the products and click on "Order". You will see a summary of your order:

Cart						CLOSE x
	SKU	PRODUCT NAME	AVAILABLE	PRICE	QUANTITY	SUBTOTAL
Hood						
x	53186	Cook Together Kitchen	174	$136.84	1	$136.84
					Drop Ship Fees:	$4.00
					Shipping Fees:	$43.05
					Subtotal:	$183.89
Lincoln						
x	538562	ABC Blocks - Plush	30	$18.28	1	$18.28
					Drop Ship Fees:	$0.00
					Shipping Fees:	$9.95
					Subtotal:	$28.23
					Order Total:	$212.12

Update Cart   **Empty Cart**   **Proceed to Checkout**

Click "Proceed to Checkout" and fill in the information from the customer who bought the product on your store. The drop shipper will ship the products to your customer.

Checkout

Shipping Information

Enter the shipping address and the name of the recipient.

*Recipient First Name:

*Recipient Last Name: *Address:

Recipient Telephone: *City:

Company/Attn: *State:

PO Number: *Postal/Zip:

Next

That's it! You have now selected products to put on your website, you have sold some, and you have told the drop shipper to ship the product to your customer (after you've charged your customer's card). You will receive confirmation of the order.

You can search your orders per ID, per date, etc…

Order ID

[   ]

Go

PO Number

[   ]

Go

Date Range

from: [   ] 🗓

to: [   ] 🗓

Go

Status Group

☑ Attention Needed

☑ Payment Pending

☑ Paid

☑ Shipment Pending

☑ Shipped

☑ Cancelled

☑ Returned

Go

When selecting products, you can select with advanced filters, such as: don't display products that are not in stock, don't display products without images, only give me products that are in stock, only give me products for which you have over 2000 in stock, etc…

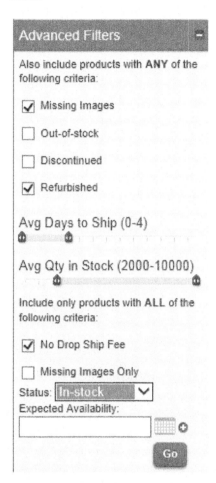

While all of this was shown from the Doba platform, for the most part, the other drop shipping product sources, such as Inventory Source and Worldwide Brands, will be pretty similar. So you can see that part is very easy and also good fun to browse products and find some winners.

Chapter 9 - Receiving and Processing Payments.

The world of online payment approval is pretty confusing and complicated at first as there is a lot to absorb, but once you have used it a few times, you will wonder why you ever found it confusing.

These days, you have the possibility to get credit and debit card approvals on your mobile phones. I have personally never done this, therefore I am not talking about that in this book. I am personally not a smart phone fanatic, as I live in the country side and reception is often extremely poor. However, I do mention "PayPal Here" later in the book, which is a service you can use to take payments with your mobile phone, but only when the buyer hands over his credit card to you and types in his PIN number, so it's not suitable for online sales.

Be aware as there are lots of fake, untrustworthy companies out there offering you this service.

Shopping carts offer different plans to accommodate your preferred method of payment processing. Some shopping carts have it all in house: a merchant account and a payment gateway so you don't have to deal with third-party providers, where integration can be a problem.

You will need "real time credit card processing". This means your customer puts their credit card information into your website and within a few seconds, the money is taken from your customer and on its way to your bank account. On top of that, an order confirmation is sent to your customer, and you get a notification that you have received an order.

You have two options for receiving payments for your online business: a third party like PayPal or a merchant account. PayPal will allow you to accept payments from any customer that has a PayPal account themselves, while a merchant account will allow you to fully process payments via debit/credit card. A customer's PayPal account can have funds from debit cards, credit cards, bank accounts, online sales of their own, etc. Both

PayPal and a merchant account come with certain restrictions and will consist of fees associated with transactions.

If you want to accept credit cards online, you will *always* need a merchant account **AND** a payment gateway. One does not work without the other. You can also, instead, or on top of that, use a third-party payment processor, e.g. PayPal. On most of my websites, I give my customers the choice to pay by PayPal OR by debit/credit card. All good eCommerce software gives you this facility.

You will find that in this chapter I explain the same things in different ways. The reason behind this is that many people don't grasp this very easily, and it is important that you understand. I am hoping if I explain it in different ways, every reader will understand the difference between a gateway, a payment processor and merchant account.

This is a VERY simplified view of how it all works (further in the book you will see the more complicated version that shows you everything that goes on in the background):

1. Your customer orders an item.

2. Your payment gateway passes on the total of the order to your merchant account.

3. Your merchant account approves the order and charges your customer.

4. You and your customer receive an order confirmation.

5. You or your drop shipper picks the order and ships it.

It sounds pretty simple and sometimes it is indeed, but it is not always that simple to set it all up.

1) Difference between merchant account and payment gateway

A question people often ask me is if they need a merchant account or a payment gateway or both.

The answer is: you need both BUT sometimes one company can provide both services.

To put it very simply: a merchant account is an agreement with a bank to let you accept credit cards, and a payment gateway is the service that authorises and processes the payment securely.

I personally use www.streamline.com and www.1shoppingcart.com as my merchant accounts, and www.worldpay.com as my gateway provider for most of my drop shipping sites. Please note that Worldpay does NOT do recurring payments if you use 1Shoppingcart as your shopping cart.

A big bonus with 1shoppingcart is that it has an affiliate program built in.

In most cases, YOU need the collect the money from your customers when you've sold an item from your website. So you will need to sign up with a debit/credit card processing company called a Merchant Account. This is not easy when you are just starting in business.

For a traditional shopping cart system, you need to be able to connect the "cart" to your bank. To do this you need a payment gateway. This payment gateway works as a guarantee that the credit card transaction occurs without any hiccups. Credit card companies like Visa or MasterCard won't process money without a "payment gateway" to guard against fraud or misuse of credit card information. The payment gateway basically protects you and the customer against getting conned—which doesn't always work, but it definitely helps. The gateway confirms that there is enough money in the account or in the available balance and charges the account. If you have seen a credit card declined for insufficient funds or the card is unauthorized for use, you can be sure that the "payment gateway" is working. This path or "gateway" is the route where the collected money gets transported back and forth, from one account to another. It serves as a way to connect your merchant account to your payment platform.

So, in conclusion, a payment gateway is an ecommerce service provider that facilitates and authorises the secure transfer of credit card information between the merchant's site and the bank. Your store cannot accept credit cards without a configured payment gateway.

As mentioned earlier, your shopping cart account generally requires a "merchant account", which collects the money from the shopping cart system through the "gateway." This establishment of a gateway serves as a way to protect credit card transactions. Getting a merchant account through your bank requires decent credit. If your credit is a little rusty, then you can use "higher risk" merchant accounts, which charge a bit more a month—though the charge is still minimal. You will also have to pay a higher percentage on your sales.

You might wonder why you need a payment gateway or processor for your transaction. Your shopping cart network serves only as a "face" to your company's ability to take orders. It specialises in setting up your products to order. The credit card company doesn't deal with any products whatsoever. The only thing the processor does is process the payment, making sure that it is a real credit card number (not a stolen one), preventing fraud, and approving the payment. Once the approval and credit card information is processed, then the money lands in your merchant account. If you are unable to get a merchant account, you can rely on services from PayPal.

When you become a drop shipper or if you have an eCommerce site, you will need to collect money from your customers. Therefore, you will need an online payment processor or a debit and credit card payment processor. This is very difficult to get if you are just starting up. You could start just by using PayPal, but many people do not have a PayPal account and may be required to sign up to pay you. This creates a barrier of inconvenience for the customer and often results in no sale.

In summary, your payment platform setup may look complicated at first, but it really isn't as difficult as it seems. Think of it as a series of "connections" so that you are able to collect money. Your payment platform comprises several parts. The "face" of the platform can be your website's shopping cart system.

You will not be able to view customer's full credit card details if you use a payment gateway and a merchant account. This is to comply with the PCI/CIPS regulations.

PCI = Payment Card Industry Data Security Standard (short for PCI/DSS)

CIPS = Cardholder Information Security Program.

The only way you will ever be able to see your customer's full credit card details is when you have a physical terminal to charge the card yourself. This is what is called a "Card Not Present" transaction. A "Card Present" transaction is where your customer hands over their card and they have to put in their PIN number in the card terminal. Often, the transaction is done by your shopping cart and payment processor and you won't see the card details.

So again, here are the pieces of the puzzle:

- **A website**. You can create this yourself or pay someone to develop this for you or use templates.

- **Payment platform:** This could be PayPal or a **shopping cart** service, such as www.UltraCart.com. It requires two additional items: a **gateway processor** and **merchant account**, which you can set up through your bank. A very popular gateway service company is www.Authorize.net. As mentioned, you also need a **shopping cart service:** This allows you to create "links" for your product, connects to your payment gateway, and notifies your drop shipper (often your fulfillment house) that they need to send the product to your customer.

If it sounds a little complicated, it is only because you are not familiar with the process. However, most people find that everyone in this process is familiar with each other, and will generally help you out. It is important to remember that everyone wants you to be successful and to get you on your feet as quickly as possible. After all, once you start making money, they start making money too—and everyone is happy!

Here is a flow chart that will help you to understand the backend of the process. Don't worry, after everything is set up, you won't have to think of it much. In fact, if you don't think about it, then everyone is doing their job. Keep in mind that everyone along this payment chain will collect some funds or make money. Your shopping chart, for example, might charge a monthly fee and maybe a small transaction fee. However, the processing gateway, such as www.Authorize.net, charges a monthly fee plus a small transaction fee for each sale.

Your merchant account also charges a minimal monthly fee. Yes, these charges add up, but they are nothing in comparison to the costs of actually opening up your own physical store, hiring employees, paying for the electricity, rent, insurance and business district fees!

There is some paperwork to be accepted as a new client and obtain a merchant account, and often one of the representatives will come and visit you. This is because of the many Internet cowboys trading on the web. The financial institutions (in the UK) now want to come and visit you, just to make sure you are a real person.

A merchant account is the company that will actually put the money into your account from your sales. Usually they charge a monthly fee and they charge a small percentage (1 to 5%) on each transaction value. This is the company that will give you a physical terminal should you need one.

A payment gateway is the company that acts from the moment your customer hits the order button until the credit card is charged. When a customer sees the screen that says "add to basket" and "checkout", that is the payment gateway screen.

Both merchant accounts and gateway accounts need to communicate with each other. If they don't interact properly, your system will fail. The first thing you need to do is check out on the merchant's website which gateways they support. There will be a list of them somewhere on the website (often difficult to find the list).

IF you have found a payment gateway that is NOT listed on the approved gateway accounts from your merchant account, you are stuck! So check this out from the start!

I advise you to find a merchant account FIRST before you find a gateway, as there are plenty of gateways to choose from but fewer merchant accounts. Once you have decided on your merchant account, you then need to find a gateway that is supported by your merchant account.

> **TOP TIP:** Find a merchant account BEFORE you find a payment gateway.

Once you have found a merchant account, they will give you a merchant account code and that's the last you probably hear from them. Of course, they will send you a bill at the end of the month, and they will also transfer your money to your bank account after each sale. It is your payment gateway processor that will give you the relevant codes that you have to link to your order buttons.

www.1shoppingcart.com supports the following gateways (only a few big ones listed):

- www.2checkout.com

- www.worldpay.com

- www.sagepay.com

- www.googlecheckout.com

- www.paypal.com

Important: if you are using membership software, make sure to choose a payment gateway that supports it! You need to check this from the very beginning! Your membership software will have a list of approved accounts.

2) What is a high risk merchant account?

In this book, I talk only about "normal" businesses. What I mean is businesses that are NOT considered high risk in the payment approval environment. If your business is high risk, it is very unlikely that you will be able to obtain a "normal" merchant account.

The banks call it high risk because there is a high risk for chargebacks (people asking for refunds), or there is a high risk for the company to "go under".

You can be considered a high risk simply because of your personal financial situation (poor personal credit history), but here is a list of the type of businesses that need a High Risk Merchant Account, even if you have a brilliant past in the finance world.

- Adult products and services

- Annual memberships

- Debt services

- Educational seminars

- Fortune telling/horoscope related products

- Insurance products

- Internet marketing products

- Lotteries

- Make money products

- Massage parlors

- Multi Level Marketing (MLM)

- Online auctions

- Online casinos and gambling websites

- Online dating websites

- Pawn shops

- Pharmaceutical products

- Sales of telecommunication equipment

- Software downloads

- Timeshare

- Travel services

- Weapons websites

- Websites that sell replica products

- etc...

There are companies that are specialised in providing services for high risk accounts. Simply Google the subject to find information. These companies are always more expensive than "normal" merchant accounts and will usually charge you a higher percentage on each sale transaction, e.g. if Streamline will only charge you 2% on a sale, these high risk companies might charge you 5% and higher.

The set-up costs for a high risk merchant account are also much higher than a normal account.

Another important note: if you are selling products in the "make money online" niche, it is virtually impossible these days to find a merchant account or a gateway that will approve you as a new customer because you are seen as a "high risk" account due to the risk of very high refund rates. The scam Internet cowboys and so-called gurus are to be blamed for this.

The only reason why I was approved by Streamline for my new product www.WorldwideSelfPublishing.com is because of their past (good) experience with my companies.

I was accepted by Streamline, but ONLY if I made it extremely clear on the sales page that the product I am selling is not a Get Rich Quick Type of Product.

I was rejected by over 20 merchant accounts and/or gateways! The reason why I tried other merchant accounts first (before Streamline) is because I had membership software that Worldpay did not approve, and Worldpay is the payment gateway for Streamline.

If you are selling a "make money" product, I can tell you that you will ***not*** be accepted by any of these companies listed below, as they all rejected me for my www.worldwideselfpublishing.com sales page, even with my positive track record in my Internet marketing business. The reason why I was rejected is because the product I am selling is considered a high risk product.

- www.2co.com

- www.2checkout.com

- www.cybersource.com

- www.authorize.net

- www.firstdatacorp.co.uk

- www.paypoint.net

- www.paymentexpress.com

- www.nochex.com

- www.sagepay.com

- www.paymall.com

- www.goemerchant.com

- www.firstdata.com

- www.globalpayments.com

- www.echeck.net

247

- www.hsbc.co.uk

- www.rbsworldpay.com

- www.g2s.com

- www.securestrading.com

- www.itransact.com

- www.netbilling.com

- www.securepay.com

- www.web.com

- www.merchantpartners.com

I could have taken the easy route and sold my videos with Clickbank, but they only approved my product for £150, and I refused to sell those videos at such a low price, as I know they are worth a lot more.

In the end, I had to change my membership site software to make everything integrate beautifully.

I can tell you that these four work together really well as I use them myself:

- ProfitsTheme as your Wordpress plugin

- Wishlist member as your membership software (one-time fee to access my videos)

- Streamline as your merchant account

- Worldpay as your payment gateway.

3) The process from order to shipment

Most online sales are done by credit card payments. In order to accept debit and credit card payments, you will need a merchant account with a merchant account provider. A merchant account can be initially expensive and will generally have a monthly fee. Some merchant accounts may even have restrictions that could limit the number of transactions that are ran in a single month or the total dollar amount that can be processed in a month's time. In most cases, these restrictions are only for the first few months. It is sort of like a probation period during which you prove your reliability as an online retailer.

You have seen the simple view of an order being processed. Here is a more complicated view of what goes on in the background when a customer clicks "Add To Basket":

1. Customer places an order on your website.

2. SSL Certification: SSL provides secure connection over the internet to merchant server.

3. Payment gateway page appears and customer enters credit card information.

4. Customer's card information is encrypted while being transferred over the web.

5. Your online store transmits the order, via your hosting company, to the payment gateway.

6. The payment gateway approves the transaction to your merchant account - your bank.

7. Merchant bank sends the authorisation request to the credit card network.

8. Credit card network sends the request to the card issuer.

9. Card issuer approves the transaction and confirms there are funds available.

10. Credit card network sends the approval to the merchant bank.

11. Merchant bank tells the merchant (you) that the payment has been approved.

12. Merchant (you) receives confirmation that transaction is successful.

13. You and your customer will receive confirmation of the order.

To this point, everything is done in a matter of seconds, but it all goes on in the background for each sale.

14. You pick goods from a warehouse, or you send the order to your drop shipper.

15. You make an invoice for customer.

16. Merchant (you) ships the goods or your drop shipper will ship the goods.

17. Inventory will be updated.

18. Merchant bank pays the money into your bank account.

19. Your customer pays the money to the credit card company.

4) Do you really need a merchant account?

With some third party gateways you don't need to have a merchant account to receive card payments.

a) PayPal

PayPal is the best known. PayPal takes a percentage of the transaction amount that is paid to you. Once the funds have cleared, you can transfer them to your business acccount.

PayPal also has PayPal Payments Pro, which is a merchant account option, suitable if you have 100+ orders per month, but I am talking here about the simple third-party platform. The commission that PayPal charges is higher than what a merchant account would charge you.

Comparison:

- Paypal charges 2.9% on each transaction and a £0.19/$0.30 fee per transaction, but they don't charge a monthly fee.

- A merchant account will charge typically 2.225% on each transaction but does charge a monthly fee of approx. £30/$48.50. The 2.225% applies for a MasterCard fee. Fees can vary per type of credit/debit card and can also vary depending on which merchant account you use.

Comparison in £:

Let's say you have 1000 sales of £95 = £95,000 in total.

£95,000 x 2.9% = £2,755 PayPal charge

£95,000 x 2.225% = £2,113 merchant account charge + your monthly charge of £30 = £2,143

Now let's work out the difference:

£2,755 You pay to payPal

- £2,143 You pay to your merchant account

_____

So you pay £612 more to use PayPal, for every 1000 sales.

Comparison in $:

Let's say you have 1000 sales of $153 = $153,000 in total.

$153,000 x 2.9% = $4,437 PayPal charge

$153,000 x 2.225% = $3,404.25 merchant account charge + your monthly charge of $48.50 = $3,452.75

Now let's work out the difference:

$4,437 You pay to payPal

-$3,452.75 You pay to your merchant account

_____

So you pay $984.25 more to use PayPal, for every 1000 sales.

I hope you can now see why it is important to work with a merchant account, as once you start selling thousands of products, it WILL save you a lot of money. Start off on the right foot and set everything up professionally.

Important to mention: lots of merchant accounts don't charge any percentage for payments from Visa Debit Cards, and in the above example we have assume that all transactions are paid by MasterCard.

Overall conclusion: you can use PayPal but it is more expensive. It also has more negatives. Read on:

Using PayPal

PayPal is probably the most popular of payment systems today. While not everyone has a PayPal account, most online shoppers do, as virtually every online store accepts PayPal payments. However, in order to accept a PayPal payment, customers must have a PayPal account. There are some exceptions, but a PayPal account is free of charge, and your customer is charged absolutely nothing when a product is purchased via PayPal. However, when the payment comes through, you are charged a fee, as you've just read.

Many customers don't like PayPal because they think you have to set up an account with PayPal.

Another big downside is that the money is not actually paid into your bank account but into your virtual PayPal bank account. If you want the money, you have to log into your Paypal account and transfer it to your bank account.

And another big negative is that the money does not come into your account as the full amount, as PayPal's commission is deducted from it. So if you have sale of £100/$161, you will receive that money minus PayPal's charges. It can be difficult to reconcile transactions. Let me re-phrase that: it can be a nightmare to reconcile transactions.

Be sure to read PayPal's Seller Protection Policy.

The Big Problem With Using PayPal

- The one thing with PayPal is that your account can be suspended or cancelled at any time, and PayPal has the right to freeze any and all of your PayPal funds. Without any notice at all, you may be unable to access your funds or accept payments for a month or longer, depending on the situation, which could leave your business in the dust. A suspension may occur on your account for a number of reasons, with the most common being "suspicious activity on the account", and although this is obscure, this is all PayPal gives you. Because of this, your business is vulnerable, which is the last thing you want. Just search for "PayPal closed my account" or "PayPal banned my account" and you will see plenty of people with their stories.

- Some retailers will never have a problem with PayPal and stand by their services, while others say they wouldn't use PayPal if it were the last payment system on the planet. So, it is always better to have more than one payment processor under your belt to ensure that your business can continue to operate smoothly no matter what happens.

- Another negative point for PayPal is that they don't have very good reporting features, e.g. sold per month, sold per customer, etc...

- PayPal can sometimes be very slow on your PC, if you haven't got a very fast internet connection.

PayPal Here

PayPal Here has been launched and I've tested it, and I must say that I am impressed. What is PayPal Here?

With PayPal Here, you can accept debit and credit cards and PayPal payments from your mobile phone! You can also log cash, make invoices and send instant receipts to your buyers.

PayPal has word class fraud management, so you're protected! So how does it work?

Well, you need 3 things:

- A PayPal account

- A Paypal Here card reader, as shown on the picture above

- A mobile phone. I've tested it on my iPhone 5s and it works quick and effortless.

The card reader is a one-off cost of £99/$158, and you need to install an app on your phone (effortlessly done in 1 minute). Once that is done, you are ready to take payments. PayPal charges 2.75% for every accepted payment.

You can only use the device for "Card Payment Present" payments. This means the customer has to physically hand over their card, you swipe it and the customer puts in their PIN number and the sale is done! It's not practical for your website, but I thought I needed to mention it here in case you are going to sell at a market stall (to test your product :-)), you can charge people's cards.

PayPal here vs Square

www.squareup.com is basically the same as PayPal Here, but the little device is called "The Square" and sits on top of your mobile phone to swipe people's cards.

The Square device itself is free, and Square charges 2.75% for every sale.

Be aware that there are lots of these little devices coming into market. My advice is to use one that is well known, e.g. PayPal, otherwise customers might not trust you and won't give you their card if you have some "strange looking device" sitting on top of your mobile without a brand name.

b) Google Wallet

This is another great starting option. Google Wallet (which used to be called Google checkout), like PayPal, does not cost anything upfront, making it a viable option to get your drop shipping business up and running. The fees are very similar to that of PayPal, with a per-transaction fee, as well as a certain percentage of the transaction amount. The actual fees, though, are based on your monthly sales volume.

All charges shown below were correct at the time of investigation.

Below, you'll see a chart of fees associated with Google Checkout/Google Wallet:

Monthly Sales Volume Via Google Checkout	Fees Per Each Transaction
Under $3,000	2.9% + $0.30
Between 3,000 and $9,999.99	2.5% + $0.30
Between 10,000 and $99,999.99	2.2% + $0.30
$100,000 or more	1.9% + $0.30

To get a Google Wallet account, you simply need to sign up through Google. Go here:

https://www.wallet.google.com

https://www.wallet.google.co.uk

You will be asked for personal contact information, as well as information related to your business. Once you are signed up, you'll need to integrate Google Wallet with your drop shipping website, which is extremely easy and can be done rather quickly.

c) 2Checkout

www.2checkout.com

Whether you are selling domestically or internationally, 2Checkout is a leader in the payment processing industry, accepting a variety of different payment methods. As an alternative to a merchant account, 2Checkout is known for their simple fee schedule, which is shown in the chart below:

Option	Cost
Application Fee	10.99
Flat-Rate Transaction Fee	5.5%
Fee Per Transaction	0.45

There are no extra fees associated with 2Checkout. There are no fees for set up, gateway, monthly, recurring billing, etc. You'll get paid weekly and do not need any special skills, such as coding or programming.

The best thing about 2Checkout is that you can give it a try before you commit to the payment processor long term.

Go to the following link and click on "Try Free Demo" to sign up for a 2Checkout Demo Account, or a 2CO Demo Account.

Sign up using this link: https://www.2checkout.com/signup.

c) And some more:

- www.stripe.com

www.payments.amazon.com or www.payments.amazon.co.uk allows only Amazon customers to securely pay on your website without entering their card information.

- www.gocardless.com allows your customers in the UK to pay via direct debit

- www.clickbank.com is easy to use

- www.E-junkie.com

- www.jvzoo.com

- www.rapbank.com

So the answer to the question "Do you really need a merchant account?" in my opinion is yes, or you will lose a lot of sales. To run a truly professional company, I advise you to get a merchant account and a gateway. You can start with PayPal; that will be the easy way, and if you start selling, look for a merchant account.

You have to ask yourself the question if the increase in sales you will create is justifiable compared to the monthly charge you will have to pay the merchant account as that charge will be the same, even if you don't sell anything that month.

Keep in mind that all the third-party accounts will charge more compared to when you set everything up with a payment gateway and a merchant account.

It is a catch 22 situation: if you don't have a merchant account, you will lose sales, but on the other hand, if you are just starting, you might not have the money to pay the monthly merchant account charge.

What are the main advantage of using a merchant account?

A merchant account offers many advantages over third-party gateways, e.g. Paypal but the most important one is that it gives your customer a checkout process without any third-party intervention. If you have a a merchant account, your store will look more professional, established and credible, which will increase your conversion rate, resulting in more sales.

Once you start selling, you will earn more as a merchant account charges less per transaction.

5) Why you need a payment processor/merchant account

You want to make certain that you choose a payment processor that is reliable, versatile and will simply get the job done for you. It is always better to go with a company that can offer you both a merchant account as well as a payment gateway. The problem is that these are difficult to find if you need three, four or more different services to interact together in a smooth manner.

What a Payment Processor Offers

In case you were wondering, this is exactly what a top-notch payment processor can offer you and your business:

Accept All Types of Payments. With a proficient payment processor, you'll be able to accept, verify and process all sorts of payment methods, from credit and debit cards to electronic and traditional checks. Some payment gateways only support Visa, others don't support debit cards, etc…

Accept Payments No Matter Where You Are. One day you may be working on your business from home in Seattle, and the next day you may be traveling to Los Angeles for a trade show. This could put a damper on accepting payments, but with a quality payment processor, payments can be accepted in Seattle, Los Angeles or even Paris. The point here is that no matter where you are, with or without Internet access, you should be able to process payments if you have a first-rate payment processor under your belt.

Have Access to Security and Fraud Protection. The best payment processors will make certain that they offer you security protection, so that you and your customer have the peace of mind to do business online. Most will use VeriSign (you won't have to purchase a VeriSign SSL Certificate on your own) and AVS or Address Verification Service to prevent credit card fraud.

Other benefits include:

- You will get paid much quicker.

- You will look professional.

- You will appear more legitimate.

- You will save a huge amount of time on billing.

- You will significantly enhance customer retention.

- You will considerably increase business sales and profit.

All in all, in being able to accept online payments, you are dramatically impacting your business's bottom line, which is a good thing in case you were wondering.

Things to Consider When Searching for an All-in-One Payment Processor

No two payment processors are created equally, so you have research to do to find a good one. As a general rule, you'll fill out an online application and wait for a phone call to talk about personalization of your account. Most have a fast turnaround time and a high approval rating, which is definitely what you want, as you want your business up and running as soon as possible. However, as with everything, some companies are better than others.

Here are a few things you'll want to look at when choosing the right payment processor for your drop shipping business:

- Pricing. Processing electronic payments on your site is not free, but it doesn't have to cost an arm and a leg either. There are plenty of fees down the line that will need to be paid, but you can stay out of the red by finding a reputable company that offers competitive rates. You'll need to think about how many transactions you are going to have a month (I know it's hard, but come up with some type of realistic number) as well as any and all additional fees that are associated with the payment processing. A low monthly fee is important, but if you are going to process a large number of transactions each month, then you'll need to make sure the per-transaction fee is incredibly low.

When you are trying to get accepted for a Merchant Account, the company will ask you how much you are projecting to sell. Make sure to prepare some figures.

- Features. Everyone will have their own preferences when it comes to features that a payment processor will provide. While you will be looking for an easy-to-use interface and management of transactions, not everyone will be looking for the recurring billing option. Therefore, if you are selling some sort of subscription that requires recurring billing, then you'll need to make certain that you choose to work with a payment processor that offers recurring payments. You will need to address your situation and determine the most essential elements so that you can choose the right company to work with. Ultimately, the more features that the payment processor can offer you, the better in the end.

- **Security**. Credit card fraud continues to be a huge concern in today's world. As a result of this, more and more customers are leery of using their credit card information online. However, there are security measures in place to protect not only you but your customer as well. If an electronic payment processor that you are considering does not offer adequate security or is not PCI-compliant, then you need to look elsewhere and cross them off your list. They will cause more harm than good in the long run. PCI stands for Payment Card Industry Standard.

- **Support**. As with any online or offline company, you want to find a company that offers a dedicated support team whenever you need them. Without this, you won't get the help you need, and sometimes it won't be easy to figure things out on your own if several sites have to integrate together.

6) What MUST work together!

In order for everything to run smoothly from the moment the customer hits the order button until payment is taken, the following seven elements MUST all work together and integrate without error messages.

1. Your bank

2. Your merchant account. This is a type of bank account you hold as a merchant, and funds from approved orders are deposited into this account.

3. Your payment gateway. This is the service that provides secure transmission and authorisation of the transactions to your merchant account.

4. Your shopping cart software

5. Your auto responder, if applicable

6. Your membership software, if applicable

7. Your affiliate program, if applicable

8. Recurring billing, if applicable

9. PayPal as payment, if applicable. It is always a good idea to give people the choice to pay by PayPal or by credit/debit card.

Believe it or not, it can take weeks to get all this working, starting from scratch. You will need a brain and some technical knowledge to do it all, as it is not always easy to make it work.

This is something that people don't tell you when they sell you overhyped rubbish. You don't actually know how complicated this can become until you actually try and implement it.

The problem is that if something doesn't integrate together, you have nine different platforms you are working with and they will all blame each other.

Luckily, there are software platforms that already have a lot of the nine points integrated so you don't have to set all of it up from scratch, which will take months! Believe me, I have done it and I am not a slow worker! My training course for my self publishing videos, www.worldwideselfpublishing.com, was set up all by me, and when you look at the page, it looks like there's not much work done behind the scenes! But a lot of work was done, as I needed to make sure ALL the above nine points were integrating beautifully, giving the buyer a pleasant experience.

These are the platforms that I've used to make it all work:

1. My bank: Natwest

2. My merchant account: www.streamline.co.uk

3. My payment gateway: www.worldpay.com

4. My shopping cart software: www.1shoppingcart.com

5. My auto responder: www.aweber.com

6. My membership software: www.member.wishlistproducts.com

7. My affiliate program: www.1shoppingcart.com

8. My recurring billing: www.1shoppingcart.com and www.worldpay.com

9. PayPal payment: www.paypal.com

How do you actually make them all work together?

Well, that is not easy to explain, but basically one platform will give you a code to paste into the other platforms. Paste the code in the wrong place or paste it with one digit missing and nothing will work!

Every good platform will have video tutorials on their site to show you how to do this. This linking from one platform to the other will be different for all eCommerce software, so I cannot give you any rules here, but the general principle will be the same for all of them: get a code and paste it in the right place.

I am giving you some screenshots, just to give you an idea how it all works.

This screenshot is from www.1shoppingcart.com.

Next to "Select Gateway", you need to choose the Payment Gateway you will work with. The selection can usually be made from a drop down menu, listing the gateways that your software can work with.

Next to "Gateway ID/Merchant login, you need to put in your ID number, which you will receive from your Merchant Account.

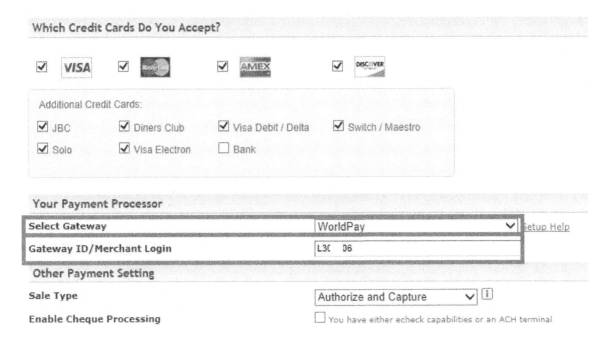

263

This next screenshot is from www.1shoppingcart.com.

Next to "Enable PayPal PDT" you will need to paste your PDT code, which you obtain from your PayPal account.

Another screenshot is from www.1shoppingcart.com.

Next to "Thank You URL", you need to past the URL your customer will see once checkout has been successful. If you are selling a digital product, you would put the download page here. Some information is hidden, as I can't show my download page for my self publishing here, now can I? :-).

Next to "2 Step Checkout" and "1 Step Checkout", you need to paste a link to which checkout page you wish to choose.

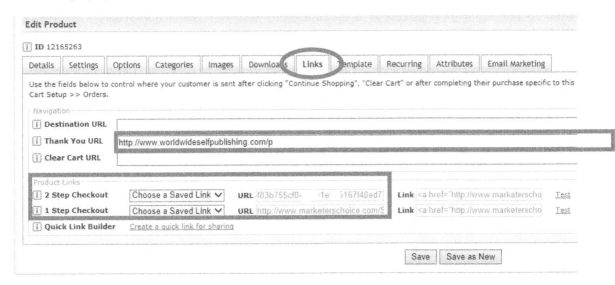

This screenshot is from my WordPress admin area, in the Wishlist Member Integration screen.

Next to "Select System", you need to choose the shopping cart you will work with. The selection can usually be made from a drop down menu, listing the shopping carts that your software can work with.

Underneath "Create a product for each membership level using the SKU (Stock Keeping Unit) specified below", you need to paste the SKU code, which you will find under the product settings in your www.1shoppingcart.com account. Each product gets a unique SKU code.

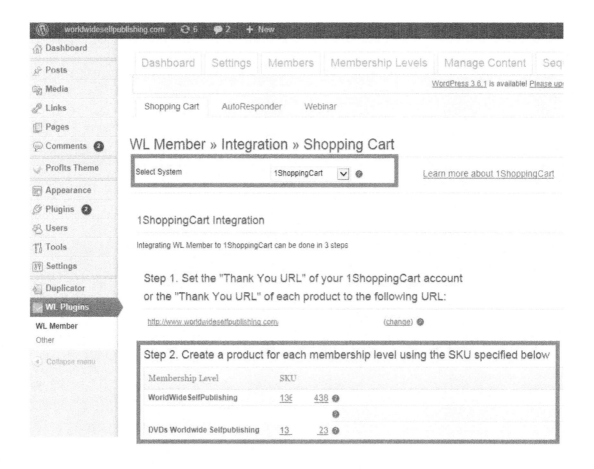

This last screenshot is from www.1shoppingcart.com.

Next to "Merchant ID", you need to paste your unique merchant ID that you receive from your merchant account.

Next to "API Key", you need to paste your API (Application Programming Interface) Key, which you will find under settings in your www.1shoppingcart.com account.

Setup 1ShoppingCart API Settings

Entering your API Settings below allows WishList Member to fully integrate with 1ShoppingCart.

| Merchant ID | 235 | |

| API Key | \2FF4   0C12191 | |

| Retry Grace Period | 3   Days |

Enter the number of days that a failed credit card should be retried for recurring payments.

| Process Upsells | ○ Yes ⦿ No |

Save Settings

A screenshot from www.ekmpowershop.co.uk, just to show you that the general principle is the same (paste a code).

In the Payment Methods you can configure your settings for payments. I have selected SecureForm and clicked Configure.

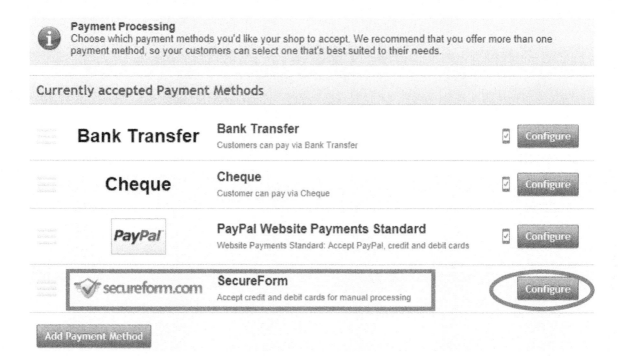

After clicking Configure, the screen below appears.

Under Key and Form ID, you need to paste your Key and Form ID in those fields, which you obtain from SecureForm, which you need to sign up for prior to filling in these fields.

Configure SecureForm

This allows you to take credit card details from your site using the SecureForm secure server, which you can then feed into your own PDQ machine to debit the money.

Visible Name
This is the name that will appear to your customers when the gateway is referenced.

    SecureForm

Username
This is provided to you by SecureForm.

    liquor

Key
This is provided to you by SecureForm.

    dc0393   b83c9a

Form ID
This is provided to you by SecureForm.

    8

Form URL
This is provided to you by SecureForm.

    https://www.secureform.com/App/f

Here is an example of how to link your order button to the right product and price: you log in to your shopping cart, go to products and click on "Links" or "Settings". Copy that code; it should look like this:

http://www.marketerschoice.com/SecureCart/SecureCart.aspx?mid=FE64CD7C-6333-4259-83F0-79F1275A4BFF&pid

This link will not work as part is cut off (1shopping cart used to be called marketerschoice).

Link that code to your order button.

So: click on your add to cart button, click on your hyperlinked item, and paste the code in the field that shows up.

Now when someone clicks on the "Add To Cart" button, your shopping cart will kick in and will know which products you've ordered and at what price. As you have linked your shopping cart previously to your gateway, the whole process now becomes automated. If you have copied one digit wrong in the above code, it will not work.

If this is all too complicate for you, I'm sorry to say that eCommerce is not for you, as you HAVE to set everything up so it integrates well.

Once the integration coding is all done correctly, the platform software will make it all work and flow well.

7) What to look for in a payment processor

While we've discussed a few things that you want to be on the lookout for when choosing to work with a comprehensive payment processor, there are plenty of other things that you need to consider, whether they are all inclusive or not. The most important thing is to make sure that all the companies you work with integrate with each other for smooth transactions.

Choosing the right merchant account and payment processor can be very difficult, boring and monotonous, but it is a task that is essential if you want to accept credit cards and other electronic methods of payment from your customers.

In just a moment, we are going to go through everything you need to know about the top merchant accounts and credit card processing services, from application turnaround times to prices to features, so that you can easily decide which one is right for you. But in case you do your own research or opt to do additional research on additional payment processors, you'll find everything you need to look for in the content below.

a) Average Approval Rating

To be clear, approval rating refers to the number of applications that are approved by the merchant company. The best merchant providers will approve 98 or 99 percent of applications that they receive. Obviously, the higher the approval rating, the better.

For example, Flagship Merchant Services approves 98 percent of their applications, while Merchant Warehouse approves 99 percent of theirs. This is excluding the high risk website applications as they have a very low approval rate.

But this shouldn't be the only deciding factor when determining which company to use for your credit card processing. There are several others factors, as discussed below, that should also be taken into consideration to ensure you are getting the most bang for your buck.

b) Monthly Cost

This is probably one of the most important factors in your decision. Money isn't everything, but if you can save money while getting the best possible service, then there's no reason to turn your back on something like that. All in all, selecting the merchant that you'll do business with is a flat-out financial decision.

All the good merchant accounts will charge you a monthly fee.

You need to check into the minimum number of transactions that the company requires on a monthly basis. Two of the best—Flagship and Merchant Warehouse—are £12/$20 and £15/$25 respectively in terms of monthly transactions. However, their monthly services cost £5/$9 and £3/$5.00 respectively with a £4.99/$7.95 statement fee for both.

c) Start-up Costs

You may think that you are going to incur hefty start-up costs when it comes to obtaining a merchant account and payment processor for your business, but the truth of the matter is that it doesn't have to be expensive. In fact, some of the greatest merchant accounts— Flagship and Merchant Warehouse, to name a couple—have zero, zilch, zip start-up costs. Therefore, you don't have to pay an arm and a leg just to get started!

d) Contract length

Most merchant accounts will want you to sign a contract with a two- or three-year commitment, but don't do this. Why would you when you can get a leading payment processor on a month-to-month basis with absolutely no contract commitments? If you sign up for one year and you decide after 6 months that you don't like eCommerce, you will still have to pay another 6 months of your contract.

e) Account set-up time

When you get your website ready to launch, you need to be able to immediately start accepting credit and debit cards as a form of payment. Unfortunately, you need to get in business with an electronic payment processing company to do this. Now, while it's true that you could have to wait a week or two weeks to get your account set up, there are shorter wait times out there. In fact, some of the best companies can get your account set up and ready to go within one or two business days. Some can get even get it set up the same business day you are approved!

f) Internet-based features

We've discussed the importance of looking at features that all-inclusive payment processors offer, but even if the company doesn't provide a comprehensive service, it is still important to have a look at the features offered.

The primary feature that you need to look at with merchant accounts is the payment gateway, as this is essentially how you will be accepting payments from your customers. You can choose to go with a merchant account that offers one payment gateway option or one that offers multiple payment gateways.

For example, Authorize.net, the leader in payment gateway companies, is offered by Flagship, while a number of different payment gateways are offered by Merchant Warehouse. Depending on your own situation, as well as how the other features rack up, you may or may not want to choose to go with the merchant that offers more payment gateways.

As long as you check out the above-mentioned factors and consider each and every one of them before making your final decision, you'll be able to choose a merchant account service company that will do you and your business good!

If you are planning to sell worldwide, you also need to check that it will be possible to check out in different currencies. Otherwise you might need a different merchant account for each currency, which of course is not ideal, and it's expensive, as each account has a monthly fee.

In my case, for my worldwide self publishing videos, I have two different merchant accounts: 1) if people pay in one payment, and 2) if people chose to pay in three installments.

Now, let's check out several of the top merchant accounts/payment gateways!

8) Obtaining your merchant account and payment gateway

www.clickbank.com is the easiest merchant account/payment processor to set up and get approved. Unfortunately, they are specialised in electronic products, e.g. eBooks, and you cannot use them for clothes or boat parts, etc. Your product will be sold in most cases through a one-page-sales-wonder. If you want to find out more about Clickbank, I offer more details in my book "From Newbie To Millionaire".

Let's turn back to drop shipping.

There are several types of eCommerce merchant accounts: third-party merchant accounts, international merchant accounts, high-risk merchant accounts, local merchant accounts, offshore merchant accounts, etc… Each one has their own conditions and policies.

As previously discussed, PayPal can suddenly close your account, and you can no longer sell anything! This is most definitely not something that you want when you are running a drop shipping business. If your funds are frozen at a moment's notice, you could run into a number of problems, such as not being able to purchase the product from the drop shipper that your customer just recently paid you for.

Therefore, let's look at some of the other merchant accounts that are available, the prices associated with those accounts, and how easy it is to sign up with them.

Before we move on, though, keep in mind that PayPal is a great way to get started accepting payments online, but it should never be the only merchant account that you utilise, as you never know what may happen to your account. But, because it costs nothing to sign up, PayPal is a great starting point.

Here is a merchant accounts comparison website: www.merchantmaverick.com. Still, make sure to check out the sites that are listed before you use them.

TOP TIP: When you apply for a merchant account, you will have to fill out some paperwork. One of the questions will be how much you expect to sell, i.e. what your turnover will be. Be aware that the higher your turnover, the lower your transaction charge. So make your forecast too high rather than too low! Your transaction fee will probably be between 1.60 and 2.99%. If you fall in a lower category of transaction fee percentage because of your turnover, you can save anything from 0.20 to 0.60%. Even if your turnover is lower than you forecasted, most merchant accounts will not change the transaction fee agreed.

a) Authorize.net

As a leader in the payment processing industry since 1996, Authorize.net (http://www.authorize.net) is a more popular online payment gateway that gives you the ability to accept electronic checks and credit cards as forms of payment via your website, as well as online auction sites. They offer free customer support that is said to be among the best, not to mention the fact that they offer other free tools, such as fraud prevention and a website seal that gives customer's the peace of mind they need purchasing from an online site, especially a new one.

Below, you'll find a chart outlining all fees associated with setting up an account with Authorize.net:

Option	Cost
Set-up Fee of Account	99.00
Monthly Fee for Account	20.00
Fee Per Transaction	0.10
Fee Per Batch of Settled CC Transactions	0.25

There are a few optional products that you can add onto your account, as shown below:

Extra Option	Monthly Cost
Automated Recurring Billing	10.00
Advanced Fraud Detection	9.95
Customer Information Manager	20.00

You can sign-up for Authorize.net from this link: http://www.authorize.net/signupnow/.

b) WorldPay

Option	Cost
Monthly Fee	31.99 (£19.95)

They like to provide their prospective business clients with customised quotes, as every person's needs are different.

www.worldpay.com: A leader in global payment processing, WorldPay is the fifth largest worldwide banking group. WorldPay is one of the more affordable solutions to both US and non-US business owners who are looking to expand their business domestically and internationally.

WorldPay accept bank transfers, credit cards and debit cards, and accepts over 140 different currencies. WorldPay is happy to accept recurring billing and offers fraud prevention tools. Recurring billing is NOT available if you use 1shoppingcart as your shopping cart. Remember that everything HAS to integrate together e.g. Worldpay does not work with 1shoppingcart.com for recurring payments.

WorldPay sends payments weekly in your preferred currency. In some cases, you may even receive payments the next business day or within two to three business days, depending on the contract.

They have a high acceptance rate, but you'll have to wait seven to ten days before being approved. There is also a one-year contract minimum. They offer multi-lingual 24/7 customer support.

WorldPay is probably the best payment processor for those in the UK and throughout Europe, as it is one of the largest payment processors in Europe and was the first-ever bank in the UK to offer a full range of Internet banking options.

Here are the links to the WorldPay sites in general, US-based and UK-based.

WorldPay Site: http://www.worldpay.com

US Site: http://www.worldpay.us/

UK Site: http://www.worldpay.com/index.php?c=UK

c) *Flagship Merchant Services*

www.flagshipmerchantservice.com: Flagship Merchant Services is the go-to merchant service provider for startups as well as existing businesses. It offers you a payment gateway as well as a merchant account, making things easy for you.

The great thing about Flagship Merchant Services is the fact that they have a high approval rating, quick and free application, low and competitive transaction fees as well as low set-up costs. The overall process of applying, integrating and processing payments online is made easy by Flagship.

Flagship has a 98% approval rate, and there are absolutely no fees to start up. There are no annual fees and no paperwork. Flagship makes it easy by offering virtually everything for free!

Here's a look at the fees you can expect to deal with when you get approved for a Flagship account:

Option	Cost
Set-up Fee	NONE!
Monthly Payment Gateway Fee	7.95
Statement Fee	7.95
Card Not Present Discount Rate	0.98 to 1.98%
Card Present Discount Rate	0.38 to 1.58%
Per Transaction Fee	0.19

Once you submit your application to Flagship, you can expect to hear back from them about your approval (or non-approval) within one to two business days, which means it only takes a couple of days before you can start accepting credit cards on your website.

A shopping cart is not included with Flagship, but can easily be found on its own.

Once setup, Flagship sends you your money two days after the online transaction from your product sale has been completed. Some other good news is that there is no yearly contract required or long-term commitment, as Flagship allows their clients to work with them on a month-to-month basis, eliminating the risk of closure or early termination fees. You'll be able to begin accepting credit cards, debit cards, gift cards, e-checks and more!

Ultimately, if you want minimal hassle and want a reputable service with a reliable payment processor, as well as the payment gateway of Authorize.net, Flagship is a good service to use.

d) Merchant Warehouse

www.merchantwarehouse.com: Known to have a good approval rate, Merchant Warehouse offers several payment options and low fees. While the application process is pretty quick and you'll receive an approval quickly, it isn't as fast as the aforementioned service of Flagship. Merchant Warehouse, like Flagship, is great for startups, as it is one of the more inexpensive solutions for being able to accept online payments. Here's a look at the charges you'll incur with Merchant Warehouse:

Option	Cost
Monthly Minimum	25.00
Statement Fee	7.95
Discount Rate	2.9%
Per Transaction Fee	0.21
Charge Back Fee	25.00
Voice Authorization Fee	0.65
Address Verification Fee	0.05
Payment Gateway Fee	10.00

There are no set-up or application fees. There are also no long-term contracts; instead, you pay month-to-month with no worry of cancellation and early termination fees.

Like Flagship, Merchant Warehouse is very quick in setting up accounts—generally within just 24 hours. The longest you can expect for it to take is 48 hours. Your previous experience and credit history will both be factors in determining your approval for an account with Merchant Warehouse.

Merchant Warehouse offer a number of different gateways, which include LinkPoint, Authorize.net, MerchantWARE Virtual Terminal, VeriSign Payflow Pro and VeriSign Payflow link.

e) National Bankcard

www.nationalbankcard.com: Like the others mentioned, National Bankcard has a pretty high approval rating. The only problem with National Bankcard is that it isn't relevant to anyone outside of the United States. Also, like the other services mentioned, there is no contract required when you sign up with National Bankcard. They have high security measures, low rates and a variety of online features.

Overall, 99% of the applications that are received by National Bankcard are approved. The application process is paperless and mostly done in-house. In most cases, you will have your account fully set-up and ready to go the very same day you apply. This makes it one of the fastest approval times. "Time is money", so the faster you can get set up, the more money you can make. While you may be able to find some cheaper options if you do your research, you won't find much cheaper than what National Bankcard can offer you. Here's a look at the fees that National Bankcard charge:

Option	Cost
Payment Gateway Fee	7.95
Statement Fee	7.95
Discount Rate	1.99%
Per Transaction Fee	0.21

As you can see from the chart above, there are no fees to get started. You simply fill out the application, get approved, and get started accepting payments from customers on your website. You'll have the fees listed above when the time comes, but there are zero costs to get started. Plus, there are no cancellation fees, either.

With National Bankcard, you'll virtually be getting everything you need to get your business going and ready to accept payments from potential customers. You'll get a payment gateway, virtual terminal and even a shopping cart—not to mention access to a number of other Internet-based features that are great for your business. They have an online system called iAccess that allows you to log in and view information related to your account, including, but not limited to, sales volumes, account balance and any incurred charges so far. It helps you stay up to date financially.

f) Leaders Merchant Services

www.leadersmerchantservices.com: With Leaders Merchant Services, you don't have to pay a single penny to get started, and they have low rates, although those low rates may not necessarily be applied to debit cards that have been issued by non-regulated, smaller banks.

Leaders are known to accept almost all applications—99% to be exact. They do prohibit applications from a few types of merchants, such as gambling and adult sites. Applications are generally approved within 24 hours, but it will take a few days to receive your gateway access. The entire process will take a few days (about three), but usually no more than five.

Each merchant (you) will receive their very own personal account representative that they can get in touch with whenever they have questions or concerns. They even offer technical support 24 hours a day, seven days a week in case you need help getting your gateway set up.

Rates will be dependent upon your specific business, but the rates are competitive. Here's a look:

Option	Cost
Payment Gateway Fee	8.00
Statement Fee	5.00+
Monthly Transaction Minimum	15.00
Card Not Present Discount Rates	0.89% to 1.99%
Card Present Discount Rates	0.49% to 1.59%
Per Transaction Fees	0.10 to 0.30

Leaders Merchant Services, as you can see, have some very competitive rates. You won't pay an application fee or a set-up fee, so the start-up costs are minimal.

They also work with Authorize.net, a leading payment gateway for processing credit cards online. Authorize.net is by far the most easy to integrate and the quickest to learn how to use. Authorize.net is secure and safe and can work with an eCommerce shopping cart or on its own virtual terminal.

While Leaders Merchant Services may not be as good as the previously mentioned payment processors, it is most definitely one worth considering, especially if you've been denied by the others.

g) Infusionsoft

www.infusionsoft.com is all-in-one-sales and marketing software and comes highly recommended, but is very expensive, starting with the basic package at £123/$199 per month and the complete package at £235/$379 per month. You can see why this is not suitable for most newbies for ecommerce.

h) Other Payment Processors

Some other reputable names for payment processing and merchant accounts include:

www.1shoppingcart.com RECOMMENDED
www.E-junkie.com
www.ibill.com
www.streamline.co.uk RECOMMENDED UK customers only
www.streamline.com

i) Examples of papers to fill in

Whichever merchant account or gateway you decide to go with, you will have to fill in some paperwork to get approved. All merchant accounts will ask you the same types of questions, e.g. how are you selling your products, do you take a deposit, how much are you planning to sell, what is the average price of your product, etc. Below, you can see the papers you have to fill in to get an account with Streamline (www.streamline.com). This is the first and the second screenshot. You will also have to sign two different direct debit forms: one for your merchant account and one for your payment gateway, in my case, WorldPay. These two forms are the third and the fourth form.

The forms are A4, and I have scanned them in, so I am hoping that they will show up well once the book is printed. If not, sorry, but I cannot do it any other way to give better results.

With NatWest: you will have to fill in these form for EACH account you want: USD transactions, £ transactions, USD recurring transactions and £ recurring transactions.

Streamline Amendment Form (Page 1 of 2) Seller Code [   ]

streamline

This amendment form relates to the Streamline Agreement (the 'Agreement') with the Merchant identified below. The parties now wish to vary the terms of the Agreement as set out in this deed (the "Deed").
For details of how We will use your information and how to give your consent, please look for the padlock symbols below and in section 19 of the Terms and Conditions (the 'Terms') for WorldPay (UK) Ltd (Trading as Streamline) and WorldPay Ltd 'WorldPay') or contact Streamline Card Centre, Victory House, 5th Avenue Gateshead, NE11 0EL.

1. Type of Application	Number of outlets [ ]	Merchant ID. [ ]	Company ID [ ]	Additional Outlet [ ]
	Mail Order/Telephone Order [ ]	E-commerce [✓]	Purchase With CashBack [ ]	

2. About your business

Legal Name ("the Merchant"/"You") [   ]

Trading Name (if different) [   ]

Trading Address** [   ]

MCC [   ]

Post Code [   ]

Landline Number (mandatory) [   ]   Mobile Number [   ]

Email [   ]   Website [   ]

Registered Number [   ] (if Limited Company or Charity)   VAT Number [   ]

Contact person (if different)   Title [ ]   First name [   ]   Surname [   ]

Position [   ]

Buying group or trade association [   ]   Member Number [   ]

Existing Streamline relationship [   ]   Merchant Number [   ]

If you have multiple outlets that are part of the same legal entity, please complete a separate copy of the Additional Outlet Form for each of your additional outlets.

3. About your goods and services (additional to main agreement)

Are the goods or services to be sold or supplied, owned or to be provided by a third party?   No [ ]   Yes [ ]

Are stocks held at any address other than the trading address detailed above?   No [ ]   Yes [ ]

Do you accept deposits prior to the supply of goods or services? (If yes, please specify in the following)   No [ ]   Yes [ ]

The size of the deposit paid in advance as X% of total transaction value [   ] %

The average time, in advance of delivery of goods/ services or full payment, that deposits are taken [   ] days

Do you levy a charge for any guarantees or extended warranties? (If yes, please specify in the following)   No [ ]   Yes [ ]

The separate percentage of card turnover on guarantees/warranties [   ] %

The average length of guarantees/warranties sold [   ] months

Percentage of goods returned whilst under guarantee/warranty [   ] %

Do you accept full payment prior to the supply of goods or services? (If yes, please specify below)   No [ ]   Yes [ ]

The % of goods or services where payment is taken prior to delivery [   ] %

The average time, in advance of delivery of goods/ services, that full payment is taken [   ] days

Do you levy a charge for memberships, subscriptions or insurance premiums? (if yes, please specify)   No [ ]   Yes [ ]

The percentage of card turnover for memberships, subscriptions or insurance premiums [   ] %

The average length of membership, subscription or premium [   ] months

Cost of membership £ [   ]

4. Card Turnover

Credit Card Turnover – Actual/Projected (delete as appropriate) £ [   ] p.a.   Average Card Transaction Value £ [   ]

Total Card Turnover – Actual/Projected (delete as appropriate) £ [   ] p.a.   Total Annual Company Turnover £ [   ] p.a.

Mail/Telephone Order/E-Commerce sales (Card Not Present) as % of total card turnover [   ] %

5. Bank Account Details

These accounts must be in the Legal Name from section 2

Primary account details   Sort Code [ ]-[ ]-[ ]   Account Number [   ]

Alternative account details   Sort Code [ ]-[ ]-[ ]   Account Number [   ]

Fill in these fields if you wish to use a separate account for Service Charges, Terminal Charges and E-commerce Charges (together "Charges", see section 7,8,9 below)

The alternative bank account is for Charges only. Separate proof of account documentation must be submitted for this account. Using an alternative bank account for Charges requires an additional Direct Debit form.

Request multiple currencies   No [✓]   Yes [ ]   This requires a separate application form and a bank account for each settlement currency.

6. Additional services (these services may require the completion of additional documents)

Do you wish to subscribe to the following services? If yes, and you are already a member, please provide Merchant ID/Ref. No.

Streamline Online	Yes [ ] No [ ]	Mobile Top-Up Yes [ ] No [ ]
American Express*	Yes [ ] No [ ]	Existing American Express Merchant ID/Ref. No. [ ]
Diners Club* (if terminal owned)	Yes [ ] No [ ]	Existing Diners Club Merchant ID-Ref. No. [ ]

*Please note that a processing charge may be levied and it may require a separate application form.

Special Instructions

Streamline Amendment Form (Page 2 of 2)

`streamline`

7. Service Charges *(Section 7, 8 and 9 are completed by Streamline)*

There is a non-refundable arrangement fee of £ [____] (+VAT) for each outlet / in total (delete as appropriate)
A charge will be applied to each transaction processed. This charge is worked out from the base rate (Base Table over).

Additional Schedule 7 attached ☐

Base Table (show charge for type of card used)

Card Type	Purchases		Refunds		TA Code [____]
Personal Cards	%	PPI(p)	%	PPI(p)	
Maestro Domestic		30.000			
Visa Debit (Electron/Debit MasterCard)		30.000			
MasterCard Credit (Maestro Int./Debit Personal Int.)	1.650				
Visa Credit (Electron Personal Int./Debit Personal Int.)	1.650				
MasterCard Signia/MasterCard World	2.250				
Commercial Cards	%	PPI(p)	%	PPI(p)	
MasterCard (All Corporate and Commercial cards)	2.250				
Visa (All Corporate and Commercial cards)	2.250				
JCB	2.250				
Diners Club/Discover Cards	2.250				

☐ Accept Contactless payments

Contactless transaction charges depend on the value of transactions and are calculated as a discount to the Purchase charges shown in the Base Table

Contactless Discounts Table

Debit Card	PPI (p) Discount
£0.00 – £2.00	7p
£2.01 – £10.00	4p
£10.01 – £20.00	N/A
Credit Card	**% Discount**
All transactions	N/A

Additional Charges Table (Additional transaction charge for nature of payment capture)
The costs associated with the following types of transactions are higher and the following transaction charges will be applied to the transaction in addition to the charges shown in the Base Table above.

Type of Transaction	Credit Card		Debit Card	
	%	PPI(p)	%	PPI(p)
Capture Method				
Magnetic Stripe				
Mail/Telephone Order sales (Card Not Present)				
E-commerce				
E-commerce Non-Secure				
Paper				
PAN Key Entry				
Authorisation				
Non Authorised				
Locality				
Inter Regional				

Is Purchase with Cashback (PWCB) on UK issued Maestro, Visa Debit, Visa Electron, and Debit MasterCard transactions allowed?   Yes ☐ No ☐

Other than for Maestro International, are Card Not Present (CNP) transactions allowed?   Yes ☐ No ☐

Authorisation charges [____] p

Min. monthly service charge (per outlet)   £ [20.00]

Polling service fee (per month per terminal)   £ [____]

☐ Enable recurring transactions

8. Terminals – If an additional terminal is required, please completed a separate agreement.

9. E-commerce Charges

For Business Gateway please complete an Ecommerce Schedule 7

Payment Service Provider [Worldpay Ecommerce]   PayPal [____]

Principal Trading Countries [____]   Country of Incorporation [____]

10. Partial Invalidity

If, at any time, any provision of this Deed is or becomes illegal, invalid or unenforceable in any respect under any law of any jurisdiction, neither the legality, validity or enforceability of the remaining provisions nor the legality, validity or enforceability of such provision in any other respect or under the law of any other jurisdiction will be affected or impaired in any way.

11. Counterparts

This Deed may be executed in any number of counterparts and by the parties on separate counterparts each of which when executed and delivered shall constitute an original but all the counterparts together shall constitute one and the same instrument.

12. Governing Law and Jurisdiction

12.1 This Deed and any dispute, controversy, proceedings or claim of whatever nature arising out of or in any way relating to this Deed or its formation, shall be governed by and construed in accordance with English law and the parties submit to the exclusive jurisdiction of the English courts.

12.2 This Deed shall take effect as a deed even if one of the parties does not execute this document in accordance with the formalities required for a deed.

IN WITNESS whereof the parties have executed this Deed as a deed on the Effective Date.

Executed by WORLDPAY (UK) LIMITED and WORLDPAY LTD acting by RON KALIFA (director)

Executed as a deed by ....

Executed as a deed by [_____]   acting by [_____]

[INSERT MERCHANT/YOU]

[NAME OF DIRECTOR/PARTNER/SOLETRADER], a [director/partner (with power of attorney to sign on behalf of partnership/sole trader]

[SIGNATURE OF DIRECTOR/PARTNER/SOLE TRADER] Director/Partner/Sole Trader (delete as applicable)

In the presence of:

Name		Signature	
Address		Date	
Occupation			

Direct Debit Form to sign for Streamline:

Please fill in the whole form using a ball point pen and send it to:

Streamline Card Centre
Merchant Records

Name(s) of Account Holder(s)

Bank/Building Society account number

Branch Sort Code

Name and full address of your Bank or Building Society

To: The Manager   Bank/Building Society

Address

Postcode

Reference

Instruction to your Bank or Building Society to pay by Direct Debit

Service User Number

FOR WORLDPAY (UK) LTD OFFICIAL USE ONLY
This is not part of the instruction to your bank or building society.

Instruction to your Bank or Building Society
Please pay WorldPay (UK) Ltd Direct Debits from the account detailed in this instruction subject to the safeguards assured by the Direct Debit Guarantee. I understand that this instruction may remain with WorldPay (UK) Ltd. and if so, details will be passed electronically to my Bank/Building Society.

Signature(s)

Date

Banks and Building Societies may not accept Direct Debit instructions for some types of Accounts

This guarantee should be detached and retained by the payer.

The Direct Debit Guarantee

- This Guarantee is offered by all banks and building societies that accept instructions to pay Direct Debits.
- If there are any changes to the amount, date or frequency of your Direct Debit WorldPay (UK) Ltd will notify you 10 working days in advance of your account being debited or as otherwise agreed. If you request WorldPay (UK) Ltd to collect a payment, confirmation of the amount and date will be given to you at the time of the request.
- If an error is made in the payment of your Direct Debit, by WorldPay (UK) Ltd or your bank or building society, you are entitled to a full and immediate refund of the amount paid from your bank or building society.
- If you receive a refund you are not entitled to, you must pay it back when WorldPay (UK) Ltd asks you to.
- You can cancel a Direct Debit at any time by simply contacting your bank or building society. Written confirmation may be required. Please also notify us.

Direct Debit Form to sign for Worldpay:

 DIRECT Debit

Instruction to your Bank or Building Society
to pay by Direct Debit

Please fill in the whole form and send it to:

WorldPay Ltd

Service User Number

WorldPay Administration Code

Instruction to your Bank or Building Society

Please pay WorldPay Ltd Direct Debits from the account detailed in this instruction subject to the safeguards assured by the Direct Debit Guarantee. I understand that this Instruction may remain with WorldPay and if so, details will be passed electronically to my Bank/Building Society.

Name(s) of Account Holder(s)

Bank/Building Society account number

Branch Sort Code

Signature(s)

Name and full address of your Bank or Building Society

To: The Manager | Bank/Building Society

Natwest

Address

Date

Postcode

WorldPay Limited: Registered in England No. 03424752. Registered office: 55 Mansell Street, London E1 8AN.
Authorised and regulated as a Payment Institution by the Financial Service Authority 504504.

Banks and Building Societies may not accept Direct Debit Instructions from some types of Account

This guarantee should be detached and retained by the Payer

The Direct Debit Guarantee

 DIRECT Debit

- This Guarantee is offered by all banks and building societies that accept instructions to pay Direct Debits.
- If there are any changes to the amount, date or frequency of your Direct Debit WorldPay Ltd will notify you 5 working days in advance of your account being debited or as otherwise agreed. If you request WorldPay Ltd to collect a payment, confirmation of the amount and date will be given to you at the time of the request.
- If an error is made in the payment of your Direct Debit by WorldPay Ltd or your bank or building society you are entitled to a full and immediate refund of the amount paid from your bank or building society.
- If you receive a refund you are not entitled to, you must pay it back when WorldPay Ltd asks you to.
- You can cancel a Direct Debit at any time by simply contacting your bank or building society. Written confirmation may be required. Please also notify us.

j) Transaction fees

On top of a monthly fee, your merchant account will charge you a fee per transaction or per sale when the customer has paid by card. How much is that charge? Well, there is no set rule, as it depends on your turnover, the kind of products you are selling and the type of card your customer pays with. You can see on this scan from my account how much I pay.

Charge Details

Invoice Number
Charges For August 2013
Page

Your Merchant ID
Store Trading Name

Cards Acquired		Number of Transactions	Charge per Transaction p	Value of Transactions £	Transaction Charge Rate	Transaction Charges	VAT Code
MasterCard Cr Per	Purchases	11		4,299.62	2.225%	95.67	
MasterCard World	Purchases	4		367.00	2.719%	9.98	
Visa Credit Personal	Purchases	7		765.38	2.494%	19.09	
Visa Debit	Purchases	132	37.880	31,400.94	0.0%	50.00	
MasterCard Business	Purchases	1		108.86	2.4%	2.61	
MasterCard Corporate	Purchases	2		392.41	2.4%	9.42	
MasterCard Fleet	Purchases	3		1,129.18	2.4%	27.10	
Visa Corporate	Purchases	5		1,829.77	2.4%	43.91	
Maestro UK (DOM)	Purchases	2	34.000	385.47	0.0%	0.68	
		167		40,678.63		258.46	E

This is what you can see on the above screenshot:

- The total of sales in August 2013 = £40,678.63/$65,732

- The number of transactions in August 2013 = 167. This makes the average transaction £243/$392 (40,678.63 divided by 167). In case you are wondering why one transaction is so high, I am selling end of line computers and high end printers on my website.

- The total of transaction charges is £258.46/$417. That's how much they charge me to process £40,678/$65.560 of orders. Not bad, eh?

- The percentages charged per transaction depend on the card the customer pays with:

2.225% for MasterCard Personal Cards

2.719 % for MasterCard World Cards

2.494% for Visa Credit Personal

0% for Visa Debit

2.4% for MasterCard Business

2.4% for MasterCard Corporate

2.4% for MasterCard Fleet

2.4% for Visa Corporate

0% for Maestro UK (DOM)

- Most used cards, in order:

Visa Debit

MasterCard Credit Personal

Visa Credit Personal

Visa Corporate

MasterCard World

MasterCard Fleet

MasterCard Corporate

MasterCard Business & Maestro UK (DOM)

9) Make it easy to check out!

Whichever payment processor you choose, make sure you make it very easy and very quick for your customer to pay and check out. Put yourself in your customer's shoes. You like quick and easy check outs—so does your customer!

Don't give your customers too many options on the checkout page, as that will distract them, and you certainly do not want that. They are ready to give you their card details, so don't distract them at this stage!

An example of a distraction would be to show a discount voucher code on the checkout page whilst you don't have any discounts running. A customer might leave your page and go find a discount voucher on the web, going away from your checkout page. The customer could come across all sorts of interesting things whilst browsing and simply never return to fill in the checkout page, and you've lost an order.

You need to create a checkout method that is quick and easy otherwise you will create checkout resistance, which will result in losing customers. Checkout resistance can also be created by any of these:

- Your site is confusing

- Your site loads too slow

- Order buttons not clearly displayed

- The checkout process is too long. I have seen shops with seven pages to fill in!

- Not enough trust in your site, e.g. security logos missing

- The wrong wording or colours on your order buttons

If you are in a niche with not a lot of competition, this becomes less important and you can use whatever buttons you like and probably still get sales, e.g. my liquorice site. I have never investigated my order buttons for that site and left the checkout process as standard checkout, without investigating any other possibilities.

Here are a few important things to mention:

a) Don't ask to create an account at check out

Instead of "create your account here", say something like "enter your shipping details here". Most people don't like "create an account", as they think it will be a long and time consuming process.

b) Check out buttons

Most eCommerce software will have a choice of order buttons, but there are a few important things to mention here.

- Different colours can create different emotions in people, but that is very debatable, e.g. some people say red is and action colour, while others say it is an "angry colour".

- Make sure the colour of the text on the order buttons goes with the colour of the actual button. You will understand what I mean once you read about the colour wheel in this book. Example: don't use red text on orange back ground.

- Don't put the credit card logos underneath the add to cart button as shown on the second picture above. In an online shop, that looks too busy.

- Do you use the text "Buy Now" or "Buy It Now" or "Add to Cart" or "Add to Shopping Bag" or "Add to Basket". Again, there is a lot of debate over this, but Amazon uses "Add to Cart" on Amazon.com and "Add to Basket" on Amazon.co.uk, so I guess these terms work for these countries, as they certainly know what they are doing at Amazon!

Of course, you can debate forever about what colour means what. I am only telling you conclusions reached by some investigative company.

c) Short checkout

Some eCommerce software gives you the choice of 1-page or 2-page checkout—or even more pages. Always, if possible, use 1-page checkout, and never more than three pages. However, with some payment gateways this is not possible. In that case, you simply do not have the choice but to accept what they offer. A bit further, you can see checkout with 1shoppingcart.com and WorldPay as payment gateway.

d) Make sure you have an https secure site

Sometimes you will see an extra "s" added to a url in the browser bar, e.g. http://www.ebay.com might change into https://www.ebay.com when you go to the checkout page.

Why is there an "s" added?

- **http** stands for "Hypertext Transfer Protocol", which is the technology protocol on the web that allows browsing and linking.

- **https** stands for "Hypertext Transfer Protocol" with Secure Sockets Layer (SSL). This is another protocol developed with safe and secure transactions in mind.

Pay attention to it: sometimes you will visit a site and pay for something and the website in your browser address bar will change to https; this means you are now in a secure session. If the extra S does not show, you are NOT in a secure session which will make you more vulnerable for credit card theft and you should stop the check-out process by abandoning the order process.

Another scenario where this can happen is when you log in to your bank account with your user name and password. Once you have logged in, the browser bar can change into https at the front of the URL, indicating that you are in a secure session.

e) Create a "Back to Home" button

When the customer has paid, put a "back to home" button on that page so the customers can keep shopping and maybe order something else OR automatically make the home page appear after the checkout procedure is done.

f) Put Google Analytics on your checkout page

By putting a Google Analytics code on your checkout page, you can see how many visitors you had on that page. If you see the page had 200 visitors and you have only received 100 orders, it is likely that a lot of customers have abandoned the checkout process, and that should be an alarm bell for you to improve the process. Some people say cart abandonment is as high as 50 to 70%. It will be difficult to find out why people are not ordering and quitting the order process, but it is important for you to investigate this as much as you can.

TOP TIP: You can put an opt-in form on your site BEFORE the customer reaches the check out page. That way, you can get the person's email address before they abandon the check out process. Of course, this is only possible if your software has this feature. www.infusionsoft.com gives you the possibility to do this.

One BIG factor is that you MUST display all shipping charges, etc. clearly before people start ordering. Also, don't forget, as mentioned, show your prices including VAT on your site.

An example of a checkout for my videos on self publishing; 1Shoppingcart as my Merchant Account and WorldPay as my Payment Gateway.

The first page after the customer has pushed the "Add to Cart" button contains all important information: price, name and address, email address, method of payment, etc.

https://www.mcssl.com/SecureCart/Checko... esprfmala F664CD7D-6333-4258-83F0-79F1: | Worldwide Self Publishing Ho... | Internet Marketing Busine

View   Favorites   Tools   Help

bank statements   Suggested Sites ▼   Google   Aweber   Neverblue   XE.com   NatWest   YouTube   7search   AmazonCom   AmazonUK

Your credit/debit card or Paypal account will be charged in your local currency at the currency exchange rat

Your Shopping Cart   Your order is safe and secure

Quantity	Product	Price	Total	Remove
1	DVD's Worldwide Self Publishing Video Tutorials. One-off payment of $997.	$997.00	$997.00	X

Coupon code (optional)

[   ] Apply

	Subtotal:	$997.00
	UK VAT 20%:	$199.40
	Total:	**$1,196.40**

Billing Information

Required fields are in bold.

First Name
Last Name
Company
Phone
Email
Confirm Email

Address
Address 2
City
ZIP/Postal Code
Country
County

[ ] Remember my information

Shipping

[ ] Ship to a different address?

Payment Information

Credit Card 💳   **PayPal** PayPal

Click the "Submit Order" button to continue

Comments/Special Delivery Instructions

[   ]

☑ **By checking this box, I affirm that I have read and agree to Internet Marketing Business's terms and conditions and the following statement:**

I authorize Internet Marketing Business to charge me for the order total. I further affirm that the name and personal information provided on this form are true and correct. I further declare that I have read, understand and accept Internet Marketing Business's business terms as published on their website. By pressing the Submit Order button below, I agree to pay Internet Marketing Business.

	Subtotal:	$997.00
	UK VAT 20%:	$199.40
	Total:	**$1,196.40**

‹ Continue Shopping   Clear Cart   Submit Order ›

You can see the https. You can also see the Norton secure logo, and you can see that the customer has the choice to pay with PayPal or with credit card.

The next page looks like this (the extra "s" on https is still shown, along with a padlock, indicating the site is secure):

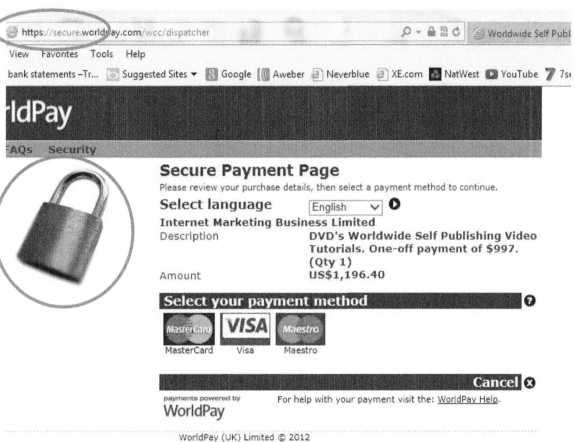

The final page looks like this:

After the customer has clicked "Make Payment", the checkout is complete and the software will send a confirmation of the order to your customer and an email to you to notify that you had a sale (if this is how you have set up the software).

For the email confirmation to your customer, don't forget to say "Thank you for your order"!

I will not go into more detail for the order confirmation, as it is obvious that it will list the description of the order, the total of the order and an expected delivery date.

10) Tell your merchant account your sales will increase

Merchant accounts are known to freeze your account if you suddenly have an unusual number of sales compared to previous months.

I have had one of my accounts frozen because I was testing out a new PPC (Pay Per Click) campaign. It was a very successful campaign and sales were flooding in. My merchant account was frozen because a red flag was raised due to "unexpected high volume of sales". Whilst this is being investigated, you can't make any sales!

TOP TIP: Inform your merchant account if you are expecting higher sales than normal.

Chapter 10 - eCommerce Software.

Rather than build a site from scratch or have it built at a huge price, it is much easier to use a Merchant Server Software Package, also called an eCommerce Server Suite, or commonly eCommerce software. This software provides all the functionality and capabilities you will need to run a professional online store, without the hefty price tag should you have one developed for you.

Some people also call these sites eCommerce site builders or shop site builders.

1) The difference between eCommerce software and a shopping cart

Many people ask me what the difference is between eCommerce websites and shopping carts. In a way, they are both the same. The difference is that one website might just need a simple shopping cart that allows customers to order and pay. In this case, all that is needed is a shopping cart. If you need software with a CMS, or Content Management System, built in, plus lots of other features, you will need eCommerce software. CMS very simply is a system that manages content. It is software that enables you to create, edit, review and publish electronic text, or content, so it lets you add products, change descriptions, etc…

As a general rule, eCommerce software is more complicated to use than a shopping cart. Some of the eCommerce software programs are so difficult to use, it will take weeks to work it all out, watching hours and hours of video tutorials.

An eCommerce solution allows you and your customers more flexibility.

The shopping cart is what your customers will use when they place orders. They add the ordered products to the cart and give you the shipping information and payment. So a shopping cart is software that acts as an online store's catalogue and ordering process. Shopping cart software is the online equivalent of a physical machine that charges your card, e.g. in a shop when you have to put in your PIN number.

If you already have a website and a payment gateway but simply want a shopping cart system, you only need a basic shopping cart.

The credit card processing is not done by the shopping cart! Most people don't know this. You will need a merchant account and a payment gateway for this. The shopping cart must connect to the credit card system.

An eCommerce site is a Content Management System (CMS) and a website application that allows your customers to buy products via transactions secured on the vendor's website. Information is usually encrypted and secured using an SSL (Secure Sockets Layer) Certificate, and orders will be processed by a payment gateway such as Protx. Protx are the leading online payment service provider in the UK.

Most shopping carts and eCommerce programs require you to have your own merchant account and merchant gateway.

There are also integrated shopping carts, but you will require advance programming skills to use these.

It is very important that you study in advance which solution you decide to use, as it will be very time consuming to set it all up again with another shopping cart, in case you decided you don't like your original choice.

If you choose a platform that is too simple, it might not be able to grow with you as your store grows.

If you choose a platform that is too complicated, you might not be able to cope with all the knowledge you need to make it work.

I cannot recommend "the" one for you, as it depends on what you are going to sell and how big you are aiming with your online store. Whichever one you decide to work with, make sure you research them thoroughly and read reviews about them.

2) Do you need eCommerce software?

We've gone through drop shipping services and payment processors. Now, if you choose to go with one of the drop shipping services that offer a fully ready-to-go website, then this isn't something you'll need to worry about. But if you are going to be choosing your own domain and hosting, uploading your own products and everything in between, then you'll need quality eCommerce software to give your customers a pleasurable experience when placing an order.

Ecommerce software has been designed to make it easy and fast for you to get your store up and running. This software has a variety of tools and features that will cover every single step of the way when it comes to setting up and running a successful online drop shipping business store.

Ecommerce software is made to help you get your website up and going, even if you don't know a thing about HTML (Hypertext Markup Language), which is a programming language for creating and designing websites, and have no clue as to which security features you should implement. The best software comes with first-rate security measures and a number of design tools to create a unique and professional looking website that attracts customers and keeps them safe.

As a general rule, a good eCommerce software solution will not just help you design your site, but will also help you register a domain name, upload your inventory, have a smooth checkout process, and ensure that your customers have a variety of payment options. All you need is some inventory, time and some ideas. Before you know it, your online drop shipping business will be up and running.

To give you one of my examples: my website www.liquorice-licorice.co.uk is built with the ecommerce software www.ekmpowershop.co.uk. The hosting is done with them as well, and so is the payment processing.

When an order comes in:

- We print the order.

- We pack the goods.

- We charge the customer's card.

- We ship the goods.

- Job done.

That's how simple eCommerce can be once all is set up, but of course, it is not autopilot income, as you have to do most of the work yourself with an eCommerce online shop (not drop shipping).

3) What to look for in eCommerce software

When it comes to selecting your eCommerce software, you need to make sure that it has all the tools and features needed to ensure your business will get up and running the right way. While it is true that everyone will be selling different products, making your particular industry different as well, you need to ensure that the eCommerce software solution that you choose has the features and tools to cater to your particular business so that you can properly design, manage, advertise and secure your online drop shipping business.

I will discuss several of the best eCommerce software solutions available later. Here is the information that was used to evaluate those solutions, which is also information that you should consider if you decide to go in search of your own eCommerce software provider.

Important: If you decide to use a WordPress shop with a blog, make sure you install Akismet (www.akismet.com) as a plugin, otherwise you will be swamped with SPAM comments. The day you sign up with Akismet is the day your SPAM comments will stop! Wordpress sites are especially vulnerable for SPAM comments and also for being hacked, so make sure to also install some protection on your site for hackers.

Search for "how to avoid SPAM comments in WordPress" for more software to stop SPAM comments. If you don't protect yourself from SPAM comments, this is how your inbox will look:

WordPress	[Christine Clayfield] Please moderate: "Leave a Comment"	15/11/2013 08:28
WordPress	[Christine Clayfield] Please moderate: "Leave a Comment"	15/11/2013 08:30
WordPress	[Christine Clayfield] Please moderate: "Leave a Comment"	15/11/2013 08:41
WordPress	[Christine Clayfield] Please moderate: "Leave a Comment"	15/11/2013 08:43
WordPress	[Christine Clayfield] Please moderate: "Leave a Comment"	15/11/2013 08:56
WordPress	[Christine Clayfield] Please moderate: "Leave a Comment"	15/11/2013 08:58
WordPress	[Christine Clayfield] Please moderate: "Leave a Comment"	15/11/2013 09:23
WordPress	[Christine Clayfield] Please moderate: "Leave a Comment"	15/11/2013 10:50
WordPress	[Christine Clayfield] Please moderate: "Leave a Comment"	15/11/2013 11:00
WordPress	[Christine Clayfield] Please moderate: "Leave a Comment"	15/11/2013 11:23
WordPress	[Christine Clayfield] Please moderate: "Leave a Comment"	15/11/2013 11:23
WordPress	[Christine Clayfield] Please moderate: "Leave a Comment"	15/11/2013 11:23
WordPress	[Christine Clayfield] Please moderate: "Leave a Comment"	15/11/2013 11:25
WordPress	[Christine Clayfield] Please moderate: "Leave a Comment"	15/11/2013 11:26
WordPress	[Christine Clayfield] Please moderate: "Leave a Comment"	15/11/2013 11:52
WordPress	[Christine Clayfield] Please moderate: "Leave a Comment"	15/11/2013 11:52
WordPress	[Christine Clayfield] Please moderate: "Leave a Comment"	15/11/2013 11:54
WordPress	[Christine Clayfield] Please moderate: "Leave a Comment"	15/11/2013 11:55
WordPress	[Christine Clayfield] Please moderate: "Leave a Comment"	15/11/2013 11:58
WordPress	[Christine Clayfield] Please moderate: "Leave a Comment"	15/11/2013 11:59
WordPress	[Christine Clayfield] Please moderate: "Leave a Comment"	15/11/2013 12:07
WordPress	[Christine Clayfield] Please moderate: "Leave a Comment"	15/11/2013 12:08
WordPress	[Christine Clayfield] Please moderate: "Leave a Comment"	15/11/2013 13:17
WordPress	[Christine Clayfield] Please moderate: "Leave a Comment"	15/11/2013 13:17
WordPress	[Christine Clayfield] Please moderate: "Leave a Comment"	15/11/2013 13:18
WordPress	[Christine Clayfield] Please moderate: "Leave a Comment"	15/11/2013 13:20
WordPress	[Christine Clayfield] Please moderate: "Leave a Comment"	15/11/2013 13:23
WordPress	[Christine Clayfield] Please moderate: "Leave a Comment"	15/11/2013 13:28
WordPress	[Christine Clayfield] Please moderate: "Leave a Comment"	15/11/2013 13:38
WordPress	[Christine Clayfield] Please moderate: "Leave a Comment"	15/11/2013 13:45
WordPress	[Christine Clayfield] Please moderate: "Leave a Comment"	15/11/2013 13:50

The above screenshot shows 31 SPAM comments on the same day, between 8am and 2pm. In order to show you the above screenshot, I have disabled Akismet for 1 day.

a) Website tools

While every software will be different, the best eCommerce provider is going to offer a variety of tools that will help you with website design and hosting as well as SEO integration. You want to find an application that consists of every aspect from creating to managing your site. It would be best to locate a software solution that offers unlimited or at least a large amount of bandwidth and online storage. If you aren't familiar with HTML, make sure to choose one that provides you numerous design templates and tools for customization to ensure that you can create a distinctive design for your drop shipping business. Luckily, most provide this.

b) Admin features

With the right features and tools in place, eCommerce software can save you a lot of time and frustration—both of which are common when you are managing your very own online business. Most software limits the number of products that you can list and sell on your site, so make sure that you choose a provider that offers enough space for your business. It also helps you to find an eCommerce software solution that allows you to sell downloadable as well as physical products—just in case you have both to sell or may sell in the future. Make sure to choose a solution that gives you the chance to create numerous reports that outline how your business is doing.

You also want to make sure that you choose a shopping cart solution that offers your customers plenty of payment options. The most popular are credit/debit cards, eChecks and PayPal; however, there are some out there that offer money orders (BACS) and cashier's checks as payment options, although the majority of online buyers will pay by card or PayPal.

c) Security features

When you have an online business, security is a must. You want to ensure your customers feel safe when purchasing products from you, so you need to find an eCommerce software solution that offers SSL and fraud protection. Some offer a variety of other security features, such as

- CAPTCHA (**C**ompletely **A**utomated **P**ublic **T**uring Test to tell **C**omputers and **H**umans **A**part) code. These are the messages you see online that say something like: "Type these characters you see in the picture" or "Verify you are not a robot and type in how much is 3 x 3".

- CVV2 (**C**ard **V**erification **V**alue Code) codes from credit cards. These are the 3 last digits on the back of your card.

d) Marketing features

Marketing is an important aspect of ensuring your online business succeeds. After all, if your store can't be found, customers won't be able to order products, meaning you won't make a profit! Marketing features offer tools that will promote your business effectively, attracting customers and ensuring customer retention. Some of the best marketing tools include gift wrap capabilities, coupons, loyalty programs and daily deals. There are some that offer affiliate programs and tools for social networking.

e) Help and support

An online business can have its ups and downs, and when you are new to the online business world, you are likely to have plenty of questions as well as concerns. Fortunately, it isn't something you have to tackle alone, as help and support are provided by eCommerce software solutions—or at least the best ones offer it. Generally, there are a number of options to get help and obtain support, including:

- Telephone
- Live Chat
- E-mail
- FAQs
- Knowledgebase
- User Guides
- Support Forum
- Video Tutorials

By making sure you are well aware of the aspects of eCommerce software and how important they are to ensuring your business is a success, it is critical that you take the time to choose the best of the best. Obviously, price will be a concern if you are just starting out, but price should most definitely not be your only deciding factor, as you want a provider that offers a variety of tools and features to make your drop shipping business a true success with minimal hassle and frustration.

Be aware: Some eCommerce programs charge you a fee to design your website and the year after they charge you the same fee again! And again the year after that! What's that all about? Completely unacceptable, but they get away with it. If you buy a computer today and you are charged for it today, would you be happy if you are charged for it again next year? And the year after again? Surely not! You will find this type of recurring billing information in the terms and conditions, that nobody ever reads!

f) Your ideal eCommerce software

There are thousands of free and cheap shopping carts that just take the order like a cashier would in a grocery store. They don't do anything to increase your sales or your ranking in Google.

Your ideal eCommerce program should include all or most of the following features:

The five as already mentioned above:

- Good SEO modules that can easily be updated

- Lots of payment options

- Must be secure

- Must have marketing tools

- Must have help and support in different forms

On top of that, your ideal eCommerce program should be able to:

- handle shipping address as billing address by default

- handle large, functional product images

- let you give a short and long description for your product

- sort product by type, by price, by size, by colour, by most popular, in alphabetical order, by newest arrival date

- let you enlarge the picture on your website

- managing of products easily and quickly, e.g. change price, add description, hide products temporarily, etc...

- handle product reviews

- sell your own products AND drop shipping products

- easy output to accounting software

- let you have multiple websites with no extra fees

- use encryption technology

- handle export of your sales reports in CVS format (for Excel) and other formats

- credit terms with customers, e.g. offer customers 30 days to pay

- multiple languages for your products

- have a 99,9% up time. Lots of them are not live due to maintenance, etc. Investigate on forums to see if this is the case for the one you are thinking of using.

- customer log in area for customers to check the progress of their order

- handle different currencies. Many will have a button on their site that says "show prices in $ or £ or Euro".

- deal with online chat

- have a search tool

- have a multiple images facility, so you can have more than one picture per product

- have a wish list feature

- have a product video library

- auto calculate when free shipping applies

- have a layered navigation for your products: put products in sub-categories and display those sub-categories as product filters

- let your customer check out on one single page, which is much easier

- let you put a search bar on the website

- let you print lots of different sales reports, e.g. sales by date, sales by card type, sales by item, sales by reference number, sales affiliate, etc...

- handle gift wrapping

- integrate with your merchant account and payment gateway. CHECK THIS FIRST if you have already decided on your merchant account.

- calculate tax and shipping automatically, depending on what product you ship to what country

- handle selling physical products as well as downloadable products, e.g. an eBook, where the customer will receive the download page immediately after purchase is made. If you are planning to sell both physical and downloadable products, you don't want to have to use two different shopping carts.

- create special offers

- create automatic confirmation emails and delivery emails

- create coupons

- can handle gift cards. You can get these at www.incomm.com.

- personalise the order form

- handle pop-up boxes. I don't mean the pop-up boxes that ask for your email address, as customers find this annoying. I mean a pop-up box that pops up when a customer looks at a product and doesn't buy it; a pop-up box can give the customer a discount on that product or suggest a very similar product to buy. This can increase your sales. Very sophisticated eCommerce software will let you do this without any special programming required.

- use encryption technology

- handles shipping via post office, UPS, DHL and FEDEX

- have an integrated sales and prospect database

- have an auto responder built in or can link to your own auto responder. My book "From Newbie To Millionaire" goes more into detail about this subject. Most shopping carts require you to export your data to other software before you can email your customers. You should choose a shopping cart that allows you to send one email to either selected customers or all customers.

- have the ability to add featured products to the checkout page, e.g. customer who bought this, also bought this—this is called upsell. "Do you want extra large fries with that?" is the well-known upsell from MacDonald's.

- have the ability to sell "related products" or "you may also like this" or "people who bought this also bought this"

- create information and analytics about your customer's buying habits, e.g. top 20 customers, etc...

- handle recurring billing if it is important for you

- create profit reports, e.g. which product has made most profit last month

- create surveys for your customers. You can learn a lot from surveys to improve your business.

- create mobile compatible stores

- create different users

- have free updates

- be easy to use for non-techies

- run on different websites, e.g. if you have one website selling candles and another website selling shoes

- handle returns easily and update the stock automatically

- print stock list, minimum stock level lists based on previous sales

- handle ad tracking

- multiple employees without giving them access to the entire software

- handle affiliate or associate programs. If you are planning to let affiliates sell for you, it is crucially important that you check this from the start. Lots of shopping carts do NOT have this feature.

Not all eCommerce programs have all the above features, but not all will be important for you. It would be difficult to find an eCommerce software program that has ALL the above features. Decide which ones are most important for you and find a program that contains all of them.

The problem is that you have to sign up for the program to really be able to see what it can do and what features it has. That's why it is a good idea to sign up with different ones and see which one you like best. This is time consuming but worth it, I think.

4) Choosing your eCommerce software/shopping cart

Choosing your eCommerce software is an important decision. It is the first thing your potential customers will see, as this is your website, so you will need to impress them in order for them to hand over their credit card details. You need to project a professional image, as your customer will have to trust you.

Each commerce software package will have its own features, and some of them come with lots of bells and whistles that nobody ever uses, but the basics are the same for all sites. Here are the things that you will have to do for each site, whichever software you decide to go with.

- Fill in the store information: your company name, address, contact details, payment methods, etc…

- Set up your website: set up your home page, your banner, logo, etc… You can outsource your banner by using a freelancer on www.elance.com or you can visit www.48hourslogo.com and have a logo/banner done for under £35/$60.

- Add crucial pages: about us page, disclaimer, privacy policy, etc…

- Add suppliers: of course you can't sell products without having a supplier, so you will need at least one supplier to start with.

- Product categories. You will always need to create a product category before you can add products, as each product will be located in a certain category.

- Add products. Try to have minimum of 20 to 30 products before you go live. Give each product a unique description, even if the products are very similar. Don't make the description too long.

- Add users. You can grant or deny access to specific users. Some people might not be allowed to see the purchasing prices, other might not be allowed to upload products, etc… You can specify this for each user.

- Add customers. If you already have customers, you can put them in manually so they end up on your mailing list, e.g. if you want to mail your customers a discounted offer for a limited period of time.

- Set up your pricing structure and discount structure. With most ecommerce software, you can choose to give your customer a discount automatically if they order over a certain amount or over a certain quantity.

- Transport charges. You will need to specify your transport charges. This can be free of charge over a certain amount or a certain quantity. This can also be calculated automatically on the total weight of the order. There are several possibilities, but these charges need to be set up from the start so when you create a new product, the software will ask you which transport charges apply for the products.

- Order processing procedure. This is where you will set if the buyer receives an email to confirm the order, when the order is shipped, when the order will be delivered, etc...

You need to do 4 basic steps, whatever software you use:

- Set up the online store and go live, once you've tested everything.

- Send traffic to your site.

- Close the sale—this means make it easy for the customer to order.

- Take payment.

TOP TIP: Very often at the bottom of shop websites on the web you will see "Powered by + the software name". This can be removed, but a lot of people leave it there. You can take advantage of that in this way:

Search for "powered by Shopping Cart Elite" or "powered by Shopify" (do the search between quotation marks). Google will then show results of ecommerce sites that are built with these shopping carts. In our example, that's Shopping Cart Elite and Shopify. Click on all the websites and see which ones you like best and which ones you think are suitable for your products.

You could also type in candles + "powered by Shopping Cart Elite", and the result will be sites that sell candles.

There are over 500 shopping carts! How the heck do you choose? Well, I can tell you that most of them are not good enough to set up a professional online business. The ones I have listed are not the only good ones but are the ones that I've used myself or people I know use them. Be aware that there are lots of unreliable companies trading on the web!

Here are a few of the top-rated eCommerce software solutions available for any online business.

a) EkmPowershop

www.ekmpowershop.com

www.ekmpowershop.co.uk

EkmPowershop has been online since 2002. They are the most popular eCommerce system in the UK, powering one in every five online shops!

EkmPowershop has all these:

- Ideal for beginners

- Free hosting

- Unlimited products

- Unlimited visitors

- Unlimited shop size

- Search engine friendly, good SEO per product

- No transaction fees

- No contract, cancel any time

- VERY affordable for what it is

- Over 150 templates (free)

- Product image light box

- Product image zoom

- Product summary in category

- Search statistics

- Recommended Retail Price (RRP)

- Live chat

- Good support

- Over 38,000 shops use EkmPowershop

- Customer reviews

- Free trial

- mCommerce as standard (mCommerce means that the shop can be viewed on a mobile phone)

- iPhone/iPad/Androids apps

- Ebay integration

- Amazon and Ebay Management

- Supports these eCommerce payment gateways: PayPal, SagePay, Cardsave, Skrill, Ogone, Amazon payments, Ukash, RealexPayments, SecureForm, Nochex, WorldPay, HSBC, Barclaycard, Netbanx, Gate2Shop, etc…

- Automatic stock control

- Multi-currency

- Social network integration

- Loyalty points

- Email to friend feature

- Block visitors

- Abandoned cart saver (You can see how many customers didn't order after they started the order process)

- Advance inventory manager

- WordPress blog

- Captcha code prevents spam

- Import/Export system

- Loyalty points

- Free UK support

- Discount management

- Password protect

- Postcode lookup

- Integration with Sage, KashFlow and BrightPearl

Building an online shop with EkmPowershop really is fast and easy.

Cost:

This really is the best thing about EkmPowershop: the cost!

Only £24.99/$39.99 per month.

One package, one price!

All the points listed above are all included in your small monthly charge.

You can see from the list above that you get a lot for your money. This really is an ideal platform to get your started.

Some negative points:

- No integration to drop shipping. EkmPowershop is only suitable if you stock products and ship them to your customers yourself.

- Does not support some well-known payment gateways.

- Doesn't have all the bells and the whistles, but you don't need all of them for a "simple" shop.

- Limited to one URL or one website. If you want a second shop, you have to pay the monthly expenses of £24.99/$39.99 again

- Can sometimes be slow when uploading new products.

- Email marketing is extra. You can either pay a monthly fee or buy a pay-as-you-go tariff, e.g. for £29.95/$48 you can email your customers once. This is ideal if you only email your customers twice per year. The monthly cost depends on the number of customers you have and starts from £19.99/$32 for 2500 customers.

My sites www.liquorice-licorice.co.uk and www.nougat-nougat.co.uk are designed with www.ekmpowershop.co.uk. I just love it, but it hasn't got all the bells and the whistles that other "bigger" platforms have.

I've set up these websites myself and I only have very basic HTML knowledge! If I can do it, so can you.

b) Volusion

www.volusion.co.uk: There is also www.volusion.com, but as I am in the UK, it re-directs me to volusion.co.uk. If you want to ensure that you create and manage a successful online drop shipping business, then you can find all the tools that you need to do so with Volusion. Volusion offers a huge selection of tools for website design, as well as shopping cart tools, marketing features and payment options. No prior web design experience or knowledge is required to fully enjoy the benefits that Volusion (recommended by Paypal!) has to offer an online business owner.

A big advantage of Volusion is that they have an affiliate program, so you can let other people do the selling for you!

Website Tools. Volusion makes it easy to create and design your website. The process is very straightforward and easy to follow. Best of all, you don't have to have any knowledge of HTML or coding whatsoever to create a customised website. Volusion offers a design wizard that will take you through the creation and design process step by step to make sure that you don't skip something important. There are dozens of pre-made templates that you can use for free. Also, if you do have knowledge of HTML, you can use the HTML editing mode to put your skills to the test and ensure your site is just how you want it. There are plenty of tools that allow you to customise your website to ensure it is unique and like no other site out there.

Volusion has free templates, but you can also buy templates with more features, ranging from £35/$56 to £575/$920. Here are some examples:

An example of a free template:

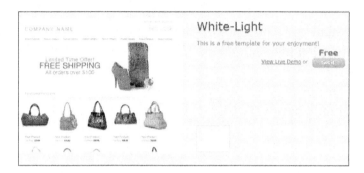

An example of a £35/$56 template:

An example of a £575/$920 template:

When it comes to adding content to your website, Volusion ensures it is quick and easy! You can create an unlimited number of article categories and add as much content as you wish because there's no set limit. There are content editing tools that give you the ability to create titles, captions and content sections for your content pieces.

Admin Features. Once your site has been created and designed, it's time for inventory. Luckily, it doesn't have to be a hassle, as Volusion offers a number of packages that cater to different inventory sizes. You can choose to have a store with no more than 25 products, all the way up to a store with no limit to the number of products that you upload. Adding your inventory is made easy by Volusion with their bulk uploader. Plus, you can add several variants to your products, including colors, lengths, sizes and more. Both physical and downloadable products can be sold.

Volusion also has plenty of tools to ensure that the process of online business management is not as overwhelming as it might otherwise be. Volusion offer tools that will allow you to keep tabs on all of your products, allowing you to see what sizes, colors and how many of a product are in stock. The software even sends you a customised alert informing you when your inventory gets low. Volusion provides a very extensive reporting tool so that you can keep track of the statistics and progress of your business. This same tool lets you see how certain aspects of your personal website are doing.

When it comes to credit card processing, Volusion offers multiple processes to capture credit card information and keep track of payments. Credit cards can be processed with Volusion in-house, or you can choose to use one or more of the different payment gateways out there. There are also tax features that let you charge tax by zip code or by state. You can even set it up to where certain customers and/or products are tax exempt. Tax calculations can be set up to be based on shipping addresses as well.

Security Features. Volusion offers a large number of security features to ensure that you can keep your site safe and secure. There is CISP (**C**ardholder **I**nformation **S**ecurity **P**rogram) and PCI (**P**ayment **C**ard **I**ndustry Standard) protection, which are used to protect credit card information.

In addition, every page has SSL (**S**ecurity **S**ockets **L**ayer) encryption to avoid any tampering with your site. Volusion offers plenty of other security features, including:

- Members-only capabilities

- Multiple logins for admins

- Ability to establish admin sections for access

- History of administration access

- Automatic cash protection

- CAPTCHA image validation for submission forms

- Only the last four numbers of a credit card number will be displayed

- Fraud score

Marketing Features. There is definitely no shortage of marketing features with Volusion's eCommerce software. Offering a wide variety of SEO capabilities, Volusion ensures that all aspects of your website are search engine optimized. They also offer:

- Social networking tools

- E-mail marketing capabilities

- Mobile features

- And more! Read on:

Volusion offers integration with eBay so that you can easily sell any of your products on eBay. In fact, it's as easy as 1-2-3. It takes only minutes to build a storefront for eBay. There's even a tool that will help you list any of your products on social networks, such as Facebook. You can place "Share" and "Like" buttons on your site. Volusion also offers the ability to create a specific Facebook theme so that it matches your website. Plus, there are tools to help you attract customers and improve your credibility as a store owner, by promoting daily deals on Facebook.

There are marketing features that make it easy to post directly to Facebook and Twitter as well as put up a video on YouTube showcasing your store's products. Social media is a good way to create brand awareness and get the word out there about your store. Volusion ensures that you can make this happen easily and quickly with their connectivity features to social networks.

Volusion also makes it so that you can optimize your website so that it can be accessed and adequately viewed on mobile devices. So, no matter where your customers may be, they can hop on their smartphone, access your website and purchase products.

Help and Customer Support. Volusion has one of the best customer support teams in the industry. Offering 24-hour support, Volusion makes it easy to contact them in the event of a crisis or non-crisis. You can reach Volusion support by live chat, e-mail or telephone.

If you'd rather search for answers on your own, there is an FAQ section and knowledgebase. In addition, there are valuable video tutorials and an excellent product manual. They all work together to ensure that you understand the eCommerce software product in and out. If you still have questions, though, you can contact Volusion and a professional customer service representative will quickly respond and answer any questions or concerns that you may have.

Pricing and Plans. There are five different plans available from Volusion, each with its own benefits. The choice will depend heavily on the number of products that you want to list in your store. Regardless of the plan, though, there are never any transaction fees with Volusion.

Here's a breakdown of the plans and prices (prices quoted are exclusive of VAT):

- **Mini Plan**. For £9/$15 per month, you can list 100 products, have 1GB of data transfer, and have access to social media tools, a Facebook store, and a mobile store. You'll only have access to online support.

- **Plus Plan**. For £19/$35 per month, you can list 1,000 products, have 3GB of data transfer, and have access to social media tools, a Facebook store, and a mobile store. In addition, you'll have access to ratings and reviews, newsletters, and abandoned cart reports. You will gain access to 24/7 phone support aside from online support.

- **Pro Plan**. For £44/$75 per month, you can list 10,000 products, have 10GB of data transfer, and have access to social media tools, a Facebook store, and a mobile store. You'll have access to ratings and reviews, newsletters, and abandoned cart reports. In addition, you'll be able to import/export product data and have access to a CRM tool and be able to take phone orders. You will gain access to 24/7 phone support aside from online support.

- **Premium Plan**. For £80/$135 per month, you can list unlimited products, have 35GB of data transfer, and have access to social media tools, a Facebook store, and a mobile store. You'll have access to ratings and reviews, newsletters, and abandoned cart reports. You'll be able to import/export product data and have access to a CRM tool and be able to take phone orders. You will also get access to Deal of the Day and My Rewards features. Plus, you'll be able to integrate your store with eBay and have your own onboarding coach to help you build your store from the ground up. You will also have Priority Phone Support with shorter waiting times.

If, for whatever reason, you need a larger plan, just contact Volusion and they'll work with you to customise a plan and pricing structure that will meet your needs.

- **Approved gateways**. These are the approved gateways that Volusion works with (if you are based in the UK): Realex, Authorise.net, Netbank, Sage pay, SKRILL, WorldPay.

- **Recurring Billing**. Volusion has a recurring billing facility, but please make sure that you choose a payment gateway AND a merchant account that can deal with recurring billing.

- Browsers. A small negative about Volusion is that you need to have an updated browser to use Volusion without any problems. Supported browsers are Firefox 13 or up, Internet Explorer 8-9, Chrome and Safari.

- Free Trial. Volusion offers a 14-day free trial (and doesn't even require your credit card to get this free trial) before you commit to one of the plans listed above.

The Verdict: All in all, Volusion in my opinion is one of the best eCommerce software solutions out there. It is straightforward, easy to use and has a large feature set for various aspects of your online business, from design to marketing to security.

c) Shopify

www.shopify.com: Another impressive eCommerce solution is Shopify. The interface is one of the most user friendly, and the feature set is astounding. Shopify truly makes it easy to create a website that is professional, unique and eye catching. All the tools and features are top notch, and there are several marketing tools to ensure you get plenty of traffic to your drop shipping business site.

If you want to get going very quickly, this one is a good choice, but keep in mind if you want access to the source code of your site, it is not possible to do this with Shopify.

Website Tools. The features that Shopify has for creating and designing the site are very extensive. There is a wizard that will take you through the process of creating your site step by step to make sure that you don't miss a beat. If you are comfortable with HTML, then you can design your own site. However, if you have no idea how to begin HTML coding, there are plenty of pre-made templates to utilise.

There are also plenty of tools to customise your site to ensure it is a distinctive design and is exactly what you want.

Admin Features. There is a set limit to how many products can be listed on your site, but you can create unlimited categories. There is a store builder interface that gives you the chance to add virtually any detail to your products, and it's incredibly easy to add descriptions and images. Both physical and downloadable products can be sold.

There is a product menu that ensures you can keep tabs on your inventory, create new profiles for products, import/export product information and more. There is even a navigation menu feature that lets you decide how your website will be displayed to your customers.

There are plenty of payment options with Shopify, from credit and debit cards to PayPal to eChecks and more! It comes with automatic shipping and tax calculators, ensuring that customers have a smooth checkout process. Unlike Volusion, there is no credit card processing in-house or a built-in POS (**P**oint **O**f **S**ale) system. This means that you'll have to get a merchant account and payment gateway elsewhere so that you can accept credit cards.

Shopify makes their eCommerce software so simple to understand and use that you can have your website up and running the very same day that you get started. Their interface is easy to navigate, and all the tools and features are easy to find.

Security Features. Being scammed online is nothing new, so you want to make sure that your customers feel safe in purchasing from you. With Shopify, you can rest assured that your customers will feel comfortable and be at ease. Not only will your web store appear professional, but it will be compliant with PCI. Shopify makes use of SSL (**S**ecure **S**ockets **L**ayer) encryption at the checkout to ensure your customer's personal information is fully protected. There's also a team of fraud prevention and protection specialists to ensure a positive experience is achieved.

Marketing Features. Shopify has a really neat feature that lets you organize a variety of information about your customers. This feature shows you who your largest spenders are so that you can target them with your marketing strategy. It also gives you the chance to reach out to any of your customers who have not shopped at your store recently. The marketing feature also lets you sort all of your customers by location, making it easy to target them for your marketing campaigns. The Shopify software also lets you import and export customer information.

Shopify also provides easy accessibility to Google Analytics so that you can keep track of statistics. This gives you insight as to which marketing campaigns and keywords are getting you the most traffic and business. It also lets you compare how well your drop shipping business site does online compared to others in the same niche and industry.

While Google Analytics is accessible to anyone, it is integrated with the eCommerce software by Shopify to make it that much easier to access and understand.

Shopify also makes it easy to generate and increase traffic and revenue for your site. Unlike Volusion, Shopify does not offer any marketing tools that make it easy to promote daily deals or a tool to create a rewards program.

Help and Support. The help and support that Shopify offers their clients is incomparable to other eCommerce software solutions. If you want to find your own answers, you can search the FAQs, wiki page and forums, as well as the support community. In addition, you can reach Shopify via phone and e-mail whenever needed.

Pricing and Plans. Shopify offers their customers four different plans:

- **Starter Plan.** For £8.75/$14 per month, you can use the starter version and upload a maximum of 25 products into your online store. You can upgrade to a plan with more features any time.

- **Basic Plan**. For £18/$29 per month, you will get the basic plan that gives you the ability to use your very own domain, unlimited bandwidth, 1GB of storage, 100 products and 2.0% transaction fees. The setup is free of charge.

- **Professional Plan**. For £49/$79 per month, you will get the most popular professional plan that gives you the ability to use your very own domain, unlimited bandwidth, 5GB of storage, 2,500 Products and 1.0% transaction fees. You will get a discount code engine and the setup is free of charge.

- **Unlimited Plan**. For £112/$179 per month, you will get the business plan that gives you the ability to use your very own domain, unlimited bandwidth, unlimited storage, 10,000 products and no transaction fees. You will get a discount code engine and real-time carrier shipping. The setup is free of charge.

Free Trial. You can try Shopify risk-free for 14 days before you actually commit to purchasing the eCommerce software. You don't even have to enter your credit card information to gain access to the 14-day free trial, which is nice.

Now, during this free trial, you need to make sure that Shopify contains all the features and tools that you feel you need to make your eCommerce business a success.

The Verdict. With one of the sleekest and simplest interfaces, Shopify is extremely easy to use and is straightforward with all of its tools and features. With its large selection of tools and features, Shopify makes it easy to get your online store running and ready to grow.

d) 1ShoppingCart

www.1shoppingcart.com is another all-in-one solution for selling online that I recommend.

- Over 3 million people are using it

- Store templates available

- Online chat

- Good support

- Email marketing included

- Flexible product options, e.g. choose size, colour, etc…

- You can sell anything: products, eBooks, services, subscriptions, etc…

- Stores viewable on mobile phones

- Customer log in at checkout

- Upsells, e.g. if you sell cupcakes, offer plates, cups, spoons as an upsell

- Get notification on your mobile when a new order is received

- Good selection of reports

- Optimised for search engines

- Coupons, discount vouchers available

- Has an affiliate program

- Social marketing buttons

- PCI certified payment processing

- Carries the security badge https, security verified

- Has a Doba catalogue with 1.5M products to sell

- No set-up fees

- Integrates with over 50 leading payment gateways; just to name but a few: 2checkout, Sagepay, WorldPay, Paypoint, Authorize.net, iTransact, etc...

Note: WorldPay cannot handle recurring billing when integrated with 1shoppingcart.

- Also integrates with PayPal

- Customer has the choice at checkout: pay with PayPal or by credit card

Pricing and plans:

Plus: £21/$34 per month

- 24/7 standard support

- Free store templates

- 500 products

- 1.25 % transaction fee

- 1 user license

- Recurring billing

- Contact management

- Mobile commerce

- 1GB storage

Premium: £62/$99 per month

- 24/7 standard support

- Premium store templates

- Unlimited products

- 1% transaction fee

- 5 user licenses

- Recurring billing

- Contact management

- Mobile commerce

- 3GB storage

- Affiliate Management

Ultimate: £156 / $249 per month

- 24/7 ultimate support

- Premium store templates

- Unlimited products

- 0.75% transaction fee

- 5 user licenses

- Recurring billing

- Contact management

- Mobile commerce

- 10GB storage

- Affiliate management

- Free domain name

There are more differences between the plans; only a few are listed above.

I am happy with 1shoppingcart. I don't use it as a shop for physical products, but for downloadable products, and the order buttons for these products are on my sales pages. Once someone clicks on the order button, 1shoppingcart takes over and everything is integrated from the moment the button is clicked until the customer gets an email with confirmation of the order. The customer also receives the download page for the product.

1shoppingcart has an affiliate program, but please note that you have to pay the affiliates yourself. 1shopping cart will let you know when payments are due to affiliates but won't pay them automatically, like Clickbank does.

e) Shopping Cart Elite

www.shoppingcartelite.com: If you want to achieve success with your drop shipping business, then you need to have the features and tools to make that happen. User-friendly Shopping Cart Elite may very well be the eCommerce software that you need, as it has an extensive selection of marketing tools, as well as features for professionally designing and properly managing your online store.

This really is a complete turnkey solution that offers absolutely everything you need to become successful, but it does come with a heavy price. This software also has a pop-up facility if you want to use it (a pop-up window that captures customers' email addresses, etc…).

Their keyword integration with Google absolutely rocks, giving you a good chance of ranking in Google search results.

Shopping Cart Elite (www.shoppingcartelite.com) has a built-in feature called Price Spy that can automate the whole process of price comparison.

Website Tools. With Shopping Cart Elite, your site design can look exactly the way you want. From images to fonts to colours, you choose how you want your site to look.

Shopping Cart Elite gives you the opportunity to customise your website header. You can even add a submenu, making it easy for your customers to find additional information, including company and site information, special offers and discounts. There's even a tool to resize images, making it easy to edit images. When product images are uploaded, this tool actually creates a thumbnail and a large image for that product automatically.

If you decide that you want Shopping Cart Elite professionals to design a website and logo for you, they'll spend 20 hours on your website design and create a custom logo for you, but unfortunately not free of charge.

Admin Features. Offering a variety of admin and inventory tools and features, Shopping Cart Elite gives you the things you need to run solid administration on your site. Unlike most other eCommerce software solutions, Shopping Cart Elite does not limit the amount of inventory you can upload to your site. Whether you just want 100 products, 1,000 products or 10,000 products, it's all possible with Shopping Cart Elite. Both physical and downloadable products can be sold.

From inventory and sales to traffic and much more, Shopping Cart Elite eCommerce software provides a variety of reports that ensure that you stay on top of your site's statistics, so that you can know how well you are (or aren't) doing. This helps you find areas that need to be improved for more traffic and business.

As for payment options, Shopping Cart Elite allows for payments to be accepted via credit and debit card, PayPal, eChecks and checks. They even provide credit card processing in-house. The software has calculators to make the checkout process smooth and quick by calculating tax and shipping automatically.

Security Features. All websites through Shopping Cart Elite are protected with a virtual proxy firewall. This just adds to the SSL security on your site. The virtual proxy firewall ensures that your site is not accessed by unsafe visitors and has the capability of detecting any form of suspicious activity. Shopping Cart Elite even offers data backup to ensure that your information is never lost in the event of a system or server crash.

Marketing Features. When it comes to marketing and search engine optimization, your site needs the best, and Shopping Cart Elite is definitely the best, going above and beyond with their marketing tools. You can use the marketing tools to ensure you are using the proper keyword density and determine quality expressions that are all search engine friendly to ensure that your content is optimized so that your customers can search for and locate products easily on your site. Not only will this help customers find your site to begin with via search engines, but it also helps them locate particular pages and products within your site.

Shopping Cart Elite has a special tool called the Blog Poster. This marketing tool syndicates your content automatically on the Internet and sends it to a variety of content sites. This automatically generates traffic to your site, while creating back links without you producing an ounce of sweat.

Your customer has the chance to compare your products with similar products from other sellers across the web. This price comparison tool actually adjusts the prices of your products so that they are at a more competitive rate, while still ensuring you make plenty of profit. This means that you don't have to keep track of the pricing of your competitors.

The search engine optimization tools from Shopping Cart Elite are unmatched by other eCommerce software providers. There are various marketing tools to help with e-mail marketing strategies so that you can properly advertise to the appropriate audience and a keyword ranking tool to see how well your site is ranking for certain keywords. There are also tools for RSS feeds, a search engine indexer, SEO on search habits of your store visitors, and a tool to help you export social networking contacts. Plus, you can keep analytics on how your visitors interact once they get on your store.

Help and Support. Clients with Shopping Cart Elite can use e-mail support at any time, plus they offer four hours each month of one-on-one live customer support. There are also plenty of video tutorials to help you learn how to properly run your online drop shipping store. If more customer support is needed, there are a couple of different packages that give you access to support reps and developers, as shown below, along with the standard plan that is included free of charge.

Pricing and Plans. There are four different plans for the Shopping Cart Elite eCommerce software. Here's a look at each of them, including what they come with and how much they cost per month.

All plans include unlimited bandwidth, storage, products and emails, as well as automated monthly updates and backups. The main differences is in the support response time, as already explained. As these plans are too expensive for many people, I am not going to explain these in detail, but here is a quick overview:

- **Basic Plan** – For £187/$299 per month, you can get this plan with two employee logins and up to 100 monthly orders.

- **Professional Plan** – For £375/$599 per month, you get unlimited numbers of employee logins and unlimited number of orders, plus better support.

- **Elite Plan** – For £563/$899 per month, you get it all.

They have a complex system of support plans (payable), ranging from four hours response time to immediate response time, etc…

In addition to the plans, there are several packages of recommended plug-ins. You really can't go wrong with Shopping Cart Elite, as it has all the necessary features you need to get your site going, from marketing and search engine optimization tools to security and design features. However, it is a bit more expensive than the others, so this may not be ideal for your startup store.

They have lots of extra's you can spend your money on.

f) Open Cart

www.opencart.com: Ideally designed for beginners, Open Cart is another easy shopping carts to use. It takes a limited number of steps to get started with Open Cart, which means you'll be well on your way to accepting orders and payments from customers. Open Cart boasts a wide range of features and tools to ensure your business gets up and running smoothly, quickly and efficiently. **Plus, it's affordable because it's FREE!** Open Cart earns money from add-ons.

Open Cart is an open source shopping cart, so you can access the source code and have complete control over your website.

One of my students has Open Cart and is not happy with it at all. He says their customer support is really bad and they never answer any questions, so be aware of that. You can see a demo store on www.demo.opencart.com . As it is free, you might as well try it.

With Open Cart, here are the major benefits:

- Unlimited products

- Unlimited categories

- Unlimited manufacturers

- Product ratings and reviews

- Template integration

- Automatic resizing of images

- Discount coupon system

- Sales reports

- Printable invoices

- Over 20 payment gateways

- Over eight shipping methods

g) Go Daddy Quick Shopping Cart

www.godaddy.com: Go Daddy is well known in the hosting industry, but they offer much more than just hosting services. The Quick Shopping Cart eCommerce software provided by Go Daddy makes it super easy for you to get your online store started; it has an extensive collection of tools and features that help you not just create and manage your store, but also promote and enhance it. Some of these include:

- Easy web store design

- Simple catalog set-up

- Multiple shipping and payment options

- Up-sells, coupons and featured products

- Manage orders as well as your customers

- Hosting and security

- Store integration

With Go Daddy, you get access to three different service levels. There are set-up fees, and a variety of features come equipped with each plan, including over 1,500 templates and colour schemes, shipping calculators with real-time rates, free 24/7 support, free hosting and the ability to accept a variety of payment methods.

Here's a look at the plans offered by Go Daddy:

- **Economy Plan**. For £3.49/$5.55 per month, you will be able to upload 20 products with one image per product, 150GB bandwidth, 1GB disk space, and free web hosting. You can add an SSL for £31/$49.99 per year and a site scanner to keep hackers at bay for an extra £4.38/$6.99 per month.

- **Deluxe Plan**. For £9.99/$15.90 per month, you will be able to upload 100 products with five images per product, 500GB bandwidth, 10GB disk space, and free web hosting. You can add an SSL for £31/$49.99 per year and a site scanner to keep hackers at bay for an extra £4.38/$6.99 per month.

- **Premium Plan**. For £17.49/$ 27.90 per month, you will be able to upload an unlimited amount of products with 10 images per product, 1,000GB bandwidth, 50GB disk space, and free web hosting. An SSL certificate is included for free, as is a United States merchant account.

h) *More eCommerce Software Solutions*

The above-mentioned are the best shopping carts for eCommerce business; however, there are a few more that are worth mentioning. After all, you may not like any of the ones listed above. Here are some you can check out on your own if you'd like:

Some good websites to design your shop:

www.ultracart.com RECOMMENDED—Ideal for drop shipping; everything is built in.
www.actinic.com RECOMMENDED
www.cubecart.com
www.pinnaclecart.com
www.3dcart.com
www.bigcommerce.com
www.agoracart.com
www.shopsite.com
www.webstore.amazon.co.uk – www.webstore.amazon.com
www.1and1.com

I believe all of these have a free trial period, so sign up and try to create a few products to see which one you like best.

If you want more examples, simply search "shopping cart software" and look at all the different companies. Review the one you are thinking of using.

5) The price of your eCommerce software.

As you have seen, you pay for what you get. A quick summary of what you can expect to pay per month:

£24.99/$39.99 for a simple one, e.g. EkmPowershop

£19.99/$29.90 for the Bronze plan of Volusion

£49/$79 for Shopify, the minimum plan I recommend

£187/$299 for Shopping Cart Elite

There are others that are £1200/$2000 per month and more!

The more bells and whistles, the more you will pay. Decide what you want and how many bells and whistles you want.

Important to mention: the "bigger" ones will have lots of features that you will probably never use.

Chapter 11 - Hosting Your Website.

1) What is hosting and choosing your hosting provider

Let's start out with setting up your site. Design is not the first step, believe it or not. In fact, it's something called hosting. You need to find a hosting company or hosting service in order to have a website. This service ultimately ensures your website is online. Without your site being on a server, your site is not online for customers to see. The foundation of a good online store is a good hosting company. Some shopping carts have their own hosting provider.

Many hosting companies will offer various tutorials and templates to help you get started setting up your website, as well as other business services, such as e-mail accounts, shopping carts, software to monitor site traffic, and more. There are a few things you will want to consider when choosing a hosting company, as discussed below.

a) Web design

Just how good are you at designing a website? If you are new to the Internet world, then you are probably going to need some drastic help in this department. You will want to choose a hosting company that caters to you and your situation. You aren't very web or tech savvy, so you need to find a hosting service that offers educational videos, tutorials, tech support and templates that are easy to customise and use.

b) Fees for bandwidth and disk space

Bandwidth refers to how much space you have for web pages to be transferred from the server to the web browser of your website visitor. Disk space refers to how much space is available to you to store your website on the server. The amount of content and graphics that you can use on your website is limited to the amount of disk space that you have been provided by your hosting service.

When searching for a hosting provider, you may find claims of unlimited bandwidth and disk space, but be sure to read the fine print, as there are generally some restrictions, such as no video or audio. Read all of the fine print and all terms of the service; otherwise, you are at risk of being charged more money or having your site shut down.

c) Server speed and uptime

The speed of your website and how often it is available to web users will depend on your hosting company. More often than not, the reason a website loses sales is because customers are unable to see a fully loaded page or the website loads at a snail's pace. Therefore, you want to make sure that your host's server is fast enough to ensure that your website loads quickly and properly every time.

As for uptime, this is the amount of time that your website is actually up and running for web users to see, as opposed to down and unusable. Uptime is generally provided as a percentage, such as 99.99 percent. You want to find a hosting company that has the largest possible percentage, as you can't make sales if the site is not up and running or uploads slow. Another important factor to keep in mind is that your store will have lots of pictures on of the products that you sell so if the resolution of your pictures is too high - for web use purposes - your site will load extra slow.

d) Number of websites

While you are probably only going to be using one website to start with, if your site and drop shipping business really kicks off, you may want to run another drop shipping site. For that reason, you may want to find a company that offers hosting for multiple IP addresses and/or domain names. This just ensures you are ahead of the game should you decide that you want another website in the future. If you opt not to start another website, no big deal, as you aren't committed to having to do so. The offer is just there if you decide to.

e) Add-on features

There are a number of add-ons that you can utilise when you choose a hosting company. A few features you want to look for in a hosting service include unlimited e-mail addresses, free software, e-mail forwarding, free photo galleries, and 24/7 tech support.

Selecting the right hosting service can ensure your business has a large number of tools and features at your disposal to keep that competitive juice flowing. You don't have to be a pro at web design, programming and coding to make your website a success, but you do need a top-notch hosting company that will help you not only create and publish your website but also maintain it for years (hopefully) to come.

2) Choosing the right type of hosting

Web hosting is a necessary component of an online website, because without web hosting, your store cannot be accessed by potential customers.

Now you know what to look for when selecting a hosting provider, but did you know that there are a few different types of hosting? If you are new to the Internet and online business world, then you probably didn't have a clue about this.

There are actually four different categories of web hosting: shared hosting, co-location hosting, dedicated hosting and in-house hosting. Each has its benefits and downfalls and will cater to a particular group of users, as they offer different services for administration and connectivity.

a) Shared hosting

Also known as virtual hosting, shared hosting is a specific type of hosting that serves more than one website on only one server. With shared hosting, you are "renting" disk space on that server from the hosting company. Each site is separate from the other, as it resides on its own section, also called a partition, of the hosting server.

Shared hosting is typically the most cost-effective way of getting website hosting, as the costs are shared amongst all users of that particular server. Therefore, you aren't paying upfront for hardware or server maintenance because it is spread out over time between you and the rest of the website owners that are using space on the hosting company's server.

You aren't responsible for these services, so to speak, as the hosting company will pay for server management, software installation and security updates, as well as technical support. This makes it ideal for smaller and medium-sized businesses, as well as for personal web users to have their own website.

Generally, the pricing for shared website hosting starts at a few bucks per month, but can vary in price based on package sizes and capabilities, such as the amount of bandwidth and disk space that is offered, add-on features, e-mail accounts, etc.

Pricing isn't the only thing to consider, though. For the most part, any type of website, whether it is a personal website, corporate website or a drop shipping eCommerce website, will work well for shared hosting. However, usage limits keep power web users from using shared hosting.

b) Co-location hosting

With co-location hosting, you can use your own server while it is in another person's data center. You will be responsible for that server in terms of maintenance and updates, but you will be provided with a dedicated IP address, a high-speed Internet connection and power for the server.

Co-location hosting is most suitable for businesses that are looking to save money on maintaining a secure server environment and want the various features and benefits that an IT department could offer. There are disadvantages, such as finding a provider and keeping up with server maintenance, which generally causes businesses to choose either shared or dedicated hosting.

c) Dedicated hosting

Dedicated hosting refers to when someone has their own server and it is not shared with anyone else. With dedicated hosting, full control of the web server is in your hands; however, the server is only being leased, so you are not the owner of it. Therefore, the owner (hosting provider) of the server will be responsible for purchasing the hardware, installing software and server maintenance.

As a general rule, dedicated hosting is used by individuals and companies that require a large amount of data transfer and need significantly high speeds. For example, Amazon may use dedicated hosting because they have thousands on top of thousands of product pages, which wouldn't be allowed on a lower-end hosting service. Dedicated hosting simply meets their specific needs.

d) In-House hosting

In-house hosting refers to when a company uses their own web servers. This is expensive, because this means that the company will purchase the server hardware, install all the software and maintain the server to ensure that it is working properly and is secure. This means that it requires well-trained technical staff. Big global corporations, such as Microsoft and IBM, generally use in-house hosting. For most businesses, this just isn't cost-effective.

It helps to understand the difference between the various types of web hosting so that you can choose the right one for your business.

The most important message regarding hosting is: don't choose one that is too cheap, e.g. £3.10/$4.99 per month, as they are certainly not the best hosting companies, and they will have restrictions.

> **TOP TIP:** Many eCommerce sites give you the opportunity to have hosting done by them and also to buy your domain name from them. Although that might be easier for you, I recommend not to do that. The reason behind my recommendations is that, if you want to change software, you are stuck with their hosting or you will have the hassle of switching hosting, which can be technically challenging.

3) Popular hosting companies

I've always used GoDaddy (www.godaddy.com) , 1and1 (www.1and1.com) or www.hostgator.com for my hosting. If you're still looking for a hosting provider, then I recommend www.godaddy.com, especially if you make mostly WordPress-based websites.

Generally I prefer www.1and1.com because I like their platform better than GoDaddy's, and in my experience they have better customer services. You can contact them late during weekdays and also on weekends. Each time I have phoned 1and1 with a problem, I had an immediate answer, but I cannot say the same for GoDaddy.

Another advantage of www.1and1.com is that you can have almost unlimited free emails for each domain name, if you choose the business option.

However, for WordPress sites, I have come across some problems with www.1and1.com, and therefore www.godaddy.com is recommended if you are planning to use WordPress.

To help you get started with hosting your website, here is a look at some of the top hosting companies. While you are free to do your own research, most consumer articles and hosting review websites stand by these hosting companies and the services that they provide their customers.

Below, you will find the name of the hosting company, the starting price of their basic hosting packages and information on what they have to offer. When possible, the rates are for regular terms and are not promotional pricing. Therefore, when you visit the hosting company, you may be able to get started at a lower price than what is shown here. These are not listed in any particular order.

I use these three hosting companies and can recommend them all.

a) Host Gator

www.hostgator.com: Offering 24/7 tech support, Host Gator is among the top hosting companies today. They offer unlimited e-mail addresses, bandwidth and disk space. They also provide free shopping cart software, message forums, membership scripts, photo galleries, site building tools and thousands of website templates. For a little bit more money, you can get unlimited domains. £6.50/$10.36 per month.

b) Go Daddy

www.godaddy.com: Despite their promotional advertising, their uptime isn't nearly as good as you could find elsewhere. However, for many, it's a deal breaker, as they offer e-mail forwards, photo galleries, forums, blogging and add-on/pre-installed software apps. £5.99/$9.56 per month.

c) 1and1

www.1and1.com or www.1and1.co.uk:1and1 is a very well-established name in the web hosting industry—and for good reason. They offer several different shared hosting packages, starting at £3.13/$4.99, and even offer virtual and dedicated web servers for larger businesses. Lower packages have restrictions on web space, e-mail accounts and SQL databases, but for a little bit more at £6.27/$9.99, you can get everything unlimited. If you choose the second- or third-level package, you'll get your domain name for free in addition to unlimited web space! Offering a user-friendly interface, 1and1 offers quality customer support, a wide selection of services, products, tools and features, as well as a professional website builder.

With 1and1 you don't pay for your email addresses.

The aforementioned hosting companies are some of the best in the industry. However, just because they are the best doesn't mean that they'll be right for you. If you've gone through the ones listed above and haven't really found a good fit for you and your drop shipping business, that's okay. But you'll need to do your own homework to find the right one, as a hosting provider is the foundation of your business, so you need to make sure it is strong.

Note: always choose unlimited bandwidth and unlimited disk space. I always choose the most expensive hosting plan to make sure all I need is included.

Chapter 12 - Your Website.

OK, you've decided on which eCommerce software you are going to use; it's time to talk about your website. An online shop needs to be attractively designed and easy to navigate for success. On top of that, you have to make sure customers can find your shop in the web's vast shopping environment.

1) Setting up your personal website

Designing your website is not easy, but it is crucially important for your success. In the first seven seconds, customers will decide to leave your site or start browsing.

Your website has to:

- Convert well: this means that people have to buy from you.

- Give customers the trust to buy from you.

- Capture customer information for future promotions to these customers, even if the customers have not bought anything when they leave your site.

- Have most of the important information, e.g. who you are, what you do, what you sell visible as soon as your customer visits your site.

- Give great customer service.

- Meet all the legislation in your country re:selling online.

- Represent your brand well.

- Be appealing so customers will come back.

- Be easy to share with social media buttons.

- Have clear Buy buttons.

343

- Easy for the customer to check out (not seven pages to fill in).

- SELL your products.

a) Who will design it?

A website can be set up a few different ways. Of course, you can do it yourself, but listed below are a few other options. If you do it yourself, you can use shopping cart software or WordPress, which also has some good plug-ins for running shops:

- www.woothemes.com

- I also like Room09 from www.themeforest.net

First of all, have a look how NOT to design a website:

www.webpagesthatsuck.com: make sure you are never listed on this site.

I believe that to outsource, you have to know yourself how to do it, otherwise you cannot check the work your outsourcer has done. I used to build my own websites, and only after I knew how it all worked did I start to outsource it all.

You can outsource the design. I always use www.elance.com for my outsourcing requirements, but there are plenty of good outsourcing websites. Here are just a few:

- www.guru.com

- www.odeskresources.com

- www.peopleperhour.com

- www.vworker.com

- www.freelancer.com

Things to know if you will outsource the development of your site:

- Choose ONE person rather than a design team. That way, only one person will work on your site.

- Make sure they are EXPERIENCED in designing online shops.

- Communication is essential. Your designer has to understand extremely well what you have in mind.

- Agree on a time scale for the development.

- Don't pay a lot in advance, only a very small sum, e.g. £31/$50 or so. Only pay when the job is completely finished, checked and tested.

- Make sure YOU are in control once the development is finished. The designer may have to show you how to do videos, how to change things on the site, etc.

- Sign an agreement or intellectual property right to make sure that the designer understands the website is 100% YOURS.

- ALWAYS, ALWAYS do the hosting yourself, not the designer!

- Don't trust anyone unless they have proven they can be trusted. Something I practice everywhere I go.

- Make sure your site will be developed in well-known computer language, not some Zulu-designed software.

- Check out his/her references and reviews.

- Never give the job to the cheapest bids.

- Make sure he/she uses a platform for your online shop that is easy for you to use.

- Ask for examples of his/her previous work.

Using a Professional

Let's assume that you don't have a clue about web design and are going to need the help of a professional. Unfortunately, web design by a professional web designer is going to cost a few thousand bucks that you probably don't have to throw around. Of course, your web designer, upon request, may show you some basic tasks so that you don't always have to contact them in the future for adding/removing content/products.

Using a Student

If you want to go the professional route, but would like to save some money, you might consider finding a college student studying web design that needs to make some extra money. Since they have no degree, they'll generally work for a lower cost. It's easier than you think to find a student—just put a quick post on www.Craigslist.com and you'll be amazed at the response that you'll receive.

Using a Template

You have another option, though, which will be even cheaper. You can opt to use a template to design your business website. Most quality eCommerce software packages offer you templates you can use. The good thing about using a template is that they are generally very easy to customise and are pretty cheap to come by. In fact, you may be able to find some for free on the web or through your hosting service. Templates are simple to update or alter when needed.

However, the downside to templates is that you have to try and make them NOT look like a template. See, other people use templates, too, which means that your customer could come to your site after visiting another site and realise that it is the exact same design. While some customers may not care, many will be turned off by this and do their business elsewhere.

So, if you decide to use a template, just take the time out of your busy day to customise the template as much as you can so that it is as unique and distinctive as possible.

One thing you need to be certain of when choosing a template and before you start customizing it is that it fits your needs. If you need drop down menus, make sure they are on there or that you can easily add them. The same goes for other features, such as a search bar and a shopping cart that allows use of more than one drop shipper. Just keep in mind that all templates are not the same, as they have different features. Choose one that meets your needs and make sure it is appropriate before you begin customizing it.

b) Purchasing your domain

If you are searching for an already developed site, you can buy ready-made drop shipping sites on www.flippa.com (put "drop shipping" in the search box). Flippa is a website where you can buy and sell ready-made websites. Be warned as transferring the site, after you've bought it, becomes a bit technical. You'll have to tell the seller of the site that complete transfer has to be included in the price before you release the funds. You will have to give the seller the login details of your hosting account, but you can create a special login for him/her so you don't need to give access to all the information in your hosting company.

Once you've made a decision as to which hosting company you'll use, you need to purchase a domain name. Your domain name is the URL address that someone will type in to reach your website. The choice is yours, of course, as to what domain you will choose but there are a number of things that you need to take into consideration when choosing your domain name. After all, it is what will represent your company and can be a very potent marketing tool. Your domain needs to be strong and evocative, as it is the first thing your customers will notice about your business. At the same time, it needs to be easy to remember.

At this point you should have chosen your niche and have a list of the keywords you're going to target (both the small easy ones and the slightly harder ones). Before you can start developing your site, you need to get a domain name and hosting.

A domain name is very important. The domain name www.insurance.com was sold for 35.6 million dollars. This was only for the domain name, not for the content of the site. *Source: www.enbeeone3.com*

Here are some tips regarding the choice of your domain name.

1. ALWAYS, ALWAYS get a domain name with the keyword in it that you want to target. This is VERY important for ranking purposes. Everybody likes their own name (almost everybody) or the name of their company, but calling a website www.JohnSmith.com or www.SmithAssociates.com if your site is about furniture does

not give Google any clues that your site is about furniture. Your domain name is one of the first things Google looks at to rank your site.

- When possible, you want your domain name and business name to be as close to the same as possible. In other words, if your business is called "Kitty Central", you want to try to get the domain name "www.kittycentral.com".

- However, for SEO purposes, if it is possible, it is always best to put a keyword in your domain name, e.g. if you only sell purple clothing, choose the domain name www.purpleclothing.com.

- As a general rule, you don't want to use acronyms for your domain name. They aren't easy to remember nor are they descriptive. Plus, they don't use a single keyword.

- I recommend that you buy your own domain name (not use a free one like yourkeyword@weebly.com). It is more professional and you have ownership and control if, say, you want to sell it.

- Put your keyword or key phrase at the beginning of the domain name, not at the end. If you keyword is "dog food in bulk" www.bulkfoodfordogs.com is an okay domain name. But this one is a much better one: www.dogfoodinbulk.com

- Domain names with model numbers in them are a good idea if there are enough searches for a certain model number, e.g. www.Hobie16Catamaran.com or www.RemoteControlHelicopters107g.com, etc...

S107G is a model number for a remote control helicopter. By using the plural helicopters in the domain name, Google will see it as helicopters **and** as the model number S107G. If the domain name would have been www.S107GRemoteControlHelicopter.com, the domain name would not rank so well for helicopters (plural) as a keyword. The important message to remember here is: always try and put as many keywords as possible in your domain name.

- Whatever domain name you choose, always check out the legalities. Some, such as Twitter, Facebook, Apple, iPad, iPod and Olympic are trademarks and cannot be used in your domain name. You don't want to spend a lot of time building a website only to have to take it down later due to trademark infringement. You can search for "keyword+brandprotection" or "keyword+registered trademarks" to find out more information.

- You could even use commonly misspelled words as domain names.

- It is always best to buy the .com or .uk or .org domain names (or the extension of whatever country you are in) ahead of .net domain names. I suggest that you don't buy extensions like .biz or .us or .info, as these are used a lot by spam websites, so search engines and visitors often ignore them.

Did you know you can also buy domain names with these extensions: .coop, .jobs, .travel, .mobi, .mil, .tel, .pro, etc?

If you have a shop that only supplies goods in your country, or you have a site that only supplies services in your country, it is best to have a domain suffix from your country, such as .co.uk or .fr or .nl.

- Avoid hyphens, symbols or dashes. However, if your keyword is not available without hyphens, it is better to buy a domain name with hyphens than to have no keyword in the domain. One reason I try to avoid hyphens is when somebody types in your domain and forgets to type the hyphens, they will go to your competitor's sites. Another reason is that Google will probably think that the domain name without hyphens is older, as domains with hyphens only started to appear when the domains without hyphens were already taken.

- Make it easy to remember.

- Make it easy to understand—people should never have to think about how to spell your domain name.

- Make it easy to say in your head and anybody else's head.

- If possible, make it easy to understand and read for the non-English or non-American people who visit your site.

- Make sure you don't make your domain name too long, such as www. howtolooseweightreallyfastandeasy.com.

- Make it easy to read in the browser bar. Letters l and i next to each other are difficult to read: ilillili. So are the letters m, n and r: mrnmrn. A vowel at the end of a word and at the beginning of the next word is often difficult to read.

- Definitely avoid double "e" e.g. www.largeenamellockets.com

- Avoid two letters the same next to each other. If someone forgets to type in one letter, they might end up on your competitor's site and never get to yours. Sometimes two letters the same next to each other also makes it difficult to read. I usually type my domain names in Microsoft Word and underline them. That way, you can see how people see it when it appears underlined as a link and decide if it is easy to read.

- Make sure that you choose "auto renew" when buying a domain name. Otherwise, if you don't pay attention at renewal time and forget to renew it, it could be gone. You should get an e-mail as a reminder for renewal, but just in case you miss the email, your domain name will still be renewed.

- If the main keywords are already taken as a domain name and you want to use "guide" or "training" after your keyword and that is also taken, use a similar word. I suggest you type in "guide" and "training" in the online thesaurus to see which other words you could use.

- If you can afford it, buy the plural of your domain name as well and/or common misspellings. This will catch customers who make a mistake, so they still end up on your website instead of your competitor's.

If you are not very creative and need some help, visit www.squadhelp.com to receive 200+ suggestions for your domain, for a small fee.

If you still aren't sure where to go with this, enlist the help of your family and friends. Give them your online business name and ask them what they think your domain name should be. You should try to create a name that is easy to spell and doesn't contain words that are commonly misspelled, as this could result in potential customers visiting a website other than your own.

You can also use software like www.marketsamurai.com or www.longtailpro.com to do keyword research, which can help you decide on a domain name. I explain Market Samurai in detail in my book "From Newbie To Millionaire".

350

The process of choosing your business name as well as a domain name for your business website can be long, overwhelming and tedious; however, it is an incredibly important aspect of marketing, branding and SEO. Therefore, it is important to brainstorm ideas and not just use the very first idea that comes to mind.

The price of a domain name can vary and depends on the extensions (.com, .co.uk, etc.), but usually is between £ 5.99/$9.70 and £9.99/$15.99 per year.

I always buy my domain names with the company who I choose for my hosting:

- www.godaddy.com

- www.1and1.com

- www.hostgator.com

However, there are plenty of other places to buy domain names.

c) *Important things to know when designing a website*

Regardless of whether you choose a professional, a student or a template to create your website, there are plenty of decisions to be made regarding the website layout and the visual appeal of the site. An attractive website is important, but don't let that take so much of your time that you forget to make sure your site is easy to navigate, as this is also of the utmost importance. Visitors will go elsewhere if they find your site too difficult to use. If your site is unprofessional looking or unattractive, they may not purchase from you.

Here are the factors that will influence the credibility of your website; numbers below represent the percentage of people saying that that particular factor is important.

Factor	Percentage of People
Design Look	46.00%
Information design/structure	28.50%
Information focus	25.10%
Company motive	15.50%
Information usefullness	14.80%
Information accuracy	14.30%
Name recognition/reputation	14.10%
Advertising on the site	13.80%
Information bias	11.60%
Writing tone	9.00%
Identy of site operator	8.80%
Site functionallity	8.60%
Customer service	6.40%
Past experience	4.60%
Information clarity	3.70%
Readability	3.60%
Performance on test	3.60%
Affiliations	3.40%

Source : Fogg / www.itu.dk

Perfecting the aesthetics of your website can be difficult and time-consuming. However, you can make things a little bit easier on yourself by checking out other comparable websites to see how they appeal to you as a web visitor. This can give you a lot of insight as to what you can do to your site to make it appeal to visitors.

You will notice that you are drawn to websites that use simple and bold colors and graphics to create their visual appeal and impression of professionalism. During your search, you will also come across sites that make you want to turn your head. When you find these, jot down what turns you away so that you can make sure that you don't do anything of the sort when it comes to designing your website.

We've spoken about the layout and appearance of your site, so now, it's time to get to the nitty gritty and talk technical stuff. I know, it's the last thing you want to talk about, but I'll try to make it as easy as possible to understand. This is information that you need to know so that you can make sure your site is designed efficiently.

You want a website design that will appeal to your visitor, to draw them in and encourage them to visit subsequent pages. You want a design that is efficient yet sleek and intoxicating, in a sense.

I am not going to go too deep into discussing web design, as that could take up an entire book all by itself. There are, however, a few important things that you should remember when designing your site. Here are my top design rules:

1. Navigation should be easy. Remember, you probably aren't a tech wizard, and neither are some of your customers. When designing your site, pretend that it is for a child—like an eight-year-old. If a potential shopper is on your website, browsing around, they want to be able to easily find what they are looking for. When they can't, they'll leave your site and find another one that's easier to use and understand to make their purchase. You'll be left in the dust without being given a second thought. Make sure all your information is easily accessible (homepage toolbar is always a good place to start). Information should include, but not be limited to: Shipping prices, Contact information and Products.

Make sure your site has a search bar at the top of the page (I sometimes put my search bar on the left), not just on your homepage, but on every page of your website. Many customers like to type in what they want instead of scouring your site for it, so having this readily available for potential customers will result in more sales.

2. Use graphics sparingly. Using graphics sparingly is certainly not easy for an online shop, as each product needs a picture. Not everyone has a broadband connection yet! Graphics (such as pictures and charts) take a long time to load. If you use heavy graphics that take a long time to load, you can lose one third of your potential customers because they will lose patience and move to another site. This is never easy: make the pictures too big and they load slow, make them too small and they will not look nice on your website. Google the subject to find out more information; search for "what is best resolution for pictures on a website" or something similar. Most software programs now have the option "save for web" to save a picture, ideal for use in an online shop.

Most ecommerce sites now will automatically convert your product image to the perfect size for their website, so you don't need to worry about your product images, but you do for all your other images on your site.

Don't make your pictures higher than 72 dpi (dots per inch), or your website will load too slowly. 72 dpi is the ideal for photos on the web.

3. Avoid using moving images and streaming video. These can also seriously limit the speed at which your website loads. These slow loading times can cause visitors to leave your site before they've even read any of your content.

You can check the speed of your website with YSLOW from Yahoo! Yslow analyzes web pages and suggests ways to improve their performance. For more information go to http://developer.yahoo.com/yslow/.

4. Simple is better. Simple is ALWAYS better! While you may want to get as much on your site as possible, even if it means cramming it all together, it makes the site look awful and often results in the customer never making it past the homepage. But, then again, they've seen everything there is to see because you've crammed it all on one page, from your contact information and shipping prices to product images, advertisements and blog extracts.

If you don't want to convert visitors into sales, then by all means, cram as much as you can on your homepage. It's the best way to steer them away. But this isn't what you want.

You want to design a simple and attractive homepage. Your homepage should clearly state your business purpose while offering a sweet and short roadmap to your site. Even if you don't do the latter, make sure that your site is simple and to the point while being appealing to the eye.

5. Creativity gets a thumbs up – but don't go too far. Creativity is how you will stand out from the rest of your competition. However, you can go too far with it, which is the last thing you want. You want a website that is unique and visually appealing, but there are some things that you shouldn't aim for. For example, shoppers are typically accustomed to having a tool bar at the top of the page, search bar in either the upper right-hand or left-hand corner, contact information at the bottom of the page, etc. When you get too creative with your web design layout, your website may become confusing, ultimately causing you to lose sales.

6. Nobody likes side scrolling. Keep your website suitable for 1366 x 768 screen dimensions, and you'll ensure that over 90% of people can see all of your content without annoying side-scroll bars. 1024 x 768 screen used to be the best dimensions, but in 2013 this changed to 1366 x 768. If you go any larger than that, there will be visitors who have to scroll left and right. You will be able to set your screen size in your web design software.

7. A word about colours. While it's true that having a clean and simple website is important, you need to consider other aesthetics of your site as well. Think of your target audience and consider the product(s) that you are selling, and then decide the graphics, colours and fonts that you believe would appeal to them while creating an image for your products and your business as a whole.

Let's do an example to help you understand a little bit better. Your customers will likely get excited with some vividly bright and bold colors; however, if you are selling spa items, then you may want some soothing, pastel colors, as bold colors wouldn't fit well. If you are drop shipping baby items, you'll also want to consider pastel colors or primary colors, as well as really cute baby graphics.

While themes are great, don't go over the top with them. Try to limit your design to no more than three main colors, and make sure each one of them complements the others. Research shows that blue is one of the most popular colors to use for commercial websites. Why? Blue supposedly signifies freedom, professionalism, security and intelligence. However, if you are selling sweet stuff, you'll want to avoid blue, as it is known to suppress appetite. Other colours to note and what they stand for:

- Green represents relaxation and wealth.

- Red denotes strength, energy and passion—it's a good one for men.

- Purple indicates luxury and sophistication. Purple is also known as the colour of the independent woman!

- Black represents elegance and authority as well as drama.

Keep in mind that if you use trendy colours, you'll need to update your site should those colours go out of style. You also want to remember that colours mean different things in other countries, so if you are selling internationally, make certain that you are careful with the colours you use. The colour of serenity and purity for those in the United States represents death and sorrow in a number of Eastern countries. So, just be careful.

Don't use lots of colours on your site or non-matching colours. Below is a chart that interior designers use. The same rules for interior design apply for websites: it all has to be pleasing to the eye and have a cosy and comfortable feel. The rule from the wheel below is: opposite colours are complementary colours. Colours that are next to each other should never be seen together. Google "colour chart" to see the colour wheel.

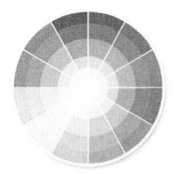

8. A logo or banner is worth your money. Essentially your virtual thumbprint, your logo or banner defines your business and your website. Your logo condenses what you provide on your website, and who you are, into one memorable yet simple design. You can design a logo on your own if you wish to tackle it, as there are numerous tutorials online that will help you learn how to design your own logo. Or you can choose to have a professional graphic designer create a business logo for you, which will cost anywhere from £31/$50 to £310/$500, depending on where you find the graphic designer and how much experience the individual has.

A logo is incredibly important, especially if you plan on expanding operations in the future. But, even so, a logo is important even if you are just starting your drop shipping business and have no plans of expanding in the future.

Your logo needs to be attractive and recognizable, but at the same time, it needs to be readable and understandable. You don't want some crazy design script that someone isn't going to be able to properly decipher. Ultimately, your logo should be basic—your company name with some type of symbol or picture.

Your logo can be used for more than just representing your company on your website, as it is can also be used on stationary, letterheads, brochures, etc. Keep in mind that the simpler a logo is, the cheaper printing will be, as a one-colour logo will be cheaper to print than a three-colour logo.

If you're not good at creating your own images and logos, then here are some places where you can get someone else to do them for you:

www.elance.com

www.20dollarbanner.com Get any website banner done for just £12.50/$20

www.kuler.com Free Adobe-recommended colour pairs and templates for design

www.designgururyan.com A great graphic designer

www.99designs.com People compete to design your logo or website, driving the price down and getting you a serious bargain

9. Formatting. Ensure that your website is formatted so that it can be viewed on all the different, yet common web browsers. These include Internet Explorer, Google Chrome, Mozilla Firefox, Opera, Safari, etc. You can't expect a new visitor to download a brand-new browser to their computer just so they can view your website. They'll find a website that has already tailored to them and is properly formatted for viewing on their current browser.

Perhaps you didn't know that there are different Internet browsers? Years ago I didn't either, but not everybody uses the same one. Wikipedia defines Internet browser like this: *A web browser is a software application for retrieving, presenting, and traversing information resources on the World Wide Web. An information resource is identified by a Uniform Resource Identifier (URI) and may be a web page, image, video, or other piece of content.*

If you do not want to download the browsers, ask a friend with a different browser to look at your site, but as a serious Internet marketer, you should download them all yourself. You will lose potential customers if your website does not view properly with Firefox or other browsers. Not all your visitors use Internet Explorer. You can easily switch between the different browsers, so you can use the one you prefer most of the time. But when you need to test your new site, you can look at it using the five main browsers.

www.browsershots.org gives a lot of information about different browsers.

10. Under construction. Never, and I mean, never, use the "Under Construction" term anywhere on your website. Don't even use it if it really is under construction. This represents to your customers that the website isn't finished, and who really wants to visit or buy from a site that is still under construction? Sites generally stay in the "Under Construction" mode for months, if not years, so it's unlikely that visitors will come back to your site often to check and see if that section of your site is up and running yet. Plus, some search engines, such as Yahoo, for example, will reject your site and will not list it in search results if a page has "Under Construction" on it.

11. Background music. Should you have background music? Most people don't like it, although there are a select few out there who would love it. The problem is that you could play metal music and cause visitors to leave your site because they don't like that type of music. The same is true with hip-hop, country or classical. Music genres are loved and hated, and it's impossible to know what each and every one of your customers is going to like, so it's better to steer clear of background music, which can often be more annoying than anything else.

Consider this: what if your customer is on the phone and browsing the web at the same time. They have their speakers on because they were listening to music a little while ago and forgot to turn them down when they got on the phone. They are surfing the web and come across your site, click on it and get blasted with roaring music. This unexpected sound is definitely unwelcome by the customer and will result in them closing your site. More than likely, they won't venture back to it. So, it's better to opt out of background music.

> If you DO put music on your site, you MUST clearly display where the visitor can turn the music on or off.

Make sure that you use royalty-free music, or you'll have to pay for the rights.

For royalty free music clips:

www.royaltyfreemusic.com

www.shockwave-sound.com

www.slicktracks.com

13. Pop-up boxes. Pop-up boxes are the boxes that appear on a website, usually rising from the bottom of the page, where you are asked to fill in your email to receive further information or to receive something free.

These are a BIG no! Sure, they may gain some sales here and there, but honestly, they are more annoying than helpful in gaining sales. They seem desperate and are often obnoxious when it comes to context. All in all, it's just better not to use them.

If you DO use pop-up boxes, use them when a visitor leaves your site without buying anything. You could offer a discount voucher or a free gift. That way, your customer will be on your list. It is better to use a subtle opt-in box than one with lots of colours.

14. Use simple fonts. Always use simple fonts that are easy to read. Don't use some drastic font just because it looks good, as it may not be easily readable, which will cause customers to leave your site. If you use unusual fonts and your visitor does not have that font on their computer, they will not be able to read the text very well.

Sans serif fonts are easier to read on a computer screen, while serif fonts are easier to read in a physical book, therefore sans serif fonts are best for use on websites.

Millionaire = Serif font = more rounded letters and curls

Millionaire = Sans Serif Font = simple letters, no decorative letters.

The best fonts for the web are:

- Arial

- Calibri

- Verdana

- Tahoma

The above-mentioned fonts are simple, professional and easy to read. If your favourite font is easy to read and doesn't have some crazy cursive or obscure approach, then by all means, use it. Just make sure it is easy to read, professional and simple. By choosing a popular, plain and simple font, it will load faster for visitors and you are guaranteed that they'll see it properly as opposed to an obscure font that many aren't even aware of, resulting in the inability to view the text on your website. Nothing is a bigger turn off for a customer than not being able to read a website. You've lost your sale immediately.

15. Your font size should be minimum 12pt. Remember that your visitors can be of all ages and older people often even find size 12 a bit too small to read. Some analysts say that font size 14pt is better. Try it and test it.

16. Flash ain't cash! Don't use Flash elements. Flash (Adobe Flash) is a multimedia platform for creating animation, video and activity on web pages. It is very often used for advertisements and games. Google can't understand Flash and so won't know what your website is about. This will be a real problem when you start trying to get on page one of the search results. A person who does not have Adobe Flash Player installed will not be able to see your site. Although sometimes Flash can look great, flashing elements can put people off.

Don't build a website full of pop-ups, flashing images and moving graphics. Research has shown that people immediately leave sites like these and, on top of that, Google cannot see fancy stuff on your site, so it is better to use the space for content and targeted keywords.

17. KISS. Remember to KISS, which stands for: Keep It Simple, Stupid. Ugly and earning money is better than beautiful and earning nothing. The key to web design is simplicity, not sophistication and overload. Don't try to look like an Internet giant; instead, focus on what makes you money.

18. Low resolution videos. If you do use videos on your website, make sure that you use low resolution ones as otherwise they will take too long to load. You can use www.handbrake.fr to convert videos.

19. Be clear. Your visitors must see in **the first few seconds** what the site is all about.

20. The 'above the fold' screen. The above the fold screen is what the visitor can see when they first open your site, without having to scroll up or down. When a visitor scrolls down, they are then looking "below the fold". The first screen visitors see is your website's prime selling space, and what you put on it can determine your success. Don't make it "overcrowded".

21. Put the opt-in box above the fold. Important headlines should always be above the fold. I also recommend putting an opt-in box above the fold if it is important for you to get people on your mailing list.

 22. Make sure a link is a link. Only underline text if it is a link. Don't underline to emphasise text, otherwise people might not click your money-making links. Make sure that a visitor can clearly see what is clickable and what isn't. The standard is to underline clickable links. You could change the colour of the links, too.

23. Leave enough white space on each page. Pages that look too busy are abandoned very quickly, and your chance of making money is gone.

24. Don't put thousands of words of text without any sub headers. Use sub headers and bullet points wherever possible. Visitors will not read every word on your site, but they will scan through it and read what interests them.

25. Text must be easy to read. No green text on a green and red floral background, please.

26. No white text on black background. Research has shown that a lot of people do not like white text on a dark-coloured background. Older people especially and people with impaired vision find it hard to read. Stick to black text on a white background, as people are used to reading it. There is a reason why big sites, e.g. Amazon, Ebay, Google, Youtube, etc. are just white background and mainly black text. Amazon and Ebay's websites have been unchanged for over a decade, and no one seems to mind. Why do they not change anything? Well, simply because it works well as it is. Why change something that works?

27. No welcome/intro/splash pages. I have never understood why somebody would want intro pages on their site. They say "enter". Yes, of course I want to see your site, that's why I clicked on it. Duh!

28. Check your content for spelling mistakes. Get friends to proofread it, as you are unlikely to see your own mistakes.

29. Include lots of internal links. Have links to your other pages at the top, left and bottom of the page because Google likes this. Learn more about this in my book "From Newbie To Millionaire".

30. Make sure that ALL the pictures, music and videos that you use are royalty free. There are institutions out there who only try to find websites that use non-royalty free products. You might get a letter in the post one day with a heavy fine if you do not abide by the royalty-free rules. The consequences could be huge and result in a lawsuit.

For that reason, you should always either buy stock photos or stock images, or make sure you use images that are under the Commercial Commons license (i.e. royalty free). Stock images are pictures on stock photo websites to be used or bought by other people. Usually you are required to provide a link to the source where you got the picture from, but read the terms and conditions of the site.

Use these sites for royalty free photographs and videos:

- www.sxc.hu The images under "results for" are free to use and royalty free. The images under "Premium results for" are payable.

- www.gettyimages.com They have a HUGE range of stock photos you can buy, but can be expensive.

- www.dreamstime.com

- www.bigstockphoto.com

- www.fotalia.com

- www.istockphoto.com

- www.publicdomainpictures.net

- www.shutterstock.com

- www.flickr.com

31. Photograph of yourself or not. A photograph of yourself on your site lets people know that you are a real person. If you don't like your own photograph, you can always create an avatar:

www.sitepal.com

www.cartoonyourworld.com

www.mywebface.com

32. Make your site trustworthy with security images. You can have the best-looking site out there, but if you don't have that image of security that customers need to see in order to hand over their credit card to you, you will lose sales.

Third-party Security Icons: This is one of the easiest and quickest ways to build that image of security and let your customers know that your site is safe to shop at. Companies such as TRUSTe will review your website. They have security standards that they follow, and if your site meets those, they will give you permission for your site to hold their icon.

You must have a legitimate website with genuine, justifiable security measures.

Security sites, such as TRUSTe, say that when their icon is posted to a website, the site's sales increase anywhere from 7 to 12 percent. If this works out for your site, then it is well worth the money that you spend to retain their permission to display their icon.

More about this can be found under "Keeping your website secure".

33. Limit your ads, concentrate on direct content. The more advertisements and irrelevant links that your site has, the more your potential customer will realise that your income is coming from affiliate links and ads rather than a quality product. Web users know what a real retail store looks like, and it isn't one covered in ads. Therefore, your content needs to be competent, direct and free of mistakes (spelling and grammar, namely). Sloppy content indicates amateurism, and most customers don't want to deal with amateurs.

Conclusion: A website must look and feel good for the visitor. The visitor must immediately have a good impression when landing on your site.

> **Remember: You never have a second chance to make a first good impression!**

d) Must have elements on your site.

Building a website is like a car: there are big cars, small cars, flash cars, posh cars, colourful cars, cars with no gadgets, cars with a lot of gadgets, nice cars, ugly cars, etc… BUT they all have one thing in common and without it, the car will not drive: they have a motor, which is an essential part of a car. A website without decent SEO and other crucial elements is like a car without a motor: it won't work!

Here are the most important things your website must have to look and feel professional, and to increase your chances of ranking for search engines. Of course SEO is the most important.

1. Disclaimer. Compulsory if you're running a site that has anything to do with health, earning money or contains information and products that could be potentially harmful.

You can download free legal policies for your website from www.seqlegal.com or search for it in Google.

2. Privacy policy. It's a good idea to have a privacy policy on your site.

3. Contact form. The minimum that should be on your contact form is your name and email address. It is better to also give your address and even phone number to create more credibility.

4. Terms of use. This is a contract that the user automatically agrees to by using your site. Make sure that all legalities not covered in the Disclaimer and Privacy Policy are included here.

5. Sitemap. A sitemap is a must-have if you want Google to accurately find all the elements on your site. Install the XML-Sitemap plugin from here or visit http://wordpress.org/extend/plugins/xml-sitemap-feed and it will be done for you. If you are not using WordPress, search for "HTML sitemap" in the help section of whatever web design software you use. Most eCommerce software has this feature built in, e.g. EkmPowershop.

6. Copyright policy. At the bottom of every page you should have: "Copyright 2014, All Rights Reserved". This helps protect your intellectual property from people who may wish to steal your content.

7. Guarantee or refund policy. If you are selling something, make sure that you always put a money-back guarantee on your website or a refund policy. The visitor will be more likely to buy when there is a money-back guarantee.

8. Testimonials (if applicable). It is important to have testimonials visible. Testimonials add social proof to your site and will help persuade your visitors into spending money on what you're offering.

Video testimonials are very effective.

If you put testimonials on your site, always put the full name and, if possible, the website from the person giving the testimonial. If possible, add a picture.

Unfortunately, testimonials are not always real (you can buy testimonials from www.fiverr.com). People get paid to do them. I am sorry if I have shocked you by saying this, but it is true. I suggest that you never use made-up, fake testimonials.

9. "About us" page. If possible, you should put a photograph of a person on the "about us" page. People want to know who they are buying from. If you say something about yourself and put a photograph on your page, you become a real person, which helps improve your credibility. After all, you don't buy just from "anybody" on the web, so compel your visitors to buy from you. Increase your chances by increasing your trustworthiness with an "about us" page.

It is estimated that 40% of your prospective customers will look at your "about us" page. Some people will make a buying decision based on what they read on this page, so it is a very important page on your site.

Putting a signature on your site also improves your credibility. You can create a signature at www.mylivesignature.com. It is free.

10. Home page. If the home page fails to tell what the site is all about, or what users can find on the site, people will leave the site more quickly.

11. Google Analytics. Google Analytics is a website statistics program that you can use for free. It is not visible to the visitor of your site. It tells you all sorts of detailed information about your site including:

Number of daily/weekly/monthly visitors

Your site's page views

Bounce Rate—when visitors leave your site without visiting another page

From which search engines your visitors came

What country your visitors are from

Which browser people use

Traffic sources

How long people stay on your site

How visitors found your site

Which keywords were used to land on your site

It's crucial to have this in place so you can see exactly how well your site's doing. It is best to put Google Analytics on EACH product page, so you can see which one of your pages no one ever visits.

You only have to sign up once and you can put Google Analytics on all your sites. The way it works is Google gives you a code, and you put that code on your website. Sign up and have a look at their tutorials: www.Google.com/analytics. It is completely free. There are some other good analytics tools available:

www.accesswatch.com - free

www.lyris.com - high-end, paid solution

www.extremetracking.com - free

www.statcounter.com - free

 www.webtrends.com - high-end, paid solution

Here is a screenshot from a Google Analytics page.

You can see where your visitors are coming from. The darker areas represent the most visitors, the lighter areas are the countries with the least visitors.

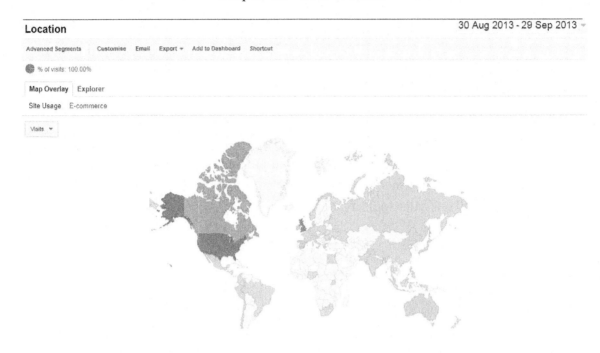

You can also see the number of visitors, how many unique visitors, how many new visitors, how long did they stay on your site, etc…

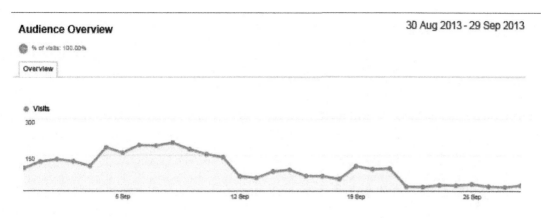

Audience Overview

30 Aug 2013 - 29 Sep 2013

% of visits: 100.00%

Overview

● Visits

300

150

| | 5 Sep | 12 Sep | 19 Sep | 26 Sep |

2,568 people visited this site

Visits	Unique Visitors	Pageviews	New Visitor ■ Returning Visitor
2,913	2,568	3,639	

Pages / Visit	Avg. Visit Duration	Bounce Rate
1.25	00:00:59	90.22%

% New Visits

86.68%

	Country/Territory	Visits	% Visits
1.	United States	1,004	34.47%
2.	United Kingdom	880	30.21%
3.	Canada	459	15.76%
4.	Spain	170	5.84%
5.	Netherlands	76	2.61%
6.	Australia	51	1.75%
7.	India	29	1.00%
8.	(not set)	29	1.00%
9.	Austria	19	0.65%
10.	Belgium	18	0.62%

12. Google Webmaster Tools

Google Webmaster Tools is a free service by Google for webmasters. It allows the webmaster to learn about the visibility for the site.

You or your webmaster have to add a sitemap to your site and submit it to Google. You can check broken links on your site, check which keywords has been indexed for your site, check which sites link to your site, etc...

I am not going into more detail, as I am sure you already have enough to absorb.

e) Why website content is so important

Content is text on your website related to your product; that is all that most people think content is, but it is much more than that and can be in all these formats:

- photos

- videos

- infographics or pictorial displays of data

- a blog post

 - pdf documents

All the above don't necessary have to be on your website. They can be somewhere else, e.g. YouTube, but referring back to your website.

In my book "From Newbie To Millionaire", there are over 40 pages all about content creation.

Valuable website content is a crucial aspect of Search Engine Optimization (SEO) as well as generating traffic, satisfying customers, building authority and trust, and customer retention. Valuable content on a specialised niche market website is 100 times more important than with a general website.

Those that are shopping in a niche market are passionate about it, which means they are on the prowl for more valuable information regarding the niche and are much more interested in developing a connection with you, the retailer. This includes reading and interacting with the site's blog or Facebook page.

Getting fresh content is not always easy and can be time consuming but is usually very important. However, my website www.micropigshed.com has NEVER had fresh content and has been on the first page in Google for over 3 years. Just shows that all you need is good SEO, regular visitors, unique content and low bounce rate. All the others methods mentioned in this book (and any other IM book) are to be implemented if your site does NOT rank well.

f) Know your conversion rates

Conversion rate is also called visitor-to-sales ratio.

A conversation rate is the number of visitors who have visited a product page on your website compared to the number of visitors who bought the product. To get your conversion rate, take the total number of visitors who have visited your page and divide that number by the total number of visitors who have bought the product that you sold on that page. Example: 100 people have visited your site and 1 person has bought something; that would be a conversation rate of 1%.

Some shopping carts can increase your conversion rate, which can make a HUGH difference in your sales. Let's look at an example:

You are selling a £31/$50 product and you have 10,000 visitors per month. If you have a 1 percent conversion rate (1000 x 1%), you have sold 100 products at £31/$50 = £3100/$5000.

If you could increase that conversion rate to 2%, you would sell 200 products at £31/$50 = £6200/$10,000, which is double the sales.

What is a good conversion rate?

Providing that you have set up the website really well as described in this book, with good SEO, good product descriptions, showing trust logos, etc., a conversion rate of 4% is generally accepted as good.

A conversion rate of 0.5% is not good and means you have work to do to increase it.

In a sales environment, there is the rule of 10: this means if you have 100 potential visitors, 10 will be REALLY interested and 1 will actually put in an order. This rule is used a lot by sales managers and their salespeople. If you are a REALLY good salesperson, you can convert up to 10 or even more.

Of course, it depends if the 100 that you started with are "targeted customers". If they are, it will be easier to get a 10% conversion.

Example: if you are trying to sell a boat to someone who is actually interested in buying a car, you are not talking to targeted customers.

On the other hand, if you had a stand at a boat show and you picked up 100 leads, these are targeted people and therefore they will be easier to sell to.

The same applies on the Internet. If you have put a keyword on a product that says "yellow shoes" and you are showing a picture of a red shoe with that keyword, the customer is unlikely to buy your shoes as he or she is not a targeted customer.

You can increase your conversions by:

- have a free shipping period

- send coupons

- have a good search tool

- display your best selling items

- display reviews - the good ones only of course.

2) Keeping your website secure

People like to see any of the above logos to show their money is protected.

People will always be skeptical when giving you their card details. How does the customer know that they are on a secure server?

Internet Explorer and Netscape have a security information pop up box that tells you that you are on an unsecured site when submitting information. In Internet Explorer and Netscape, customers will see a **locked** padlock in the browser bar when visiting a secure site.

A secure site will also show https in the browser bar instead of http, without the S.

Regardless of the reason you have started your own business and regardless of the type of website that you are going to be setting up and running, you are going to need to ensure that it is safe and secure. While web hosting services will provide plenty of security for you, as will other services that you'll need, there are still plenty of issues that could arise that may call for an extra layer of security. In order to maintain a proper level of security for your website, it is important that you enforce protocols and regulations to enhance your website's level of security. Below, you'll find a few threats that may or may not affect you that you should be aware of as you venture into the world of online business.

a) Credit Card information protection

If you are going to be selling products, which you are if you are running a drop shipping or eCommerce business, you'll need to make sure your customer's credit card information is safe once they input it into your website. There is generally an encryption service in place, which will usually come with your eCommerce software and/or payment processor; however, it never hurts to double-check this. The majority of websites will use VeriSign or TrustE as their primary provider of security protection, as they run SSL protection, which ensures that electronic criminals cannot read online transactions.

You are getting access to customer's credit card details if you are running an eCommerce site and/or charging the customer via a physical terminal. It is therefore your duty to protect the customer's card details as much as possible. I therefore recommend:

- Install Norton or a similar trustworthy anti-virus and security protection package. I always use Norton 360, which is the most professional package and includes protection of card details of customers. NEVER use the free ones, as they simply are not as good as the "official", well-established and well-known ones.

- Install spyware software on top of the anti-virus software. You also need anti-spy software. I use www.superantispyware.com. NEVER use the free ones, as they simply are not as good as the "official" ones.

- Always update your anti-virus and anti-spyware software.

- Make sure your payment gateway complies with PCI.

b) Understand you are at risk for hacking

It takes a lot of time and effort to get your website ready to go, so you would hate it if someone were able to hack into your site and ruin everything you've put together. The more visitors that you begin to have at your site, the higher the risk that you'll have people targeting you. There are some people out there that will do everything they can to take out their competition, so be careful and make sure that your site is secure so this doesn't happen to you.

WordPress is known for having sites hacked. So if you do use WordPress, make sure you put plugins on to protect your site from hackers.

c) *Implementing virtual firewalls*

Firewalls are the first step in protecting a computer and its contents. Your website should have a strong and reliable firewall in place the moment it goes live. As the first line of defense, firewalls can block attacks and ensure that same threat does not return again.

d) *Limit access*

Don't give a lot of people the ability to access your website admin dashboard. In fact, don't let anyone but yourself and your business partner, if you have one, do so. When a large number of people have admin access to your website, you are more at risk for a breach or things going wrong. Only one person has to change something minor in the settings by accident and the whole website can stop running smoothly, resulting in losing sales.

e) *Update software*

New versions of software are always being created by manufacturers, and this is one thing that you want to make sure you stay on top of. These updates are generally related to security vulnerabilities. Update your software regularly or you are at risk from these vulnerabilities.

f) *Change passwords*

You and anyone with admin access to your site need to update passwords on a regular basis. This helps you stay a step ahead of hackers, as they use key logger technology, which can create millions of password combinations in seconds. By changing things every now and then, you make it that much more difficult for them to actually gain access to your site.

Along with your web hosting company, you can keep your website safe and secure. It is possible to keep electronic criminals away, you just need to realise that you are at risk and understand the security measures that you can take to ensure your site's safety.

g) https

Make sure you have an https site, as previously discussed, providing your customers maximum security.

h) Use a Verification Code

The best payment processors will make certain that they offer you security protection, so that you and your customer have the peace of mind to do business online.

This is the text printed on the left hand side of the screenshot below: "Verified by Visa (VbV) and MasterCard SecurdeCode (MSC) often referred to as 3D Secure or Payment Authentication, are the latest fraud prevention initiatives launched by the card schemes as a more secure method for authenticating you, the cardholder, at the time of the transaction. Both schemes work in the same way - by using personal passwords, set by you, the cardholder, to add an extra layer of protection when you shop online"

The instructions that you see on the right hand side of the screenshot below are coming direct from your card issuing bank, e.g. Halifax, Natwest, etc,, and any information that you submit on these authentication screens are securely passed to your card issuing bank for them to approve the information given.

It will be an extra step for your customer to fill in before the order will be processed, but the vast majority of customer will be happy to do this as they know it gives them extra security.

This is what the customer will see if you use a payment processor that offers verification code as standard, without a charge:

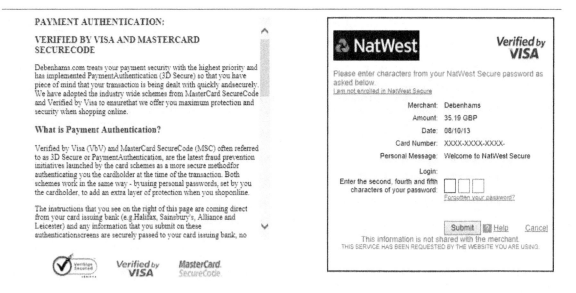

3) Google Trusted Stores Program

You can apply to the Google Trusted Stores Program, and if you are approved, you are allowed to use their logo on your site. This gives your customers an extra security, as it is pretty hard to get their approval. You need to be a merchant with a very high service score and you need to be an established store, processing lots of orders. The Google Trusted Stores on your website is a sign of trust between you and your customers, so your customers will have take comfort in knowing that their orders will ship on time and that any potential problems will be dealt with immediately.

4) Make some easy money with Adsense.

Many visitors to your site will leave without buying anything. You can still make money from these customers by putting Adsense on your site. When people click on one of the ads, you have made money.

Word of warning: as soon as your visitor clicks on any of the links, they are leaving your site. This applies for Adsense. You can put other money-making links on your site and set them up in a way that they open up in a new browser window when someone clicks on the link.

You could put the ads underneath the following text on your site: "You may also be interested in these sponsored links". Amazon also has sponsored links at the bottom of their site:

Sponsored Links

1. **Top-selling Liquorice**

2. **Every Kind Of Retro Sweet**

3. **Do you love liquorice?**

4. **Black Liquorice Company**

- What are Adsense and Adwords?

Google Adwords is the largest PPC (Pay per Click) network. Google has two different types of network: the search networks (Adwords) and the content networks (Adsense, now displayed as "AdChoices" or "Ads by Google"). As a default, Google places your ad on both networks. The search network is the one that you have probably seen often when searching with a keyword. The websites shown in the boxes below have paid for an Adwords campaign. In this case, the keywords "dog training" show these sponsored links when somebody searches for those keywords. When somebody clicks on the sponsored ad, the advertiser or the person who is running the *adword campaign has to pay Google money.*

Adwords look like this:

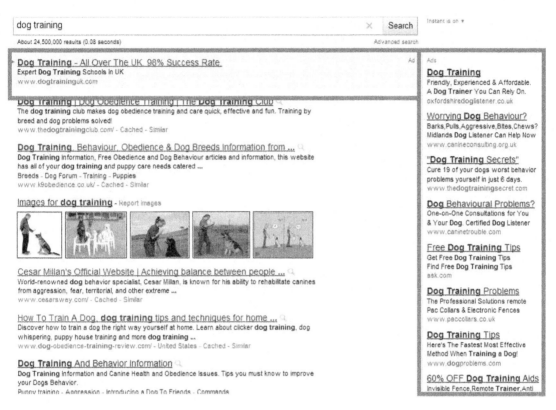

The content network places your ads on relevant websites. In other words, Google places ads and images automatically on the websites that have chosen for ads to be placed on their sites. When somebody clicks on those ads, *the website owner gets paid by Google.*

PPC is explained in detail in my book "From Newbie To Millionaire".

Adsense looks like this :

Put Your Website To Work
Making Money With Your Website Is Easy -
Find Out How & Sign Up!
www.Google.com/AdSense

The Widows Dating Site
Online Dating For Widows. Join Now To Meet
1000's Of Our Members
www.OnlineSeniorDates.com/Widows

Racing Pigeons Lofts Sale
Save on Racing Pigeons Lofts 100s of Shops
& 1000s of Brands
www.shop.com

Largest Pigeon Loft
Find Great Deals to Save Up To 50% On
Largest Pigeon Loft Here!
Largest-Pigeon-Loft.Best-Price.com

Ads by Google

Adwords = a website owner paying for his website to be shown in the searches. Each time somebody clicks, **the website owner pays Google** per click.

Adsense = a website owner decides that he wants Google to place relevant ads on his site. Each time somebody clicks the ads, **Google pays the website owner** per click.

If a website owner pays $1.00 per click for Adwords and opts for search networks **and** content networks, he can decide an amount he wants to pay for Adwords ($1.00) and a separate amount he wants for Adsense ($0.60).

5) Make some easy money with affiliate sales.

Find some affiliate products and put them on your site. You could put these links underneath the following text on your site: "You may also be interested in these links".

If your customers are not going to buy anything, you might as well try and earn something out of them.

Word of warning: websites with too many obvious links on to other products are often not liked by your visitors, so don't overdo it!

6) Make money with an exit page.

When your visitor leaves your site, you could put an exit page on. This is a page where customers can fill in their email address. That way, you can email those people with promotions or a newsletter, and they might visit your site again in the future. You can email them a discount voucher for the product they looked at.

This exit page will have to be set up by your webmaster or search for how to do it yourself.

The exit page could say something like this: "I am sorry to see you go, simply fill in your email address and I will email you a discount voucher."

These customers who fill in their email address with be added to your list and you can make money from them at a later stage, although they did not buy anything when they first visited your website.

Chapter 13 - eCommerce Website Templates.

1) What to look for in eCommerce website templates.

You want your first drop shipping business to be successful, and for that to happen, it must have a professional, high-quality website design. Unfortunately, it's highly unlikely you have the funds to cough up to pay for a custom web design, and that's okay. Instead, you can use a ready-made website template. You may find something that you fall in love with and never plan on changing—at least not in the near future. With that said, when you are scouring the web for website templates for your eCommerce web store, you want to consider a few things to ensure that the template can accompany your growth to avoid a template change or redesign in the future.

Here are four primary factors to consider when choosing a website template for your drop shipping website:

1. Flexibility. Ask yourself whether the template that you are eyeing will work for any niche or brand. Just starting out, you probably aren't sure where your business is going or what you really want out of it. However, if you want to keep a fun, youthful attitude, then make sure your template showcases this particular approach. The same is true if you want to keep a professional approach, in which case you would want to choose a more business-oriented template.

2. Scalability. Make sure that you choose a template that will still work with your online store when you decide to add lots of new products. Your template needs to be able to grow with you as you grow your store. So, while you may find a template that is suitable for your current setup, check that it will not limit you when business goes well and you need to expand.

3. Customisable. More than likely, you'll find plenty of templates that you really like, but there are just small things about them that you hate and you want to be able to change. By finding a template that you can customise, you can eliminate the areas that you dislike while keeping the bulk of the template intact. This goes for content, color schemes, logos, and more.

4. SEO-friendly. Because you are building a brand-new online store, you need as much SEO as you can—the easier you can achieve higher rankings in the search engines, the better. By opting for an SEO-friendly website template for your eCommerce site, which includes title and meta tags, you can rank better in all search engines for your targeted keywords.

While there's plenty more that you could look for when choosing your drop shipping website template, these four are the most important. Never forget these four as you search for a template, be it free, paid or within your drop shipping or eCommerce software solution. With the right template, you are priming your drop shipping site and brand for overall better sales performance now and in the future.

2) Finding quality drop shipping/eCommerce website templates

You may not have a lot of money to spend when starting your new venture. Sure, there are costs associated with your new drop shipping business, but at least you won't have to pre-purchase inventory and have somewhere to stock it until a customer orders. So, ultimately, that's free. And so is your website design—at least at first, if you want it to be. Utilizing free website templates can be extremely beneficial to you as you get your drop shipping business started. You won't have to spend a single penny for your web development. You may be able to obtain free templates that are included in the cost of your domain and web hosting or as part of your eCommerce software or drop shipping service package.

If you don't like the ones offered by your hosting, eCommerce or drop shipping provider, then you can utilise the Internet to find other options. You can find free website templates that are perfect for a drop shipping or eCommerce store all over the web. These will be discussed in this chapter.

a) Free store-specific templates

Here are a few different templates.

1. WordPress Plug-in – If you are using WordPress to power your site, you can download an eCommerce plug-in that is state of the art, with a primary focus on aesthetics and usability. It boasts social networking features as well as marketing features. You can find this one by visiting this link: www.instinct.co.nz

2. Prestashop – This is an open-source and professional shopping cart solution that is available for use at no charge. The sophisticated interface offers a variety of customisable themes. You can find this one by visiting: www.prestashop.com

3. All sorts of templates – On www.freewebsitetemplates.com you will find templates for Interior Design, Hairstyle Salon, Law Firm, Gardening, Hair Design, Pet Shop, Cake Shop, Shoe Store, Nightclub, etc... There are hundreds of websites here.

b) *More eCommerce drop shipping site templates*

Here is a link to a site called Blogger Mint. They created a post a while back highlighting 16 different templates that would make for an ideal website template for your drop shipping store. There are a variety of templates in this post, ensuring that there is just about something for everyone's preferences and taste.

Blogger Mint Post – www.bloggermint.com/2011/08/16-gorgeous-free-eCommerce-templates/

Now, here is a list of sites where you can find even more drop shipping/eCommerce website templates. Each of these sites offers quality templates, but make sure that before you try to upload one to your site that it is compatible with your current software. This is especially important if you are actually purchasing a template instead of finding one to use free of charge.

Here are a few places where you can find free eCommerce website templates that would work well with your drop shipping business:

- **Template Monster** – www.templatemonster.com

- **Quack It** – www.quackit.com/

- **Templates Box** – www.templatesbox.com

- **Free Website Templates** – www.freewebsitetemplates.com

c) Paid website templates

A few sites where you can find high-quality website templates that you have to pay for are as follows:

- **Square Space** – www.squarespace.com (free trial)

- **Template Mela** – www.templatemela.com

- **Ecommerce Templates** – www.ecommercetemplates.com

- **Template World** – www.templateworld.com

Don't forget to check that your template has to integrate with your drop shipper's feeds e.g. pictures, descriptions, etc...! However, you can also manually add each product.

Chapter 14 - Rising Above the Competition With SEO and Content.

1) What is SEO and the importance of SEO.

SEO = Search Engine Optimisation, or how to rank in Google by following certain rules.

SEO is very important in making sure that customers keep finding your shop and that you do not end up hidden on the fifth page of Google.

SEO is talked about a lot among webmasters because it is very important. For a newbie, it can be a bit confusing. SEO is not an exact science, and it will take you a considerable amount of time to create a site that is worthy of a good search engine ranking.

SEO is something that any new online business must familiarise themselves with. After all, when it's done correctly, it is your ticket to true online success. There are a few SEO tools online that you can gain access to for free or at a nominal fee—some of which are described in this book in brief.

While you don't have to be a complete expert at SEO to start building your website business, it will be extremely helpful if you are somewhat familiar with SEO and what it can do for you. Therefore, I strongly recommend at least reading the Beginner's Guide to SEO on www.moz.com before delving too deep into launching your business. You'll be amazed at how much it can help you build your site, research competition and market your site later on.

None of the SEO rules apply if you are planning to send traffic to your site with PPC ads or with social media. SEO is only important if you want Google to show your website when someone types in your keyword.

Before I start this SEO chapter, I have to tell you that I believe ranking in Google is overcomplicated by many people. I will give you some examples of my sites, where very basic SEO has been applied and these sites have been ranking on page one since I've published them, years ago. I have NEVER touched any of these sites as I believe in the following: "if something works, leave it alone". Panda or Penguin have never bothered me for the sites listed below.

The liquorice and the nougat sites listed below are also good examples that an ecommerce does NOT need to be very big to rank. Of course, I am not making £22,000/$35,000 per month from these sites, but they do give me a nice monthly income with little work.

The micro pig site is not a typical ecommerce site but was built with the only purpose of selling my book about micro pigs. Therefore, in a way, it is eCommerce, as I am selling something. This site creates an average of 350 book sales per month (eBook, hard copy and Kindle combined) and ranks in google.com as well as in google.co.uk

So here are three of my sites:

1) www.liquorice-licorice.co.uk I have intentionally built this site NOT to rank for the word liquorice on its own, as the competition was too large, but for the keywords listed below. The site is shown on page one in google.co.uk for all these keywords:

- Double salt liquorice
- Double salt liquorice UK
- Triple salt liquorice
- Triple salt liquorice UK
- Triple salted liquorice
- Pure hard liquorice sticks
- Pure liquorice
- Italian liquorice
- Italian liquorice sticks
- Liquorice for diabetics
- Dutch liquorice
- Belgian liquorice
- Buy liquorice online
- Buy liquorice
- Gelatine-free liquorice

- Sugar-free liquorice

Note: searches vary, therefore every day different websites are shown by Google.

Why did I choose that domain name? It is one of those words that is difficult to spell for some people. Some people will type in 'liquorice' and others will type in 'licorice'. Liquorice is the way it is spelled in the UK and licorice is the American way. I have used both in my domain name to rank for both markets, although the keywords that I have targeted are mostly intended for the UK market, as most of my customers are in the UK, but some UK customers will also search for "licorice".

2) www.nougat-nougat.co.uk This site ranks on the first page of Google for the following targeted keywords:

- Italian nougat cakes

- Belgian nougat

- Wedding nougat cakes

- Gelatine free nougat

- Nougat in bulk

This is a very small store but still has, on average, about 20 orders per month. Most people order enough for free delivery: £49/$82.

The total turnover for this site is approx. : £49 / $82 x 20 = £980 / $1640. With large profit margins, say 50% for ease of calculation, I still earn £490 / $820 per month from this store. Worth keeping as I never touch the store and my staff processes and ships the orders therefore no work for me at all.

3) www.micropigshed.com This site creates income from book sales and from Adsense and ranks on the first page for the following targeted keywords:

- Looking after a micro pig
- Micro pigs care
- Micro pig care
- Micro pig
- Micro pigs
- Caring for a micro pig
- Keeping micro pigs
- Micro pig diet
- How to keep micro pigs
- How to keep micro pigs as pets
- Micro pig food
- Micro pig food UK
- How big is a micro pig
- Micro pigs book

Well, I hope they are still ranking well when you are reading this book.

2) What does Google like and not like.

Let's first have a look at what Google does like to see.

If you have a look at the websites mentioned on the previous page, you will note that there are no videos on these sites, no reviews, no like buttons, no links, but they still rank. In my experience, the following is most important to rank in Google on the first page and stay there:

- Apply good, basic SEO.

- Use keywords that people actually type in! This might sound obvious, but I do very regularly come across sites that use "145zddk47" as an image tag! No way! Not if you understand SEO.

- Be in a market/niche where it is possible to beat your competition, after your research.

- Use keywords in the content. Example: page title has keyword salt liquorice, so all other tags and keywords on that page need to be salt liquorice.

- Have regular visitors, both unique visitors and repeat visitors

- Have a low bounce rate—a high bounce rate means that a visitor opens your site and immediately leaves the site. For Google, this is a red flag as Google will conclude that there is nothing interesting to see on your site, therefore it will not show it again if you have repeatedly high bounce rates.

Now this might look a little bit too simplified for a lot of readers and difficult to believe, but I have proof that it works: my liquorice site, my nougat site and my micro pig site.

- Valuable content is important for more than just satisfying your customers and complementing a sale, as it is the backbone of your SEO.

Ultimately, Google looks for quality backlinks, content, keywords, social media links and more. The process that Google utilises changes regularly, but it is a process that works to eliminate the numerous websites online that are spammy or have very poor content. Because of this, you need to understand what it is that will get your website considered as spammy.

Google does like links to high PR directories or sites.

So, here are a few things that you need to avoid and stay clear of to avoid Google not showing your site or even de-listing your site (never showing again).

- **Too Many Backlinks, Too Quickly**. Backlinks have always been considered as the thing that truly helps your website get high in rankings; however, if you have too many, especially low-quality ones, your website may actually suffer. So, it doesn't necessarily mean that you have too many links, but within the links that you have, there are too many that are low-quality, poor backlinks rather than high-quality, first-rate backlinks. One note: stay away from automated forum and blog comment programs, as these are the bad links that your site doesn't need to have.

- Poor Quality Content. When you have a blog or even when you are creating your website content, you should strive for at least 300-350 words per posted piece. Your blog will help keep your site freshly updated with brand-new content, which is something that the search engines—including Google—love. Stay on topic, be direct and keep the content concise while being informative and interesting. Never repeat topics. This is a great way to not only grow your business, but to connect with your customers as well.

- Poor Website Design and Layout. Poor designs will also have your site considered as spam by Google. You need a professional looking, easy to navigate and sleek interface that represents your business appropriately. It's okay to use free templates, but make sure it resonates well with your overall business and future goals. Your online website should be top notch when it comes to design and layout and should properly represent your business and what you are trying to convey to your customers. Remember, the design is likely to be what has your visitors staying on your site to shop or leaving to find a more eye-appealing site to shop on.

Here are some more things to avoid:

- Automated content

- Not enough content

- High bounce rate

- Paid links

- Excessive link exchanges

- Links to low quality directories or bookmark sites.

- Anything done by automation: content, links, articles, etc...

- Duplicate content

All in all, you need to focus on building your business's foundation and its future right from the start. By taking the time to create high-quality web and blog content, working to increase good backlinks and ensuring your site is easy on the eyes and simple to navigate from page to page, you should be good to go when Google's "spider" comes around checking out your website.

> **TOP TIP:** Most important: NEVER EVER EVER do anything automated on your site, e.g. automated articles, automated link building, automated website building (that will have the same duplicate content), automated video distribution, automated Facebook likes, etc. This applies for ANY site, not just for eCommerce sites.

3) What about Penguin, Panda and Hummingbird Updates?

Google changes the way it ranks websites on a regular basis, and when it does that, some people call it a "Google dance" and sometimes, if there are major changes, the Google dance gets a name, e.g. Penguin update, Panda update and the latest one, Hummingbird, as of September 2013. Websites that rank for months can all of a sudden no longer rank.

There is a lot of debate going about "old-fashioned" SEO not working anymore after the Penguin and Panda updates from Google.

A lot of my sites (you've seen a few) are doing even better for the main reason that I have always done my SEO really well and NEVER used anything automated. For some of my keywords that have little competition, the SEO on my one-page-sales-wonders is not even THAT good on my sites, but that is done intentionally because I can better that if need be to higher my rankings.

The Penguin update (second Panda update):
- penalises sites with keyword stuffing (which I have never done)
- penalises sites with automated link building (which I never use)
- penalises sites on which the backlinks are created too many too fast. I explain in my book to create backlinks ONLY to the extent that it is humanly possible to do.
- quality content is also very important (which I apply if appropriate, not for a sales page)
- penalises sites with black hat SEO (which I have never used)
- penalises sites with high bounce rates (when your visitors don't stay on the site for long)
- penalises sites with domain names not relevant to the content

- penalises sites with poor onsite optimisation (no internal links)
- and more … but the above are important.

The Hummingbird update is Google's attempt to better service their user's needs. The update:
- Focuses on long tail keywords
- Focuses on conversational searches/verbal searches, e.g. how to cook a fish, why does my dog bark. Google will pay attention to the words like why, when, where, how, etc…
- Puts less emphasis on matching keywords and tries to understand more precisely what searchers want to see.

We all have to type in more words to try and find exactly what we are looking for. Google knows this and therefore acts upon it.

My micro pig keywords are still ranking as described earlier, as I have always done my SEO with long tail keywords and conversational searches.

It is exactly what I say in my "Newbie To Millionaire" book: NEVER buy anything automated, never do keyword stuffing and always use a domain name with the keywords in it and put appropriate content on the site with internal links. My opinion is that good SEO is more important now than it ever was. The methods in my Newbie book (and partly explained in this book) can now be applied with even more success than before (if that is possible).

If you apply exactly the same principles as explained, you will most probably rank in Google, regardless of Panda , Penguin or Hummingbird updates, and if you are targeting the "keywords with potential".

When Google "does one of their dances", I just adjust my dance moves so I can stay in the game. If you don't use anything automated, you can do the same.

4) The difference between On-Page SEO (OPSEO) and Off-Page SEO (OFFSEO)?

The sort of SEO we will cover here first is OPSEO—this is On-Page Search Engine Optimisation. This is very important for Google ranking. On-Page SEO means designing your website in a search engine-friendly way, by using keywords throughout the site, title tags, meta tags, header tags and more. This is also called internal and external web optimisation. You can't do one and not the other to rank highly in Google. The OPSEO (internal) are changes you make ON your website and OFFSEO (external) is the stuff that you do outside of the design of your site.

By doing OPSEO correctly you have a good chance in the SERPs = Search Engine Result Pages, or the listings pages returned when you search for a keyword.

Have you ever wondered how search engines decide how to rank your website in their results pages? Or how they know exactly what's on your page and what it's about?

They send out robots (or "bots") that crawl your site, paying particular attention to the elements we are about to discuss. If you get these things right, then you stand a much better chance of appearing in the search results for the keywords you want. **Use your keywords mostly on the top and the bottom of each page.**

TOP TIP: use commonly misspelled words or model numbers as keywords in either your domain name, title tags or meta description. The person who typed in the misspelled word probably does not know how to spell it correctly anyway. It is amazing how many visits I get on pages with a misspelled word. Google Analytics gives me this information.

Off-Page SEO refers to work done outside the design of your website or when the website is finished to help you rank in the search engines. Off-Page SEO is a continuous process: it means getting back links to your site and promoting your site on other websites, building your credibility online. It can also be done through article marketing, joining forums and so on.

To summarize: On-Page SEO is important when you build your site and Off-Page SEO is about getting traffic to your site, once it is online.

In order to develop a successful site you need to keep two things in mind: you are aiming to please Google, but you must also aim to please the searcher, and you must know what searchers are looking for and what keywords they use. According to recent studies, Off-Page SEO is now more important to Google than On-Page SEO: 30-40% for On-Page SEO and 60-70% for Off-Page SEO. A few years ago, On-Page SEO was clearly the most important (about 90%).

The three sites I have just mentioned (liquorice, nougat and micro pigs) totally contradict this as I have NEVER done any Off-Page SEO for these sites. You see, it is not that difficult to rank in Google! All I did was get these sites to the first page of Google and it had regular visitors and low bounce rate therefore they have been on the first page for many years. No social media, hardly any links, no work to send traffic! Orders just come in for doing nothing. I took me about 3 months to get to page one in Google with my liquorice site after tweaking my SEO. Once it was there, it stayed there! The same applies for my micro pig site.

5) Simple SEO to implement

Here is some SEO information to help you get started. These steps are basic, simple to implement and are needed in the beginning stages of your website and your drop shipping business. The need for SEO is because if you aren't on page one or two for your keywords, it's unlikely that someone will find your website, which means you won't make a sale.

What makes a good keyword to target?

A basic explanation is: one with low competition AND high searches

There are two types of keywords:

- Information gathering keywords—people looking for information, not to actually buy something.

- Buying keywords—the visitor has made up their mind that they want a product, and you just need to guide them to your page to make the sale.

Both of these can earn money: *buying keywords* can get you sales, while *information gathering keywords* can earn you advertising revenue, if you put money making links on your website. This is explained in detail in my book "From Newbie To Millionaire".

Buying keywords and key phrases are things like:

- buy horse box

- purchase horse box

- horse box reviews

- compare best horse boxes

- Top 10 horse boxes

- which horse box is best

Information gathering keywords are much broader. Some of these keywords may indicate the person is leaning towards making a purchase, like:

- horse box benefits

Some keywords are a strong indicator that the searcher has no intention of buying anything, such as:

- funny horse videos

- horse riding pictures

Basically, we need to look at three things when we're choosing our niche:

1. Demand

2. Profitability

3. Competition

6) Must have elements for SEO Success

SEO is very detailed and you can get books just on this subject. I am only going to cover the most important basics. If you apply these rules, you should be able to rank in Google on the first few pages; assuming your site will get lots of visitors, it might stay on the first page for years.

1. Keywords in the URL

Along with keywords in your site's page titles, keywords in the domain name and URL are hugely important if you want to rank quickly. URL stands for Uniform Resource Locator and is basically the name of your website.

One of the quickest ways to rank for a keyword is to have that keyword in your domain name, i.e. http://www.YourKeyword.com

I recommend naming your domain after your broad niche so that you can have a wide range of items and information available, while still benefiting from the keyword-rich domain name.

This means, for example, you could have the domain: *http://www.horsetacks.com* rather than *http://www.yellow-metal-horse-tacks.com* so you can sell lots of other horse tacks, not just yellow ones.

- In my research, I have concluded that shorter URLs usually perform better in the search results.

- Shorter URLs are also more likely to be used by other Internet marketers for links and so on.

- Bad URLs make it unclear for Google what your site is all about. With good URLs, you tell the search engines what you want your page to be ranked for.

An example of a bad URL : www.hypnosis.com/index.&?89=76=ahtr?52

An example of a good URL : www.hypnosis.com/list/coverthypnosis (covert hypnosis is the page name)

2. Page title tag

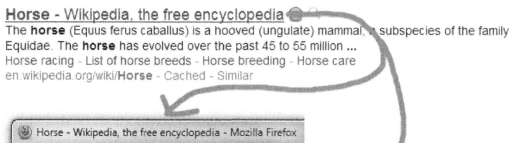

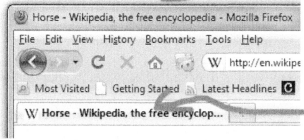

The title tag is one of the most important parts of SEO to get right. Make certain that your keyword is there, as it's what Google places a lot of weight on. It's what your users will see in Google and it's what will appear on the top of the browser window.

Do not go over 70 characters in length for your page title.

Give each page a title (or tag) containing a keyword. You can give your page two titles by putting a "|" between the two keywords or phrases, e.g. How to design a logo | logo design. This will count twice as a keyword for Google. To get the "|" key, use shift key plus the key on the left of the letter Z on your keyboard (on my QWERTY keyboard, it might different on yours).

TOP TIP: Do not include stop words in your keywords and search phrases. Google ignores these and considers them irrelevant. Do not use stop words in your meta title, meta keywords, links or header tags. Here is a list of some commonly used stop words.

And	Be	I	In	Me	Of	On	The

> **TOP TIP:** The keyword that you want to rank for in the page title needs to be early in the title. This is important for Google. So do NOT use this: "Secret Tips Revealed about how To Stop Your Dog From Barking". Instead use: "Stop Your Dog From Barking Secret Tips Revealed" because the "Stop Your Dog From Barking" is more important than "Secret Tips" in the search.

3. Meta description or meta tags

In Google's search results, your meta description will appear in bold under your title. The 'meta tags' or 'page description' are the two lines that appear in Google underneath the 'title tag'.

You need to write a good description because it is the one thing that users have to decide whether or not to visit your page.

Do not go over 350 characters in length.

Horses and **horse** training, care, **tack**, and supply info.
Horses, horse information, horses for sale, horse classifieds. We answer some of the most common questions about horse breeds, horse care, **horse tack**, ...
www.horses-and-horse-information.com/ - Cached - Similar

Title tag = the underlined text = Horses and horse training, care, tack, and supply info.

Meta tag or page description = Horses, horse information, horses for sale, etc.......

4. <H> tags or header tags

<H> tags tell the search engines what is a heading on your website. H1 is the page heading, H2 is a sub heading and H3 is a sub, sub heading.

> Every page should contain ONE H1 tag (no more, no less) which must contain your target keyword.
> Next you need ONE OR MORE H2 tags also containing the keyword.
> And, lastly, ONE OR MORE H3 tags containing your keyword.

Some web design programs call them Title, Header, Subtitle. In your WordPress post/page editor, these different H tags are called Heading 1, 2 and 3 and can be accessed by clicking the drop-down box that says "paragraph":

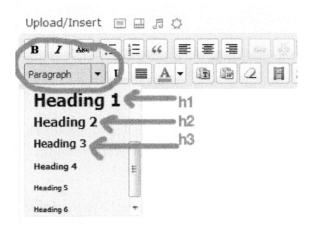

Microsoft Word headers:

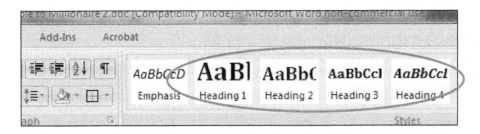

All web design software that I have come across has these headers built in. So if you call a page name "covert hypnosis" as your page title tag, you would also put a header on that page with "covert hypnosis".

It is always a good idea to use the following in the Page Title Tag, Meta Tag and Header Tag: Product Name + Keyword + Company name, e.g. Camera154 + Digital Camera + Sony Digital Camera.

5. Images should have the keyword in their filename and as their alt tag

Google, or any other search engines, cannot recognise pictures on your website (not yet anyway), but if you give each picture a keyword, Google will recognise the keyword.

Each page should have at least one image on it, and that image's filename should be in this format: your keyword.jpg/.png/.gif (suffix depends on file format).

When you insert the image onto your site, you also need to set the "alt tag" as your keyword. This is easy to do in WordPress, as shown below:

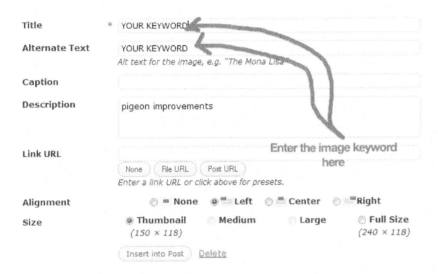

If you are not using Wordpress then you should put the alt tag in manually. The code for it is:

```
<img src="http://www.yourdomain.com/images/your-keyword.png" alt="your keyword" />
```

If you're using a website design program, then try right-clicking the image and clicking "properties". There will be a section marked "alternate text" or "alt text". That's the box into which you enter you alt tag keyword.

You must give every picture on your website a name because Google counts it as a keyword.

Do the test on your website, or on other websites. When you see a picture on the page and you move your mouse over the picture, you will see the picture name either on the screen or at the bottom left corner of your browser window. That is the Image Alt Tag. If no name appears when you hover over the picture, it means that no Image Alt Tag was used or, in other words, the picture was not named with a keyword in the title.

Google's picture search won't find your picture of a Ferrari 658 if you put it on the web with a reference "DCMB999002". It might show it if you give your picture a name like "My Ferrari 658".

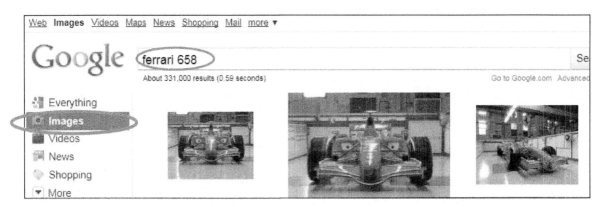

Five Easy Tips for Product Image SEO

Many overlook this very important factor in SEO. For each product that you are selling on your drop shipping website, you have an image for that product. Instead of just uploading the product image, try uploading it and creating a name for it that is search-engine friendly. By doing this, your product images will appear in search results across the world and will appear in Google image search. Here are a few tips to help you with product image optimization:

- Use the keywords/product name in the image file name. Just as it is important for the URL of your product to contain the keywords/product name, it is important to incorporate the same into your image file name, as this will help search engines determine your site's relevancy. For example, you wouldn't want to use this image file name: "StockPhoto_48317681507SM.jpg". As you can see, this file name doesn't add much value to the image or to your site. However, a file name for your image such as this one will: "Red Zebra Print Velvet Evening Handbag.jpg." This image name accurately displays what the product is (handbag), the type of material that the purse is made out of (velvet), the actual type of purse it is (evening handbag) and the printed material used and its color (red zebra print). It's very descriptive.

- Develop descriptive ALT text. Search engines use every possible tag and text associated with your image to determine its relevancy. However, unlike web pages, search engines can't figure out the image text. As a result, they use captions, file names and all other image-related tags and text to determine its content.

- Create appropriate anchor text. If you use images in linking, then you need to make certain that your anchor text is descriptive so that search engines can properly identify and rank your images and site. It's also helpful for your visitors.

- Ensure each image is relevant to its content. This means your alt text, image URL, anchor tags, etc. This ensures that search engines can see that your site is not spam and that the image is actually of high quality and is content-relevant.

- Do NOT over-stuff keywords. Just as with web page and blog content, you do not want to overstuff keywords into your image descriptions, text and tags. Make sure that all text description is short and to the point. It's just better for ranking in search engines.

> **TOP TIP:** if you want to sell in a specific area, e.g. in Detroit, include Detroit in your page title to maximise rankings when people search for "Ferrari in Detroit".

An example:

With an online stores, you are going to have numerous products ,each product will have a separate page. In order for these pages to get indexed in Google and to attract potential customers, there are a few SEO steps you need to take. Now, don't worry; these aren't hard, but they are extremely important if you want to have success with SEO. On-page SEO is more important than you think and it starts with these easy implementations:

- Make sure you add the product name/keyword into the product description. Here you want to add as many relevant keywords as possible and other known relevant names without sounding too spammy or sales-y. It also doesn't hurt to add in "free shipping" and other common terms that are associated with online products into your text.

- Consider adding additional product pages per color of a product. For example, many will search for products by their color (iPhone 4Gs white, zebra print handbag, etc.) instead of simply searching for the product by itself. By optimizing your pages for those customers, you'll reach a lot more potential customers.

- Make sure to use local keywords. Even in drop shipping, it doesn't hurt to localize some of your content, whether it be locally to you or in large cities that may find more use out of your product. Try implementing this strategy: Dallas iPhone 4gs or Seattle mirror décor.

The aforementioned basic SEO tips will help bring you more traffic as well as significant return on investment (ROI). By not implementing these tips into your drop shipping website, you are only hurting yourself and helping your competition.

I love www.ekmpowershop.co.uk and use this platform for many of my shops. It is all optimised for SEO: each page can have a header with a keyword and so can each product. You simply create a product under a specific category, give it a description, upload a picture, set a price and voila, it's done.

EkmPowershop automatically pulls out the keywords from the title and the description that you give your products. You don't have to do a thing if you don't want to.

It's pretty easy to get started. Here are a few screenshots from Ekmpowershop, to show how the platform looks once you are inside. Most eCommerce software has good SEO tools built in.

Screenshot 1: You can see that you can give each category a description with keywords. Each product can be altered simply by clicking edit or delete, or you can change the order of appearance on the site.

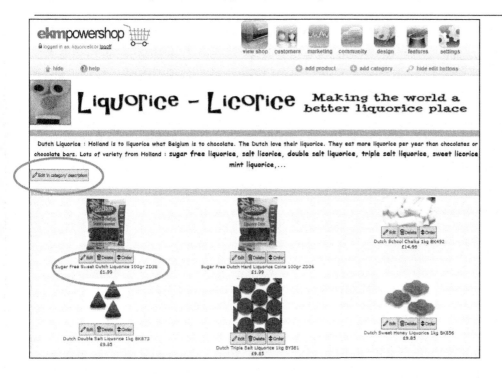

Screenshot 2: You can give your product a title (with keywords) and a product description with keywords.

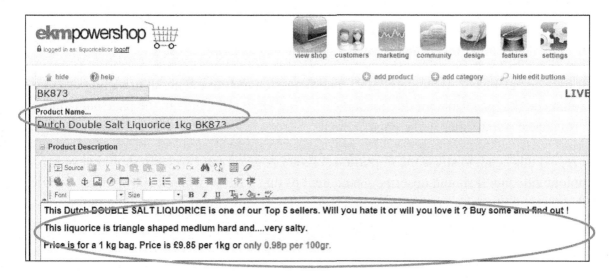

Screenshot 3: For each product, you can create a Meta Title, Meta Description and fill in Meta Keywords. That is brilliant for SEO !! I really love www.ekmpowershop.co.uk, and their service is brilliant too.

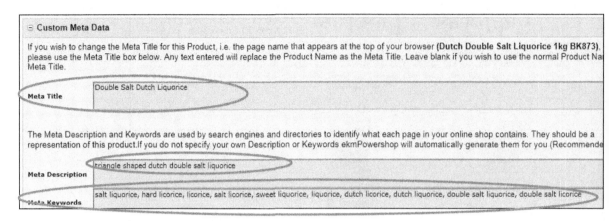

Never give your product a title with a reference number **only**. You **must** always give your product a name with the **keyword**. Nobody will search for BK873 (my reference number for the product), but people will search for "Double Salt Liquorice". So my product name or title in www.ekmpowershop.co.uk is "Dutch Double Salt Liquorice BK873". Many people ignore this aspect with eCommerce, which is vital for SEO.

6. The pages must be named according to the content that is on them

If the page name is "safe dog collars", make sure you are talking about or selling dog collars on that page and not dog medallions. Your keyword that is in the page name must also appear a few times in the page content.

I repeat this again to stress the importance: Every page on your website should have a unique title tag. It should describe the content of that page so when it shows up in Google, the visitor will find what they expected to see. This is important for Google ranking, because if every visitor leaves the page in a matter of seconds, Google will notice this and might rank you lower.

> **TOP TIP:** Forget the one-word keywords and try to rank with long tail keywords. It makes your SEO job a lot easier and you will rank more quickly. Always design a separate page for each long tail keyword on your site, and use that same keyword on each page in your content. Example: You are building a site on muscle training. Instead of trying to rank for "muscle training", you try and rank for "muscle training for legs". The title tag of one page should then be "muscle training for legs". On that page, use the keyword "muscle training for legs" spread out all over that page. Do the same for "muscle training for arms", etc…

7. Keyword density.

Aim to have the keyword make up somewhere between 2 and 4% of the text on each page of your site. Any more than this and Google may consider it "keyword stuffing" (the practice of repeating a word over and over again to try to influence your Google position) and ignore your page. Any less than this and Google may not realise that your page is about this keyword.

Always put your keyword in the first AND last sentence of each page.

Always make some of your keywords **bold** or *italic* on each page, to emphasise them to Google, as Google does recognise bold text.

8. Activity

This is a tricky thing to quantify. Since one of the latest Google algorithm updates, Google now looks at "activity" as one of the factors it takes into account when ranking a website. This could mean a number of things: comments your blog posts receive, frequency of updates, forum activity (if you have a forum on your site), or the time people stay and browse on your site. The general rule of thumb is to update your site, or have some form of user interaction, at least once a week. This is in total contradiction to my micro pig site www.micropigshed.com as I have NEVER updated that site for years and it is still on the first page for several keywords.

9. Number of links per page

Google will only scan a maximum of the first 100 links on a page, maybe even fewer than that. Keep the amount of links to around 50 (with over 25 of them as internal links).

More about links later in this book.

TOP TIP: Make some of your keywords on your pages Bold, Italic or Underlined in order for Google to see them easier.

TOP TIP: Use your targeted keyword in the first sentence and in the last sentence of each page.

---

10. Social Media Buttons

This is something I do not personally practice, but everyone I know in the Internet marketing environment thinks it is very important these days.

Social Media Buttons are buttons that look like this:

When clicked, these will link directly to your Facebook, Twitter or LinkedIn account.

The only websites I have put these on are my Internet marketing related websites, as I am "expected" to know the importance of them as they are generally accepted as being important. However, I know for a fact that social media is NOT that important to make a lot of money online, as I am personally not a social media fan at all. I sometimes do force myself to visit my Facebook page, but I have never made any money with Facebook and I am NOT interested when someone is having a bath or a cup of tea! I have several sites that rank on the first page that DON'T have any of these links on; here are a few: www.liquorice-licorice.co.uk, www.nougat-nougat.co.uk, www.micropigshed.com

Perhaps I would sell more if I put social media buttons on my sites. I must admit, I have never tested it because if something works, leave it alone is my motto.

The main concern I have with these social media links is that IF you only have 20 friends on Facebook or you only have 5 likes, this will put people OFF buying from you. If I want to buy a product and I come across a website that has 5 likes and I come across a website that has 500 likes, I will trust the latter one more.

HOWEVER, and this is a BIG HOWEVER: you can't believe in likes anyway. You can buy likes! You can buy friends! You can buy software that will give you 500 friends in the next month, BUT these are automated friends and Google will soon find out and punish you for it! On top of that, these friends will not be targeted friends, so they are a waste of space and time. What's the point of having friends that hate fish when you are selling fish?

IF you can build your friends HONESTLY, it would be different, but this is very time consuming.

So, unless you want to devote lots and lots of time convincing people to like your pages, I advise you not to put these buttons on your site. That's only my opinion! I know most people think differently, but I like to earn money as much as possible on autopilot, without having to spend hours and hours trying to find likes.

I just don't like begging people to like me! You like me or you don't ! Having said that, go and like my Facebook page :-).

The same applies for a blog; there is always work to be done to keep it updated. If I visit a website in 2013 and the last post was November 2010, I immediately move on, as I assume the webmaster doesn't really care if he gets business or not.

If you believe in social media, sure, put the buttons on. Perhaps you can make it work for you, but I have never made the time to make it work for me as I am doing OK without it.

11) Internal links

Have links to your other pages at the top, left and bottom of the page because Google likes this. Learn more about this in my book "From Newbie To Millionaire".

Summary of SEO :

Remember: where do your keywords go?

1. In URL, best at the beginning

2. In Page Title, best at the beginning

3. In Meta Description or Meta Tags, best at the beginning

4. In Header tags H1, H2, H3, etc....

5. In Alt Text (pictures), best at the beginning

6. Name the pages according to the content on them

Important: Make one separate page on your site per keyword you want to target. Focus on one long tail keyword on each page.

7. In Content: keyword density is important

8. Activity is important

9. Low bounce rate is important

10. Regular visitors is important

11. Links are important; Authority Site Links are brilliant

12. Social Media Buttons (if you like social media or are planning to use it a lot)

13. Put several internal page links on your site

- Example layout of a website, showing best practice on-page SEO. The following is for a page optimised for the key phrase "micro pig feed".

<title> tag *(less than 69 characters)*	Micro Pigs | Micro Pig Feed
Meta Description tag *(less than 156 characters)*	Find the best micro pig feed at the Micro Pig Shed.
Meta Keyword tags *(your webpage keywords)*	Micro pig feed, micro pig feed, micro pigs feed, micro pigs feed, feed for micro pigs, what to feed micro pig, what do micro pigs eat, what do micro pigs eat
<h1> tag *(most important title should only be one per page)*	Basics of Micro Pig Feed
<p> tag *(body text paragraph)*	Basic micro pig feed should contain several basic elements… Whenever possible, provide your pig with unlimited grazing on chemical-free grass. If this is not possible, add high-quality hay such as alfalfa or oat to the micro pig feed. This roughage is very important, but feed within reason!
<img> tag	IMAGE - given the alt. tag "micro pig feed"
<h2> tag	What Should Be In Micro Pig Feed?
<p> tag	Fifty percent of the balance of the micro pig feed should be a good-quality commercial pig food. There are pelleted foods on the market specifically for miniature pigs. Feed pig starter to pigs under two months, and adult food to all others. Since you are not planning to send your pig to market, do not use pig grower or finisher.
<h3> tag	Know what micro fig feed you're looking for?
<p> tag *(links to other pages on your site)*	• Micro Pig Feed Product A • Micro Pig Feed Product B • Micro Pig Feed Product C • Micro Pig Feed Product D

If you want to design a page on "micro pig training", you would replace "micro pig feed" with "micro pig training" and of course change the content accordingly.

411

- Another example layout of a website. The following is for a page optimised for the key phrase "horse tack trunk" (paragraph content taken from Wikipedia):

<title> tag *(less than 69 characters)*	Horse Tacks | Horse Tack Trunk
Meta Description tag *(less than 156 characters)*	Find the best horse tack trunk for you at our horse tack site.
Meta Keyword tags *(your webpage keywords)*	Horse tacks, horse tack trunk, horse tack trunks, best horse tack trunks, cheap horse tack trucks
<h1> tag *(most important title - should only be one per page)*	Horse Tack Trunk Basics
<p> tag *(body text paragraph)*	Horse tack trunks are a place to store away all the horse tacks you have probably accumulated over your years' horse riding. Tack is a term used to describe any of the various equipment and accessories worn by horses in the course of their use as domesticated animals. Saddles, stirrups, bridles, halters, reins, bits, harnesses, martingales, and breastplates are all forms of horse tacks.
<img> tag	IMAGE - given the alt. tag "horse tack trunk"
<h2> tag	More About The Contents Of Horse Tack Trunks
<p> tag	Saddles are seats for the rider, fastened to the horse's back by means of a *girth* (English-style riding), known as a *cinch* in the Western US, a wide strap that goes around the horse at a point about four inches behind the forelegs. Some western saddles will also have a second strap known as a *flank* or *back cinch* that fastens at the rear of the saddle and goes around the widest part of the horse's belly.[1]
<h3> tag	Know what type of horse tack trunk you're looking for?
<p> tag *(links to other pages on site)*	• Horse Tack Trunk A Horse Tack Trunk C • Horse Tack Trunk B Horse Tack Trunk C

Depending on the amount of content you have in between your <p> tags, you may want to put your key phrase in once or twice. You want to aim for an overall keyword density of about 4% (meaning that around 4% of the content on the page is your keyword).

- The "perfectly optimized page" for the example keyword phrase "chocolate donuts".

Page Title: Chocolate Donuts | Mary's Bakery

Meta Description: Mary's Bakery's chocolate donuts are possibly the most delicious, perfectly formed, flawlessly chocolaty donuts ever made.

H1 Headline:
Chocolate Donuts from Mary's Bakery

Image Filename:
chocolate-donuts.jpg

Photo of Donuts
(with Alt Attribute):
Chocolate Donuts

Body Text: _____
_____chocolate donuts_____

_____donuts_____

_____chocolate donuts__

_____donuts_____

chocolate_____

_____chocolate donuts_____

_____chocolate_____

_____chocolate donuts_____

Page URL: http://marysbakery.com/chocolate-donuts

7) Components of Google's Ranking Algorithm

On the Pie Chart Below you can see the importance of the keyword on page optimization.

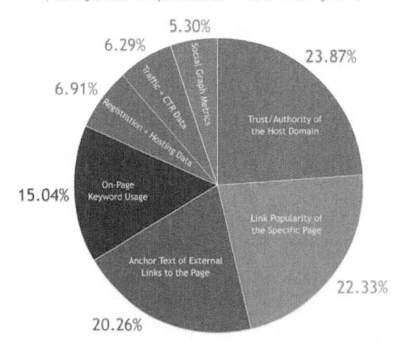

Source : http://moz.com/blog/visual-guide-to-keyword-targeting-onpage-optimization

First: 23.87% Trust/Authority of The Host Domain. A trusted domain with lots of visitors, lots of content and inbound links. Three things to remember as the most important: domain age, good content, quality links.

Second: 22.33% Link Popularity of the Specific Page. The quality and the quantity of the inbound links are very important. This will be covered later in the book. You cannot control who links to your site, but you can control who you link to. When getting backlinks, only ever link to relevant sites.

Third: 20.26% Anchor Text of External Links to the Page. It is important to have anchored links coming into your page. You need the correct anchors from quality sources. If you point to a relevant page on a website, you should use keyword rich anchor text, e.g. instead of "click here". Here are some stop-dog-barking tips is much better than Click Here for Tips. It is better for two reasons: firstly because the visitor immediately knows what to expect when clicking the link, and secondly because for search engines the anchor text is another link with relevant keywords. So instead of using Anchor Text, use Descriptive Anchor Text, like this one: Here are some stop-dog-barking tips.

Fourth: 15.04% On-Page Keyword Usage. Keyword density should be about 2 to 4% maximum. Not enough and your site might not rank, too much and it is considered keyword stuffing. Trial and error is the only way to find out.

Fifth: 6.91% Registration – Hosting Data. Google likes old domain names. They know that spammers will never register a domain for longer than one year. Google also does not really like .info websites because very often these are used by spammers as .info domain names are cheaper to buy. If your target market is Australia, you must make sure that you have a .com or .au website and also an Australian server.

Sixth: 6.29% Traffic – Click Through Data. You have done a lot of work and your website ranks in Google, BUT most visitors who visit your website immediately hit the back button. To Google, this means that the information on your site was not interesting enough for the visitor to stay; Google will therefore rank it lower. Unless you work really hard on the content, the website will not rank on the first pages again. Google will also keep a record of the amount of times your website is shown and clicked on.

Seventh: 5.30% Social Graph Metrics. Google never used to take this into account. If Google finds out that your website is liked by a lot of people, it will show higher in the rankings. This is where social networking and the backlink strategies discussed later in this book are important. You need to open an account with Facebook,LinkedIn, Google+ , and so on and get people talking about you or pointing to your site.

SEO Conclusion: On-page SEO takes a long time if you want to do it right BUT it will pay off. It is the most important thing for getting free traffic. Your hard work will be worth it once you type in your keyword and your website is listed first! You will probably never forget that moment. I still remember the first time I ranked on the first page with my keyword. That's when I realised that if I can achieve it for one site, I can duplicate my method for other sites or outsource the building of more sites.

Some of the most important things that determine your ranking success with Google:

- SEO: keywords in domain name and on your site

- Content: you must have good unique content

- Links: you must have other sites that link to yours

- Reputation of your site, mostly coming from social media, e.g. YouTube, Facebook

- Activity on your site: if nobody ever visits your site or if visitors stay only briefly, Google will be not be impressed.

It is not enough to have an extremely well-optimised website with ON Page SEO, as there is more work to be done, all of which will be discussed in this book.

TOP TIP: You need to investigate your keywords BEFORE you start the design of your site. Design your site around your keywords.

---

8) Number of results myth resolved

There are different ways of searching for a keyword, which is important to remember for your keyword research in any search engine. Suppose we search for: *race horses for sale.*

- **Broad match:** only type in the words in the search engine, without putting the words between "" or [ ]: the searched for words will show up in any order. Not always relevant searches will show. So your search would include the following:

- race horses for sale
- horses race sale for
- sale for race horses
- for horses sale race

- **"Phrase match"**: the order of the words has to be correct to show. Other words can be included on either side of the phrase, but no other words are allowed in between any words of the search words. You type your search like this with quotation marks or inverted commas at beginning and end: "your search word or phrase here". Your search would include:

- *race horses for sale* in England
- help me with finding *race horses for sale*

It will not show: race horses and dogs for sale (because "and dogs" is in the middle)

- **[Exact matches]**: your exact phrase will show and nothing else. You type your search like this with square brackets at beginning and end: [your search word or phrase here]. Your search would include:

- *Race horses for sale* and nothing else. Nothing else will be shown, not even this: race-horses for sale, or racehorses for sale.

Broad match = keywords without "" or [ ] = any words or any order of words will show.

"Phrase match" = "your keywords" = order of words has to be correct and no words in between.

[Exact] = [your keywords] = only exact wording searched for will show

---

TOP TIP: As an Internet marketer, it is very important to always search for keywords in "phrase match" or [exact match].

Even if you are not going to be an Internet marketer, never search for more than one keyword with broad match as you will get more accurate search results.

The following two screenshots show you what a difference the two different searches can make: 17,500 results against 184,000 results shown.

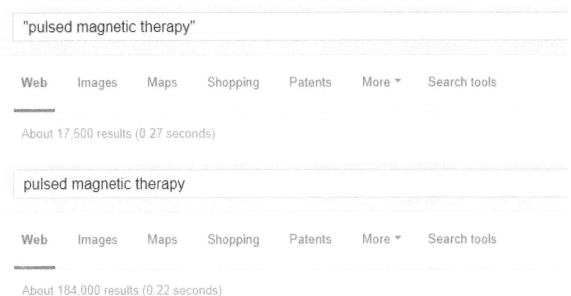

The following information is especially useful to newbies. When I first started online, I was confused. Suppose I searched for horse and got 185,000,000 results, does this mean that I have to compete with over 185 million pages about horses? Surely that is not possible!

No, it is indeed not possible, but that's not how it works. Let me explain.

The number of results doesn't say much in terms of competition. If there is a large number for the results, then there is a lot of interest in the subject. The search results will include ALL the websites with the word "horse" on any page , this means websites selling DVDs with "horse" in the title, or horse riding holidays, etc... all *irrelevant* to the horse tack niche. The only websites that you have to compete with are the first eight pages of results, so that's a maximum of 80 websites. The reason for this is that Google will list lots of websites that have the word horse in it but that are poorly SEO optimised. Google will also show pages with a lot of unrelated stuff. The bottom line is the only ones you have to worry about are the ones that are listed on the first eight pages. To show you how important long tail keywords are, here's an example.

Google shows 339,000,000 for the exact search for "Mercedes":

Google shows 55,100 for the exact search for "yellow Mercedes"

Conclusion: your competition is immediately less if you refine your keywords and want to rank for "yellow Mercedes" compared to "Mercedes".

To close the SEO section, here are a few ways to **never** rank highly:

- No title tags or very bad title tags

- Irrelevant domain names

- Using link farms

- Using lots of Flash all over your website

- Irrelevant content or not enough content

- Using wrong keywords on different pages, e.g. giving a page a title tag "stop dog barking" and then not using any of these three words on that page.

- Black Hat SEO (keyword stuffing)

What is Black Hat SEO?

These are techniques some people use to try to get higher search engine results in an unethical way. Some of the Black Hat SEO techniques were acceptable many years ago but not anymore. When these techniques are applied, they can result in high Google ranking very quickly. But it can also be for a short time, if Google decides to ban or never show your site.

White Hat SEO is what we have discussed so far in this book. Google likes White Hat SEO, and it's worth pleasing Google. If it does not like your website or marketing technique it can simply ban your site.

Where does the term Black Hat SEO come from?

Remember the good old Western movies? Generally the bad cowboys wore black hats and the good ones wore white hats.

To avoid being banned, you must follow the advice below at all times. These techniques are generally known as Black Hat SEO techniques:

- Never use link farms.

- Never copy other people's content. Not only can you be banned from Google, but you can be taken to court for violation of copyright laws for stealing other people's content.

- Never cloak. Cloaking is when you try to fool Google by sending visitors to one site and sending Google to another site. This can be done very easily with redirects and some clever programming. Google hates it. If you type 'dogs' in your search, you do not want to open a website on crocodiles. A Google employee can manually check if you are cloaking by visiting your website. Google will not warn you before it bans you.

- Do not overstuff your page with keywords. One example of overstuffing would be to use two keywords in each sentence of your site.

- Do not use keywords not related to your content. A list of 40 keywords from a thesaurus listed at the bottom of your website is not going to do you any good.

- Do not use hidden text. Ten years ago this used to work: put a yellow banner on a site and stuff it with yellow text as your keywords. The website visitor would not see the keywords, but Google would think they are all good keywords. Not anymore: Google doesn't fall for that trick any longer.

- Do not distribute any viruses, Trojans or other malware.

- Do not use automated link submission programs. This is totally against Google's terms of services.

- Do not use Adwords with a landing page that is not 100% designed around Google's regulations for its landing pages. Your website can be banned from Adwords overnight without any warning. You must read Google's landing page requirements.

- Do not stuff it with SPAM. Other websites can report you, and you risk being banned.

So, don't try to cheat your way to the top. Design a White Hat SEO site and put some decent content on it. Work on getting links to get traffic. The lazy way often means the banned way!

If you are banned, you can ask to be included again, but often it is simply better to forget the banned website and start a new one.

9) Perfect SEO for eCommerce websites

Source: www.moz.com

On the following picture you will see all the elements that are important for an eCommerce product page for on-page optimisation.

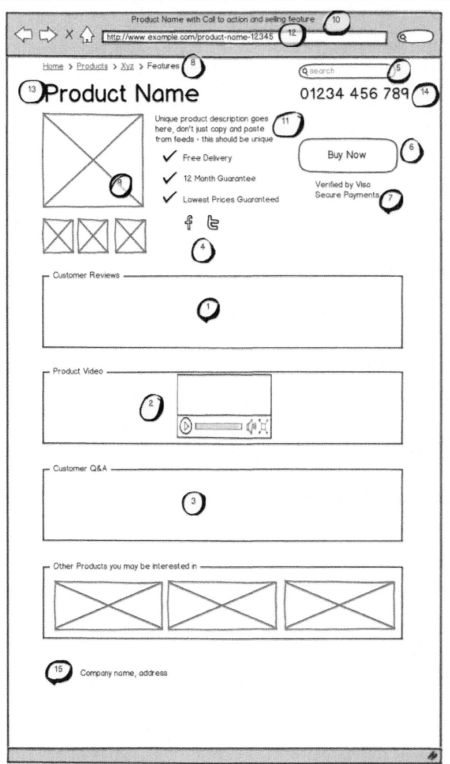

Product Name with Call to action and selling feature — 10

http://www.example.com/product-name-12345 — 12

Home > Products > Xyz > Features — 8

search — 5

Product Name — 13

01234 456 789 — 14

Unique product description goes here, don't just copy and paste from feeds - this should be unique — 11

✓ Free Delivery

✓ 12 Month Guarantee

✓ Lowest Prices Guaranteed

Buy Now — 6

Verified by Visa
Secure Payments — 7

— 9

— 4

Customer Reviews — 1

Product Video — 2

Customer Q&A — 3

Other Products you may be interested in

15 — Company name, address

created with Balsamiq Mockups - www.balsamiq.com

Here is a brief explanation of the different elements:

1) Customer Reviews. If possible, always put a customer review on your site. Video reviews are the best one, as previously discussed. Ideally reviews should overcome buying objections, e.g. if a potential customer might think that the product looks too big, you could ask the person who does the review to say on the review: "I thought to start with that it was too big but it is not at all when you see it."

2) Product Video. This is not easy to do but worth doing as it will convert into more sales. Have a look at www.zappos.com. There are lots of product videos on that site.

Google likes videos, so if you put a video on your site, optimised with your relevant keywords, you have a chance of Google showing it in the search results. Product videos are great for good content. www.wistia.com is a great website for video optimisation.

3) Questions and Answers. It is not always easy to create content for product pages, but a questions and answers blog is a brilliant tool to use.

4) Social Sharing Buttons. A great way to let others do your advertising, this definitely applies if you have a website where youngsters are likely to hang around and buy. If they buy something and like it, they will share it with their friends. Google likes sharing and likes at the moment, but that might not stay that way forever. I would not put sharing buttons with the idea of ranking but more with the idea of letting other people sell your products by sharing them.

You don't necessary have to have this on each product page, and if you decide not to put sharing buttons on your website, you can consider sending your buyer an email a day after the delivery date and ask in the email to share/like your product/website.

5) Search Options. A search box on an eCommerce is absolutely essential so visitors don't have to keep clicking on different pages to find what they are looking for.

6) Call to Action. As discussed, SEO is crucially important, but once visitors are on your page, you need to make sure that they can see the order button at all times.

You can use these sites to measure and improve your call to action:

www.clicktale.com

www.crazyegg.com

7) Security Images. As already discussed, you are asking people to hand over their credit card information, so they need to be able to trust you. Put logos on your site, e.g. Verified by Visa or Truste Certified, etc…

8) Breadcrumbs. No, I don't mean breadcrumbs from bread, I mean breadcrumbs in web design. Yes, there is indeed such a thing! The term originates from the fairy tale Hansel and Gretel, when the two children drop breadcrumbs to find their way back home. The same applies on a website: breadcrumbs offer an easy way for the visitor to go back to their starting point or to the page they want to visit again.

On websites with a lot of pages, breadcrumb navigation can make it much easier for your visitors to navigate your site. ECommerce website is an ideal scenario where breadcrumbs can be applied because there are usually a lot of product pages. If you want to find out more, go to www.moz.com and search for breadcrumbs.

9) Images. Of course you need a product image on your site for each product. Ideally you need a magnifying glass option so people can enlarge the image. Most ecommerce software and templates will convert the images automatically to a suitable size for the product. Make sure your images look clear and not too dark.

Important to remember is the resolution of your images: if the resolution is too high, your site won't load fast and potential customers won't have the patience to wait so they will exit your site, visit another site (that *does* load quickly) and order from another store!

10) Meta Title. I have already covered this. If you have thousands of product pages, it is not really feasible to customise all of them. Some good software packages will do this automatically when you simply give the product a name.

11) Product Description. Naturally, the product description cannot be too long. It has to be to the point and explain the basics about the product. Use keywords in the description. It is important for SEO purposes that you make every product description unique. Don't just copy it from your wholesaler's website as other retailers might do the same, and the content of your website won't be unique. Remember that Google likes content to be unique.

12) Page URL. I have already explained this, so I won't go into detail here. Important here is not to include categories or sub-categories in a page URL. It is always a good idea to use the product name as a code for the URL e.g. www.yourwebsite.com/product name 5687.

13) H1 Tags. Some people debate that these have become less important. As it does not take a lot of time to implement this, I believe it is still worth doing. In some eCommerce software, you can set it in a way that your product name automatically becomes the H1 tag for that page.

14) Phone Number. People will simply trust you more if you add a phone number, so if possible, do put a phone number in a visible spot on your site. Not many people will phone you, and the ones that do will be potential customers, so you should be glad you do get calls.

15) Company Details. I have already mentioned this in your must-have elements for your site. It is another trust sign, and Google can also see where you are based, so that might help your rankings for those keywords, e.g. if someone types in "shoes in Manchester" and Google can see you are based in Manchester, you have one extra good point with Google.

Hopefully you will take some, or all, the above points into account when building your site.

10) Good SEO resources

SEO is very complex and would require another book all on its own. Here are a few great resources that are really helpful in teaching even the most illiterate person how to properly use SEO to their advantage.

www.moz.com This is definitely the go-to source for beginners and professionals alike. Moz provides literally everything you need to know about SEO and using it to make your website work. There is a Beginner's Guide that is crucial when you first start out and a blog that you should follow up with frequently. The site offers a wide variety of tools, some of which are available for free members and others that are only available to paying members. Many find that Moz is well worth the price of a membership to gain access to everything that they have to offer.

www.seobook.com This is probably the second-best SEO resource out there. They have a great blog with tons of information as well as plenty of information available on the initial website.

www.semrush.com

www.seoquake.com

www.seohat.com

www.searchenginejournal.com

www.imnewswatch.com

www.searchengineland.com

www.whichtestwon.com (interesting site)

11) Add good value content to your site

While the ease of navigation and function as well as the visual appeal of your site are all important, one of the most important aspects of your site is how much value you are providing the customer.

What can customers expect when they visit your website? Will they get hard to come by products? Mind-blowing deals? Educational information? Advice and tips?

You have to give your customers something, so this is just as important as knowing what you are going to sell.

There is a complete chapter on Content in my book From Newbie To Millionaire.

What is Valuable Content?

Valuable content comes in many forms. You can provide customers with valuable content with product reviews, articles, blog posts, newsletters, tips of the day/week/month, and more. The thing with valuable content is to make sure that it is informative and attention grabbing, while being non-promotional. A sales pitch for one of your products is nowhere near being considered valuable content; however, if you were to write a non-biased product review, truly outlining the pros and cons of one of your products, this would be considered valuable content to your reader, who is also your prospective customer. Content should always be updated on a regular basis and should never, ever be copied from another source.

An example of good content: if your product has been in the news, put it on your website and send an email to your customers telling them to go and have a look at your site.

In my case, there were 2 article in a leading newspaper in the UK in October 2013 that I've put on my liquorice website. News like this will immediately increase your sales if you use it in your advantage. You can email your customers, telling them to look on your website for the articles.

Liquorice slows skin cancer cells

LIQUORICE could hold the key to beating the most lethal form of skin cancer, scientists have discovered.

Researchers identified a compound in liquorice root that slowed the growth of cancer cells.

Now they hope the substance can be developed into a drug to combat malignant melanoma.

Previous studies found another anti-cancer chemical in liquorice called glycyrrhizin. But attempts to turn it into a medicine were hampered because long-term consumption of glycyrrhizin can cause high blood pressure and swelling on the brain.

Experts at the University of Minnesota in the US have now found another ingredient – isoangustone A – which has the same benefits without the dangerous side effects.

Malignant melanoma kills around 1,700 people a year in the UK and is

By **Pat Hagan**

the third most common cancer in people aged 15-39.

Over-exposure to the sun's rays is the biggest cause and since the mid-1990s there has been a 24 per cent increase in cases.

Some evidence suggests even a few bouts of sunburn in childhood can trigger cellular changes that lead to skin cancer later in life. Cancerous mole cells start to divide, eventually spreading through the body.

The research, published in Journal Cancer Prevention Research, found isoangustone A slowed the rate at which melanoma cells reproduce, partly by blocking certain proteins needed for them to flourish.

When the extract was given to mice with skin cancer, it had the same effect of suppressing growth of tumours.

Taking a liquorice pill may help cool down hot flushes

CONSUMING liquorice may help tackle hot flushes.

In a new trial taking place in Israel, 120 women are taking a daily liquorice pill for 20 weeks while scientists measure the effect it has on their hot flushes.

This follows a small pilot study which suggested the pill produced an 80 per cent drop in hot flushes after eight months. How

exactly the liquorice works is unclear, but one theory is that it contains a compound called glabridin which has oestrogen-like effects.

Oestrogen levels in the body decline after menopause, resulting in symptoms such as hot flushes.

If the trial is successful, the team hope to perform a larger study comparing liquorice with a placebo.

Creating Your Content

Answering people's questions is always a good form of content. Visit some Questions and Answers websites and find what problems people have in your niche e.g. www.answers.com or www.theanswerbank.com.

In my book "Finding Niches Made Easy", I list 177 places to visit to find niches. Most of these places are also excellent to find ideas for content.

Not everyone has a skill for putting pen to paper—or fingers to the keywords—so hiring a freelance writer may be needed so that you can get top-notch, informative and interesting articles. You will find freelance writers working for anywhere from £3.10/$5 to £18.80/$30 per article, depending on the quality of work you want. Always ask for a sample first to make sure that they can really write well. Freelance writers can be found on sites such as Elance.com, oDesk.com and WriterAccess.com. You can even post a "gig" on Craigslist to grab the attention of writers.

Another option you have is inviting guest writers and bloggers to write articles for your site. As a general rule, guest posts are free for you, but you have to be willing to give the writer something in return. In most cases, they want you to allow a link or two back to their website within the article or at the end of the article with a resource box that gives a brief background of themselves and/or their business.

You need content to survive on the web, but it has to be quality content or it doesn't offer much value for your business and sure as heck isn't effective in marketing and making your site known in search engines.

Quality content attracts web traffic, builds relationships with customers and improves SEO, which is what we are talking about next.

www.marketsamurai.com This software is one of my favourite tools for online research. It offers brilliant keyword research and search engine optimisation tools. It gives a deep insight into keywords and competitors for that keyword. Every Internet marketer should get to grips with it. It is the best possible investment you could ever make when it comes to making money online. You'll easily make the money back because you'll be able to find the keywords that you can easily dominate, and it costs just £60/$97 (*one off payment, free upgrades and support for life*). The advertised one-off payment is £92/$147, but if you subscribe for a seven-day trial you automatically get $48 discount.

www.longtailpro.com is another keyword research tool I have used.

You can also use Google Keyword Planner to find keywords to target. Just Google the subject. In order to use Keyword Planner, you need to sign up for a Google Adwords account. You do not have to spend any money in order to use Keyword Planner.

There are a number of other keyword tools available, so it is a case of finding one that you like. Examples of other tools:

www.goodkeywords.com

www.longtailpro.com

www.keyworddiscovery.com

www.keywordelite.com

www.keywordspy.com

www.micronichefinder.com

www.ppcwebspy.com

www.senuke.com

www.webmaster-toolkit.com

www.wordtracker.com

Chapter 15 - Things to Do Before Sending Traffic.

OK, you know what products you are going to sell, you know what software you are going to use for your online shop and you know how to put SEO on your site. Now there are four vital things you must do or must know before sending any traffic to your site.

1) You must publish your website.

When you design your website with eCommerce software, you don't have to worry about this too much as the software should do this automatically for you.

Okay, now that you have finished designing your site, it looks goods and you have tested to make sure that everything works, you must publish it. It is now in finished mode sitting on your computer, but as we mentioned before: 10,000 people are not going to come to your office or lounge to look at your site, so it needs to be published for the world to see.

This is done by a protocol called *FTP: File Transfer Protocol*. It is a way of sending files securely from one computer to another. We are all involved in FTP without realising we are doing it. If you buy a song or an eBook from the web and download it to your computer, you are using FTP because you are transferring the files from the host computer to your computer.

There are three ways to publish a site:

- When using WordPress, publishing is done automatically, so you do not need to do it. Press "F5" and the latest version will be visible online or click the "Update" button.

- When using a web design program like Webplus or Microsoft Expression Web, there is a "publish to" button. You need to fill in some technical information that your hosting company will be able to give you. The information that you will need will be available from your account with your hosting company. Most of the time, all you need is your username, password and IP address.

430

- If using Filezilla, you drag the files from your computer to the Filezilla server.

Filezilla is FTP software and it is free. There's a huge amount of help available on the site, where you can also download it: www.filezilla-project.org.

Filezilla looks a bit scary to start with but believe me, it is easy after you have used it a few times.

Unfortunately it is impossible to explain in detail how each web design program publishes your site. Simply Google how to do it and there will be videos on YouTube to show you.

Note: The homepage of your website *must* always be called index.html when using Webplus.

I suggest that you submit your site for publishing to these search engines:

- Submit your site to Google here: http://www.google.co.uk/submit_content.html (or just Google "add url"). You must submit every website, even if you have designed it with WordPress. From experience I know that Google will see your site much quicker if you submit it.

- Submit your site to DMOZ (PR8) here: http://www.dmoz.org/add.html. DMOZ is a huge database of human-added websites. A backlink from them to your site is a great thing to have and will greatly increase the amount of traffic you receive. If you do not get listed here at your first attempt, make some changes to your site and apply again to be listed. It will be worth the effort.

- Submit your website to Bing: http://www.bing.com/toolbox/submit-site-url

- Submit your site to Yahoo (PR8): http://search.yahoo.com/info/submit.html

Once you have submitted your site, you can check if Google has found it by typing in Google site: www.yourwebsitehere.com and Google will show your site and the pages it has indexed. If Google displays a message "Your site did not match any documents", it means that Google has not indexed your site yet.

You can also just type your URL in the search box at www.google.com. If your site appears in the results, Google has indexed it. If three weeks after submission, your site is still not indexed, I suggest you submit it again. The best way to speed up getting indexed is by submitting to social bookmark sites and by getting backlinks to your site.

You can focus your submission efforts based on your target market, with this interesting information according to www.hitwise.com:
- Yahoo! searchers are younger and affluent
- Google searchers are often older, male and have a larger income
- Bing searchers are often female, within the best converting to buyers ratio

Although 88% of all searches are through the top three search engines, below is a list of some other search engines that you can submit your site to.

www.dogpile.com

www.entireweb.com

www.exactseek.com

www.excite.com

www.gigablast.com

You could also use www.addme.com for manual submission to 14 search engines.

You can find a list of the smaller search engines here: www.thesearchenginelist.com.

Be prepared to receive a lot of follow-up emails or SPAM from several search engines after you have submitted your site. Do NOT submit your site until your site is up, running and ready to take orders from customers.

My book "Finding Niches Made Easy" contains a lot more search engines, including advances search techniques.

2) You MUST TEST all the links on your website

All steps you take to make your online shop a success are useless if no one can find your website.

No traffic = No visitors = No profit

Before sending traffic to your site you need to TEST, TEST, TEST everything on your site.

TEST – TEST – TEST – TEST – TEST – TEST

This is crucial; I cannot stress this enough. Have you ever come across websites with "error 404" or other errors? Or pictures that are only half shown? Or text that runs over a picture? Of course you have. Very often this is because the webmaster does not check the website regularly. You have no chance to earn money with links that do not work. You need to you check your links on a regular basis—your page links as well as your affiliate links.

When you re-organise files on your computer, check your site. Depending on which company or host you use and how you have published your site, this can affect the website. When pictures have changed folders on your computer, those pictures might not show up on your website. The pictures will show as a blank frame with an "x"—very unprofessional.

This is what you have to check regularly:

1. Check that all your internal page links are working.

2. Click and test "Add to Cart" buttons on your pages. All good shopping carts have a feature called "Test run" where you can make a test purchase to see if all runs smoothly. After you have done that, you go back and click the "Go Live" button.

This is how it looks in 1shoppingcart: L3011 means the system is Live. If you want to do some testing, simply change it to T3011 (T for Test) and that means you are in test mode and you can test the order buttons on your website. Don't forget to change it back to L3011 when you're done testing, otherwise customers will receive error messages saying their payment cannot be processed.

Your Payment Processor	
Select Gateway	WorldPay ⌄
Gateway ID/Merchant Login	L3011
Other Payment Setting	
Sale Type	Authorize and Capture ⌄ ⓘ

3. Check that all your pages display as intended.

4. Check that your email auto responder is working properly. Opt-in with your own email address for testing purposes.

5. Check that all hyperlinks to internal pages are linked to the correct page.

6. Check that customers can see in a few seconds what the site is all about.

7. Can the customer see the contact information easily?

8. Check that all your videos are playing correctly and load quickly.

9. Check if your website looks good opened with the different Internet browsers: Internet Explorer, Firefox, Google Chrome, Opera, Safari (for Apple computers) and so on.
10. Ask three friends to look at your website for their comments and criticism. Looking at a website from other people's point of view can teach you a lot. Other people will see things that you don't.

3) You must make sure that you can check how your website is doing

Now that your website is tested and published, you must make sure that you can see how it is doing. When you have made it to the first page of Google, you need to stay there. Once you are on the first page does not mean that you will stay there forever.

If you just want to know how many visitors have looked at your site, you can place a visitor counter on your page. Just search for "visitor counter" and you will find plenty. The visitor counter websites will give you a code that you put on your site.

I have already covered Google Analytics in this book (www.Google.com/analytics), but there are some other very good websites you can use:

-www.site24x7.com is a great website monitoring service, and you will get instant alerts when your site goes down (not free).

- Visit www.websitegrader.com (or any other analytics website) and type in your website and your competitor's site. Look how many links your site has compared to your competitor's site. Analyse and learn.

- www.google.com/webmasters/tool

- www.quantcast.com

- www.siteluck.com

- You also need to get more and more back links—slowly but surely.

- You must ALWAYS keep an eye on your competitors to make sure they do not overtake you.

- Visit www.delicious.com and see how many people have bookmarked your site and your competitor's site. Analyse and learn.

- Visit www.facebook.com to see who has most fans. Analyse and learn.

- Visit www.compete.com and compare both sites. Analyse and learn.

- Visit www.google.com/alerts and put your three main competitors on alert. Google will let you know when your competitors are active on the web.

Analyse and Learn from your competition!

4) You must avoid being banned by Google.

If you follow only the guidelines in this book, you are fine and your site should not get banned. However, your site can be banned by Google for several reasons. One reason is by applying Black Hat SEO to your site, which I've explained previously. Also, NEVER use link farms or automated back linking.

Whilst talking about being banned: if possible, when you first start out, open 3 or 4 different PayPal accounts if you have different bank accounts. That way, when one of your accounts is banned, you can learn from it and use one of the other accounts.

It is VERY difficult to set up a new account if your account has been banned once as PayPal can check your IP address and know it is you again, opening a new account.

Chapter 16 - Analyse and Learn From Your Competition.

You want to find out how your competitors ended up on the first pages of Google, where you want your site to be. There are several ways to do this, and that's what I will talk about in this chapter. You want to find out if your niche is a profitable one, and one that you can break into in a relatively short period of time, or if it is going to take you years to break into the first page of Google.

1) Learn from your competition

In any business, online or off line, you need to keep an eye on your competitors and try to better them. You can find out what keywords they rank for on the first pages.

Search with your keyword and look at the first three pages to see which domain names show. Click on each domain name and once on the website, put your cursor anywhere on the page, right-click and choose "view source". This will give the web page's source code, which will look something like this:

```
ww.pettag.co.uk/acatalog/Tags_for_Horses.html - Original Source

Format

<HTML><HEAD><TITLE> Pet Tag Engraving Horse Tags Horse Tags</TITLE><Actinic:BASEHREF
 VALUE="http://www.pettag.co.uk/acatalog/"/><META NAME="ACTINICTITLE" CONTENT="Horse Tags"><META HTTP-
 Type" content="text/html; charset=iso-8859-1"> <META NAME="Keywords" CONTENT="Horse Tags, Horse Ident.
 Horse ID Tag, Pet Tag">
<META NAME="Description" CONTENT="Pet Tag Engraving Services - Horse Tags">
<META NAME="ActinicKey" CONTENT="fe4b34e8eae9d5de86a1d6d5818f89ef0">
<META NAME="Generator" CONTENT="accxecom5">
 <SCRIPT LANGUAGE="JavaScript" SRC="actiniccore.js" TYPE="text/javascript"></SCRIPT><script language=
<!--
function MM_swapImgRestore() { //v3.0
var i,x,a=document.MM_sr; for(i=0;a&&i<a.length&&(x=a[i])&&x.oSrc;i++) x.src=x.oSrc;
```

Now you can see the page how Google sees it. You need to view the source code of a minimum of ten first domain names, but it's better to do all 30 of the domains from the first three pages of your search. Either copy and paste all the information next to TITLE TAG, META KEYWORDS, META DESCRIPTION or do a print screen of all the websites (my software www.printingyourscreen.com is ideal for this). Analyse and learn. See what keywords your competitors use to get on the first few pages of Google.

ONLY look at those websites that DON'T have a showroom, so the websites that only sell their products online and nowhere else, as those are your main competitors.

You can also do the opposite. Go to pages 20 to 30, right-click "View Source" and see why those sites are *not* ranking on the first pages of Google.

You can find out how well optimised your competitors' sites are by using www.webceo.com or www.spyfu.com (not free).

To better your competition, you need to develop your website so that Google sees it as more relevant. You might have to do better SEO or optimise your site better. You might just beat them with that extra link. There is no golden rule that applies here: you just have to research and learn.

Yahoo Site Explorer gives information about your competitors' sites.

www.marketsamurai.com has a great tool to learn about your competition. You can evaluate the top 10 sites in your niche, and Market Samurai also gives your competitors' anchor text.

TOP TIP: Apply good SEO to your site first. Providing that you are in a low competition niche, you will probably rank in Google. If this does not work, check out how your competition made it to the 1st pages (by doing "view source" on their site) and work on your SEO. If that fails, you can use traffic methods to drive traffic to your site to increase your chances of Google ranking.

---

2) Assess the quality of your competitor's site

First things first—visit your competition. Pretend you are a customer looking for a particular product in that niche. Type in the keyword and visit the first few sites.

The fact that your competitor's site is showing on the first page means they have done a good job getting it there, so you can learn from them. Analyse their site, their keywords, and their SEO, and see if you can do the same, or better it.

Here are a few questions that you want to ask yourself while you are visiting your competitor's site:

- Is the site easy to use and navigate from one page to another?

- Does the site offer valuable information relevant to the product(s)?

- Are the product descriptions complete and detailed with quality images, or are there tiny pictures and poor quality or short descriptions of the products up for sale?

- For which keywords are your competitors' sites shown in Google?

- Do they advertise with Google Adwords?

- How likely is it that you would purchase a product from that particular site?

The quality of the site has a lot to do with how much business you will receive. If the design is poor and not visually appealing, the images are unclear and hard to see, the descriptions are short with little to no important details, the site is hard to move from one page to another, and/or the site does not offer any sort of value to the product, then the site is less likely to succeed in the industry.

Sites that offer high quality, visually appealing web designs, clear images, concise yet informative descriptions, easy navigation and valuable content will have more sales than a site that does not offer these things to its customers.

In looking at the top few sites, you will want to see if there is anything that you can do to differentiate yourself from them. If the sites are excellent, then you may have your work cut out for you. However, if there are a lot of improvements that could be made to the sites, then you probably stand a chance of creating a site that will stand out from the competition, adds value and gains sales—all of which are required for success.

3) Page Rank and Backlinks

As you become more familiar with SEO, you'll quickly learn what Google Page Rank is.

Page Rank is measured on a scale between 0 and 10 (10 being a handful of the biggest sites on the Internet) and gives you an idea of just how important Google thinks a website is. The higher the Page Rank (typically called PR), the higher up in the search engine results the site will appear.

In order to measure Google Page Rank, you'll need to add a browser plug-in. For Chrome, it is the Page Rank plug-in, and for Firefox, it is the SearchStatus plug-in. You can download Firefox at www.mozilla.org. If you use Firefox as your browser, the page rank for each site will be shown. Note: Firefox can slow down searching .

Here's a screenshot from the information that you will see once you have downloaded the necessary plug-ins:

- When you hover your mouse over PageRank, you will see that Amazon has a page rank of 8/10.

- The 2M that you can see in the circle is the Unique linking domains Amazon has to their website.

You can learn a lot more from this screenshot, but that is too much to talk about now.

Your site will start with a PR 0, and it will be harder to appear on the first page of Google than a similar site with a higher PR. If all the sites on the first page have PR of over four, you'll find it tough to beat them.

Let me explain it with an example. Suppose you have a website on hypnosis, but it is not getting many visitors because it isn't on the first page of Google for any keywords. Google thinks that your site is not important because it's not getting any traffic—it's kind of a Catch 22. Google gives your site a low PR, or Page Rank, and your site now has a PR0 because it has no backlinks at all. Page Rank is mostly based on quality of backlinks and domain age.

However, some people may find your site and link to it from their site. When people link to your site and your Page Rank goes up, and then might be PR1. However, a link from a small insignificant blogger does not really mean a lot to Google.

All of a sudden the National Hypnosis Centre, which is a high authority website with a PR 8, finds your website and links to your page. That immediately means that your Page Rank, or Authority, will go up because Google can see that someone important likes your site. If you can get a number of links from High Authority sites in your niche, your PR might suddenly rise.

Search engines do like to see sites linking to other relevant sites. The more links Google can see, the more chances your site has to be ranked. The more inbound links that point to your site, the more people will visit it and Google will then rank you higher.

Conclusion: the higher your page rank, the more important Google thinks your site is.

A backlink is a link from one site to another. For example, this link to YouTube (YouTube) would count as a backlink to that site, with the anchor text "YouTube" (the text that's been turned into a hyperlink or link). Just by underlining it, it does not become a link. You need to set it as a link in whatever web design program you use. Most hyperlink icons look like this:

When Google looks at the backlinks to a site, it checks:

- **The Page Rank** of the site that the link is coming from—a backlink from a site with a Page Rank of 9 will be much more valuable than a backlink from a site with a Page Rank of 1.

- **The "anchor text" of the back link.** In the example above, the anchor text was "YouTube". It's important to understand the concept of anchor text because it's one of the ways Google decides on how relevant your site is for different terms.

A good analogy of how this works is to think of all the sites competing for a keyword as politicians trying to get elected into Parliament or Congress. Each backlink is a vote for that candidate. Google would look at my link to YouTube above and say "okay, this counts as one vote for YouTube.com to be top of the search results for the keyword *YouTube*".

The winning candidate will be the one with the overall highest number of votes (there are other factors that also decide on the search result listings, but this is a good start).

If your competitor's search shows only sites on the first page that have a PR of between 0 and 3, that is good for you as it might be do-able for you to beat them. The same applies for sites with a low number of backlinks.

So how do you get these backlinks? Usually it's done by contacting websites in the same niche as yours and asking them to put a link on their site to yours. You can also do it yourself manually. If you are lucky, people will find your site and put a link on their site to yours.

If someone mentions your website with a hyperlink, e.g. on Facebook, Google can see that too and that will be an extra vote for your site.

4) Measure Incoming Links

Still working with the competition, you now want to see how many incoming links (better yet, domains) the site has. You will do this by using the Site Explorer offered for free by www.moz.com. By knowing this figure, you will determine how much work you'll need to do to rank similarly in the search engines. A number of factors are used when determining ranking, but the number of linking domains plays a heavy role in determining PR.

Backlinks are an imperative part of getting on Google's first page, along with content. Many people say it has become less important to rank, but I know a lot of people who still practice backlinking with success.

What is a "backlink" and how do they work?

To simplify: a backlink is a link from one site to another site. Backlinks are like votes. If you want to be on the first page of Google for the phrase "horse tacks" then you'll need to get backlinks to your site with the keyword "horse tacks" in them. The higher the Page Rank of the site that's linking to you, the more useful the back link.

These links to your site will do the most good if they're from sites that are *relevant* to your site. This means that a horse site would do best getting backlinks from high Page Ranking horse-related web pages.

Links to your site must be keyword links. The quality of the backlinks is more important than the quantity. In other words, if you have 100 links from a hypnosis site to your dog-training site, Google will ignore these. If you have only two links to your site from a PR8 dog training website, Google will like it.

Let's take a look at this, including a backlink from another site to our site:

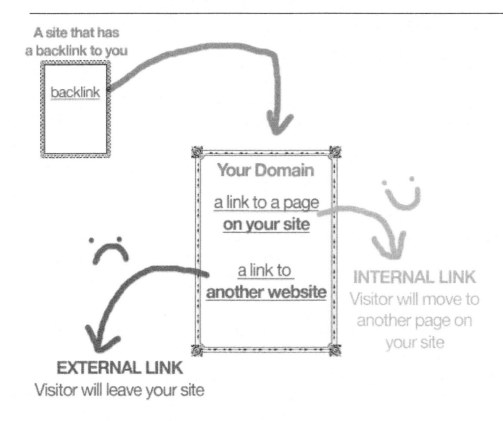

When a visitor comes to your site, they will see a number of links that they'll want to click. If they click a link that takes them to someone else's website, then you lose them.

> **TOP TIP: Always try to make your external links open in a new browser window. This way you won't risk your visitors moving away from your site. You can do this by adding the target="_blank" attribute to the link.**

If the link takes them to a page on *your* site, then you keep them, and so have more opportunities to sell to them.

In most web design programs, there will be a choice to open a hyperlink in a new window or the same window. Here is a screenshot of how WebPlus does this:

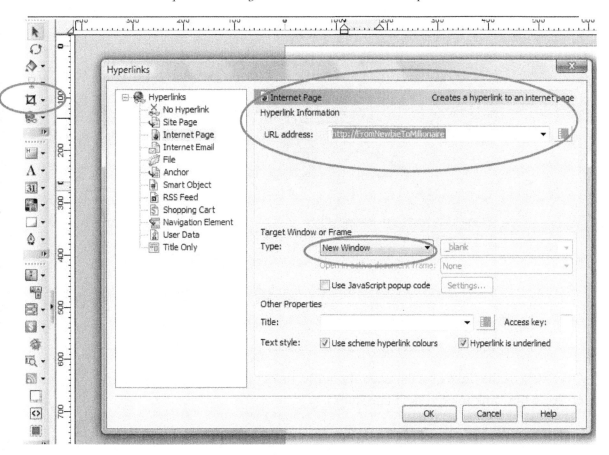

This is one of the reasons that, on each page, there should be more internal links than outbound links.

One of the ways Google calculates Page Rank is by using a concept built on "more inbound than outbound links".

To explain this it's best to think of your website as a series of buckets. Each page or post is a different bucket.

Imagine that each backlink you get to your site pours a small amount of liquid (that we'll call "link juice") into the page's bucket. Now imagine that any link on that page is a hole. An internal link is a hole that will pour your link juice into one of your other pages and keep it on your domain. An outbound link will take your link juice and lose it.

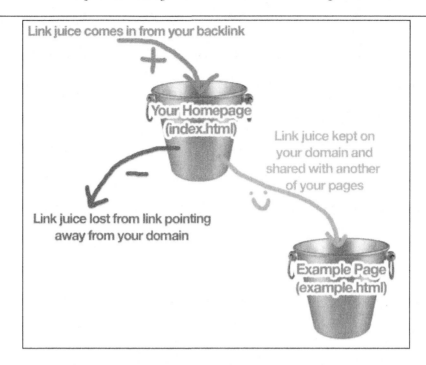

Over 50% of the links on each page should be links to other pages on your site. This helps preserve the "link juice" (aka Page Rank).

Quick backlinking methods

There are many tools on the Internet that are supposed to work wonders for you and automate links. Please investigate carefully before you commit to buy. Search for reviews on the software before you decide. NEVER EVER use automated links on your site.

A link farm is any group of websites that link to every other site in the group. Most links are created by automated programs and services and will be considered SPAM. Link farms are websites created mainly for the purpose of creating links to a page. These websites are not real and are mostly automatically created by software.

TOP TIP: You should NEVER use link farms that randomly link thousands of sites to your site. Another name for these link farms is FFA or Free For All sites. Your site might get banned altogether and never be shown again.

WARNING REGARDING BACKLINKS STRATEGY

Keep the number of backlinks you get each day low at first, and then slowly build more and more per day. Google doesn't like people creating their own backlinks in large numbers because it's manipulating the search results. Steadily increasing your number of backlinks will look more natural and will avoid being penalised by Google. That is one of the reasons why sites that sell thousands of links an hour are useless and might damage your site.

IMPORTANT RULES REGARDING BACKLINKS STRATEGY

If you cannot get any backlinks from high PR, educational or government sites, you should get as many backlinks as possible on any websites related to your niche.

> **TOP TIP: It is always good to include some .edu, .gov or .org sites in your outbound links. Even if they do not link back to you, they could have some value for Google.**

There are some rather expensive but good websites that offer personal link-building services. Just search for them, but remember to check them out first.

The best sites to get back links from:

- A site that has a minimum of one keyword that is the same as your site

- A site that has a minimum of one search term that is the same as your site

- A site that has text content on the page, not only links

- Links from well-known websites

- Links from sites with a high Page Rank

- Links from .edu, .gov or .org websites

Links that you do NOT need:

- Links from non-relevant pages

- Links from unethical websites full of spamming content

- Links from websites with hundreds of unrelated links on the page

- Links from adult sites

Keep in mind that most of the Automated Link Strategies Packages do not abide by the above rules.

> **TOP TIP:** Only work to get backlinks from relevant websites. If you have a website about dogs, it will be totally useless to get backlinks from a website about furniture!

Incoming links are supposed to be a huge factor that influences your rankings massively. Where this might be the case for many websites, in my experience, my "simple" websites still rank in Google without lots of links, external or internal.

Examples:

- my website www.liquorice-licorice.co.uk has been on the first page of Google for over 3 years for its relevant keywords

- my website www.nougat-nougat.co.uk has been on the first page of Google for targeted keyword since it was developed, years ago. This is a good example that you don't need a large site to rank.

Type in the web address of the first site listed in your Google search when you did a search for your competitors. Let's say that we are searching for hair extensions. Here are the first four sites listed in the Google search:

1. http://www.hairextensions.com/

2. http://www.amazon.com/

3. http://www.sallybeauty.com/

4. http://www.greatlengths.net/

As you can see, you'll be competing against Amazon, which is a big site. But, let's start with the first site. Type in www.hairextensions.com into Open Site Explorer: http://www.opensiteexplorer.org, which is a search engine for links. You will see that it shows 588 linking root domains (at the time of the screenshot).

Page Metrics:

Page Authority	Linking Root Domains	Total Links
58/100	588	9,509

Let's go ahead and look at Amazon. Type in www.amazon.com into the Open Site Explorer. You will see that the linking root domains jumped dramatically to 152,000.

Page Metrics:

Page Authority	Linking Root Domains	Total Links
97/100	152k	3.65m

That may be a little scary, but keep in mind that is for the site as a whole, not necessarily the keyword "hair extensions".

Now, If you use the specific link that was shown in Google searches, rather than the primary URL, you will type in www.amazon.com/b?ie=UTF8&node=702379011. This will show only two linking root domains, which means that you stand a chance at competing with such a big website.

Page Metrics:

Page Authority	Linking Root Domains	Total Links
48/100	2	15

If a page has fewer than 50 incoming domains

As a general rule, it will take up to a year to achieve this. If you can have some really great content, you should be able to get 50 incoming linking domains within 12 months or less. As far as the site that you are visiting goes, having so few incoming linking domains may mean that the competition in this market isn't as fierce as you once thought. It could also mean that the demand is low for this particular niche. So, be careful when following through.

If a page has 50 to 250 incoming domains

As a general rule, it can take a year or a little more to reach this many links, but is an ideal range when looking for a profitable niche. In a short period of time, you can use long tail keywords to really generate traffic to your site. It may take longer to make it to the #1 spot, but you'll be on the first page of Google in no time with the right approach.

If a page has 250 to 500 incoming domains

Generally, it would take a couple of years to reach this many incoming domains, although it isn't impossible. Once you reach this amount of linking domains, the payoff will likely be huge. However, it will take more time on your part to achieve this. If this is your first site, it is recommended to find a niche that has fewer liking domains so that you can reach success faster.

If a page has 500 or more incoming domains

This is going to require some heavy work, probably taking several years to get up there and compete—definitely not what you are looking for with your first eCommerce store.

Now, keep in mind that these are just basic figures. You may be able to achieve this within a smaller amount of time, or it could take you longer. It all depends on the quality of the content that you deliver and the various approaches that you use.

5) Authority Links

When it comes to ranking high in Google, authority really matters. You can have fewer links from highly respected websites, such as the New York Times and CNN, and rank higher in Google than if you had 100 low-quality links from unknown domains.

While the link count that you just learned about is useful, the whole picture is not shown. There is more to it than the number of linking root domains. As you've probably noticed when using the Open Site Explorer, you can view page authority for the link that you enter. However, there is some more information regarding Google Page Rank that you should be aware of so that you can appropriately interpret the PR when studying your competition.

PR0 to PR2

These are the lowest of the pages, but are honestly relatively average. If the sites rank high for a certain niche and only have a Page Rank between 0 and 2, then there may be a lack of demand for the niche or lack of competition.

PR3 to PR4

Top sites are more frequently within this range than any other PR range. This is the type of niche that you want to get into, as it will be the easiest to get to the top, but the market still has enough of a demand for you to make a profit. With excellent site content, a visually appealing and easy to navigate web design, and some effort, you can tap into the market and become a top contender in a couple of years (depending on your approach and how great your content is, it may take less time).

PR5

If your competition is a PR5, then your work will be a little bit harder, but it is still possible to reach that bar. If most of the sites are PR5, then you should be careful, as it will take a few years to really break into this market, even with value and backlinks.

PR6+

If your top competitors are a PR6 or higher, then it's not recommended to enter the market for this one. These guys have been around for years and years and the competition is incredibly fierce—so fierce that you don't want to get involved, at least not with your first-ever site.

6) Exceptions to the rule

As with everything, there are exceptions to the rule. This means that there are a few exceptions to the above-mentioned information.

Keep in mind that Page Rank is a measure of authority for an individual page and the website domain as a whole. In other words, it's possible for a primary web domain to be at PR8, but one of the secondary pages only be at PR1.

Getting on Page One of Google

While you might think that the first two or three sites on page one of the Google search results are the most important, the truth of the matter is that there is still another one that is just as important, if not more important. The site that it is in the last spot, the #10 spot, on the search results page. You see, you don't have to be the first, second or third site for a keyword, although it is beneficial, but you do want to make sure you are on the first page of Google as soon as possible. Most web users will not go beyond the first page of search results, so it is critical that you work to achieve page one. Once you've accomplished this, you can then target your site to become one of the top three or so leaders for the keyword.

Anyway, you want to check out the linking domains for the last site on the first page of Google. If the number is significantly lower than the top few sites, then you are in a good spot, because that means that the competition is not too deep in this particular market. With a fraction of the incoming domain links that the top few sites have, you can make it to page one of the search results, gaining more exposure. It is harder to rank higher the closer you get to the top spot, but it's nice to know that getting to the bottom of page one is ultimately within your reach.

Alternatively, if the #10 site on page 1 of Google has just as many incoming domain links as the top sites have, then you may be in trouble. You are going to have to fight, and fight hard, to reach the first page, not to mention one of the top spots for a keyword. If this is the case, then you might want to start out with a different market or target a different keyword so that you can reach success within a shorter period of time.

Deep Linking

The majority of a website's traffic comes from long tail keywords. These are also easier to rank higher for than the generic keywords. During your keyword research, if you discovered several long tail keywords, then you'll want to take the time to uncover some more information about them. We have all become better in searching over the years, so most people will type in multiple keywords instead of just one word.

Due to the fact that long tail keywords are easier to rank well with, it will be in your benefit to pursue some links to your non-homepage pages, which are known as secondary pages. This is especially true if the niche you are targeting is pretty saturated. For example, instead of fighting for the #1 spot for "patio furniture," you can focus on reaching the top with "wicker patio furniture", "cushioned patio furniture" and "wood patio furniture." Not only will you get more targeted traffic, but your conversion rate will also be higher.

In all honesty, this is probably the best SEO strategy that you can use to your advantage, especially when you are first starting out and need that extra boost. Linking to web pages that are not the home page is known as "deep linking" and is ultimately the perfect way for one to build and market their brand new drop shipping and eCommerce website.

Now, if you remember, you typed in Amazon into the Open Site Explorer. This is what you got:

Page Metrics:

Page Authority	Linking Root Domains	Total Links
97 /100	152k	3.65m

You then went on to use a secondary page, other than the homepage, to determine how many linking root domains there were for the hair extension page that popped up in the primary search results for the keyword "hair extensions". To refresh your memory, though, and to keep you from going back a couple pages, this was the link: www.amazon.com/b?ie=UTF8&node=702379011. And when you put this in the Open Site Explorer, this is what you got:

Page Metrics:

Page Authority	Linking Root Domains	Total Links
48 /100	2	15

With only two linking domains, you can actually compete with one of the largest websites online for this particular keyword.

Chapter 17 - Getting Traffic to Your Online Shop.

There are over 100 traffic methods in my book "From Newbie To Millionaire". I will discuss a few here.

Of course, if you are so lucky (like I am with some of my sites) that your site ranks on the first page of Google, you won't have to do much to get traffic in order to get sales.

Have you ever seen a Tesco or a Wal-Mart on a dirty old road, in the middle of a forest? I haven't! Why not? Simply because there is no traffic. In Internet marketing and in eCommerce, traffic equals sales.

If you think you've done enough to try and get traffic: do some more! You can never get enough traffic. Providing your store meets most of the important criteria you have learned so far in this book, you should receive orders, and the more traffic gets to your site, the more orders you will receive. You don't have to be a genius to work that one out.

Here is the result of an interesting study regarding the media that influences consumers to start searching for products online.

Media	Percentage of Respondents
Magazines	47%
Reading an article	43%
Broadcasts TV	43%
Newspapers	41%
Face to face communications	39%
Cabe TV	36%
Coupons	36%
Direct Mail	30%
Radio	29%
In store promotions	27%
Online Advertising	26%
Email advertising	25%
Online communiteis	19%
Outdoor billboards	12%
Blogs	10%
Instant messaging	8%
Mobile phone	7%
Yellow pages	7%
Text Messaging	6%
Other	6%
Mobile video or pictures	4%

Source : RAMA- Retail Advertising & Marketing Association

Note that 36% of people start searching online with a coupon. You can also see that email advertising is important as it influences 25% of people! Start building your list and put your email marketing skills into practice.

Another important thing to note is the mobile phone at only 7%. I am sure my daughters do agree with this, as they constantly tell me that neither them nor their friends take any notice of all the advertising that appears on their phones. The same applies for Facebook ads. I asked my daughters to ask all their friends how many of them ever click on the ads on their mobiles or on Facebook and the result is: nobody.

Did I miss Facebook on the above list or is it not there? :-) With all the over-hyped stuff about making money on Facebook, why is it not on this list?

As you already know, I am not a social media person. I analyse and learn. To give you one example: I follow several big gurus and I am on their mailing lists.

One guru organises events regularly. In February, he announces an event that is in March four times on Facebook.

In April, he announces another event twice that is in June.

In August, he organises another event but does NOT announce it on Facebook. Now why is that? Surely because it didn't give him any sales the first two times he announced the events. If he would have had a lot of sales for tickets for the event, he would KEEP announcing it on Facebook every time he had an event, wouldn't he?

There are PLENTY of examples I could give you similar to this one.

Here are some ways to get traffic.

1) Improve your SEO

Always try and improve your SEO if you are not ranking high enough. Small changes can make a big difference.

2) Free traffic from shopping directories and trade associations

A directory is a great way to source links for your site. A directory is a website that has a list of links to other sites and usually categorises them in a certain order.

This is fairly simple and quick to do. Search for

- "your keyword" + "directory", e.g. jewelry + directory

- "your keyword" + "directories"

- "your keyword" + "trade associations"

- "your keyword" + "meta-indexes" for sites with master lists of directories

You can also simply search for "list of shop directories" and you will lots of them.

Then look at all the websites that might be of interest to your niche. Sign up if need be and submit your website to the directories. Most of the time, these submissions are free, but even if it costs you a few dollars or pounds a year, it might be worth investing for that extra link to your site. Directories are a very good resource for generating backlinks to your site.

- www.dmoz.org (PR8) A listing on DMOZ is worth fighting for as Google loves this directory. Make sure you choose the correct category. If your submission is rejected, try again three months later. A listing with DMOZ would give you higher rankings almost immediately.

Shopping Directories:

- www.pricegrabber.com

- www.megashopbot.com

- www.shopping5.com

- www.shopping.com

- www.shopzilla.com

- www.ukbuyonline.co.uk

Price comparison sites:

One of the first things potential customers do is go to price comparison sites.

- www.moneysupermarket.com

- www.kelkoo.com

- www.pricerunner.co.uk

- www.twenga.com

- www.twenga.co.uk

- www.idealo.co.uk

- www.nextag.com: for .uk and .com

3) Free traffic from Google Merchant centre

Google Merchant Center is how you can have your products listed in the Shopping Results of Google when someone searches for your keyword. You upload your product data to Google and make it available to Google shopping and other Google services.

You need to create an account here: www.google.com/merchants. When that is done, create a feed and submit the feed to Google with your Google Merchant account.

4) Free traffic from Google Places

If you have a physical shop people can visit, submit your site to Google Places.

5) Free traffic from Google image results

Always give your images a keyword.

Google will automatically display the well-optimised images in the search results for images.

6) Free traffic from Google news.

www.news.google.com

www.news.google.co.uk

If you have something really important/different/unusual to tell, submit it to Google news.

7) Free traffic from press releases

Press releases are syndicated content, which means that when you post one, a lot of other sites will automatically take it and post it onto their web pages too.

Most Internet marketers don't realise the importance of press releases and therefore under-use them, but they are a fantastic way to get extra visitors to your site.

You can use these to promote products, the launch of your site or a new section, or just to raise awareness of what you're offering. Plus, optimising the press release for the keywords you're targeting will also allow it to rank in Google almost overnight!

Google loves press releases, but only if they follow a certain set of rules:

- The information you're giving must be newsworthy and specific - promoting a product, a service, a site launch, a new eBook or book and so on.

- It should not be written like a sales letter - write it as if it was going to appear in a broadsheet newspaper. It needs to be factual and well worded.

- Craft the best possible headline and then use that headline in the first sentence. You have to make your headline sound like a newsworthy topic. "Announces" or "review" or "interesting result" are good words to use. The headline should ideally not be longer than ten words.

- In the first paragraph you should make it clear who you are and what you're offering. The body copy should be between 250 and 300 words.

- Explain why the reader should care—Why/how/when/where are you promoting this?

- Avoid using sensationalist adjectives like "insane", "crazy"—again, this is NOT a sales letter.

- Include ALL your contact details.

- Include city and date of the release.

- You MUST spell check and proofread.

You can outsource the writing of your press release. Help is available here: www.writinghelptools.com or www.elance.com.

Most press release sites are free, but sometimes if you pay a one-off fee they guarantee that yours will be picked up by the major search engines. From my experience, the paid press release sites give more results.

Some good free press release sites:

www.businesswire.com
www.free-press-release.com free submission to online news feeds
www.i-newswire.com
www.prfree.com
www.prlog.com will automatically send press releases out to a large number of other sites for you, including (potentially) Google News (free service)
www.prnewswire.com
www.prweb.com
www.webwire.com

To find more press release sites, just Google: "free press release distribution" or "press release submission service" or "press release submission directory".

8) Free traffic from video marketing

You can hire someone on www.elance.com to do a video for your shop.

I must admit, I don't do enough video marketing myself at the moment but I am planning to work on that in 2014. Google loves videos at the moment, therefore putting videos on your site, and on other sites all over the web, will be an extra vote for you for Google's ranking.

You can submit your videos, mostly with a link to your website, to the video websites listed below. If you cannot put a link with your video, make sure your URL is shown on the video itself. You might have to become a member first before you are able to submit a video. Most of these websites are free but for some you will need a paid account.

Always use your keywords in the title and description when submitting a video. Some video sites to upload to are:

- www.youtube.com YouTube is the most popular site, but lots of other sites are getting tons of traffic and are worth submitting your video to.

- http://video.Google.com Google also has a free batch uploader, which enables you to upload more than one video at once.

- www.vimeo.com This is a very popular video site. The BEST thing: no ads! Yes, no ads! Who-ever watches the Youtube ads anyway?

- www.buzznet.com

- www.dailymotion.com has high Alexa ranking.

- www.flixya.com

- www.gofish.com

- www.screenjunkies.com

- www.metacafe.com

- www.viddler.com

- www.instant-traffic-geyser.com

- www.tubetoolbox.co.uk

- www.video.yahoo.com

- www.tubemogul.com Tube Mogul: sign up here to have all your videos automatically uploaded to up to 20 video hosting sites all at once.

You can search for "video hosting sites" and "video classifieds" to find more Video Hosting websites.

Informative: www.viralvideochart.com gives you a chart of the most popular viral videos. If your video is on the top 10 chart, you know you've done well! ☺

9) Free traffic from blogs and forums

Search for

- "your keyword" + "blog", e.g. jewelry + blog

- "your keyword" + "forum", e.g. jewelry + forum

Join some blogs and forums and mention your site now and again.

10) Free traffic from affiliate marketing

Learn about affiliate marketing if you have an eCommerce site (not a drop shipping site) and a shopping cart that has an affiliate program. Let others do the selling for you.

11) Free traffic from social media

I am putting this last as I am personally not a great social media person. I can see it is great fun to socialize, but I cannot see the money in it for me. I believe it is better to spend more time on other traffic methods rather than spending hours on Facebook but hey, I could be wrong. Try it and see what you think; maybe you can create extra sales with Facebook.

TOP TIP: Don't use software that automatically gets you thousands of followers/friends on Twitter, Facebook or any other social networking site. Normally the followers will be bogus in some way, either fake accounts or people who have been spammed to death. The only way you will ever get any real, potential buyers is by doing it the good old-fashioned way—yourself!

12) Free traffic from email marketing.

Email marketing, if done right, can create lots of extra sales. I suggest you study how to do it correctly, as I cannot include it all in this book.

Spam is a big problem and spam is ignored by many people. Take a look at the following chart. In 2012, 72.1% of emails received by people were spam according to a study from Kaspersky Lab.

On the positive side: this is 8.2% less than in 2011.

Trends in 2012

Lower spam volumes

The amount of spam fell throughout the course of the entire year. At the close of 2012, the percentage of spam settled at 72.1%, or 8.2% less than in 2011.

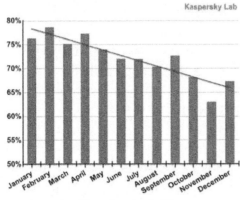

Percentage of spam in mail traffic

source: www.kaspersky.com

13) Run promotions on a regular basis

Once you have your customer's email addresses, you need to make sure that they will not forget about you, so they need to hear from you now and again. A brilliant way of doing this is by running promotions. Before you run a promotion, make sure you check that your software can handle it. There are different types of promotions you can do; here are a few.

- Free gift. You can give away a box of (preferably Belgian) chocolates to anyone who spends over a certain amount.

- Buy one, get one 1/2 price

- Free return for a certain period

- Free postage and packing for a certain period

- Give a percentage of your profits to a charity

- Gift cards promotions

- Email a discount voucher

- Give a coupon code

Make sure you make it clear when the promotion ends.

14) PPC = Paid Traffic

The type of paid traffic we will discuss here is PPC (Pay Per Click) traffic. PPC advertising is my favourite form of paid traffic but ONLY with the smaller search engines.

As the name implies, this kind of traffic will cost you money for every person that clicks on your ad and visits your website. The cost of each click may cost anywhere from £0.04/$0.03 to £59/$80, depending on the keywords you want to target.

If you can start an ad campaign for only $0.03/£0.04 per click, there is a chance that you can make good profit from your site. £59/$80 per click is for "the big boys" or only suitable if you are selling very expensive products, otherwise you will probably never make any money.

Do not bid on open keywords as that will be more expensive. Find your golden keyword or long tail keyword and bid on that keyword. The days when you could earn money from PPC with a keyword like "dog" or "insurance" (open keywords) are long gone. You need to find more specific, which means cheaper, keywords to bid on, e.g. how to stop my dog barking.

If you decide to use Google Adwords, I suggest you have a look at their Google Traffic Estimator tool. This will tell you how much traffic you can expect, how much your keyword is going to cost per click and how much your estimated daily cost will be.

In my experience, it is more difficult to earn money with PPC if you run a drop shipping site, as your profit margins are usually smaller than with your own eCommerce site, where you stock the products that you sell.

In my book "From Newbie To Millionaire" is a spreadsheet that shows you when you will make money with PPC and when you won't. I never run a PPC campaign without using that spreadsheet.

Be aware with paid traffic: you can lose a lot of money. Only spend money you are prepared to lose. It may take you a while to find something that works well.

Chapter 18 – eBay.

If your sites is not ranking very high in Google, you can always sell your products on other websites. If you can't get any traffic, go where the traffic already is, e.g. eBay, Amazon and other big online shops.

I always recommend creating multiple streams of income. We'll look at eBay first, followed by some other online shops in the next chapter.

1) Selling on Ebay

Setting up your own personal website does take time and money. Therefore, it is important that you don't set up your own website until you are positive about what you plan to sell, you've chosen your supplier, and you know your target audience. It would be a huge bummer if you had to scrap the website because you changed your niche market.

Your website will take some time to get off the ground because you'll need to generate web traffic to your site and improve your ranking in search engines, so that when people search for your niche, they will actually find your website. It's possible that money will not be made immediately, but in the long run, the profit can be remarkable. It is because of this that you may want to give eBay a try when you first start out.

Lots of eCommerce software now have a "Push to eBay" feature, which means, in a matter of minutes, your products are listed on eBay.

a) Using eBay to sell

www.ebay.com, www.ebay.co.uk. To sell on eBay, you'll need a PayPal account, which is super easy to get. You'll also need to set up an eBay account so that you can begin posting your items for sale. This chapter is dedicated to using eBay to sell your products, a great place to get started.

eBay is ideal to help you learn the process of online sales, test your products to see which ones sell easily and well, and test drop shipping and/or wholesale services.

b) *Maintaining your eBay customer rating*

When it comes to eBay, you have a customer rating, which will need to be kept in tip-top shape if you plan to use eBay for selling. Each time that you sell a product to someone, the buyer will be able to rate their experience with you.

Your customer rating is incredibly important to having success on eBay. Subsequent buyers will be able to see your customer rating, which will ultimately provide prospective customers with your reliability and what they can expect if they do business with you. In addition, if you hope to ever have you very own store on eBay, then you'll need a high rating.

You may run into problems on eBay with customers. One customer may have a dumb reason for wanting to return an item that they purchased, or maybe you made a mistake when you posted an item causing you to take a loss on the product. Sometimes, it's better to take a loss here and there because that rating cannot be changed once it is done.

Even if you are just using eBay to really get started and don't plan on using it in the future, you want to make sure you keep a high customer rating, because you never know when you might decide to use eBay again.

c) *Using eBay to promote your website*

A decision to use either eBay or a personal website does not have to be made, as it is possible to use both for selling your products. In fact, many online retailers use both. Your eBay listings can actually help you get traffic to your personal website. Of course, you can't just openly promote your personal site on eBay, but there are a couple of ways that you can get around that:

- You can use your eBay "About Me" profile section to link to your website. A number of prospective customers on eBay will review your information and will click on the link and visit your website. This inbound link also helps give your search engine ranking a much-needed boost.

- You can use e-mails and/or a newsletter to invite eBay customers to visit your site. While you don't want to be rude or pushy, a good way to go about doing this is using a thank you e-mail after a purchase. You can thank your customer for purchasing with you and let them know you appreciate their business and offer your website link for future purchases. You could say something like this:

"Thank you for selecting Crowns & Jewels for your jewelry needs! We truly appreciate your business today! Please visit us again at www.crownsandjewels.com."

How effective using eBay is to promote your website depends solely on the number of sales you can make and how happy the customers are with their experience with you. In other words, eBay cannot be your only marketing tactic, but it is a good way to get started marketing your personal website. You can use both to make your drop shipping business really work.

It is a good idea to start with eBay for your drop shipping business. Basically, eBay acts as classroom instruction. It will allow you to learn about having an online business and test the popularity of your products—all before you expand your business. When you reach a specific amount of experience on eBay, you can get an eBay store (more on this in the next section) or opt to operate your own website.

Even when you get your own website up and running, you can still use eBay for selling your products, especially when holidays come around, as a number of people turn to eBay to find gifts. It's a great place to sell seasonal products that you have a limited supply of and products that you obtained at crazy clearance prices, which would be more appropriate for eBay than your own site, as your personal website is for your regular supply of products.

2) Selling used items on eBay

Yes, this book is about drop shipping, but you never know when it might come in handy to know a little bit about selling used items on eBay. For one, you may want to sell new and used items that are relevant to your niche, in which case you would get your new items from a wholesaler or drop shipper and your used items from garage sales, thrift stores or various other locations. It is a great way to become known for your product on eBay, which is exactly what you want and need.

You could sell your returned items that you've sold from your online shop on eBay if the products has been unwrapped, making it, in theory, a secondhand item.

Cashmere is one of the top sellers on eBay, and is something that hardly ever loses its value. A premium fabric, cashmere is in high demand all over the world and comes in limited supply in a number of locations. The best thing about it is that its value holds true practically forever regardless of how old it is or how many individuals it has gone through. You could purchase cashmere items, such as scarves and sweaters, via wholesale or use a drop shipper, and sell them on eBay individually.

Alternatively, you could sell used cashmere items that you picked up at a thrift store or a local yard sale.

Cashmere from the 1950s sell for amazing prices, so if you come across any vintage cashmere, it is imperative to hold on to it, refurbish it, and re-sell it on eBay. It's unbelievable the prices that you can get for these types of items.

If you really want to make a specific market work on eBay, you should sell new and used items as well as vintage and antique items to really capitalize on demographics.

Combine used items and wholesale items to start with when selling on eBay.

Why not just sell used items?

You are probably thinking that sounds easy, so why don't I just do that instead of drop shipping. Well, the truth of the matter is that selling used items takes a lot of time and effort on your part—much more than you are probably willing to give, especially when you can sell new items much easier. You see, with used items, you have to spend hours and hours scouting yard sales, bazaars and second-hand stores to find the items that will sell well on eBay.

However, for a day or two a week, you can find a few items here and there that you can sell on eBay to supplement your income and to complement your wholesale or drop ship items while expanding your customer base.

Lots of eCommerce software packages and templates have an automatic feed to list products on eBay, saving you tons of time.

a) Tips for finding quality used items to sell on eBay

If this is something that you decide to do, here are some tips:

- **Shop Larger Events**. You can spend a lot of time driving from one house to another to find a garage sale worth your time. The best thing for you to do is visit larger events, such as fundraisers and bazaars, where a ton of different things will be from various homes. Sometimes, businesses will donate brand new items to these events, giving you the chance to get a new item at a fraction of the cost, which you can then turnaround and sell as a new product for full retail. You can learn about these events in your local newspaper, a community website or even on Craigslist.

- **Shop the Richer Areas**. If you visit garage and yard sales in larger, upscale neighborhoods, you may find some really good eBay sellers, such as name brand clothing, china, premium colognes and perfumes and more. Even if the items have been used and the cologne or perfume bottle is only ¾ full, it will still sell on eBay.

- **Get There Early**. Showing up to a yard sale late is like showing up to an interview late: you are left in the dust and don't stand a chance. You need to get there early so that you can get the best stuff; otherwise, all the good stuff will be gone when you get there that afternoon.

- **Have Cash and Don't Be Afraid to Bargain**! People have garage sales because they need to get rid of the stuff that they have no need and no room for. They just figure they might as well get a few bucks for the things that they don't need. Be sure to show up with cash, and when you find something you want, bargain with the seller to get it a little lower. The best time to do this is at the end of the day when the seller is getting ready to close up shop and needs to get rid of whatever is left. Make sure you have the cash in your hand so that the seller sees visibly that you have money and are serious about buying. You could compare it to having a piece of candy in your hand while you tell your child to clean their room. It's obvious that they'll get the candy if they clean their room, just as it is obvious to the seller that if they go lower on their sale price, they'll get rid of their unwanted things. One of the best ways to get bargaining to work is to offer to buy a larger box of items, whether it be books, cosmetics, or other items, for one low price.

b) Secondhand items that usually sell well on eBay

While I can't guarantee that if you have one of these items, it will sell on eBay, the items listed here are items that generally sell really well when listed on eBay. It's a great way to supplement your drop ship or wholesale products.

- Designer Clothes

- Leather: jackets, coats, briefcases, purses, belts

- Children's items: bedding, clothing, small toys

- Designer perfume

- China: dolls, dishes

- Wedding dresses

- Cowboy boots: ostrich, lizard, embroidered, bright colours

- Sports equipment

- Vintage items: any

- Brand name cosmetics: sell better if unopened

- Brand name kitchen items

- Anything with a tag or still in the box

Due to the time and effort involved in selling used items, I recommend only using it as a supplement to your wholesale or drop ship products. It's an excellent way to add some income and build a name for yourself in a specific market on eBay. It's also a great way to get that customer feedback rating and get some experience under your belt regarding the eBay process.

c) Step-by-step guide for drop shipping on eBay

1. Sign up to a supplier site. You may need to supply your credit card details in order to get a verified sellers account. Don't worry, this is just a security check.

2. Search for an item that you want to research and, possibly, sell. As soon as you start searching you'll see the huge range of products available; you'll just have to try to choose!

3. Research, research, research. Log in to eBay and search for the item you're researching.

4. Check "Completed listings" on Ebay.

This allows you to see items that have sold, in green, and auctions that ended unsold, in red:

* Note the items that received bids, but did not sell. This indicates items that had interest, but where the reserve price was set at more than people were willing to spend. If you find lots of instances of your chosen item going unsold, but getting bids, you could dominate the market by underselling the reserve prices other people are setting (assuming you can do this and still make a profit).

1) Search the list of results. If you find that the vast majority of the item you want to sell is finishing as "Sold", then this may be a great product to sell. If you find that your item is a hot seller then that's even better. Check how many items are selling every day and every week. Your best bet is to find lots of items that are selling at the "Buy It Now" price, because this makes it easier to calculate how much profit you'll make.

2) Find an item you want to sell on any of the supplier's sites you have signed up with. Keep an eye on the minimum orders that these suppliers ask for. Some will require a minimum order of 10 to 1,000, which won't be possible if you're just starting out. You want to find someone who allows you to order single items or, if you think the item will sell well, 10 at most.

3) Contact the seller. Sometimes the price per unit won't be listed, so you'll have to get in touch to find out their pricing; you'll also need to make sure that they have the item in stock.

4) Now to create the listing: search back through the listings that ended with the item being sold and copy and paste it into your new listing but re-word it. Add any information

from your supplier that's missing in the listing, your Terms and Conditions and refund policy, and you're good to go!

You can type in any keyword in eBay and research if the items are selling well and find similar items to sell.

> **TOP TIP**: Do not "oversell" your product. If you're completely honest about what you're selling, then you'll get fewer refund requests. This doesn't mean you should undersell yourself, just don't say anything that isn't 100% true.

5) Now that your listing is live, you'll have to answer any questions that you're sent, and sit back and watch as the bidders go crazy for what you're offering!

6) When the item sells you need to remember that PayPal will hold your funds for around 15 days, or until you get positive feedback.

7) Order the item(s) from the supplier and request that they're sent to the addresses you've received from the buyers. Make sure you tell the supplier not to put the price anywhere on the packaging!

8) Rinse and repeat! If you find that your initial few items sell really well, then attack it hard and put up a lot of the same item. He who dares wins!

Keep tabs on what sells and how much profit you make overall for each item. I'd recommend setting up a spreadsheet with the time and date that each of your items sold, along with a running total of the profit you've made. This will allow you to keep track of the rate at which these are selling, and to notice when sales are starting to slow down. Depending on the eCommerce software you use for your store, these reports might also be available from within your software.

Aside from the initial investment in the first batch of stock, you should not put any more of your own money into selling these. If you stick to that, you will increase your chances of making money.

> **TOP TIP**: If your supplier says it will take two days for the product to be sent to the customer, then on your sales page state "four days for delivery". This way, if your supplier requires a minimum order, you have two days in which to sell the minimum order amount. If you feel it will take you more than two days, then add more days for delivery. Be careful not to make it too long, though, because this will definitely put some people off buying.

d) Ship international or not?

Once you've decided for sure to sell on eBay, you need to consider where you'll ship your items to. Do you want to stick to shipping only in your country or will you be open to shipping internationally?

You will have to investigate which shipping company is best for you, e.g. UPS, FedEx, DHL, Royal Mail, etc…

Shipping international is more complicated than shipping domestically. When you ship overseas, you'll need to adjust your shipping fees accordingly and fill out customs forms. The fraud risk is greater and there is ultimately a greater chance of your items getting lost in the mail if uninsured. So make sure you unsure everything that you ship internationally.

Your product could ultimately decide whether you ship domestically or if you ship internationally. Consider cashmere—did you know that more than three-quarters of cashmere sales on eBay are to international buyers? The reason for this is that cashmere is not as readily available in other countries as it is in the United States. Some products are simply more popular outside of the United States or cannot be found, so they are sold easily to international buyers. This is something you'll need to research, as if you aren't offering your products to international buyers, you could be missing out on a large percentage of sales.

If you make the decision to ship internationally, you'll want to offer multiple locations in your eBay listing for where you will ship to you, along with relevant shipping prices. Be selective, though, so as to protect yourself from potential fraud.

There is seller protection available via eBay as well as PayPal, but you aren't always protected. If an account number or credit card number is found to be fraudulent, the funds can be revoked without notice to you. If you've already shipped the product, then it's at your loss. If you accept money orders (BACS payments) from an international country, make certain it is from a reputable company, such as American Express, MasterCard or Visa. You can also receive payment via wire transfer, but it should be to an account solely for this purpose only. The money should be removed immediately, before the product is shipped. This is just to ensure your safety and security.

Chapter 19 - Selling From Other Online Venues.

We have talked about selling on eBay. We have talked about selling on your own personal website. Now, we are going to talk about selling on various other online venues.

While eBay is still one of the most popular places to sell and to buy, there are downsides to it: fees, competition, etc. So, you might want to consider using other online venues to sell your products as well. Of course, Amazon being the biggest one.

Below, you will find a short list of a few different online places where you can sell your products that you have bought from a wholesaler. Along with each venue, you will also find a brief overview of what the site is and what it has to offer you as an online retailer selling wholesale or drop ship products. The first several go into greater detail, then you'll find a few extras that have a brief description of the site. You will find that you can save money with many of these sites when compared to eBay.

1) Bonanza

www.bonanza.com With cheaper selling fees than eBay and no listing charge, Bonanza is an auction venue that is for more unusual, off the beaten path items. Therefore, it's not like eBay; it's a place to sell items that are unique and out of the ordinary. Bonanza believes heavily in communication between the buyer and seller, and for that reason, they offer chatting and instant messaging, resulting in more real-time communication and negotiations. Their customer service is said to be significantly better than eBay. Small Business Computing and Ecommerce Guide have both listed Bonanza as the best alternative to eBay.

You'll find some of the lowest selling fees here, which is great if you are worried about overhead costs. However, the site does not offer auctions and isn't as well-known as some similar sites, such as eBay.

The only downside is that Bonanza isn't widely known. It doesn't have the traffic and popularity that eBay does; therefore, your sale volume might not be quite as large. Although, it is quickly becoming one of the more popular alternatives to eBay.

2) Craigslist

www.craigslist.com All major cities, even outside of the United States, have a dedicated Craigslist site. Craigslist offers no auctions, so products are at fixed-price rates. Most people go to Craigslist to find a job, a cheap sofa, or a house or apartment for rent, but plenty of people sell products there for pretty decent prices.

With Craigslist, there are no listing fees, no sign-up fees, and no percentage of profit to be paid. It's all simply free of charge. Many people can post a product in the morning and have it sold by that afternoon. Products can be used, new, vintage, antique, etc. It doesn't matter; it all sells.

The major caveat with Craigslist would be scammers. As with numerous other sites, Craigslist is almost like a magnet for scams, especially since buyers do not have to be verified or even have an account with Craigslist in order to respond to one of your posts. So, you must be careful when selling on Craigslist.

Here are some basic tips for Craigslist:

- Never provide banking account information to someone, especially from another country, who says they need it in order to send you a bank wire transfer. It's in your best interest not to make the sale, even if it was possibly legitimate, because nine times out of 10, it is a scam to drain your bank account for every last penny.

- In many cases, Craigslist is better for selling products locally. Sometimes, prospective buyers want to see a product before they actually hand over their hard-earned cash.

- Don't post too many things at once, because Craigslist may think you are scamming and may block your account. You can't use Craigslist as you can eBay, posting 50 products at once, so keep that in mind to ensure your account stays open, active and usable.

3) Amazon

www.amazon.com or www.amazon.co.uk or any of the other Amazon worldwide. While you can't have an auction on Amazon, you can still sell some of your products in their Stores section.

Amazon isn't really known for used products, but if you are drop shipping items, then you are probably going to have more new items than used. The great thing about Amazon is that they'll even act as drop shipper for you, but you'll need to send a bulk shipment to them which they will store for you. Then, when a product sells, they'll pack and ship it for you.

You can sell in different ways on Amazon (not all listed):

Find more info here: http://services.amazon.co.uk/ or http://services.amazon.com

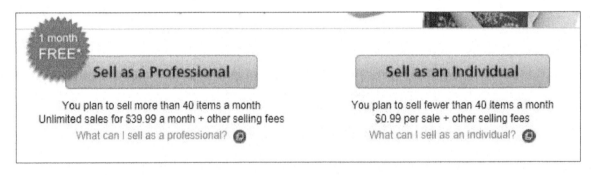

- you can become a reseller, just sign up and sell what you want, obviously following the rules and regulations

- you can have an Amazon store

- you can create a seller account

- you can become a Vendor. This is where Amazon stocks your product e.g. they will order100 ties from you and sell them from their stock. Once their stock goes down to, say 10, they will order another 100 from you to fulfill their orders from stock. Amazon will collect the money from their customer and ships the goods. You will invoice Amazon for every order you have shipped to them.

It is not easy to become a Vendor, and usually you will need to visit your local Amazon office to discuss terms and prices. I am an approved Amazon Vendor for some products.

They make their administrative procedures so complicated for approved vendors that they organise one day training seminars for it. Once you are accepted as a vendor, you will have to go through very complicated procedures:

- filling in spreadsheets with information about your products, including barcode number

- filling in complicated spreadsheets with selling prices, RRP prices, bundle prices, their profit margins, etc…

- provide a picture in exactly the format they want it and upload each picture with THEIR reference number.

Once all the start-up procedures are approved (not easy—takes weeks), they will start ordering from you.

Make sure that you put your profit margins pretty high when you decide on your pricing (how much you will charge Amazon for your products), as they will send you invoices each month for the following:

- 5% SNS accrual fund

- 6% traffic marketing

- 6% operations—damage allowance

These percentages are calculated on the total amount that Amazon has bought from you each month—so their turnover for your products.

That is a total of 17%!

If you add 30% profit to your purchasing price, you only actually earn 13%, as the 17% they charge you has to be deducted from your profit.

One other negative aspect for being an approved vendor is that Amazon pays pretty slowly: 60 days end of month or longer.

If you would like your payment faster, you can give away (another) 2.5% by giving them a 2.5% discount if they pay before 60 days.

That is 60 days from the end-of-month invoice date! So if your invoice date is June 2, the 60 days start to count and the end of the month June, so you will get your money 60 days after end of June; in other words, the end of September. As you can see, if you don't have the funds to overcome the period where you had to pay for the stock and Amazon pays you, you will create cash flow problems, and cash flow is a killer in any business!

4) ArtFire

www.artfire.com Featured in The New York Times, Reader's Digest, Fox Business and CNNMoney, ArtFire is a newer online marketplace that focuses primarily on craft supplies, crafts, fine art and vintage items. It does cost to have a seller account, but it's just under £8.15/$13.00 a month, and you get a customisable eCommerce store that allows unlimited listings with as many as 10 images per listing. The site offers a number of valuable tools, including a coupon feature, SEO tools and integration of Google Analytics. Their customer service is said to be pretty exceptional. In 2011, it was ArtFire that was selected by customers as the top marketplace.

5) eCRATER

http://www.ecrater.com/ eCRATER is very similar to eBay, but you won't be paying listing fees or crazy final value fees that make selling your product virtually worthless. But they've got to make their money somewhere, right? Of course, and they do that by charging a price for premium product positions. There are mixed reviews online in regards to eCRATER, so proceed with caution. But, it wouldn't hurt to post an item on there and see how it does. If it works well for you, then keep on selling.

6) Online Auction

www.onlineauction.com This site allows for unlimited listings, but you'll have to pay a fee to do so. But, it's only £5/$8 per month. Online Auction is similar to eBay and is actually quite popular. There are mixed reviews about this site, just as there are with ECrater; however, there are a lot of satisfied sellers and buyers.

7) Etsy

www.etsy.com This is an online venue that is for buying and selling handmade products, so it may not necessarily work well with your drop shipping business, unless you can find quality handmade items to re-sell; it is a site to keep in mind should you begin to sell handmade products in the future. It's a great place to sell craft supplies and vintage items as well. Just don't forget to check their restrictions, as all items must be more than 20 years old, be handmade, or be handmade or commercial crafting supplies. Storefronts are free, but you'll pay a fee to list an item.

8) Ruby Lane

www.rubylane.com An online venue to sell vintage, collectibles and high-end antiques; however, it can be a little bit expensive to get started with a £47/$75 set-up fee in addition to other fees each month. But if you have high-end and vintage items, it may be worth the money, as you'll easily reach your target market.

9) Madbid

www.madbid.com is relatively new and it is a penny auction site. From a commercial point of view Madbid is very cleverly done. I am pretty sure they are raking in the money! They've have been in the press a lot due to the incredible bargains people have won. You cannot use the site without having to buy credits. Every time you bid on an item, your credit goes down.

Have a look, if you are lucky, you can buy things here for ridiculously cheap prices and sell them on Ebay or Amazon. You can snap up goods, from cars to mobile phones for 80 percent less than the normal price. But....you will have to be patient as you will need to constantly watch the bidding, it can take hours to win a bid. Personally, I haven't got that sort of patience. I like things to move fast: bid, pay and done!

10) More Alternatives

While the aforementioned are some of the more popular online sales venues, there are numerous others. It would take mountains of pages to list them all here, but we'll list a few with briefer descriptions.

- **Adflyer.co.uk** – www.adflyer.co.uk An eBay alternative for the British with your own customisable shop window. Allows items to be imported from eBay. No listing fees, just a six percent commission fee at the time of sale.

- **iOffer** – www.ioffer.com An online auction site with more bargaining (a swaps and trades platform) and no auction end times. Upgrading gets you a free storefront with fees only being paid once an item sells.

- **TIAS** – www.tias.com Offers only fixed-price listings for jewelry, arts and crafts, collectibles and antiques. There are minimum fees, though, or commission on products, depending on the situation. They also offer eBay submission and uploading of listings to classified ad sites.

- **My Store** – www.mystore.com Easy to use and no fees unless you use features for advanced sellers.

- **BidStart** – www.bidstart.com A great place to sell collectibles with fees being half of that of eBay.

- **StoreEnvy** – www.storeenvy.com A completely free online platform with hundreds of thousands of different products.

Chapter 20 - How Much Does It All Cost?

Now that you know what you need and where to get it, it's time to have a look at how much everything will cost you. The total cost will depend on who you choose to work with. In my spreadsheet below, I am working with Streamline as my merchant account, WorldPay as my payment gateway and EkmPowershop as my eCommerce software or shopping cart.

Monthly Expenses	£	$	Euros
Hosting	£9.99	$16.00	€ 11.89
Streamline Fee	£30.00	$48.50	€ 35.70
Streamline Annual Management Fee	£2.49	$4.00	€ 2.93
Worldpay Fee	£19.95	$32.00	€ 23.75
EkmPowershop	£24.99	$39.99	€ 29.75
Aweber Auto Responder	£11.75	$19.00	€ 13.99
Total	£99.17	$159.49	€ 118.01

So for only £99.17/$159.49, you can run your own profitable business from home. That is very affordable compared to starting up a brick and mortar business.

EkmPowershop does NOT have all the bells and whistles, but I can highly recommend it for newbies. Once you decide you like eCommerce, you can always change to more expensive eCommerce software and build another shop with more bells and whistles.

You have to pay £99.17/$158.24 per month whether you sell anything or not. So better get selling!

Notes on the spreadsheet above:

- The Streamline monthly fee does NOT apply once you go over the threshold in the turnover agreed with your bank, e.g. you might have agreed that if your transaction charges on your sales are over £25/$40.45, this monthly fee does not apply.

485

- All figures are excluding VAT/TAX.

- Hosting fee is based on a PROFESSIONAL hosting company.

- You don't need Aweber auto responder if you use eCommerce software that has an auto responder built in and you want to use that one.

- If you do want to use Aweber, the monthly cost depends on how many subscribers you have and starts from £11/$19 per month for up to 500 subscriber and goes up to £80/$130 per month if you have between 10,000 and 25,000 subscribers.

- Because this is important, I decided to give you European readers the total in Euros.

- $ and Euro prices depend on currency fluctuations.

The above are fixed monthly fees. On top of that you will have to pay a percentage of the selling price of the product for your payment processing company. This can be anything between 2 and 9% depending on your negotiating skills and how many products you sell per year. Debit cards in the UK don't carry a transaction fee.

One-off expense: Set-up Fee for Streamline Merchant Account : £245/$395

If you want to avoid the above expenses, you can just start selling with PayPal. They don't charge a monthly fee. You won't need a merchant account or a payment gateway. In this case, your monthly expenses are only £34.98/$55.99 (see spreadsheet below). However, some people don't like paying with PayPal or don't have a PayPal account or might not have any funds in their PayPal account. You will lose sales if you only use PayPal as payment method, but you can always do this to get you started. Your total monthly expenses if you only use Paypal and no auto responder are:

Monthly Expenses	£	$	Euros
Hosting	£9.99	$16.00	€ 11.89
EkmPowershop	£24.99	$39.99	€ 29.75
Total	£34.98	$55.99	€ 41.64

You will also have to pay a one-time price per year for your domain name, e.g. £5/$9, but as that is ignorable, I am not putting that on the expenses list.

I am assuming you will be working from home, so I have not gone into much detail about your expense in this book, but here are a few not to forget, as your business will grow:

- Your wages!

- Rent and business rates

- Hosting

- Mortgage

- Insurance

- Loans, e.g. car

- Warehousing expenses

- Computers

- Cameras

- Phones

- Accountancy fee

- Software licenses

- VAT or taxes (often forgotten)

- Merchant account monthly fees

- Payment gateway monthly fees

- Auto responder fees

- Outsourcing fees

It is interesting to know your total cost per order:

- Add up all the costs for the last 12 months.

- Divide that total by the numbers of orders you have received in the last 12 months.

- That will give you your total cost per order.

You can also calculate your average spent per customer:

- Add up the numbers of orders you had last year.

- Divide that number by the number of people who bought from you last year.

- That number is your average order per customer.

Variable expenses

You have seen the fixed overheads (expenses that don't change), but on top of that you have your variable expenses:

- Petrol/Diesel

- Marketing expenses

- Travelling expenses

- Stationery

- Bank charges

- Transport costs

- Packing materials, e.g. bags, cartons, tape, bubble wrap etc…

- Advertising

- Letterheads, business cards

- Utilities (gas, electricity & water)

- Vehicle expenses

- Petty cash

- Stamps

- Written-off stock and returns

- Depreciation—your accountant will sort this out. I hope you will soon have a business big enough so you will need an accountant.

- Your merchant account transaction fees; Let's have look at how much that can be.

In August 2013, the total of my transaction fees is £258.46/$417

streamline

Charge Details

Invoice Number
Charges For August 2013
Page

Your Merchant ID
Store Trading Name

Cards Acquired		Number of Transactions	Charge per Transaction p	Value of Transactions £	Transaction Charge Rate	Transaction Charges	VAT Code
MasterCard Cr Per	Purchases	11		4,299.62	2.225%	95.67	
MasterCard World	Purchases	4		367.00	2.719%	9.98	
Visa Credit Personal	Purchases	7		765.38	2.494%	19.09	
Visa Debit	Purchases	132	37.880	31,400.94	0.0%	50.00	
MasterCard Business	Purchases	1		108.86	2.4%	2.61	
MasterCard Corporate	Purchases	2		392.41	2.4%	9.42	
MasterCard Fleet	Purchases	3		1,129.18	2.4%	27.10	
Visa Corporate	Purchases	5		1,829.77	2.4%	43.91	
Maestro UK (DOM)	Purchases	2	24.000	385.47	0.0%	0.68	
		167		40,678.63		258.46	E

* For a breakdown of Acquired, Premium transaction charges, please refer to your
Management Information package.

Miscellaneous Charges	Number or Value	Charge Rate	Charge Amount £	VAT Code
Streamline Online Monthly Fee	12.00	Per Month	12.00	S
Retention terminal rental	13.00	Per Month	13.00	S
			25.00	

Note the monthly fee of £25.00/$40, which is your monthly fee. That fee at the moment is £30/$48 if you don't make any sales. I also have a physical card terminal so I am charged the monthly rent for that: £13/$21.

The invoice received from Streamline that will automatically be debited from my account looks like this:

Streamline Merchant Services

Invoice

Invoice Number	
VAT Reg Number	
Invoice Date	01 September 2013
Charges For	August 2013

Your VAT Reg Number
Your Store Reference

Your Merchant ID
Store Trading Name

If you have any queries
please call us on

Charges Summary	Charge Amount £
Transaction Charges - Cards Acquired	258.46
Transaction Charges - Cards Processed for Other Acquirers	0.00
Miscellaneous Charges	25.00
Total Charges	283.46
VAT	5.00
Total Due	**288.46**

The amount shown will be debited from account no.
at branch   on or after 18 September 2013

VAT Analysis	VAT Code	Net Amount £	VAT Rate	VAT Amount £
	S Standard	25.00	20.0%	5.00
	E Exempt	258.46	0.0%	0.00
	Total VAT			5.00

Note that the miscellaneous charges of £25/$40.40 are added to the total of the transaction fees, which makes a total of £283.46/$458; and on that amount, the VAT is charged, where applicable, (only £5/$8) making the total payable £288.46/$466.

Chapter 21 - How Long Does It All Take?

1) How long does it take to get a merchant account and payment gateway?

In theory, it takes between 3 and 4 weeks to get a merchant account. You will find that whichever company you contact, they will tell you it takes one month to set it all up but it can take MUCH longer. However, some merchant accounts can approve you much quicker, but usually it takes three to four weeks before it is all set up and working.

2) How long does it take to find products to sell?

After you have signed up with drop shippers or wholesalers, you can find new products, suitable to sell, in an hour if you are lucky, or it can take you two days. When you are thinking of selling a product, you need to do your research as described in this book, e.g. check the competition, is there a market for the products, etc…

3) How long does it take to build your website?

Of course this depends how quickly you can work and how quickly you can absorb information and put it into practice. How many hours will you work on the site daily?

My site www.liquorice-licorice.co.uk was set up completely by myself and it took me approx. 2 weeks to set up from scratch. Note that there are not that many products on that site.

4) How long does it take to rank in Google?

If you don't submit your website to Google, it take on average between 4 and 6 weeks before Google will index your site. If you submit your site, as explained in this book, your site might rank in a few days.

Don't forget, in order to rank in Google, you need to do your SEO very well, otherwise your site will simply never show in the first 10 pages of Google, meaning you won't sell much. In that case, you can start sending traffic to your site.

5) How long does it take to start selling?

This really depends a lot on the answer under question 4). You could start selling within one week of submitting your site.

Providing your website is designed following the recommendations in this book and providing you have selected good products and are selling at good prices, you could start selling the same day your site is on page one of Google.

You will still sell if you are on page two or three but not so much. If you are on page 10, you will probably not sell anything at all.

Work towards your goal of selling loads, don't stop until you've reached your goal and work hard, even on bad days.

You can't get much done in life

if you only work on the days when you feel good!

Chapter 22 - You Must Keep a Record Of Everything.

As you get more and more orders in, it really is very important to get a system going! A good system!

Just because everything is done online, you still need to keep records and file stuff *properly* so you can find things immediately when you want them.

In the UK, by law (as far as I am aware the law hasn't changed), you need to keep paper records of your outgoing invoices (to customers), incoming invoices (from suppliers) and bank statements for 10 years.

It will not be easy to reconcile everything if you don't keep records. I suggest you make a filing place for:

- your outgoing invoices, or your sales

- your incoming invoices from your suppliers

- your bank statements

- your merchant account sales

- your complaints not resolved

- your complaints resolved

- your to do list

Let me give you an example so you can see that it is not always easy to reconcile amounts. You need to put your thinking cap on when you reconcile your bank statements.

1) At the end of the day, you enter into your accountancy software how much money you have received that day. You will input this per order (see screenshot from my Sage accountancy software). I had six credit card sales (I input my credit card sales as CC) on 1.8.2013 and the total is £1403.10/$ 2,238.65, but it doesn't say the total in Sage, as the sales are listed individually.

562227 SR	01/08/201. 2604	CC2604	Sales Receipt	161.75
562228 SR	01/08/2013 3166	CC3166	Sales Receipt	201.53
562229 SR	01/08/2013 2724	CC2724	Sales Receipt	208.12
562230 SR	01/08/2013 3034	CC3034	Sales Receipt	405.89
562231 SR	01/08/2013 2796	CC2796	Sales Receipt	207.87
562232 SR	01/08/20 3 1802	CC1802	Sales Receipt	217.94

Now have a look when your bank statement comes in:

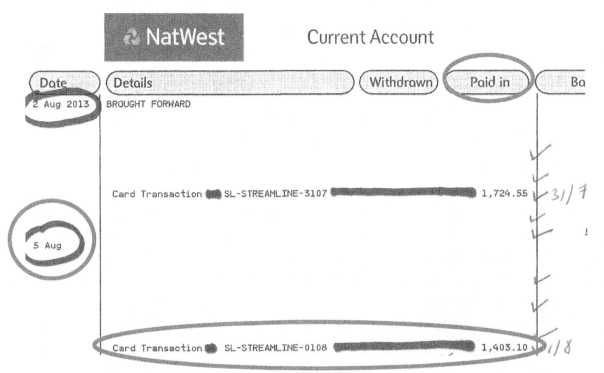

On 5 August it says paid in £1,403.10 with no other details at all on the bank statement.

You can learn 3 things from my bank statement:

1) The date I've charged the customer's card is NOT the same date as the money was paid into my account, as the cards were charged on 1 August and the money was actually in paid into my bank account on 5 August (there was a weekend in between). Usually the money will be in your account the next day.

That's why you can see my secretary has scribbled 1/8 next to the amount of 1,405.10 to say that amount represents the total of the cards charged on 1 August.

2) At the end of each day, you must keep a record of the total sales.

3) Your bank statement does NOT show each transaction individually, but the total of all the transactions done in one day.

Now let's have a look at how the paperwork looks from your merchant account, which you will receive at the end of each month if you work with Streamline. You can see that on their paperwork, the transaction is dated 2 August, but the money was received in my account on 5 August.

Batch Totals	Batch Start Reference	Gross Value £	Adjustment £	Net Value £
01 August 2013	002341	1,724.55	0.00	1,724.55
02 August 2013	002342	1,403.10	0.00	1,403.10
05 August 2013	002343	315.24	0.00	315.24
06 August 2013	002344	4,046.57	0.00	4,046.57
07 August 2013	002345	1,894.07	0.00	1,894.07
08 August 2013	002346	2,242.51	0.00	2,242.51
09 August 2013	002347	1,712.70	0.00	1,712.70
13 August 2013	002348	2,955.34	0.00	2,955.34
14 August 2013	002349	2,550.59	0.00	2,550.59
15 August 2013	002350	1,386.77	0.00	1,386.77
16 August 2013	002351	2,099.74	0.00	2,099.74
20 August 2013	002352	2,173.28	0.00	2,173.28
21 August 2013	002353	3,472.80	0.00	3,472.80
22 August 2013	002354	1,279.16	0.00	1,279.16
23 August 2013	002355	2,302.91	0.00	2,302.91
27 August 2013	002356	2,286.35	0.00	2,286.35

So there you go, now you have some idea about how confusing it can all become if you don't have a system!

I am only showing you one day of transactions, but these transactions come in on a daily basis, so you will have hundreds of transactions every month and thousands per year. Begin as you mean to continue, and start with a system the moment you have your first sale!

On top of the above sales, you will have to be able to tell which supplier has supplied the items for the above sales so you can keep an eye on your profit margins.

- ALWAYS, ALWAYS check your suppliers' invoices to make sure you are invoiced at the correct price and for the correct quantities. LOTS of suppliers try and charge you more, by accident or intentionally.

Chapter 23 - Taxes, Legal Requirements and VAT.

A word about taxes.

Just because you are selling online doesn't mean you don't have to pay tax. I speak to people and they tell me "I love my little side business". As soon as I mention the word taxes, they change their mind and all of a sudden it becomes "their hobby" instead of a little side business.

Whether it is a little side business or a hobby is irrelevant. You are earning money from your sales, therefore you need to pay tax on that income. You might look at it as a hobby or having some fun selling, but the tax people will have a different opinion on that matter!

The rules are clear: you must pay taxes on all business and personal income. That also applies if you are selling on eBay or Amazon by the way.

In the UK, you have to pay tax on ANY income if it's higher than the limit of £9,440/$15214 per year.

You have to register for VAT if your turnover is over £79.000/$127,000. If it is lower, you don't have to worry about VAT. You can voluntarily register if you wish to claim VAT back.

http://www.hmrc.gov.uk/rates/it.htm

http://www.hmrc.gov.uk/incometax/should-you-pay.htm

http://www.hmrc.gov.uk/vat/start/register/when-to-register.htm

I am not going into detail about how much tax you need to pay as that is different in every country and a thousand rules apply. I know it is too much in the UK!

A word about legal requirements and VAT.

- You must be a legitimately registered business in the UK and in the US; you will need a State Tax ID number (USA) or register for a VAT number (UK) to claim back VAT on your products or expenses.

- It is easiest for your buyers if the price you sell for on your website is TAX/ VAT inclusive, otherwise the customer will get a surprise at the checkout when this is added. If you mostly sell to companies that are VAT registered, you can put the prices on your website + TAX/VAT, but make sure to display somewhere on your website that the prices do not include TAX/VAT.

- It is impossible for me to list all the legal requirements in all the countries that this book will be available in. Therefore, check your official government sites or give a local accountant a call. A local accountant will probably answer some questions free of charge hoping that he will win your business once you are successful.

Here is a quick overview of what applies in the UK:

- You must send an order confirmation.

- Delivery of the product must be within 30 days of order date, unless otherwise stated.

- Your customer has a 7-day, money-back guarantee.

- A refund must be done within 30 days of the request for the refund.

There are more rules.

- A lot of people ask me how it works with setting up a company and how to set up an Internet marketing company. Basically setting up an Internet marketing company is the same as setting up any other company: you will need to get a business name, register your business, pay taxes, etc…

I suggest that you not worry about this at all at the beginning of your Internet marketing venture. Set up a website (or two or three), see if you are actually making money and if you do, start worrying about setting up a business, income taxes, VAT, etc… You might not enjoy being an Internet marketer or a drop shipper, therefore it would be silly to set up a registered business right from the start. However, it will be easier to be approved by a merchant account if you do have a business.

In order to work with some suppliers, you will need to prove that you are a company, so if you haven't, you won't be able to deal with those suppliers; remember, you can't buy from a REAL wholesaler if you are not a company. You could pretend you are a company: that is up to you. I am sure some people do just that, but if they ask for your VAT number you will be stuck.

- Check the legalities concerning the products you want to sell. Some products, e.g. liquids, precious metals, etc. have to be approved by certain organisations before you are allowed to sell them.

-The taxes/VAT can be different depending on the location where you are invoicing to and where you are shipping to. Some products have taxes/VAT in some countries and might not have VAT in other countries. You need to investigate this for the products you are selling and charge your customer accordingly

- Once you are successful and you are making money, you need to find out how to set up a business in your own country. This is very easy, affordable and straightforward these days (well, it is in the UK) and all aspects of it can be done online.

- Once you have found out how to set up your own business or how to run a business from home as a sole trader, start working towards even more success.

- You must comply with all legal requirements regarding sales taxes and so on. Just because you are selling online does not mean you do not have to pay taxes on your income.

- Taxes/VAT are different in all countries and different for a lot of products. To give you one example: if you are selling online video tutorials from the UK, the following applies:

- If you sell them to a UK buyer, VAT of 20% applies.
- If you sell them to another EU business, e.g. Spain, there is no VAT providing that you have PROOF that the company you sell to is indeed a business. The VAT

registration number of the customer needs to appear on your invoice in order for it to be a zero rated VAT sale.

- If you sell them to another EU business and the buyer is an individual, not a company, VAT applies to the sale.
- For all sales outside the EU, there is NO VAT.

The big problem here is that often you will receive a sale and you do not know where the sale came from, e.g. when people order with a gmail email account (a gmail account can be anywhere in the world). In that case, you need your customer's address from the order paperwork.

That's why it is important to use a shopping cart that automatically charges VAT or not, depending on what country the sale is made to. You can set these settings with any good shopping cart.

Internet marketing sales/income and VAT/Taxes can sometimes become pretty complicated and confusing. That's why my accountant does it all! I have not come across an accountancy program especially for Internet marketers and eCommerce owners who own several shops.

When you are becoming a "BIG" shop, you will have to deal with VAT; whether you like it or not, it is a legal requirement!

Always play the game following the rules!

The following text (from here to the end of this chapter) is copied from www.ekmpowershop.com and it is important to read:

There are many worldwide and country specific rules, regulations and laws that govern how websites and in particular ecommerce enabled website should be presented, work and what content should feature on them.

This is a quick guide to the main issues which effect ecommerce businesses using shopping cart software. This is in no way a complete guide and you should always seek proper legal advice from professionals if you are unsure about any legal issues with your website or online shop.

In the UK if you are running an ecommerce enabled website there are three major acts and directives that you must comply with. These acts and directives are:

- Data Protection Act 1998

- Distance Selling Act 2000

- Ecommerce Directive 2002

We have covered the basics of each of these acts and directives below along with contact information should you wish to learn more about them.

Data Protection

(a) You must register under the Data Protection Act if you collect any kind of information about people, these could be your customers, employees or potential customers. This information includes names, addresses, telephone numbers and email addresses.

(b) You must state what you do and intend to do with your subject's data and not deviate from that statement.

(c) The Act is applies to any size of business.

(d) You must not export the personal data outside the EC (European Community) without permission from the people you are collecting data on.

(e) You must ensure that all information is held securely and must be revealed or deleted upon request from the subjects of the information.

(f) You must only record data which is pertinent to your prime business needs.

For more information, search for: The Data Protection Act 1998

Consumer Protection (Distance Selling) Regulations

The Consumer Protection (Distance Selling) Regulations 2000 apply to many ecommerce websites. However, they are not applicable to 'business-to-business' transactions.

(a) You must provide clear information about your products and services before purchase.

(b) You must be clear about postage and packing costs and whether VAT or any other tax is included in the prices shown on your website.

(c) You must provide a written confirmation of order following purchase, for example a confirmation email.

(d) You must allow a "cooling off" period where by the customer can change their mind and cancel or return the order within 7 working days for most goods. Certain exclusions do apply with items such as perishable and digital goods.

(e) You must inform your customers of their right to cancel their order with no loss other than return postage and packing.

For more information, search for: The Consumer Protection (Distance Selling) Regulations 2000

Ecommerce Directive

(a) You must display the name of your business, the company registration number (or proprietor's name), geographical address (not a PO Box number), contact information e.g., telephone number and email address, VAT registration number (if registered).

(b) You may refer to trade or professional schemes if applicable.

(c) You must provide clear information on price, tax and delivery to buyers.

(d) You must clearly display your site's Terms and Conditions.

(e) You must acknowledge all orders.

(f) In commercial communication with your customers, you must clearly identify any electronic communication designed to promote your goods or services.

(g) You must clearly identify the sender of all electronic communication.

(h) You must clearly define any promotional offers and the qualifying conditions regarding these offers.

(i) If you send unsolicited emails, you must clearly identify them as unsolicited.

For more information, search for: The Electronic Commerce (EC Directive) Regulations 2002

Information Commissioner's Office e-privacy directive (ICO Cookie Law)

This law relates to the storage of, or gaining access to information stored in the device of a visitors/users on your website. This means the use of cookies and similar technologies for storing information.

(a) Your website must provide clear and comprehensive information about the purposes of the storage of, or access to that information.

(b) You can 'assume' consent has been given for your site to use cookies, as long as the above point has been carried out (clear and prominent information made available to visitors, on the cookies used by your site).

(c) Cookies used for functional purposes do not require consent. Cookies used by ekmPowershop.com for instance, which make the cart and other aspects work properly do not require consent/opt in.

For more information, search for: Information Commissioner's Office e-privacy directive.

Find more legal information in the USA here:

www.e-comlaw.com

www.hg.org

www.ibls.com (Internet Business Law)

Conclusion: Make sure you understand all the legalities in your country.

Chapter 24 - Crucial to Succeed.

Here's a list of the most important things that you will HAVE to watch.

- Good SEO is vitally important.

- You must have fresh and unique content, unless your competition is very low. This does not apply for my own small eCommerce websites as I haven't done anything (other than removing and adding products) to them for the last two years and they still rank.

- Get your pricing right.

- Watch your competition and learn from them. Sign up on their email list and see what you receive from them in your inbox.

- Consider having an opt-in box on your website in order to practice email marketing.

- Email your customers on a regular basis with promotions.

- Make sure you have a quick checkout process.

- Respond VERY QUICKLY, e.g. matter of minutes or hours to any customer queries. Don't ever leave it two days to reply. Remember to treat other people like you want to be treated yourself and remember the shoes picture!

- Put yourself in your customer's shoes and treat them like you want to be treated when you order something online.

- Choose the ecommerce or drop shipping software most suitable for you.

- Keep your site secure.

- Check ALL your links on a regular basis

- Send traffic to your list if you are not ranking in Google yet. The more visitors you receive, the more chances you have of Google showing your site on the first few pages. Just because you are not on page one today, doesn't mean you can't be there tomorrow.

I will never forget the days I saw some of my sites in the Top Three! It is a reward for your efforts. If you don't put the efforts in, you will never be rewarded.

- Keep your site updated/optimised all the time.

- Keep learning from your mistakes or from your competitors.

The whole process discussed in this book can be summarised as follows:

- Find a good, well-analysed niche in a market with a need.

- Find products that you can sell with a good profit.

- Find suitable eCommerce software for your needs.

- Sort out your Merchant Account and your Payment Gateway.

- Build an easy-to-use website that is pleasing for the eye.

- Drive traffic to your site.

- Start pocketing profits.

The most crucial thing you need to succeed is to have a winner's attitude!

Winners don't quit and quitters don't win!

Put the knowledge you have learned from this book into action!

Knowledge that isn't applied **is not more valuable than no knowledge**

Chapter 25 - Your Checklist.

O Sign up for free with some drop shippers. Play around, sell a few items to start with, see if you like the whole concept. Start small with PayPal-only order buttons.

O Set up your business—if you want to scale this up to a REAL business

O Set up your business bank account

O Find a niche in which you will sell your products

O Source products

O Decide who your supplier will be for your products

O Decide on a domain name

O Buy the domain name and hosting

O Get a Merchant Account

O Get a Payment Gateway

O Make sure you have all the pictures for your products

O Make all the descriptions for your products

O Decide on your selling price for each product

O Build an online store

O Put SEO on your store and products

O Test everything on your store

O Publish your store

O Decide on a courier to ship your products if you don't use a drop shipper

O Send traffic to your store

Looks pretty simple doesn't it? You will soon find out it is not THAT simple.

Chapter 26 – Conclusion.

Phew, I got there in the end! This book is (almost) finished!

Congratulations, you have made it to the end of the book. You are now ready to start creating your own online store(s). I really appreciate you reading this far and I hope I have given you a lot of useful information.

I can't promise you bundles of money overnight. That's why I am different from all the other scam artists. I am telling you the truth and the truth is that it will take work and determination to make this work for you, but it CAN be done. I know because I did it! I know you can do this too!

If you decide to work with one of the drop shipping services and/or eCommerce providers outlined in this book, then you are already equipped with some of the tools and features that you need. Research companies very thoroughly if you decide to work with others.

I hope this book has provided you with everything you need to know to get your drop shipping business started from the ground up, and I sincerely hope you will be successful.

Don't be afraid of failure.

The only difference between try and triumph is a little umph!

It can happen that you fail, but it's okay to start over, try things a little bit differently and try again. This is one of the many reason starting an online business is so great, because you won't be stuck with a lease for an expensive building for 10 years and you won't have to worry about any other aspects of a brick-and-mortar business that would be emptying your pockets.

Don't give up too quickly if you can't get it to work or can't earn any money. I never made ANY money during the first year I was an Internet marketer.

Remember:

- **Customer is King**

- **Content is King**

- **SEO is King**

- **Cash is King**

- Build your email list as soon as you can so you can keep in touch with your customers on a regular basis.

- Get into social media if you believe in social media.

- Enjoy it!

Start working towards your goal; if I can do it, so can you!

So what's next?

You need to believe in yourself. If you think you can do it: you will!

You need to get organised.

You need to set yourself a realistic goal.

You need to set up a system, a step-by-step process of what you are going to do—Starting Today!

You too can enjoy financial freedom with the money making possibilities of the web and with the Power Of The Internet!

What will the future of online shopping bring in 2014/2015?

According to www.forbes.com, there are 10 trends to watch for online shopping.

Many online shops are competing with the big boys, e.g. Amazon, Asos, Sears, Walmart, etc. so they must try and offer the same products and services.

1. In-store pickups. It is sometimes difficult for people to stay at home when they are expecting a delivery. People like ordering online, but they don't like to organise their lives around a delivery time. It would be convenient for people to order online and pick it up on their way home from work.

2. Pick up depots. Some big retailers are planning to build large pick up depots for the same reason as mentioned in point 1.

In Florida, Farm Sores let their shoppers order their groceries online and they the customer can pick them up at a drive-thru.

3. Mobile Apps. More and more people "live" with their smart phone and so will also shop more and more with their mobile phones. However, personally I don't think you can easily browse products, etc. as the screen is simply too small.

4. Less flash more function. Virtual dressing rooms have been tested, but didn't get a good consumer response. You don't need to make your site all flash and posh, just make it a functional site. When virtual dressing rooms work perfectly, maybe you will see them on more stores.

5. Video. Customers can take videos of their clothes or their purchase and put it on your website. You can use the video as a review for your product.

6. Social Networking. Social networking is important to many people. Facebook won't remain the only big one. More and more networks are popping up, and one of them will someday take over from all the existing ones. There are already very big ones that are in competition with Facebook. So if you will use social media to promote your site, don't JUST use Facebook.

7. Daily deals and flash sales.

- www.onekingslane.com is a site where products are listed for 72 hours only. One Kings Lane is the leading new eCommerce company for the home, offering the best of top-brand, vintage and designer items at exceptional values. Many more similar websites are expected to appear soon.

- www.ibood.com offers daily deals on the principle "Gone is gone". A certain number of items are for sale, and when they're sold out, you can no longer buy them.

8. Retail-based social network. This is where one company tries to create a social network of its own customers. Walmart has tried but failed. Maybe some new ones will succeed.

9. International. Lots of little online shops are selling products abroad. I am one of them. I sell and ship liquorice products to Norway, USA, Spain, Holland, Finland, etc… More and more companies will ship overseas in the future.

10. Deal aggregators. There are a few well-known websites that inform customers of where there are special deals going on. Some examples:

- www.fatwallet.com

- www.dealnews.com

- www.ConsumerSearch.com

There a lot more, just search for them.

Personally, in the future, I would like to see "Trust" buttons to appear on lots of sites; "Trust" videos would be even better as you can buy as many likes as you want, therefore you can also buy "Trusts"! It will be more difficult to buy "Trust" videos, as the videos will have to have people on! More and more people carry smartphones with easy video recording, so it will be a matter of minutes for someone to "quickly" record something about a company and a person and put it as a video on the web.

You never know who you can trust at the moment. Who knows? Perhaps "Trust" videos will be a thing in the future?

You have seen screenshots of some of my accounts. Important to mention: Total income/turnover does not mean total profit. There is a big difference! VAT needs to be deducted where applicable, and all expenses need to be deducted from the earnings in order to calculate the taxable profit. On top of that taxes need to be paid, after which your net profits can be calculated.

11. Drones. Amazon is testing their drone delivery system. Who knows, one day your orders will be delivered by a drone. Search for "Amazon drones" on Youtube to see what I mean.

A few end notes:

- *Be human on your way to the top*

Once you are making good money, don't forget to enjoy it with your family and friends! Help your friends and family when you can. Make somebody happy with your money. Be rich but be human. Never become a money robot and forget the most important things in life: health, love and happiness.

The Best Things In Life Are Not Things.

Measure your wealth by things you have that no one could buy at any price.

- *Remember your friends*

Don't let the money go to your head and look down on your friends or family. The friends you had before you made money should still be your friends. Make sure you tell your friends that you are still the same person, just with more money.

- *Look after your health*

Sit on your computer in an ergonomic chair and in the correct posture. If you can afford it, go to www.breakremindersoftware.com and buy it, which will help prevent office-related injuries (not available for Apple computers). www.workpace.com is a similar, more sophisticated software and I believe available for Apple computer.

- Read the www.PainInTheThumb.com book about Repetitive Strain Injury. You will be shocked by the real-life horror stories. The book is also available on Amazon.

- *Don't ever forget the art of giving back*

I give to charities every month. I strongly suggest that you donate a percentage of your income to a charity. It will make you feel good, it will keep you going and keep you focused and there's no reason to be the richest person in the cemetery. You can't do any business from there ☺.

- *Back up your data*

It is vital to back up all your data at least once a week and if possible once a day. Back up everything relating to your sites. You will spend a lot of time building your site, and you certainly do not want to lose it all if your computer crashes.

- *Put a review on Amazon please*

If you have enjoyed reading this book, please, if you can make the time, put a 5 star review on Amazon. You are helping a hard working woman by doing this:-).

Good luck in your drop shipping / eCommerce business! I really hope that you make it big time!

Christine Clayfield.

www.ChristineClayfield.com

Christine Clayfield

Author, Entrepreneur, Infopreneur, Internet Marketer, Book Publisher, Public Speaker

Here are some of my favourite quotes; if you practice them, you will get far! A lot further than a lot of people you know.

- No bees no honey, no work no money!

- Don't give up, don't ever ever give up! (Churchill's famous words)

- A goal without a deadline is nothing more than a wish!

- All our dreams can come true, if we have the courage to pursue them. (Walt Disney)

If you like this book, tell your friends, family and colleagues about it. For any suggestions or comments (good or bad) about this book, email me:
Christine@dropshippingandecommerce.com

There is no support system set up for this book as I am not selling some sort of automated software that needs a support line. I have written the book, now it is up to you to put it into action!

Having said that, I am very happy to answer your questions, but please don't ask me questions for which you can find the answer in this book or in Google. I have to think about my health.

Join me on:

If you would like to be notified when I have written a new book, please opt-in on www.FromNewbieToMillionaire.com.

> **I am planning to make videos about drop shipping and eCommerce, showing you step by step how to set it all up, upload products, connect everything to shopping cart, merchant account, etc. I will set up a shop and record it all on video so you can SEE how it is all done. If you are interested in this, please visit www.DropshippingAndEcommerce.com/yesvideos.html. If a LOT of people are interested in the videos, I will do them and you will be notified when they are ready.**

Make Money With This Book

I hope that you have enjoyed reading this book and that you have learned a lot. There are two ways that you can earn money with this book:

1) www.Amazon.com and www.amazon.co.uk Sign up with Amazon as an Associate and search for "Christine Clayfield" in the book section or search for "Drop shipping and ecommerce. What you need and where to get it". Get your affiliate code and put it on your website or email the affiliate code to your friends, family and colleagues.

2) www.Clickbank.com There will be an eBook version of this book on Clickbank. Just search for "Drop shipping and ecommerce. What you need and where to get it". You will receive a very large commission on the sale of the eBook.

The sales letter is here: www.DropshippingAndEcommerce.com. Simply get your affiliate code and put it on your website or send it to your friends, family and colleagues.

There will be an affiliate page on Clickbank (at the bottom of the sales page) with pictures and keywords, articles, etc. for you to use. You can also get your Clickbank affiliate link here: www.DropshippingAndEcommerce.com/affiliates.html

Make Money With My Other Products.

1) My Internet Marketing Success System explained step by step. Product: "From Newbie To Millionaire".

Buy the eBook here: www.FromNewbieToMillionaire.com

Buy the hard copy book: search for it on Amazon.

Read what people say about the book: www.FromNewbieToMillionaireTestimonials.com

Earn money as an affiliate: www.FromNewbieToMillionaire.com/affiliates.html

Make Money Online, Work From Home

From Newbie to Millionaire

Internet Marketing Success System Explained Step By Step

Foreword by ROBERT G. ALLEN

Over **100** Traffic Methods

MAKE MONEY ONLINE SUCCESS

by Self Made Millionaire **Christine Clayfield**
Best Selling Author

2) *My book explaining how I find new niches*: "Finding Niches Made Easy".

Buy the eBook here: www.FindingNichesMadeEasy.com

Buy the hard copy book: search for it on Amazon.

Earn money as an affiliate: www.FindingNichesMadeEasy.com/affiliates

3) *My Self Publishing Success System explained step by step in video tutorials.*

Product: Worldwide Self Publishing Business Training. The very best Self Publishing Training available. I know because I bought all the other ones!

I publish a new book, on average, every 6 weeks. These books are all in different niches and I outsource all aspects of the book, including writing and cover design, except for the publishing, which I do myself. You can found out how I find new niches and how I self publish my books here: www.WorldwideSelfPublishing.com.

I have books in all of the following niches: ice fishing, tarantulas, micro pigs, hypnosis, racing pigeons, recording studio, food processors, organic gardening, panic attacks, standup comedy, cyclists, golf trolleys, bladeless fans, horses, iguana, discuss fish, wedding planning, cat training, green house, body building, magnetic therapy, sports injuries, peafowl, African pygmy hedgehogs, puffer fish, dementia, bone spurs, flying squirrels, hoarding, and a lot more!

Buy the video tutorials to watch online: www.WorldwideSelfpublishing.com

Read what people say about the videos: www.WorldWideSelfPublishingTestimonials.com

Earn money as an affiliate: www.WorldwideSelfpublishing.com/affiliates.html

4) My Break Reminder Software

I have to try and reduce the time I spend on my computer due to my neck-injury. I used to use www.workpace.com, which is software that forces you to take breaks whilst on your computer. I had my own simplified version developed, which you can buy here: www.BreakReminderSoftware.com. Sorry, not available (yet) for Apple computers.

Earn money as an affiliate: www.BreakReminderSoftware.com/affiliates.html

5) My Print Screen Software

When I was looking for a very simple screen software application, without all the bells and the whistles, I couldn't find it, therefore I had my own developed.

You can buy it here: www.PrintingYourScreen.com

Earn money as an affiliate: www.PrintingYourScreen.com/affiliates.html

Printing Your Screen, Screen Capture

The Software that Makes Printing Screen Shots And Saving Screen shots *instant*.

Appendix

Drop Shipping Services

Worldwide Brands – http://www.worldwidebrands.com

Doba – http://www.doba.com

SaleHoo – http://www.SaleHoo.com

Drop Ship Access – http://www.dropshipaccess.com

Drop Ship Design – http://www.dropshipdesign.com

DropShippers.com – http://www.dropshippers.com

Wholesale2B – http://www.wholesale2b.com

Sunrise Wholesale Merchandise – http://www.sunrisewholesalemerchandise.com

Product Sourcing – http://www.productsourcing.com

ATS Distribution – http://www.atsdistribution.co.uk

Sites That Drop Ship

Alternative Health Care – http://www.althealthcare.com/

Anatex – http://anatex.com/

Aura Fragrance of Paris – http://www.aurafragrancesofparis.com/

Big Discount Fragrances – http://www.bigdiscountfragrances.com

Crealle – http://www.crealle.com

Cutting Edge Products – http://www.cuttingedgeproducts.net

Fish Click – http://www.fishclick.com/

Fitness Cash – http://www.fitnesscash.com

Guardian Survival Gear – http://www.wholesalesurvivalkits.com

Hobby Tron – http://www.hobbytron.com/dropship.html

Halloween Select – http://www.halloweenselect.com

iiSports – http://iisports.com

Jewelry Sprite – http://www.jewelrysprite.com/

Pet Stores USA – http://www.petstoresusa.com/drop-ship

Real Action Paintball – http://www.rap4.com

RMF Scrubs Wholesale – http://www.rmfscrubswholesale.com

Safety Technology – http://www.safetytechnology.com

Sensual Mystique – http://www.sensualmystique.com

Sos Eyewear – http://www.soseyewear.com

TboTech – http://www.tbotech.com/distributor.htm

TeeShirtsRock – http://www.teeshirtsrock.com

Upright Golf – http://www.uprightgolf.com

Viking Wholesale – http://www.vikingwholesale.com

Vitabase – http://www.vitabase.com

WMS Clothing – http://www.wmsclothing.com

Buying Wholesale

DHGate – http://www.dhgate.com

AliExpress – http://www.aliexpress.com

AliBaba – http://www.alibaba.com

Wholesale Fashion Square – www.wholesalefashionsquare.com

Apparel Showroom – http://www.apparelshowroom.com

Cosmopolitan Cosmetics –http://www.cosmopolitanusa.com/

BooJee Handbags –http://www.boojeehandbags.com/

Buy 4 Less Electronics –http://www.buy4lessinc.com/

Noah's Ark Distribution –http://www.shopnoahsark.com/

Wholesale DVDs for Less – http://wholesaledvdsforless.com/

DMA Incorporated –http://www.dma-inc.net/

Self Defense Supply –http://www.selfdefensesupply.com/

Master Cutlery – http://www.mastercutlery.com

Payment Processors/Gateways

Google Wallet - https://www.wallet.google.com or .co.uk

AuthorizeNet – http://www.authorize.net

1ShippingCart - http://www.1shoppingcart.com

Infusionsoft - http://www.infusionsoft.com

Streamline - http://www.streamline.com (UK and Europe)

2Checkout – http://www.2checkout.com

WorldPay – http://www.worldpay.com

Flagship Merchant Services – http://www.flagshipmerchantservices.com

Merchant Warehouse – http://www.merchantwarehouse.com

National Bankcard – http://www.nationalbankcard.com

Leaders Merchant Services – http://www.leadersmerchantservices.com

Ejunkie - http://www.ejunkie.com

iBill - http://www.ibill.com

eCommerce Software/Shopping Cart Providers

Volusion – http://www.volusion.com

EkmPowerShop - http://www.ekmpowershop.com or .co.uk

1Shoppingcart - http://www.1shoppingcart.com

Shopify – http://www.shopify.com

Shopping Cart Elite – http://www.shoppingcartelite.com

Go Daddy Quick Shopping Cart – http://www.godaddy.com

Open Cart – http://www.opencart.com

Ultracart - http://www.ultracart.com

Actinic - http://www.actinic.com

Cubecart - http://www.cubecart.com

Pinacclecart - http://www.pinnaclecart.com

3D - http://www.3dcart.com

BigCommerce - http://www.bigcommerce.com

AgoraCart - http://www.agoracart.com

ShopSite - http://www.shopsite.com

Amazon Webstore - http://www.webstore.amazon.co.uk or .com

1and1 - **http://**www.1and1.com

Hosting Providers

Host Gator – www.hostgator.com

Go Daddy – www.godaddy.com

1and1 – www.1and1.com

Auction Sites and Alternatives to eBay

eBay – http://www.ebay.com

Amazon – http://www.amazon.com

Overstock – http://www.overstock.com

Bonanza – http://www.bonanza.com

Craigslist – http://craigslist.org

eCrater – http://www.ecrater.com

ArtFire – http://www.artifire.com

Online Auction – http://onlineauction.com

Etsy – http://www.etsy.com

Ruby Lane – http://www.rubylane.com

Adflyer.co.uk – http://www.adflyer.co.uk

iOffer – http://www.ioffer.com

TIAS – http://www.tias.com

MyStore – http://www.mystore.com

BidStart- http://www.bidstart.com

StoreEnvy – http://www.storyenvy.com

SEO Tools

Moz – http://www.moz.com

SEOBook – http://www.seobook.com

Open Site Explorer – http://www.opensiteexplorer.org/

Index

CPSIA information can be obtained at www.ICGtesting.com
Printed in the USA
BVOW08s1301241014

372222BV00016B/218/P